W9-AFR-369

DATE DUE

Oppositional Defiant Disorder and Conduct Disorder in Childhood

Oppositional Defiant Disorder and Conduct Disorder in Childhood

Walter Matthys and John E. Lochman

(W)WILEY-BLACKWELL

A John Wiley & Sons, Ltd., Publication

This edition first published 2010
© 2010 John Wiley & Sons Ltd.

Wiley-Blackwell is an imprint of John Wiley & Sons, formed by the merger of Wiley's global
Scientific, Technical, and Medical business with Blackwell Publishing.

Registered Office
John Wiley & Sons Ltd, The Atrium, Southern Gate, Chichester, West Sussex, PO19 8SQ, UK

Editorial Offices
The Atrium, Southern Gate, Chichester, West Sussex, PO19 8SQ, UK
9600 Garsington Road, Oxford, OX4 2DQ, UK
350 Main Street, Malden, MA 02148-5020, USA

For details of our global editorial offices, for customer services, and for information about how
to apply for permission to reuse the copyright material in this book please see our website at
www.wiley.com/wiley-blackwell.

Library of Congress Cataloging-in-Publication Data

Matthys, Walter.
  Oppositional defiant disorder and conduct disorder in childhood / Walter Matthys and
John E. Lochman.
    p. ; cm.
  Includes bibliographical references and index.
  ISBN 978-0-470-68231-9 (cloth) – ISBN 978-0-470-51088-9 (pbk.)   1. Oppositional
defiant disorder in children.   2. Conduct disorders in children.   I. Lochman, John E.
(John Edward)   II. Title.
  [DNLM: 1. Attention Deficit and Disruptive Behavior Disorders.   2. Child.
WS 350.6 M443o 2010]
  RJ506.O66M38 2010
  618.92′89–dc22

                                                                                2009033757

A catalogue record for this book is available from the British Library.

Set in Minion 10.5/13 pt by SNP Best-set Typesetter Ltd., Hong Kong
Printed in Singapore by Fabulous Printers Pte Ltd

1 2010

To Paula and Linda

Contents

About the authors

Walter Matthys, MD, PhD, is Professor of Aggression in Children at Utrecht University, The Netherlands. His clinical work as a child and adolescent psychiatrist is based at the Department of Child and Adolescent Psychiatry, University Medical Centre Utrecht. His research at the Rudolf Magnus Institute of Neuroscience focuses on the neurobiological and psychological characteristics of children and adolescents with aggressive behaviour and disruptive behaviour disorders, and on interventions to prevent and treat these disorders.

John E. Lochman, PhD, ABPP, is Professor and Doddridge Saxon Chairholder in Clinical Psychology at the University of Alabama, where he also directs the Center for Prevention of Youth Behavior Problems. He has served as a Special Professor at Utrecht University. He is Editor-in-Chief of the *Journal of Abnormal Child Psychology*, serves on the Board of the Society for Prevention Research, and is President of the American Board for Clinical Child and Adolescent Psychology. His research interests encompass risk factors, social cognition and intervention and prevention with aggressive children.

Preface

This book offers a brief but comprehensive overview of empirical knowledge and associated clinical information regarding oppositional defiant disorder (ODD) and conduct disorder (CD) in children aged 3–14 years. Since the amount of research in this subject is vast, we have avoided presenting an extended review of the literature of some areas while neglecting others. Instead, we have given priority to conciseness and clarity in the presentation of a broad array of topics.

The book opens with an introductory chapter on relevant terms. We then present the developmental psychopathology perspective (Chapter 2). The section of the book on aetiology starts with a chapter on basic issues (Chapter 3) followed by two detailed chapters on individual and environmental characteristics (Chapters 4 and 5). We then describe the clinical assessment from a decision-making point of view (Chapter 6). The section on intervention opens with a chapter on general issues (Chapter 7), followed by chapters on behavioural parent training (Chapter 8), cognitive-behavioural therapy (Chapter 9), pharmacotherapy (Chapter 10) and multicomponent interventions (Chapter 11). Finally, issues relating to the delivery of intervention are discussed in Chapter 12.

This synopsis is intended to be a guide for professionals and will be useful for students and researchers as well. Some information, for example on genetics, will serve as background information for clinicians and will be relevant for their accurate general understanding of the initiation, development and maintenance of the disorders. The background aetiological chapters can also help clinicians in understanding subsets of the children they see. Students and beginning researchers will find a quick overview of the whole field, while advanced researchers may find essential information on topics that are not their primary focus of interest and expertise.

For decades, the research fields of ODD and CD (and aggressive and antisocial behaviour) on the one hand and attention deficit/hyperactivity disorder (ADHD) (and hyperactive, impulsive and inattentive behaviour) on the other have been split as if these two groups of disorder and problem behaviour are independent of each other. In fact, however, they often co-occur. The separation of research areas of ODD/CD and ADHD has hampered our understanding of these two groups of related disorders. Fortunately, the last decade has seen an integration of the research fields of these disorders. In this book, we have paid much attention to the relation between these disorders, with respect both to aetiology, assessment and treatment, and to neurobiological factors in ODD and CD, as information on this topic has grown rapidly over the last few years and is essential for an accurate understanding of these disorders.

In reviewing the literature, we pay particular attention to recently published studies and meta-analyses, if available, without neglecting older, high-quality studies. The selection of studies, of course, reflects our own view on the subject. Likewise, we give personal comments on issues. We include our clinical and research experience in the chapters on clinical assessment and interventions. To make the book accessible, we have included a conclusion in the form of summary points at the end of each chapter.

We would like to thank the publisher Wiley-Blackwell for the invitation to write the book and the many people associated with the publisher for their assistance: Carole Millett, Emma Hatfield, Holly Myers, Al Bertrand, Darren Reeds, Anne Bassett, Annie Rose, Carrie Walker and Helen Baxter. We would also like to thank Karen Shield for her assistance in manuscript delivery, and Martin Schmidt, Dennis Schutter, Louk Vanderschuren and Sarah Durston for their detailed comments on earlier drafts of the chapters.

Walter Matthys
John E. Lochman

Foreword

The authors of this important book, Professors Walter Matthys and John E. Lochman, need little by way of introduction; they are known to a wide professional readership for their prolific empirical, clinical and theoretical studies of Disruptive Behavior Disorders (DBD) and other challenging behavior problems of childhood and adolescence. Certain children, as early as two or three years of age, drive their parents to despair by the intensity of their tantrums and aggressive outbursts, the intransigence of their defiance, and the wilfulness of their demands. During the school years teachers struggle to cope with their violation of classroom rules, and the disruption that results from (inter alia) their inattention, hyperactivity, bullying, and cheating. Many go on to an adolescence marked by violence, vandalism, theft, and other delinquent activities. These children, diagnosed early on as presenting Oppositional Defiant Disorder (ODD) and later Conduct Disorder (CD), cause much harm to society. As they grow up they enter, exit and almost invariably return, through the 'revolving doors' of mental health, educational, social services, and justice departments. Carers and teachers endure ongoing distress and demoralisation, while the State is forced to raise vast sums of money for damage limitation and repairs, and the costs of assessment and treatment agencies.

Clearly, the need to support families, teachers and workers from the social and mental health professions is urgent, and represents a compelling rationale for the book. The authors state that their aim is to write for professionals, students, and researchers, a concise guide to the aetiology and the assessment of ODD and CD, as well as to evidence-based interventions, and their short and long-term outcomes, Focusing on children aged 3 to 14 years, the book provides in twelve chapters, a overview of aetiology, assessment, prevention and treatment of ODD and CD, with particular attention given to recently published studies and meta-analyses. High quality studies from the past are not neglected. The introductory guides and final point-by-point summaries to each chapter, the provision of technical and conceptual definitions, plus comprehensive referencing, ensure that child and adolescent psychiatrists, clinical psychologists, and trainees, have access to a store of useful empirical information and practice wisdom. There is another group of professionals who also benefit, as they acquire familiarity with subjects which are not necessarily their primary focus of interest and expertise.

The authors explore several theoretical domains that are pertinent in a study of behavioral pathology: psychiatric taxonomy; developmental psychopathology; behavior genetics; pharmacology; neurobiology; conditioning; social learning; and cognitive science. A consistent theme of the book is an insistence on empirical knowledge and evidence-based practice. This philosophy leads to a search for reliable and valid assessment methods, several of which are described and analysed fully. Alongside this inquiry is an exploration of clinically efficacious and effective interventions. Several have been demonstrated to have 'significant effects' (a term that is explained) on particular disruptive behavior problems, after treatment and at longer term follow-up. Most of them emerge from areas including cognitive behavior therapy, ecological (systemic) multi-component treatment, behavioral parent training, and psychopharmacotherapy. Multi-component programs may combine psychopharmacotherapy and psychosocial treatments; in general they are most effective if they provide the treatment to both child and parent. With regard to the question of how 'cost-effective' (a term also explained) the interventions are, the initial findings are encouraging. Given the popularity of computers and video games for young people, it is not surprising that electronic media have an established role in an increasing number of treatment programs.

What sets this book apart from many others of its genre is the space given to the factors (ranging from macro-level influences of social policy and environmental advantages or disadvantages to microlevel factors such as adverse temperamental and personality traits) which encourage or prove antipathetic to the delivery of successful interventions. Outcomes for evidence-based interventions may often be less promising when they are exposed to the vicissitudes of real-life 'scenarios' and settings, such as community agencies, schools and clinics. There are many other potentially adverse contingencies: a recurring difficulty, for example, is the failure of many parents to engage in treatment programs, despite imaginative efforts to promote their attendance at sessions. On the basis of 'received wisdom' in some areas it is assumed that there is therapeutic value in the use of a collaborative approach to treatment and the use of booster sessions at the end of treatment sessions. There is, in fact, very little research to guide clinical practice in these areas. Methodological bias in empirical investigations may produce misleading conclusions. For example, constitutional factors such as Attention Deficit Hyperactivity (ADHD) often occur at the same time as DBD. An understanding of the two conditions was hampered by considering them in earlier studies as separate entities. An integration of the research fields in the last decade has produced valuable insights into the nature of both disorders.

In conclusion: I have had only sufficient space to comment on a fraction of the book I read in its entirety. Professors Matthys and Lochman have, in

my opinion, written an outstanding review of an extensive, and at times difficult, clinical literature. By skilful organisation and thoughtful defining of
terms and concepts, they have produced a pleasurable read without sacrificing
intellectual rigor. They have stuck throughout to a clear set of aims and objectives. Whereas psychotherapy with children and adolescents has traditionally
involved the application of many empirically unsupported methods, the
authors have committed themselves to evidence based studies of childhood
interventions – a basis essential for effective and thus ethical clinical
practice.

Martin Herbert
Professor Emeritus, Exeter University

1

Behaviours and disorders

All children refuse to comply at some time or other. And a lot of children occasionally get involved in fights. Also, various children lie at times. Although these behaviours are inappropriate, from a clinical point of view they need not be of great concern if they occur infrequently and in an isolated manner. When, however, these behaviours occur in a cluster and repeatedly in a particular child, there is reason to be worried. In this chapter, we first look at the various types of socially inappropriate, disruptive behaviour that have been discerned, and then consider related clusters of behaviours or diagnostic categories that have been distinguished. Finally, we discuss appropriate behaviours that may be underdeveloped in children with maladjustment.

Disruptive behaviours

Oppositional behaviour

Oppositional behaviour or non-compliance is behaviour in which a child resists a caregiver. A range of oppositional behaviours may be discerned, from passive to active forms of non-compliance (Kochanska & Aksan, 1995). Thus, children may ignore a parental direction, which is an example of passive non-compliance, but they may also directly refuse a parental command, which is a form of mildly active non-compliance. In addition, children may angrily reject parental commands or prohibitions, which is a form of severe non-compliance or defiance. In preschool children, moreover, a distinction needs to be made between normative non-compliance and clinically significant non-compliance or oppositionality (Wakschlag & Danis, 2004). Normative non-compliance reflects the young child's self-assertion and is driven by the desire to do something autonomously (Wakschlag & Danis, 2004). Normative or self-assertive non-compliance is generally short-lived, whereas clinically significant non-compliance is more intransigent (Wakschlag & Danis, 2004).

Oppositional Defiant Disorder and Conduct Disorder in Childhood   By Walter Matthys and John E. Lochman
© 2010 John Wiley & Sons, Ltd.

Aggressive behaviour

Aggression is behaviour deliberately aimed at harming people (Parke & Slaby, 1983). Hitting other children is an example of physical aggression. There are, however, other forms of aggression. Words also may harm people, either as a possible precursor of physical aggression such as in verbal threats, or as a means to denigrate or provoke another child. This occurs, for example, when children call each other names. Relational aggression is another form of aggressive behaviour that has been investigated in recent years (Crick & Grotpeter, 1995). It is defined as damaging interpersonal relationships or feelings of inclusion. Malicious gossiping and threatening to withdraw friendship are examples of relational aggression. In this book, when we use the term 'aggression', we understand this as physical or verbal aggression. When relational aggression is discussed, this is made explicit.

Among these various forms of aggressive behaviour, the distinction has been made between reactive and proactive aggression (for reviews, see Dodge, 1991; Kempes *et al.*, 2005; Vitaro *et al.*, 2006). Reactive aggression is an impulsive aggressive response to a frustration, a perceived threat or a provocation. On the other hand, proactive aggression is controlled aggressive behaviour that anticipates a reward. Reactive aggression also has been called defensive or 'hot-blooded' aggression, whereas proactive aggression has been called instrumental or 'cold-blooded' aggression.

When considering aggression, one may distinguish differences in the underlying motivation (or the 'whys' of aggressive behaviour) from differences in the various forms of aggression (the 'whats' of aggressive behaviour) (Little *et al.*, 2003). Thus, the distinction between reactive and proactive aggression (the 'whys') may be applied both to physical, verbal and relational aggression (the 'whats'). One example of verbal reactive aggression in children is to get angry and swear at adults when corrected. One example of physical reactive aggression is to strike back when teased by a peer. A child threatening another child in order to get his or her own way is an example of verbal proactive aggression. To incite other children to act against a child whom he or she dislikes is an example of proactive relational aggression. Although reactive aggression and proactive aggression are highly correlated, correlations drop dramatically after the distinction has been made between the form and the motivation of aggression (Polman *et al.*, 2007).

Antisocial and delinquent behaviour

Antisocial behaviour is defined as behaviour by which basic norms, rights and rules are violated. Thus, when children lie they violate the norm of speaking the truth, when they steal they violate the right of the protection of one's property, and when they are truant they violate a rule. 'Antisocial behaviour' is often used as a general term for the various inappropriate behaviours such as oppositional and aggressive behaviour. When children repeatedly resist in response to requests, instructions or corrections given by adults, they indeed violate the norm to be obedient to their parents or teachers. And when children beat their peer, they violate their peer's right of physical integrity.

When antisocial behaviours are legal violations, they are called delinquent behaviours. Depending on the age of the child, behaviours such as theft, running away, truancy from school and setting fires are considered to be delinquent. Legislation between countries, and among states within countries, largely varies, so that the same behaviour, for example drinking alcohol, is considered as illegal in one country or state but not in another.

Psychopathic features and callous-unemotional traits

There is one other term that is relevant here – psychopathy. Psychopathy refers to personality characteristics such as an absence of empathy, an absence of guilt, an absence of anxiety, shallow emotions and the inability to form and sustain lasting relationships (Cleckley, 1976; Hare, 1993). Thus, psychopathy does not refer to a specific set of behaviours but to underlying characteristics of individuals.

The construct of psychopathy in adults consists of various dimensions. The dimensions that have been found to be useful in children and adolescents are callous-unemotional traits (for a review, see Frick & White, 2008) and narcissism (Barry *et al.*, 2007). The affective factor of psychopathy – the callous-unemotional trait – consists of lack of guilt, lack of empathy and callous use of others for one's own gain, and has been found to have moderate stability in longitudinal research (Pardini *et al.*, 2007; Barry *et al.*, 2009).

Disruptive behaviours

The above discussed inappropriate behaviours also are called disruptive behaviours. These behaviours not only disrupt child–child interactions and child–adult interactions, but when these behaviours occur frequently, the relations between children and the relations between children and adults are disrupted as well. 'Externalizing behaviour' is another general term for these inappropriate behaviours (Achenbach & Edelbrock, 1978). It is used to distinguish these behaviours from overcontrolled or internalizing behaviours such as withdrawal and anxious behaviours.

There are, however, more behaviours that are disruptive than the ones discussed above. Impulsive behaviours such as interrupting others and having difficulty in waiting a turn indeed are clearly disruptive. Hyperactive behaviour such as running about in the living room or leaving one's seat in the classroom and during meals at home, are troublesome as well. Finally, attention problems such as difficulty in sustaining attention may occur unnoticed, but other behaviours related to attention problems, such as not following through on instructions, are quite upsetting.

Diagnostic categories

Disruptive behaviours may occur either infrequently or in isolation in individual children, and in these cases the behaviours can then be considered as 'normative'. However, they may also occur as clusters. These clusters of co-occurring patterns of inappropriate behaviours or syndromes form the basis of the psychiatric categories from the classification systems of the *Diagnostic and statistical manual of mental disorders*, 4th edition (DSM-IV; American Psychiatric Association, 1994), or its revised form DSM-IV-TR (American Psychiatric Association, 2000), and the *International classification of diseases*, 10th revision (ICD-10; World Health Organization, 1996). Although these syndromes originate from hypotheses about co-varying symptoms or behaviours derived from observations of patients by clinicians, factor analytic studies of child and adolescent problem behaviour support how these behaviours are associated to each other (see later in this chapter).

The disruptive behaviours are distinguished from other disorders such as pervasive developmental disorders in DSM-IV-TR. Indeed, the former group of disorders is described under the general heading 'Attention deficit and disruptive behaviour disorders'. These disorders consist of: (1) attention deficit/hyperactivity disorder (ADHD), with characteristic features of hyperactive behaviour, impulsive behaviour and attention problems; and (2) the two disruptive behaviour disorders (DBDs) – oppositional defiant disorder (ODD) and conduct disorder (CD) – with characteristic features of oppositional, aggressive and antisocial behaviour. It is generally accepted that ODD and CD are different age-related manifestations of the same condition, with ODD already occurring in young children and CD occurring more often in older children and adolescents (Loeber *et al.*, 2000). Therefore, in this book for purposes of brevity ODD and CD are often referred to as the DBDs.

Although the subject of this book is the DBDs, we also will pay attention to ADHD. The DBDs and ADHD are related to each other with respect to their symptoms, and these disorders also often co-occur or are comorbid. Indeed, the odds ratio of DBD–ADHD comorbidity in a meta-analysis of community based samples was 10.7 (Angold *et al.*, 1999). Or to put it in another way, about 50% of children and adolescents with a DBD have comorbid ADHD, and vice versa (Kutcher *et al.*, 2004). In the assessment of children who are referred because of disruptive behaviour problems, clinicians therefore need to consider whether the child's inappropriate behaviours or symptoms are part of a DBD or of ADHD, or whether both disorders can be diagnosed. As we will describe in later chapters, the treatment of DBDs

---

Box 1.1 Symptoms of oppositional defiant disorder

- Loses temper
- Argues with adults
- Actively defies or refuses to comply with adults' requests or rules
- Deliberately annoys people
- Blames others for his or her mistakes or misbehaviour
- Is touchy or easily annoyed by others
- Is angry and resentful
- Is spiteful or vindictive

---

comorbid with ADHD is different from the treatment of DBDs without ADHD comorbidity.

Oppositional defiant disorder

In DSM-IV-TR, ODD is defined as 'a recurrent pattern of negativistic, defiant, disobedient, and hostile behaviour toward authority figures'. An overview of ODD symptoms is given in Box 1.1. Whereas DSM-IV-TR differentiates the various symptoms of CD into distinct groups such as 'Aggression to people and animals' and 'Serious violations of rules' (see Box 1.2, below), subgroups of symptoms are not formally identified for ODD.

However, in our view, a close consideration of the eight symptoms or criteria of ODD shows that they are very heterogeneous as well. Indeed, two symptoms are clearly oppositional and defiant in nature: 'Actively defies or refuses to comply with adults' requests or rules' and 'Argues with adults'. There are two symptoms of emotional dysregulation: one is mild ('Is touchy or easily annoyed by others') and one is more severe ('Loses temper'). There is one emotional symptom, and it is specifically about anger: 'Is angry and resentful'. There is one symptom of provocativeness: 'Deliberately annoys people'. And, finally, there are two symptoms of hostility: one is mild ('Blames others for his or her mistakes or misbehaviour') and one is severe ('Is spiteful or vindictive').

Thus, among the eight symptoms of ODD, there are only two oppositional and defiant symptoms. Consequently, a child may be diagnosed with ODD without showing any clear oppositional or defiant behaviour. Furthermore, the issue of heterogeneity of symptoms of ODD is important as inconsistencies in results of studies might be caused by differences between sample characteristics. The heterogeneity of samples is even increased when subjects with CD also are included, which is often the case.

Importantly, DSM-IV-TR specifies that manifestations of ODD are almost invariably present at home and need not be present at school or in the

Box 1.2 Symptoms of conduct disorder

Aggression to people and animals

1. Bullies, threatens or intimidates others
2. Initiates physical fights
3. Uses a weapon
4. Is physically cruel to people
5. Is physically cruel to animals
6. Steals while confronting a victim
7. Forces someone into sexual activity

Destruction of property

1. Sets fires
2. Destroys others' property

Deceitfulness or theft

1. Breaks into someone's house or car
2. Lies to obtain goods or favours, or to avoid obligations
3. Steals without confronting a victim

Serious violations of rules

1. Stays out at night
2. Runs away from home
3. Truants from school

community. The opposite symptom pattern, however, such as the presence of four symptoms at school but none at home, does not preclude ODD. Thus, according to DSM-IV-TR, symptoms need not be present in more than one setting.

The prevalence of ODD, i.e. the percentage of cases at a given point in time, varies considerably between studies, with a median of 3.2 (Lahey *et al.*, 1999). Although gender differences for ODD are quite inconsistent across studies, most data suggest either somewhat higher rates in boys than in girls or no gender difference (Loeber *et al.*, 2000).

Conduct disorder

In DSM-IV-TR, CD is characterized as a 'repetitive and persistent pattern of behaviour in which the basic rights of others or major age-appropriate societal norms or rules are violated'. Four groups of behaviours are distinguished: (1) aggressive conduct that causes or threatens physical harm to people or animals; (2) non-aggressive conduct that causes property loss or damage; (3) deceitfulness or theft; and (4) serious violations of rules (Box 1.2). Although the symptoms of ODD are all within the capacity of preschool children to perform, some of the symptoms of CD, such as forcible sexual activity, use of weapons and breaking into houses, are not (Wakschlag *et al.*, 2007).

DSM-IV-TR distinguishes two types of CD: the childhood-onset type with the onset of at least one symptom prior to age 10 years, and the adolescent-onset type, with an absence of any symptom prior to age 10 years. The distinction between these two types is supported by various studies (Moffitt, 1993; Lahey *et al.*, 1998; for a review, see Moffitt, 2003; see also Chapter 2). This childhood-onset group has been shown to have relatively poorer outcomes when compared with the adolescence-onset group. Because of this outcome, the childhood-onset type has also been called the life-persistent CD subtype (Moffitt, 2003).

Some longitudinal studies suggest that, among the children with early-onset CD, some lack the continuity of conduct problems from childhood to adulthood; these children have therefore been termed 'childhood-limited conduct problem group' (Moffitt, 2003). However, to date there is not enough evidence to further divide the childhood-onset type into a life-course-persistent versus a childhood-limited group (Moffitt *et al.*, 2008).

ODD and CD are both related to and different from each other. The association between these disorders needs to be considered from a developmental point of view. Longitudinal studies give the opportunity not only to prospectively follow children (follow-forward studies), but also to examine earlier diagnoses in adolescents who meet the criteria of disorders (follow-back studies). With regard to the relation between ODD and CD, follow-forward studies have shown that most children with ODD do not develop CD, whereas follow-back studies have shown that most children with CD had prior ODD (for a discussion of this issue, see Moffitt *et al.*, 2008, and Chapter 2). Importantly, most children who meet the criteria for childhood-onset CD also meet criteria for ODD (for a review, see Lahey *et al.*, 1992). Therefore, the rules of DSM-IV-TR specify that ODD is to be excluded if CD is present.

The prevalence of CD varies considerably between studies, with a median of 2.0; CD is more common in boys than in girls (Lahey *et al.*, 1999).

Other relevant disorders

Other diagnostic categories are relevant here for two reasons. First, some characteristic behaviours of these disorders are similar to symptoms of ODD and CD. For example, 'Does not seem to listen when spoken to directly' is a criterion of inattention in ADHD but is related to refusing to comply with adults' requests, which is a symptom of ODD. Also, a depressed mood, characteristic of a dysthymic disorder, in children may manifest as irritability. This expression of irritability may be related to the ODD symptom 'Is angry and resentful'. Second, some disorders often co-occur with ODD and CD. The most prevalent comorbid disorder of the DBDs is ADHD (Angold *et al.*, 1999). This comorbidity is highly important both with respect to the aetiology of the DBDs (see Chapters 3 and 4), the assessment (see Chapter 6) and the treatment of the DBDs (see Chapters 8–11).

DSM-IV-TR provides lists for two types of ADHD symptom: inattention and hyperactivity/impulsivity. Thus, three ADHD subtypes are distinguished: predominantly inattentive (I), predominantly hyperactive-impulsive (HI), and combined (C). An overview of ADHD symptoms is given in Box 1.3.

Also important is comorbidity with other disorders and developmental conditions, including mood disorders (Angold *et al.*, 1999) such as dysthymic disorder, anxiety disorders (Angold *et al.*, 1999) such as separation anxiety disorder, learning disorders and academic underachievement (Frick *et al.*,

---

Box 1.3 Symptoms of attention deficit/hyperactivity disorder

Inattention

1. Fails to give close attention to details or makes careless mistakes
2. Has difficulty sustaining attention
3. Does not seem to listen
4. Does not follow through on instructions and fails to finish schoolwork or chores
5. Has difficulty organizing tasks and activities
6. Avoids, dislikes or is reluctant to engage in tasks that require sustained attention
7. Loses things
8. Is easily distracted
9. Is forgetful in daily activities

Hyperactivity

1. Fidgets
2. Leaves his or her seat
3. Runs about or climbs
4. Has difficulty playing or engaging in leisure activities quietly
5. Is 'on the go'
6. Talks excessively

Impulsivity

1. Blurts out answers
2. Has difficulty waiting a turn
3. Interrupts or intrudes on others

1991; Hinshaw *et al.*, 1993), communication disorders and borderline intelligence. We will pay attention to these comorbid disorders and conditions when discussing the assessment (see Chapter 6) and treatment of the DBDs (see Chapters 8–11).

DSM-IV and ICD-10

Besides DSM-IV-TR, the ICD-10 (1996) of the World Health Organization is used in many countries. It should be noted, however, that little research has been conducted into ICD-10-defined disruptive behaviour problems. Over the years, differences between both systems have diminished, but important distinctions still remain. First, ODD is not a distinct category in ICD-10 but is instead a subtype of CD, along with the socialized and unsocialized subtypes of CD. Second, hyperkinetic disorder in ICD-10 is quite different from ADHD in DSM-IV-TR. Hyperkinetic disorder requires symptoms in three domains (hyperactivity, impulsivity, inattention), whereas DSM-IV-TR distinguishes various subtypes depending on the occurrence of symptoms of inattention and hyperactivity/impulsivity. Thus, hyperkinetic disorder is a narrower concept than ADHD. Third, one of the subtypes of hyperkinetic disorder is hyperkinetic conduct disorder. Thus, in contrast to DSM-IV, in ICD-10 the co-occurrence of CD (of which ODD is a subtype) with hyperkinetic disorder is not considered a comorbidity but a subtype of hyperkinetic disorder, i.e. hyperkinetic conduct disorder.

Factor analytic studies support the distinction that DSM makes between ODD, CD, ADHD and other disorders. Factor analysis is one statistical technique that can search for patterns in co-variation among a group of behaviours. Using exploratory and confirmatory factor analyses with data from various questionnaires in population and clinically referred samples, Hartman *et al.* (2001) investigated the internal construct validity of a DSM-IV-based model of ADHD (inattention, hyperactivity/impulsivity), ODD, CD, generalized anxiety and depression. The factorial structure of these syndromes was supported by the data. However, the DSM-IV model did not meet the absolute standard of adequate model fit, leaving substantial room for improvement. Findings from another study support the four-factor DSM-IV model (ODD, CD, hyperactivity/impulsivity, inattention) of the DSM-IV-TR 'Attention deficit and disruptive behaviour disorders' (Lahey *et al.*, 2008a). In addition, this model fitted better with the data than models based on ICD-10 and the Child Behavior Checklist (Achenbach, 1991).

Socially appropriate behaviours

It is also important to pay attention to appropriate behaviours, because children with DBDs may not have these behaviours in their repertoire. There are a number of social behaviour skills that children use to cope adequately with everyday problem situations. These skills include entering a group, starting a conversation, asking questions and listening to others. Other socially appropriate behaviours such as showing interest, comforting, sharing, helping and donating are more clearly prosocial in that they are intended to benefit other persons (Eisenberg & Fabes, 1998). Empathy is related to prosocial behaviour (Eisenberg & Miller, 1987). Empathy is defined as the understanding of, and sharing in, another's emotional state (Hoffmann, 2000). Strictly speaking, empathy is not behaviour. Instead, it is an emotion. Empathy involves a matching of emotions between the child and the other person, i.e. feeling with another person.

Summary points

- Among oppositional behaviours, one may distinguish passive forms of non-compliance (e.g. ignoring parental commands) from mild active forms (e.g. refusing parental directions) and severe active forms or defiant behaviour (e.g. angrily rejecting parental commands).
- Aggressive behaviour may manifest in various forms: in physical aggression, in verbal aggression and in relational aggression, i.e. damaging interpersonal relationships or feelings of inclusion.
- When considering the underlying motivation in aggressive behaviour, the distinction can be made between reactive, defensive or 'hot-blooded' aggression, and proactive, controlled or 'cold-blooded' aggression.
- The affective factor of psychopathy – callous-unemotional traits – consists of a lack of guilt, lack of empathy and callous use of others for one's own gain.
- The symptoms of ODD are very heterogeneous, with only two symptoms that are clearly oppositional in nature, and, furthermore, two symptoms of emotional dysregulation, one on anger, one on provocativeness and two on hostility.
- Symptoms of ODD need not be present in more than one setting in order for a child to qualify for ODD.
- In CD, the distinction is made between the childhood-onset type of CD, with an onset of at least one symptom prior to age 10 years, and the adolescent-onset type of CD, with an absence of any symptom prior to age 10 years.
- Some symptoms of ADHD are clearly disruptive, such as not following through on instructions (inattention), leaving the seat in the classroom (hyperactive behaviour) and difficulty waiting a turn (impulsive behaviour).
- Follow-forward studies have shown that most children with ODD do not develop CD, whereas follow-back studies have shown that most children with CD have had prior ODD.
- The most prevalent comorbid disorder of the DBDs is ADHD.

2

Developmental perspectives

This chapter will describe the normal development of child compliance, anger and aggression during the childhood years. Using a developmental psychopathology perspective, the developmental course of the problematic externalizing behaviours that comprise ODD and CD, and of subtypes of children with conduct problems, will be described. A specific focus will be placed on the development of early starters versus late starters, of aggressive-rejected versus aggressive-nonrejected children, and of children with psychopathic traits.

Development and developmental psychopathology

The first textbook on developmental psychopathology appeared in 1974 (Achenbach, 1974). In the subsequent 35 years, the benefits of using a developmental psychopathology approach have been increasingly recognized by the scientific community, and research on the causative factors and treatment of childhood mental health difficulties such as conduct problems has been advanced and expanded under a developmental psychopathology framework (Lochman et al., 2008a). Developmental psychopathology includes a focus on understanding causal processes, understanding the role of development, and understanding the continuities and discontinuities between normality and pathology.

The need for a developmental psychopathology approach arose out of a growing recognition of the limitations of traditional developmental and psychological perspectives (Rutter & Sroufe, 2000). At the same time, emerging research demonstrated that developmental pathways were complex and dynamic, involving both individual and environmental factors (Rutter & Sroufe, 2000). An inclusive framework, allowing the examination of a

Oppositional Defiant Disorder and Conduct Disorder in Childhood   By Walter Matthys and John E. Lochman
© 2010 John Wiley & Sons, Ltd.

multitude of factors on developmental processes, was needed to integrate the growing bodies of information from diverse disciplines such as psychology, psychiatry, sociology, biology and epidemiology. By taking a developmental psychopathology perspective, clinicians and researchers attempt to understand the processes by which behaviours, both normative and atypical, arise and are maintained (Luthar *et al.*, 1997).

Development of behaviour and processes over time

A knowledge of normative developmental processes and behaviours corresponding to different developmental levels is imperative to understanding maladaptive behaviours and disorders (Sroufe & Rutter, 1984; Essau & Petermann, 1997). At the most basic level, problems can be identified by making contrasts between expected abilities at a given stage of development and an individual's actual functioning (Edelbrock, 1984). For example, physical aggression is common among preschoolers, but steadily declines with age to become almost non-existent by the end of adolescence (Bongers *et al.*, 2004). In a developmental psychopathology perspective, the processes involved in development are also crucial considerations. For example, the influences of genetic and environmental factors must be analysed in the context of ongoing developmental processes within the individual (Rutter & Sroufe, 2000). There are normal variations at points in time, and especially over time, in externalizing behaviours and related emotional characteristics (Lochman *et al.*, 2008a). In this section, we will review normal development of compliance behaviours, anger and aggression in children, all of which are key characteristics associated with the disruptive behaviour disorders (DBDs).

Compliance behaviours

All children at every age exhibit both compliant and non-compliant behaviours, and non-compliant behaviours, by themselves, are not causes for referral or diagnosis (Lochman *et al.*, 2008b). However, the frequency, intensity, form and effects of such behaviours set apart normal and abnormal expressions of non-compliance. Clinical manifestations of non-compliance are categorized as symptoms of ODD and were described in Chapter 1. This section will outline patterns and contributing factors in normal compliant and non-compliant behaviours.

Although most people involved in the care of children have an idea of what is meant by compliance and non-compliance, these behaviours often prove difficult to define operationally. In their treatment manual for non-compliant children, McMahon and Forehand (2003) use the definition 'appropriate following of an instruction within a reasonable and/or designated time' to operationalize compliance, noting that it is important to distinguish between the initiation of compliance and the completion of the specified task (Schoen, 1983). Five to 15 seconds is suggested as a reasonable period for the initiation of compliance. McMahon and Forehand (2003) define non-compliance as the refusal to initiate or complete a request and/or the failure to follow a previously stated rule that is currently in effect. In defining compliance and non-compliance, it is also important to recognize that these are not stand-alone behaviours on the part of the child, but are bidirectional interactional processes between adult and child. Parenting behaviours can affect a child's likelihood of compliance, and child characteristics and responses can in turn affect parenting behaviours.

Children first begin to understand the consequences of their own behaviour between 6 and 9 months of age, and may also learn to recognize the word 'no' during this time. Increasing physical development, cognitive abilities, social skills and receptive language skills lead to improved abilities to respond to verbal directions, and children are generally able to follow simple instructions by the age of 2. Nonetheless, non-compliance with commands is very common for 2- and 3-year-old children, possibly due to parental expectations (i.e. 'the terrible twos') and parents' failure to train their young children to comply (Brumfield & Roberts, 1998).

Compliance levels are expected to increase with age in typically developing children (e.g. Lahey *et al.*, 2000). Although specific normative data for compliance do not exist because of complex issues about sample characteristics and measurement (Brumfield & Roberts, 1998; McMahon & Forehand, 2003), the expected progression of compliant behaviours in young children as they age has generally been found, with some exceptions (Smith *et al.*, 2004). Vaughn *et al.* (1984) reported increases in compliance with maternal requests between 18 and 30 months of age, and Kochanska *et al.* (2001) found that children's committed, eager compliance to maternal directions increased from 27% to 56% during the 14 to 33 months of age period. Brumfield and Roberts (1998) reported that, whereas 2- and 3-year-old children only complied with 32.2% of maternal commands, the compliance rate for 4- and 5-year-olds reached 77.7%. However, Kuczynski and Kochanska (1990) reported no change in overall compliance with maternal requests between toddlers (1½ to 3½ years old) and 5-year-olds, but did find variations over time in specific non-compliant behaviours. Direct defiance and passive non-compliance decreased with age, and simple refusal and negotiation (an indirect form of non-compliance that requires more autonomy and social skill) increased.

By the time they reach school age, children are expected to comply with adult requests the majority of the time. McMahon and Forehand's (2003) review of studies suggests that compliance rates are around 80% for normally developing children. Patterson and Forgatch (1987), however, report lower compliance rates in a sample of 'nonproblem 10- and 11-year-old boys': 57% to maternal requests and 47% to paternal requests.

In adolescence, non-compliant behaviours often again increase, and go above childhood levels in typically developing youth. Developmental changes in cognition and social skills, combined with adolescents' growing independence and need to establish their own identity, may lead to increased parent–adolescent conflict. Conflict tends to be at its highest during early adolescence, and to decline from early adolescence to mid-adolescence and from mid-adolescence to late adolescence (Laursen *et al.*, 1998).

Boys and girls differ in their normative rates of oppositional, non-compliant behaviours, with boys demonstrating higher levels than girls during childhood. However, the gender difference closes with age, and boys and girls demonstrate increasingly similar rates as they progress through adolescence (Bongers *et al.*, 2004).

Anger and aggression

Like compliance and non-compliance, angry and aggressive behaviours are common to all children, representing clinically significant problems only when frequent and severe enough to disrupt a child or family's daily life (Lochman *et al.*, 2008b). Not surprisingly, children who are identified as angry by parents and teachers are more likely to display externalizing behaviours (e.g. Denham *et al.*, 2002; Bohnert *et al.*, 2003; Rydell *et al.*, 2003). Relations have also been reported between child anger and internalizing problems (e.g. Eisenberg *et al.*, 2005) and between child anger and being victimized by their peers (Hanish *et al.*, 2004).

The presence or absence of anger is often a defining factor in the classification of aggression. Anger is a key feature of *hostile aggression*, which carries the intent to harm and is accompanied by emotional arousal, but not *instrumental aggression*, which is motivated by external reward rather than by emotional arousal. In a similar distinction, as noted in Chapter 1, *reactive aggression* is emotionally driven and takes the form of angry temper outbursts, whereas *proactive aggression* is instrumentally driven and takes the form of goal-driven behaviours (e.g. domination of others or obtaining a desired object; Dodge, 1991; Dodge *et al.*, 1997).

Anger and development

Anger is one of the earliest emotions to appear in infancy. Between 2 and 6 months of age, infants engage in recognizable displays of anger, including a characteristic angry cry, and by 7 months facial expressions of anger can be reliably detected (Stenberg *et al.*, 1983). Caregivers tend to respond to infants' anger expressions by ignoring them or reacting negatively, thus beginning the socialization process against anger expression (Malatesta *et al.*, 1986; Huebner & Izard, 1988). As children learn what is socially acceptable, their displays of anger may diminish. By 24 months of age, toddlers are able to modulate their expression of anger and are more likely to display sadness, which is more likely to elicit a supportive response from a caregiver (Buss & Kiel, 2004).

Angry feelings are likely to be accompanied by physically aggressive behaviour in very young children, but with increasing age and developmental level, expressions of anger change in typically developing children. Dunn (1988), for example, found that physical aggression and teasing were equally prevalent in 14-month-old children, but by 24 months children were much more likely to tease. During early childhood, children are expected to learn appropriate ways to manage and express their anger. Young children acquire a progressively larger emotional vocabulary and an increased understanding of the causes and consequences of feelings (Ridgeway et al., 1985; Denham, 1998). By the time they reach elementary school age, children have generally developed a sophisticated understanding of the types of emotional display that are appropriate and functional in a given context (Shipman et al., 2003). In regard to anger, Shipman and colleagues reported that children in the 1st through 5th grades identified verbalization of feelings as the most appropriate means of expression, followed by facial displays. The children identified sulking, crying and aggression as equally inappropriate ways to express anger. These findings are consistent with other research demonstrating that, with age, children become increasingly less likely to engage in expressive displays of anger as they come to recognize that their ability to maintain emotional control is important to their social functioning (Underwood et al., 1992).

The types of circumstance that elicit anger in children also change with developmental level. Very young children are likely to react angrily when someone or something interferes with their attempts to reach a goal, whereas anger in older children is more often precipitated by a threat to self-esteem. This change is accompanied by increases in older children's self-awareness, understanding of social norms and the importance they place on others' perceptions of them.

Aggression and development
An understanding of normal developmental patterns in aggressive behaviour is an important starting point in identifying clinically significant problems for children of a given age. In typically developing children, aggressive behaviours follow a declining trend with age during childhood and adolescence. Large-scale longitudinal and cross-sectional studies have demonstrated that rates of aggression decline during childhood and adolescence, with the highest levels of physically aggressive behaviour occurring in the youngest children, perhaps at age 2, and the lowest levels corresponding to late adolescence (e.g. Stanger et al., 1997; Nagin & Tremblay, 1999; Keiley et al., 2000; Bongers et al., 2003, 2004).

Declining trajectories of aggression over time hold for children of both genders; however, at any given point in childhood, boys tend to display higher rates of overt aggressive behaviour than girls. In fact, boys may display twice as much aggression as girls during childhood. These gender differences appear to be present very early on, prior to 4 years of age, and are therefore unlikely to be due to socialization effects associated with school attendance. Aggressive behaviour declines more quickly for boys and, by late adolescence, the rates of aggression in males and females are indistinguishable (e.g. Bongers *et al.*, 2003, 2004). Aggressive acts are nearly non-existent in typically developing late adolescent-aged youth of both genders.

Another classification of aggression differentiates between physical aggression and relational aggression. Girls are more likely to have a higher proportion of their aggressive behaviour that is relational or indirect in nature. Relational aggression involves efforts to cause harm by damaging others' relationships or threatening to do so (e.g. spreading rumors, social exclusion; Crick & Grotpeter, 1995), and the spreading of rumours about peers and gossiping can be considered to be a form of bullying (Ireland & Archer, 2004). Boys engage in about as much relational aggression as girls, but the largest portion of their aggressive behaviour (in contrast to girls) consists of overt or physical aggression.

Development in problematic externalizing behaviours

Due to a number of factors that will be further elaborated in later chapters (see Chapters 4 and 5), some children fall outside the normal or typical variations of externalizing behaviours (Lochman *et al.*, 2008b). A chronic trajectory of overt conduct problems that starts as early as 2 years of age is evident among some children, although other 2-year-olds have desisting conduct problems over time and are of less clinical concern (Shaw *et al.*, 2005). Aggression is one of the most stable problem behaviours in childhood, with a developmental trajectory towards negative outcomes in adolescence, such as drug and alcohol use, truancy and drop-out, delinquency and violence (Lochman *et al.*, 2006a). Children's aggressive behaviour patterns may escalate to include a wide range of severe antisocial behaviours in adolescence (Loeber, 1990). The negative trajectory may even continue into adulthood, as demonstrated by Olweus' (1991) finding that 60% of adolescents identified as bullies had their first criminal conviction by age 24 (Olweus, 1991). Continuities between childhood DBD and adulthood disorders are far from simple (Rutter *et al.*, 2006a). On the one hand, many antisocial adults have a history of disruptive behaviour in childhood (Robins, 1966). On the other, many children with a DBD do not become antisocial adults. Thus, there is both continuity and change in these behaviours.

Aggressive behaviour can lead to serious and negative legal and relational consequences for the child engaging in the behaviour. The negative effects are not limited to the aggressive individual, however, as aggressive behaviour, by definition, has the potential to cause harm or injury to others. In schools, aggressive bullying, which may be verbal, physical or psychological, has been recognized as a serious problem (Rigby & Ian, 1996). Bullying is a deliberate act with the intent of harming the victims (Farrington, 1993). Examples of direct bullying include hitting and kicking, charging interest on goods and stealing, name calling and intimidation, and sexual harassment. The victims of bullies can tend to be shy (Nabuzoka & Smith, 1993). However, it is important to note that aggressive children are often the victims of others' aggression as well (Smith & Ecob, 2007; Moffitt & Scott, 2008) and are thus 'bully-victims'.

Researchers have observed that the manifestations of antisocial behaviour generally change over time across the life-span (Loeber & Hay, 1997). For example, a toddler may bite, hit and throw temper tantrums, while a child in his late school years may shoplift and skip school. Likewise, an adolescent may sell drugs and steal, while an adult may commit fraud and violently aggress against others. Researchers with a developmental perspective have recognized these developmental variations in antisocial behaviour and have explored the degree to which early forms of antisocial behaviour portend later forms (Lochman *et al.*, 2009a). There may be not only continuity within the same disorder (homotypic continuity), but also continuity that involves different disorders (heterotypic continuity). For example, in the Dunedin study, ODD and CD were associated with an increased risk of later substance abuse disorder and antisocial personality disorder (homotypic continuity), as well as adult depression, anxiety disorders, eating disorders, schizophreniform disorders and mania (heterotypic continuity) (Kim-Cohen *et al.*, 2003).

As a result, subtyping approaches have emerged that divide the population of antisocial individuals into groups on the basis of developmental variations in antisocial behaviour, age of onset of conduct problems and course of antisocial behaviour over time. Decades of research have verified that conduct problems co-occur with other adjustment problems at a much higher rate than would be expected by chance (Angold *et al.*, 1999). Comorbid diagnoses include ADHD, and internalizing problems such as anxiety and depression. Several hypotheses have been proposed for the high rate of comorbidity (McMahon & Frick, 2005). In one proposed pathway, additional adjustment problems may stem from conduct problems if, for example, a child's disruptive behaviours lead to peer rejection and resulting feelings of depression or anxiety. Finally, common risk factors, such as social-cognitive deficits, may be causal sources of conduct problems and other disorders.

Subtypes of disruptive behaviour disorders

Antisocial behaviour in children and adolescents can be subtyped on the basis of developmental variations in behaviour and the age of onset for conduct problems. This subtyping approach is reflected in the *Diagnostic and statistical manual of mental disorders*, 4th edition, text revision (DSM-IV-TR; American

Psychiatric Association, 2000), including the diagnoses of ODD and CD (see Chapter 1). ODD symptoms in general emerge earlier than CD symptoms. While many children exhibit oppositional/disruptive behaviours (ODD) and ultimately desist in these behaviours over time, a substantial subset of these children gradually progress to more delinquent acts (Loeber & Farrington, 2000). CD is diagnosed when these delinquent acts include behaviours that violate societal norms and/or the basic rights of others. While symptoms of CD generally emerge in middle childhood or early adolescence, they may also appear in early childhood (American Psychiatric Association, 2000). Consequently, the DSM-IV-TR presents two subtypes of CD based on age of onset – a childhood-onset type characterized by onset prior to age 10, and an adolescent-onset type characterized by onset after age 10 (American Psychiatric Association, 2000).

Many researchers have acknowledged that these age-of-onset distinctions have important implications for the course of antisocial behaviour over time, and are consistent in many ways with research on early starters versus late starters.

Early starters versus late starters

Within this subtyping approach, one group of offenders, termed 'early starters' (Patterson *et al.*, 1989) or 'life-course-persistent' offenders (Moffitt, 1993; Loeber & Stouthamer-Loeber, 1998), commit their first transgression early and persist in offending throughout the life-span. This book primarily focuses on these 'early starters'. As McMahon *et al.* (2006) observe, individuals with childhood-onset CD likely fall within this subtype. Patterson *et al.* (1989) maintain that, for these 'early starters', antisocial behaviour is a developmental trait that emerges consistently throughout life but manifests itself differently at each developmental stage. Early manifestations of antisocial behaviour often predict later manifestations of antisocial behaviour (Patterson *et al.*, 1989). Patterson *et al.* (1998) clarified these relations further. They demonstrated that high levels of antisocial behaviour in childhood significantly related to early arrest (before age 14) and that early arrest significantly related to chronic offending by age 18. More specifically, Patterson *et al.* (1998) found that the majority of chronic offenders (71%) evidenced antisocial behaviour in childhood, followed by early arrest, along their path to criminal offending.

While many researchers have noted the stability in antisocial behaviour over time, others have acknowledged that a small group of individuals do not exhibit early patterns of antisocial behaviour but begin their criminal careers later in life. Epidemiological data, for example, suggest that the prevalence of antisocial behaviour spikes in adolescence (Moffitt, 1993). Moffitt (1993) explores these data further and notes that the prevalence rate of antisocial behaviour in boys hovers around 5% at age 11 but jumps to 32% at age 15.

These prevalence rates continue to increase until the mid-20s, when most individuals are believed to desist in their antisocial activities (Moffitt, 1993). This subtype of offender has been termed 'late starters' (Patterson *et al.*, 1989), 'adolescent-limited' offenders (Moffitt, 1993) or 'limited-duration' offenders (Loeber & Stouthamer-Loeber, 1998). Individuals with the adolescent-onset brand of CD probably fall within this subtype (McMahon *et al.*, 2006).

Many researchers have argued that these two subtypes – the early and the late starters – differ in terms of their associated risk factors. In a long-term longitudinal birth cohort study in Dunedin, Moffitt and Caspi (2001) found that life-course-persistent offenders could be differentiated from adolescence-limited offenders on the basis of risk factors related to parenting, greater peer difficulties, IQ, neurocognitive functioning and child temperament and behaviour. Moffitt and Caspi (2001) demonstrated that children on the life-course-persistent track experienced significantly higher levels of childhood risk in these three domains than their counterparts on the adolescent-limited trajectory. The early-onset group was found to have significant difficulties in domains of violence, mental health, substance abuse, work and family life when the Dunedin cohort was followed into adulthood (Moffitt *et al.*, 2002; Odgers *et al.*, 2007b). The distinction between the two groups of children has been replicated in longitudinal studies within a dozen countries (Moffitt, 2006; Moffitt & Scott, 2008).

Aguilar *et al.* (2000) also distinguished between early-onset/persistent offenders and adolescence-onset offenders on the basis of childhood risk. However, their results substantially diverge from those highlighted by Moffitt and Caspi (2001). More specifically, Aguilar *et al.* (2000) did not find any significant group differences in early temperament variables. Moreover, they did not find any early group differences in neuropsychological functioning; these differences only emerged in late childhood and early adolescence. Despite the lack of significant, early differences in the temperamental and neuropsychological domains, Aguilar *et al.* (2000) did identify a number of group differences in psychosocial areas. More specifically, they found that early-onset/persistent offenders were significantly more likely to come from single-parent homes characterized by high levels of stress than adolescents in the 'never antisocial' and childhood-limited groups. These early-onset/persistent offenders were also significantly more likely to have evidenced avoidant attachment with caregivers at age 12 and 18 months and to have experienced abusive, neglectful or otherwise inadequate parenting (Aguilar *et al.*, 2000).

Patterson *et al.* (1989) also emphasize the impact of ineffective parenting practices on children's engagement in the early-starter pathway. Additional parenting factors such as parental convictions and parental transitions have been linked to the early-onset course of antisocial behaviour in girls (Leve & Chamberlain, 2004). In sum, it appears clear that many factors increase a child's risk for initiating and continuing along the early-starter pathway.

Although risk factors described in the prior paragraphs seem to be influential in placing some children onto the early-starter pathway, the concept of social mimicry has emerged as the primary explanation for why others pursue antisocial behaviour later in life. Moffitt (1993) maintains that social mimicry occurs when a subgroup of adolescents observes the antisocial behaviour exhibited by their life-course-persistent peers and subsequently follows suit. Moffitt (1993) asserts that these adolescents are motivated by the desire to assert their independence and acquire mature status. Although these offenders were expected to gradually desist in their antisocial behaviours as they gained access to more adult roles and began to perceive delinquent activities as resulting in punishing rather than rewarding consequences (Moffitt, 1993), recent longitudinal research indicates that the late starters do have some continuing problems with criminal and substance-using behaviour into young adulthood (Moffitt *et al.*, 2002; Odgers *et al.*, 2007). Conceptual and empirical elaborations of the basic distinction between early versus adolescent-onset youth patterns have suggested that these two classifications may exist on a continuum rather than being qualitatively different (Lahey & Waldman, 2003). These elaborations have also identified a third group of aggressive children, the child-limited group, who do not progress to serious delinquent behaviour (Raine *et al.*, 2005; Odgers *et al.*, 2008).

Aggressive-rejected versus aggressive-nonrejected youths

Peer status is another social dimension in which subgroups of aggressive children have been found to differ (Bierman, 2004; Conduct Problems Prevention Research Group, 2004). There is a considerable body of literature demonstrating that aggressive behaviour is a strong predictor of peer rejection, particularly among boys (Coie & Dodge, 1998), and that aggression and peer rejection together predict a range of poor adolescent outcomes, including delinquency (Coie *et al.*, 1992; Lochman & Wayland, 1994). However, this literature also indicates that the relationship between aggression and social status is complex, as not all children who exhibit high rates of aggressive behaviour are rejected by their peers, and a significant portion of children who are rejected by their peers do not exhibit high rates of aggression.

To better understand the relationship between aggression and peer status, Bierman *et al.* (1993) compared the characteristics of aggressive boys who were rejected with those who were not. Although both groups showed higher rates of physical aggression than rejected non-aggressive and comparison (neither aggressive nor rejected) peers, the aggressive-rejected boys exhibited more diverse and severe types of conduct problems than the aggressive-nonrejected boys. The more diverse types of disruptive behaviour exhibited by aggressive-rejected boys tended to reflect greater impulsivity and worse behavioural control (e.g. verbal aggression, rule violations, hyperactivity). In addition, the aggressive-rejected boys exhibited lower adaptive skills on teacher and peer ratings of attentiveness/perceptiveness.

Bierman and colleagues' (1993) findings are consistent with subsequent studies, which have found that peer rejection in childhood is strongly associated with ADHD, and that children with co-occurring ADHD and aggressive behaviour are at greatest risk for peer rejection (Hinshaw & Melnick, 1995). While they often have 'controversial' social status, children exhibiting proactive aggression without co-occurring ADHD are less likely to be rejected by their peers (e.g. Milich & Landau, 1988). The relationship between peer rejection and aggressive and antisocial behaviour appears to be bidirectional. Not only does aggression predict social rejection in childhood, but peer rejection during childhood has also been causally linked to persistent and escalating levels of antisocial behaviour in adolescence (Coie *et al.*, 1995a). One potential mechanism underlying this relationship is that children who are rejected by their mainstream peers may be increasingly likely to affiliate with deviant peers, from whom they receive reinforcement for aggressive and delinquent acts.

Changes in psychopathic traits over time

Although there has been an increased interest in understanding the development of callous-unemotional (CU) traits in youth, longitudinal research in this area is sparse (for an exception, see Frick *et al.*, 2003). To address the lack of longitudinal research investigating the possible interactions between child anxiety and parenting practices in predicting the development of CU traits in school-aged children, Pardini *et al.* (2007) examined the development of CU traits across a 1-year period with a sample of 120 moderately to highly aggressive children. Consistent with prior research, CU traits in children displayed a moderate degree of temporal stability and predicted increases in antisocial behaviour across time. However, CU traits were changeable across this relatively brief developmental span and were affected by certain protective factors. Specifically, children who were exposed to lower levels of harsh punishment and perceived their parent as warm and involved exhibited decreases in CU traits over time. These parenting practices were also related to reductions in antisocial behaviour, suggesting that the co-occurrence between CU traits and antisocial behaviour might be partially due to shared environmental influences. In contrast, lower levels of anxiety were uniquely related to increases in CU traits over time, particularly for children who describe their caregiver as exhibiting relatively little warmth and involvement. The results suggested the important protective role of certain parenting practices, especially parent warmth and involvement, in moderating the development of CU traits during these preadolescent years.

In another recent longitudinal study (Barry *et al.*, 2008), 80 moderately aggressive preadolescents were followed for three annual assessments and, similar to the prior study, had moderately stable psychopathic characteristics over time. This study examined whether children's social relations might affect the development and change of psychopathic traits over time. Although consistent findings were not evident at all time points, partial evidence for moderation was found. The stability of narcissism was affected by the child's perception of his or her social competence, and, in contrast, the stability of impulsive conduct problems (i.e. the behavioural dimension of psychopathy) was influenced by the child's social competence based on teacher ratings and their social preference based on peer ratings. As expected, greater impairments in these social areas were associated with more stable and persistent psychopathic characteristics, including narcissism and impulsive conduct problems, whereas better social functioning was associated with decreasing levels of psychopathic characteristics across time. These two longitudinal studies both suggest important parent and peer contextual factors that can buffer against, or enhance, the likelihood of psychopathic traits increasing in strength over time.

Developmental models and aetiology of disorder

Developmental psychopathology is concerned with the question of how causal processes operate to result in a given outcome (Rutter & Sroufe, 2000; Lochman *et al.*, 2008a). Questions of nature versus nurture and of the relative contributions of genetic and environmental factors are considered under the umbrella of causal processes, and we will explore these issues in Chapters 4 and 5. Research conducted from a developmental psychopathology perspective has demonstrated the complex interactions of genes and environment in normal and abnormal behavioural variations (Plomin & Rutter, 1998; Rutter, 2008). In the study of causal processes, the developmental psychopathology approach also incorporates the principles of equifinality (i.e. the same outcome through different pathways) and multifinality (i.e. different outcomes through the same pathway). Developmental psychopathology focuses on certain classes of variable that influence trajectories of behavioural development: risk factors (such as smoking during pregnancy, which predict the likelihood of problems emerging or being maintained across time), protective factors (such as parental warmth, which alter and influence the relationship between a risk factor such as neighbourhood violence and subsequent negative outcomes; Masten, 2006; Patel & Goodman, 2007) and promotive factors (which are positive variables such as family communication that contribute to the development of positive social behaviours; Youngblade *et al.*, 2007).

Summary points

- Developmental psychopathology examines developmental processes in children from the point of view of diverse disciplines such as psychology, psychiatry, sociology, biology and epidemiology.
- Non-compliant child behaviours by themselves are not a cause for referral or diagnosis, but the intensity, form and effects of such behaviours, along with the child's age, can indicate abnormal levels of non-compliant behaviour.
- Normatively, physically aggressive behaviour occurs frequently in young children, but the rates of physically aggressive children begin to noticeably decline after 2½–3 years of age.
- Children with aggressive behaviour are at risk of severe antisocial behaviour in adolescence, and of antisocial personality disorder in adulthood.
- 'Early starters' are children who begin displaying delinquent and antisocial behaviour during childhood and are at risk of continuing to persist in offending throughout the life-span.
- Children who are both aggressive and highly rejected by their peer group are at particularly high risk for negative adolescent outcomes.

3

Basic issues on aetiology

In this chapter, we discuss some essential issues on aetiology in order to provide an adequate foundation for the review of individual and environmental aetiological factors in Chapters 4 and 5. Because dysfunctions of the brain play a role in the development of all psychiatric disorders, including the disruptive behaviour disorders (DBDs), we will first clarify how to conceptualize the functioning of the brain in relation to the functioning of the mind, and the role of social experiences in this relationship. We will then discuss the essential difference between the concepts of 'correlate' and 'risk factor'. Specific attention will be given to comorbidity of attention deficit/hyperactivity disorder (ADHD) in the DBDs. Finally, we will provide a general aetiological framework for the DBDs.

The brain–mind–environment relationship

In a seminal paper, Kandel in 1998 outlined a framework for psychiatry. Some of his ideas are relevant here. First, since all mental processes (or 'mind') derive from operations of the brain, psychiatric disorders are disturbances of brain function, even when the causes of the disturbances are environmental in origin. Second, as genes and their protein products are important determinants of the pattern of interconnections between neurons in the brain, genes contribute to the development of psychiatric disorders. Third, just as genes contribute to behaviour, so behaviour and social factors can exert actions on the brain and its (psychological) functions by modifying the expression of genes and thus the function of nerve cells. Learning, including both learning that results in dysfunctional behaviour and learning within the context of psychotherapy, produces changes in synaptic connections.

Oppositional Defiant Disorder and Conduct Disorder in Childhood   By Walter Matthys and John E. Lochman
© 2010 John Wiley & Sons, Ltd.

In other words, the causal relationship between brain and mind is bidirectional (Kendler, 2005). Not only do changes in the brain directly affect psychological functions, but the training of psychological functions may produce changes in the brain as well. The latter mind-to-brain causal relationship is demonstrated in studies on brain function following psychotherapeutic intervention (for a review, see Etkin *et al.*, 2005). For example, patients with obsessive compulsive disorder who responded to behaviour therapy (which trains response prevention after exposure) showed greater decreases in right caudate metabolism than patients who did not respond (Schwartz *et al.*, 1996). Both selective serotonin reuptake inhibitor and behaviour therapy have produced changes in brain functioning in obsessive compulsive disorder (Baxter *et al.*, 1992). Thus, learning may alter brain functioning.

Not only do social experiences affect the functioning of the brain, but the environment also affects the functioning of genes (Hernandez & Blazer, 2006; Rutter, 2006). Briefly, the DNA, which carries the inherited genetic information, specifies the synthesis of messenger RNA. The latter specifies the synthesis of polypeptides, which will ultimately form proteins. However, only a proportion of the genes in any one cell are 'expressed'. Indeed, the effects of genes are dependent on whether they are functionally activated; this is called gene expression. Here the environment may play a role, not in affecting the DNA but in affecting the transcription and translation processes, i.e. the process by which the DNA directs the synthesis of messenger RNA (transcription) and the process by which this transcribed messenger RNA is translated into a polypeptide (translation). Although we can currently only speculate about the implications of the emerging field of gene expression on the aetiology of DBDs, we are far moved from the debate about nature versus nurture (Rutter, 2006).

Risk factors and the causation of disorders

The various factors involved in the causation of psychiatric disorders almost always act in a probabilistic rather than a deterministic fashion. In other words, the factors increase the likelihood of the specific disorder but do not determine it. These factors are therefore called 'risk factors'.

Risk factors need to be distinguished from correlates in that they precede the outcome, such as a disorder (Kraemer *et al.*, 1997). Many individual and environmental characteristics have been shown to be associated with children with DBDs, antisocial or aggressive behaviour, as will be discussed in Chapters 4 and 5. However, it has not always been demonstrated that the risk characteristic preceded the occurrence of the DBD or maladaptive behaviour. Only studies using a longitudinal design can differentiate between correlates and risk factors.

Moreover, many risk factors do not indicate the mechanisms that actually cause the disorder (Rutter, 2003). Thus, for example, some prospective studies of low autonomic arousal have shown that this characteristic is associated with an increased risk of aggressive and antisocial behaviour (Venables, 1989; Raine et al., 1997a). Although hypotheses about the specific mechanisms involved (e.g. fearlessness, sensation-seeking) have been generated, these have not been rigorously tested. Therefore, the precise mechanisms involved with low autonomic arousal as a factor in the development of aggressive and antisocial behaviour are unclear.

To be called a causal factor or an active mechanism influencing the development and maintenance of the disorder, a risk factor should be manipulable and, when manipulated, the risk factor should be shown to change the risk of the outcome (Kraemer et al., 1997). Psychotherapeutic interventions can be used to demonstrate whether changing individual or environmental characteristics, such as the school child's social problem-solving skills or the parents' discipline skills, result in decreases of maladaptive behaviour. Thus, studies of the mediation processes in psychotherapy have the potential to contribute to aetiological models of psychopathology.

However, findings that changes in a child's social problem-solving skills and in the parents' discipline skills are related to and precede decreases of maladaptive behaviour may only mean that these skills play a causal role in the persistence of an already established DBD. In other words, it may be likely that these skills were not involved in the initial causation of the DBDs but instead may play a causal role in the maintenance of the disorder. In our view, in the discussion about the aetiology of psychiatric disorders, the distinction between processes involved in the initiation of the disorder and processes involved in the maintenance of the disorder has been neglected.

We also need to differentiate proximal from distal risk factors. Proximal risk factors directly affect the child's behaviour, whereas distal risk factors operate via proximal factors. For example, inappropriate parenting skills such as inconsistent discipline are proximal to the child's antisocial behaviour but are embedded in a larger matrix of distal contextual variables such as maternal depression, marital disharmony and low socioeconomic status.

In Chapters 4 and 5, many empirically supported risk factors are discussed, and these factors may operate in conjunction with each other in two ways. They may add to each others' effects (additive) or they may interact with each other (moderating). Factors operate in addition to each other when each factor (e.g. a large family or broken home) operates as a risk factor, and the various factors (both large family and broken home) provide an accumulated risk. Factors operate in interaction with each other when a factor operates only in the presence of another factor, for example when the effect of exposure to an environmental risk such as physical abuse depends on a child's genotype.

Although our knowledge about the individual and environmental factors involved in the development and persistence of the DBDs is growing, we are still far away from a full understanding of the specific causal processes underlying the development of the DBDs over time. Moreover, our growing insight only relates to the DBDs at a group level. Thus, we do not yet know where the disorder comes from for each individual child. Therefore, in the assessment of an individual child, we cannot aim at a full understanding of the causation of the disorder (see Chapter 6). Nevertheless, a thorough knowledge of risk factors involved in the causation of DBDs is important for clinicians, either as background information that serves as important foundation for interventions, or in order to generate a hypothesis of the possible processes involved in the development of the disorder in a particular child. The latter hypothesis can be used to guide and adapt manual-based interventions to fit the primary risks experienced by specific children.

The comorbidity between the DBDs and ADHD

For many years, the research fields of the DBDs (and antisocial or aggressive behaviour) and ADHD (and hyperactive, impulsive and inattentive behaviour) have been split as if these two groups of disorders and related behaviours have been independent of each other. Studies on correlates and risk factors in the DBDs did not take into account the possible co-occurrence of ADHD symptoms, and vice versa. Even today, studies on the aetiology of antisocial, aggressive and delinquent behaviour sometimes omit to control for the possible role of hyperactivity-impulsivity and attention problems in their statistical analyses. This separation of the research areas of the DBDs and ADHD has hampered our understanding of these two groups of related disorders. Fortunately, the last decade has seen an integration of the research fields of the DBDs and ADHD.

This is urgently needed as there is greater comorbidity between the DBDs and ADHD than would be expected by chance. Indeed, as already mentioned, the odds ratio of oppositional defiant disorder/conduct disorder (ODD/CD)–ADHD comorbidity in a meta-analysis of community sample based studies is 10.7 (Angold *et al.*, 1999). As comorbidity is probably higher in clinical samples than in community samples (see, for example, Reeves *et al.*, 1987), some authors state that, at least in everyday clinical practice, DBD–ADHD comorbidity is the norm rather than the exception (Kutcher *et al.*, 2004).

There are various hypotheses for the causes of this comorbidity. According to the three independent disorders model (DBD, ADHD, DBD–ADHD), the comorbid disorder is a separate disorder. Support for the three independent disorders model has been found in family prevalence studies (e.g. Faraone *et al.*, 1997). In contrast, the correlated liability or correlated risk model hypothesizes that there is a continuous relation between the liability to one disorder and the liability to the other disorder. Behavioural genetic studies using the twin method suggest that there is a substantial overlap between the genetic influences on ADHD and the genetic influences on the DBDs (e.g. Nadder *et al.*, 2002), supporting the correlated liability model.

In a twin study, the three independent disorders model and the correlated liability model were tested using a model-fitting approach that has been shown to have the potential to validly discriminate between the two models (Rhee *et al.*, 2008). The hypothesis that comorbidity is due to the presence of a separate CD + ADHD disorder could be rejected, whereas the hypothesis that there are shared genetic and environmental influences on ADHD and CD that explain the comorbidity between CD and ADHD was supported. There thus seems to be more evidence for the correlated liability model than for the three independent disorders model.

An aetiological framework

Many individual and environmental factors have been identified that may play a role in the initiation and persistence of the DBDs in children; these will be discussed in Chapters 4 and 5. These factors operate with each other in ways we only partially understand. Although we are far remote from an integrative theory to explain the development of DBDs, we can outline here the structure of an overall aetiological framework.

The development of the ODD and childhood-onset CD often starts in the toddler years, and maybe even in infancy. At 1½ to 3 years of age, children may show problem behaviours such as restlessness, negativism and irritability (i.e. temperamental characteristics) that are genetic or environmental biologically determined (e.g. from smoking during pregnancy). In the preschool years (3–6 years of age), these problem behaviours may develop into symptoms of DBD due to neurobiological factors on the one side and the negative parenting behaviours that the child's problem behaviours evoke on the other side.

Indeed, coercive parent–child interactions do develop from the preschool years onwards. These coercive interactions are elicited by the child's maladaptive behaviours, but personality characteristics in the parents such as impulsivity contribute to these interactions as well. Negative parent–child interactions together with negative peer interactions evoked by the preschool and school child's maladaptive behaviours sustain the symptoms. These negative interchanges also result in deviant cognitive and emotion-regulating capabilities that, in turn, sustain the symptoms. Moreover, the functioning of the parents, the peers and the child is also affected by contextual factors such as the neighbourhood and the school. Importantly, neurobiological factors that have played a role in the initiation of the DBDs go on playing a role in the maintenance of the disorders.

One important characteristic of this aetiological framework is that causality is considered to be multidirectional instead of linear. Thus, the preschool and school child's non-compliant behaviour and anger outbursts may lead to parental disagreement about how to manage the child's misbehaviour. This disagreement may result in inconsistencies in parenting that reinforce the preschool and school child's misbehaviour.

Although prospective longitudinal studies with young children suggest that the DBDs start much earlier than at school age (see Chapter 2), it should not be ruled out that there actually are children with a typical development until, say, the age of 7 or 8 years who only then start showing disruptive behaviours associated with academic underachievement or environmental factors such as insufficient monitoring.

Finally, heterogeneity in the DBDs not only is manifested in the large variety of symptoms and associated disorders (see Chapter 1), but also applies to aetiology. Thus, different sets of causal pathway may lead to different manifestations of DBDs.

Summary points

- Genes contribute to the development of psychiatric disorders because genes and their protein products are important determinants of the pattern of neural interconnections in the brain.
- Not only do dysfunctions of the brain manifest in dysfunctions of the mind (mental processes), but the mind, through the individual's experiences in the environment, affect brain functioning as well. In other words, social factors exert actions on the brain and its (psychological) functions by modifying the expression of genes and thus the function of nerve cells.
- The various factors involved in the causation of psychiatric disorders almost always act in a probabilistic rather than a deterministic fashion. In other words, the factors increase the likelihood of the specific disorder but do not determine it. These factors are therefore called 'risk factors'. These need to be distinguished from correlates in that risk factors precede the occurrence of disorders.
- Proximal risk factors (e.g. inappropriate parenting skills such as inconsistent discipline) directly affect the child's behaviour, whereas distal risk factors (e.g. marital disharmony) operate via proximal factors.
- In order for a risk factor to be called causal or an active mechanism influencing the development and maintenance of the disorder, it should be shown to be manipulable, and, when manipulated, it should be shown to change the risk of the outcome.
- In the discussion about the aetiology of psychiatric disorders, the distinction between processes involved in the initiation of the disorder and processes involved in the maintenance of the disorder has been neglected.
- There is more support for a correlated liability model than for a separate disorder model when explaining DBD–ADHD comorbidity.

- The development of ODD and childhood-onset CD starts in the toddler years, and maybe even in infancy. Genetic or environmental biologically determined problem behaviours such as restlessness, negativism and irritability that manifest in toddlerhood may develop into symptoms of DBD during the preschool years due to neurobiological factors on the one hand and coercive parent–child interactions elicited by the child's problem behaviours on the other. Over the years, negative interactions between the child and others result in deviant cognitive and emotion-regulating capabilities that sustain the symptoms. Furthermore, the functioning of the parents, the child and peers is also affected by contextual factors such as the neighbourhood and the school. Neurobiological factors that have played a role in the initiation of the DBDs go on playing a role in the maintenance of the disorders.

4

Individual characteristics

Children with disruptive behaviour disorders (DBDs) differ from typically developing children in a large number of individual characteristics. Most of these characteristics are correlates, only a few may be considered to be a risk factor playing a role in the onset of the DBDs, and some may be considered factors playing a role in the maintenance of the DBDs. These characteristics are very different in nature, varying from genes to psychological functions.

We start this chapter with an overview of behavioural genetics. We then present research on temperament, a biobehavioural construct that may provide a bridge between behaviour and the functioning of the various neural systems such as the autonomic nervous system (ANS) and the hypothalamus–pituitary–adrenal (HPA) axis. After discussing studies on the latter systems, we present research on molecular genetics, neurotransmitters and neurocircuits. We then review research on executive functions (EFs). These higher-order psychological functions, which are subserved by the neurocircuits, direct lower-order psychological functions, among which are problem-solving. Before presenting research on social problem-solving and social information-processing, we discuss the issue of intelligence and language development in the DBDs. Finally, we discuss anger and anger regulation associated with DBDs.

Behavioural genetics

In behavioural genetic research, the relative strength of effects of genes and of environmental influences on the variation within populations with respect to some trait or disorder is estimated. Behavioural genetic research has shown that we should not separate nature and nurture. Instead, this research has increasingly illustrated the interplay between genes and environment, i.e. how

Oppositional Defiant Disorder and Conduct Disorder in Childhood   By Walter Matthys and John E. Lochman
© 2010 John Wiley & Sons, Ltd.

each operate and how they influence one another (Rutter, 1997, 2006; Moffitt, 2005a; Rutter *et al.*, 2006). This interplay is described in terms of gene–environment correlations and gene–environment interactions. We first discuss research on estimates of heritability.

Estimates of heritability

Twin and adoptive designs are used in behavioural research. Rhee and Waldman (2002) conducted a meta-analysis based on more than a hundred twin and adoptive studies on antisocial behaviour. The overall heritable estimate of antisocial behaviour was 41%. The distribution of heritability estimates across studies was also examined by Moffitt (2005b), and the peak was around 50%. A heritability estimate of 40–50% is considered moderate. However, heritability estimates for young children are higher, maybe because the effect of environmental factors such as peer influence on antisocial behaviour is less in preschoolers than in adolescents and adults. For example, the heritability coefficient for aggression among 3-year-olds is 69% (Van den Oord *et al.*, 1996). Similarly, the heritability coefficient for antisocial behaviour that is pervasive across settings among 5-year-olds is 82% (Arsenault *et al.*, 2003). These findings suggest that the environment naturally moderates (in good and bad ways) the effects of genes as children get older.

Moreover, genetic influence is probably stronger for the DBDs comorbid with ADHD than for the DBDs only. The heritability estimate for ADHD symptoms is indeed higher than that for antisocial behaviour, with percentages ranging from 60% to 88% (Waldman & Rhee, 2002). Most, if not all, of the considerable overlap between hyperactive-impulsive-inattentive and antisocial behaviours can be ascribed to the genetic influences they share (for a discussion of this issue, see Moffitt, 2005b). Another characteristic that may be associated with DBDs and is relevant to mention here is the psychopathic or callous-unemotional trait. It has been shown that antisocial behaviour is more heritable among 7-year-old children with callous-unemotional traits (heritability estimate 0.81) than in children without these traits (heritability estimate 0.30; Viding *et al.*, 2005). Thus, when considering the estimate of heritability in preschool and school-age children with DBDs, we should take into account the presence or absence of comorbid ADHD and callous-unemotional traits.

Furthermore, externalizing disorders run in families. Therefore, whether the family transmission of adolescent CD and adult antisocial personality disorder, alcohol dependence and drug dependence is due to a general or a disorder-specific vulnerability, and to what extent this vulnerability is heritable, has been examined (Hicks *et al.*, 2004). Results indicate that parents pass to the next generation a general vulnerability to the spectrum of externalizing disorders rather than an increased risk of a particular disorder. Moreover, this vulnerability appeared to be highly heritable, the estimate being 80% (Hicks *et al.*, 2004).

Because these heritability estimates account for only a portion of the variance in predicting externalizing and antisocial behaviour, it also means that there are environmental influences. A distinction has been made between shared (common, family-wide) environmental influences and non-shared (unique, person-specific) environmental influences. Shared environmental influences, for example inappropriate generalized parenting behaviour used with all the children in a family, make children within the same family more alike. Non-shared environmental influences, such as being the unique target of sexual abuse, make children within the same family more unalike. In Rhee and Waldman's (2002) meta-analysis, the estimate of shared environmental influences was 16%, whereas the estimate of non-shared environmental influences was 43%, indicating that the bulk of environmental effects on children's behaviour varies for different children in the same family. These environmental influences should be considered in relation to the effects of genes.

Gene–environment correlations

There are various types of gene–environment correlation (Moffitt, 2005a; Rutter, 2006). First, a passive gene–environment correlation occurs when the child's disruptive behaviour and the inconsistent discipline provided by the parents are correlated because they have the same origins in the parents' genotype. Parents indeed may both transmit to their child a genetic liability for disruptive behaviour and provide inconsistent discipline that is symptomatic of their genetic liability for disruptive behaviour. Thus, genetic transmission may confound a cause-and-effect interpretation of the association between inappropriate parenting and children's disruptive behaviour, and there is some evidence that this is the case (Moffitt, 2005a).

Second, active gene–environment correlations refer to the processes by which individuals select or shape their experiences. There is much evidence that individuals with antisocial behaviour act in ways that increase the likelihood that they will experience high-risk environments later in life, such as marrying a partner with criminal behaviour or substance abuse, unemployment and alcohol abuse; however, little is known on the role of genetic factors in these effects (Rutter, 1997).

Third, an evocative gene–environment correlation occurs when the child's disruptive behaviour and the parenting the child receives are correlated because they have common origins in the child's genotype. Bell (1968) was the first to draw attention to the child's effect on the parents' behaviour. This child effect may be under genetic influence. Thus, a genetic child effect that evokes inappropriate parenting may confound a cause-and-effect interpretation of the association between inappropriate parenting and children's disruptive behaviour (Moffitt, 2005a). Three adoption studies demonstrated that, compared with adoptees at low genetic risk for aggression, adoptees at high genetic for aggression, because of their biological parents' antisocial behaviour, received more discipline and control from their adoptive parents. Furthermore, it was shown that the link between these children's genetic risk and their parents' parenting was mediated by the children's aggressive behaviour (Ge et al., 1996; O'Connor et al., 1998; Riggins-Caspers et al., 2003).

However, this evidence for a genetically mediated child effect only applies to parenting within the normal range, as adoptive parents do not show severely inappropriate parenting such as physical maltreatment (Moffitt, 2005a). Therefore, in the E-risk longitudinal study, in which one-third of families were selected to oversample families who were at risk, it was assessed whether a genetic child effect evoked extreme forms of inappropriate parenting (Jaffee et al., 2004b). It appeared that children's genetic factors played a significant role in explaining why some children were more likely than others to experience normative physical disciplinary practices such as spanking. However, the study also showed that factors leading to injurious maltreatment did not lie within the child but within the family environment.

These studies on evocative gene–environment correlations are important for our understanding of the mechanisms underlying the aetiology of the DBDs. In her discussion of these studies, Moffitt (2005a, p. 540) concludes that 'the observed association between normative parenting [i.e. parenting within the normal range] and child aggression is in large part a spurious artefact of a third variable that causes both, namely the child's genotype'. Moffitt goes on to state that 'Scarr (1991) may have been correct when she argued that parenting in the normal range will not produce significant changes in children because the associations between ordinary parenting and child outcome are not causal'.

We think that two issues with respect to the relationship between ordinary parenting and the child's aggression or disruptive behaviour should be distinguished: first, the processes involved in the initial causation of the DBDs, and second, the processes involved in the maintenance of the DBDs. We agree with Moffitt and Scarr that the results of the studies on evocative gene–environment correlations suggest that ordinary parenting does not appear to play a primary role in the onset of the DBDs in many children. This, however, does not exclude the possibility that non-optimal parenting within the normative range plays a role in the persistence of the DBDs. Indeed, the parents of children with DBDs need more than ordinary parenting skills to respond adequately to frequently occurring inappropriate behaviours of their children. For example, parents are likely to reinforce the disruptive behaviours of their child by responding to them, whereas ignoring these behaviours would be more appropriate (see Chapter 5). This parenting skill – ignoring – is an important focus in behavioural parent training (see Chapter 8). Studies on the effectiveness of the training of this and other parenting skills (e.g. using time-out, praising appropriate behaviours) suggest that an improvement in these skills results in a decrease in children's disruptive behaviours (see Chapter 8). Thus, it is likely that inappropriate parenting (which should be distinguished from maltreatment) plays a role in the persistence of the DBDs, as the improvement of parenting skills results in a decrease of disruptive behaviours. In addition, unusually harsh or inconsistent parenting, outside of the normative range, may play a role in the development of DBDs, and can have deleterious effects even when a child is not at genetic risk.

Although a more differentiated interpretation of the results of gene–environment studies than the one given by Scarr and Moffitt is, in our view, needed, the associations between environmental risk factors and behavioural outcomes in general nevertheless shrink by at least half when controlled for genetic confounders (Turkheimer & Waldron, 2000; Moffitt, 2005a). However, even a small effect for an environmental risk factor can be important as the risk for antisocial behaviour accrues when individuals accumulate a number of risks, such as teenage parents, large family size and a broken home (Rutter *et al.*, 1998).

Gene–environment interactions

Gene–environment interactions occur when the effect of exposure to an environmental risk factor on the child's behaviour depends on his or her genotype. Gene–environment interactions were first demonstrated in behavioural genetic studies. In the Iowa adoption study, for instance, adversities in the rearing environment were measured by the adoptive parents' characteristics, such as marital problems and substance abuse, and genetic liability was measured by the biological parents' antisocial personality (Cadoret *et al.*, 1995). It appeared that adversities in the environment had no effect on aggression and conduct disorder (CD) in adoptees without a biological risk.

However, in behavioural genetic studies, genetic liability relies on an inferred liability, based on differences between individuals (e.g. monozygotic and dizygotic twins) in a specific sample. In contrast, in molecular genetic studies, genetic liability is measured in relation to an identified susceptibility gene (Rutter, 2006). Molecular genetic studies may thus show more specifically that the effect of exposure to an environmental risk on the child's behaviour is conditional on the child's genotype, or that the effect of the child's genotype is dependent on the presence of environmental adversity.

Caspi *et al.* (2002) tested the hypothesis of a gene–environment interaction effect using child maltreatment and a polymorphism (i.e. an alternative form or allele of a gene at a particular locus) in the promoter region of the gene encoding monoamine oxidase A (MAOA), i.e. an enzyme involved in the metabolic degradation of dopamine, noradrenaline (norepinephrine) and serotonin. It was shown that maltreated children whose genotype conferred low levels of MAOA expression more often developed adolescent CD, adult aggression personality characteristics, symptoms of adult antisocial personality disorder or adult violent crime than children with high levels of MAOA expression. This study was replicated using parental neglect, interparental violence and inconsistent discipline as the environmental risk instead of maltreatment (Foley *et al.*, 2004). MAOA genotype and environmental risk interacted significantly. In these two studies, the MAOA genotype was unrelated to antisocial outcomes; however, its effects were revealed only in the presence of environmental risks.

A gene–environment interaction was also demonstrated in a study on the role of the dopamine transporter (DAT) gene (the dopamine transporter regulates the distribution of dopamine in the extracellular space) in adolescents with ADHD symptoms (Laucht *et al.*, 2007). It was found that environmental risks moderated the impact of genetic variation in the DAT gene effect on the development of ADHD symptoms, revealing an effect of DAT only in those individuals exposed to psychosocial adversity. Thus, research on gene–environment interactions suggests that environmental risks can strongly affect children who are genetically vulnerable (Caspi & Moffitt, 2006).

The path from genes to behaviour is long and complex. Genes and their protein products determine the pattern of interconnections between neurons. Before discussing the characteristics of the various neural systems in children with DBDs, we will consider temperament, which is affected by genetic factors.

Temperament

Temperament refers to enduring behavioural traits that are comparatively pure in early childhood and become modified with increasing age. From a clinical point of view, temperament is a useful concept to describe behavioural patterns in toddlers who are still too young to diagnose with a DBD or ADHD but are nonetheless at risk of the development of DBDs with or without ADHD.

A large number of studies, the first of which was the New York Longitudinal Study conducted by Thomas and Chess (Thomas *et al.*, 1968), have demonstrated that specific temperamental features precede the occurrence of DBDs, i.e. that these characteristics are true risk factors. In the Dunedin longitudinal study, the dimension 'lack of control' (consisting of emotional lability, restlessness, a short attention span and negativism) at ages 3 and 5 was specifically associated with antisocial behaviour at ages 9 and 11, and with CD at ages 13 and 15, as well as with hyperactivity and inattention at ages 9 and 11, and with attention problems at ages 13 and 15 (Caspi *et al.*, 1995). Similarly, in the Australian Temperament Project, children who at 7–8 years displayed both aggressive behaviour and hyperactivity had more difficult temperamental characteristics even at 4–8 months and increasingly at 32–36 months, i.e. they were more irritable and less cooperative-manageable than normal controls and hyperactive children (Sanson *et al.*, 1993). Finally, maternal ratings of infant fussiness, activity level, predictability and positive affect during the first year of life each independently predicted maternal ratings of conduct problems during ages 4–13 years (Lahey *et al.*, 2008b).

There has been much theorizing on temperament. Temperament is a biobehavioural construct that may provide a bridge between behaviour and the functioning of the various neural systems: the peripheral or ANS, the HPA axis and the neurocircuits in the brain. Nigg (2006a) has developed a framework of temperament based on neurobiological theories by Gray (1982), Fowles (1980) and Beauchaine (2001). According to Nigg, there are two basic incentive systems – approach and withdrawal. Approach is defined as a willingness to approach possible incentive or reward, whereas withdrawal is conceptualized as a readiness of withdrawal-related behaviour in potentially unrewarding or uncertain contexts; it is associated with fear and anxiety. In addition, a regulatory system known as constraint has been identified by Nigg. Finally, Nigg distinguished an affiliation or empathy system related to the capacity to recognize and feel negative emotions (sadness, anxiety, fear) in others.

The autonomic nervous system

The ANS comprises the sympathetic and the parasympathetic branches. The parasympathetic nervous system is concerned with the conservation and restoration of energy. In contrast, the sympathetic nervous system prepares the body for fight or flight. Thus, the ANS regulates life functions on a moment-to-moment basis.

The effects of the sympathetic and the parasympathetic branches on the heart are antagonistic. Activation of the sympathetic branches results in an acceleration of the heart rate, whereas activation of the parasympathetic branches results in a deceleration of the heart rate and an increase in the ebb and flow of the heart rate during the respiratory cycles (Beauchaine, 2001). Over the years, many studies of resting heart rate have been conducted. In a meta-analysis by Ortiz and Raine (2004), the effect size for resting heart rate in children and adolescents with antisocial behaviour was −0.44, indicating that the means of the group with antisocial behaviour and the group without antisocial behaviour were 0.44 of a standard deviation apart, the group of children and adolescents with antisocial behaviour having a lower heart rate.

Lorber (2004) has subsequently conducted a meta-analysis of heart rate effects in groups of children with more specifically defined forms of antisocial behaviour. Thus, the effect size of resting heart rate was computed in children with aggressive behaviour and in children with conduct problems. The effect size of resting heart rate in children with aggressive behaviour was −0.51, whereas in children with conduct problems it was −0.34. Studies have also been conducted with clinical populations. For example, school-age children with DBDs have been found to have a lower resting heart rate than normal controls (Van Goozen et al., 2000a).

Findings of a lower heart rate as evidence of autonomic underarousal, however, are difficult to interpret. Two hypotheses have been generated to interpret reduced arousal in children, adolescents and adults with antisocial behaviour. The fearlessness theory argues that low levels of arousal are markers of low levels of fear (Raine, 1993). In contrast, stimulation-seeking theory claims that low arousal represents an aversive physiological state and that individuals therefore seek out stimulation to raise their arousal to a normal level (Zuckerman, 1979). Unfortunately, there is no research that has rigorously tested these two theories in one study.

Moreover, resting heart rate reflects both parasympathetic and sympathetic nervous system reactivity. In contrast, there are two psychophysiological cardiac measures that are uniquely related to either the parasympathetic or the sympathetic nervous system. Respiratory sinus arrhythmia, i.e. the degree of ebb and flow of the heart rate during the respiratory cycle, is parasympathetically mediated and indexes emotional regulation (Beauchaine, 2001). Boys between the ages of 8 and 12 with conduct problems who were also aggressive showed lower baseline respiratory sinus arrhythmia than controls (Beauchaine et al., 2008). Likewise, adolescent males with antisocial behaviour have been found to have reduced respiratory sinus arrhythmia (Mezzacappa et al., 1997). Thus, emotional dysregulation in children and adolescents with antisocial behaviour and conduct problems may be associated to parasympathetic or vagal hyporeactivity.

The other psychophysiological cardiac measure is the pre-ejection period, an index of sympathetic nervous system activity (Beauchaine, 2001). It has been used as a peripheral marker of reward sensitivity. Pre-ejection period non-reactivity to monetary incentives has been shown in preschoolers with ODD and ADHD (Crowell et al., 2006), in male school children and adolescents with conduct problems (Beauchaine et al., 2007) and in aggressive boys with conduct problems (Beauchaine et al., 2008). These results suggest reward insensitivity in aggressive boys.

Skin conductance activity also exclusively reflects sympathetic activity and is considered to be a marker of punishment sensitivity (for a critique, see Fowles, 1980). In Lorber's (2004) meta-analysis, it was found that children with conduct problems had lower basic skin conductance activity ($d = -0.30$). School-age children with DBDs have also been found to have lower basic skin conductance level than normal controls (Van Goozen et al., 2000a). In addition, in a follow-up study of children who at the age of 7–12 years had been treated for DBDs in an inpatient and/or day-treatment setting, basic lower skin conductance activity before treatment was a predictor of externalizing problems and of (maintenance of) DBD in adolescence (Van Bokhoven et al., 2005). Finally, lower basic skin conductance and decreased skin conductance reactivity have been found in preschool children with aggressive behaviour

(Posthumus *et al.*, 2009). If basic skin conductance is indeed a marker of punishment sensitivity, young children with low basic skin conductance activity would be at risk of developing DBDs, and older children with DBDs would be at risk of maintenance of DBDs, because of the reduced responsiveness to negative feedback on their misbehaviour.

However, studies on electrodermal reactivity in anticipation of, and in response to, aversive stimuli are more informative than studies on basic skin conductance level. Reduced skin conductance responsivity in anticipation of punishment is a robust finding in psychopathic adult individuals (Fowles, 2000). Likewise, reduced electrodermal activity in anticipation of, and in response to, an aversive stimulus has been found in psychopathy-prone adolescent boys (Fung *et al.*, 2005). These findings suggest a lack of anticipatory fear and reduced responsivity to punishment, which may hinder fear conditioning and socialization. However, differences did not emerge when antisocial non-psychopathic boys were compared with antisocial psychopathy-prone boys. Thus, as discussed by the authors, it might be the antisocial behaviour component of the psychopathy that is associated with the lack of response of skin conductance.

With respect to ADHD, children with ADHD who were compared with controls showed smaller heart rate differences when responses to positive feedback (reward, escape of punishment) and negative feedback (punishment, losing reward) were contrasted (Crone *et al.*, 2003). Thus, children with ADHD showed reduced psychophysiological responses. Similar heart rate results were found in a study by Iaboni *et al.* (1997). Children with ADHD habituated more quickly to reward and showed lower heart rate responsivity to the reintroduction of reward following extinction. The results of both studies are in line with the theory of an elevated reward threshold in ADHD (Haenlin & Caul, 1987). According to this theory, children with ADHD, compared with normal children, require higher amounts of reward in order to perform optimally due to an elevated reward threshold. Importantly, studies on pre-ejection period non-reactivity to monetary reward by Beauchaine and colleagues (2007, 2008) and Crowell *et al.* (2006) also suggest reward insensitivity in aggressive boys.

Although there is evidence of a genetic effect on resting heart rate (Ditto, 1993), and measures of electrodermal activity are influenced approximately equally by genetic and non-shared environmental factors (Crider *et al.*, 2004), these psychophysiologial characteristics should to date be considered correlates rather than risk factors as the results of a few longitudinal studies are inconsistent. On the one hand, a predictive value of a measure of skin conductance (i.e. skin conductance response half-recovery time) at age 3 on fighting at age 9 (Venables, 1989) has been demonstrated. Similarly, a low resting heart rate at age 3 has been found to predict aggression at age 11 (Raine *et al.*, 1997a), and a low resting heart rate at age 9 has been found to predict increases in aggression and delinquency 2 years later (Clanton *et al.*, 2009).

On the other hand, however, a low heart rate measured at 14, 20, 24 and 36 months of age did not predict externalizing behaviour problems at age 7 (Van Hulle *et al.*, 2000).

The hypothalamus–pituitary–adrenal axis

The HPA axis regulates the individual's response to stress. Cortisol secretion by the adrenal cortex is under control of adrenocorticotropic hormone from the pituitary, which is regulated by corticotropin-releasing hormone from the hypothalamus. Corticotropin-releasing hormone is released in response to stress and the subsequent activation of cortical (e.g. prefrontal cortex) and limbic (e.g. amygdala) inputs. In terms of temperamental dimensions, stress response is a key feature of the withdrawal dimension, i.e. the readiness of withdrawal behaviour in potentially unrewarding, uncertain or threatening contexts. Children with DBDs are thus expected to have lower basal cortisol and lower cortisol reactivity to stress.

Van Goozen *et al.* (2007) calculated effect sizes for studies that had investigated the relationship between basal cortisol and DBDs or aggressive behaviour in children and adolescents. The weighted mean effect size was −0.40, indicating that the mean of the group with DBDs or aggressive behaviour was 0.40 of a standard deviation lower than the mean of the control group. Thus, there is evidence of reduced basal cortisol secretion in children and adolescents with aggressive behaviour. Van Goozen and colleagues also calculated the effect sizes for studies that investigated cortisol reactivity during stress. The weighted mean effect size was −0.42. Importantly, the specificity of low cortisol responsivity in oppositional defiant disorder (ODD) was demonstrated in a study that also involved children with ADHD and healthy controls; the ADHD group showed the typical stress-induced cortisol response of the healthy control group, but children with DBDs had a blunted response (Snoek *et al.*, 2004).

Why would the cortisol response in children with DBDs be blunted? It has been suggested that chronic negative experiences, in part due to adverse rearing circumstances (see Chapter 5) but also elicited by the children's own disruptive behaviours (see research on evocative gene–environment correlations, above), results in a habituation to stress and thus in low stress reactivity (Van Goozen & Fairchild, 2008). Although this has not yet been tested, the plasticity of the HPA axis has been shown in a preventive study with preschool children at risk of DBDs because of a sibling being adjudicated for delinquent acts (Brotman *et al.*, 2007). Indeed, relative to controls, children who together with their parents participated in behavioural parent training (see Chapter 8) had increased cortisol levels in anticipation of a social challenge when compared with preintervention levels. Thus, this study showed that a preventive behavioural intervention may alter the stress response in preschool children at risk of DBDs.

Finally, when studying HPA axis functioning in aggressive children, it seems obvious to pay attention to the distinction between reactive or hot-blooded and proactive or cold-blooded aggression. In one study, it was shown that reactive aggressive children had a heightened cortisol response to stress, whereas proactive aggressive children tended to have a response to stress that was comparable to that presented by non-aggressive children (Lopez-Duran *et al.*, 2009). Clanton and Lochman (2009) found that, following a laboratory-based provocation in computer game play, children who had been rated by teachers and parents as having greater reactive aggression were less likely to have their cortisol return to baseline levels during a 20-minute recovery period.

We should currently consider these deviances in HPA axis functioning in children with DBDs correlates rather than risk factors as most studies are cross-sectional in nature. However, two longitudinal studies with older children with aggressive behaviour have shown that low cortisol is a predictor of persistent aggression (McBurnett *et al.*, 2000; Shoal *et al.*, 2003). Thus, there is some evidence that HPA axis dysfunctioning plays a role in the persistence of aggression and, probably, in the maintenance of DBDs. However, no longitudinal studies in young children have been conducted in order to demonstrate that deviances in cortisol precede the occurrence of disruptive behaviour.

Androgens

Males have higher concentrations of androgens and display higher aggressive behaviour than females. Therefore, testosterone and its precursors, including dehydroepiandrosterone sulfate (DHEAS), have been examined in animal and human aggression studies.

Connor (2002) reviewed studies conducted since 1980 on testosterone in children and adolescents. Nine studies found a significant positive correlation between higher testosterone levels, measured in either serum or saliva, and aggression or delinquency. Four cross-sectional studies found no significant correlation between testosterone and aggression. Studies supporting a significant correlation between testosterone and aggression have included pubertal and postpubertal adolescents and young adults in their samples, whereas in the studies that failed to find this association, sample populations tended to be prepubertal. Moreover, there is also some evidence that testosterone levels in children and adolescents are related to social dominance rather than aggression (Rowe *et al.*, 2004).

Interestingly, a moderating effect of cortisol on the relationship between testosterone and overt aggression has been demonstrated in adolescent boys.

A significant relationship between testosterone and overt aggression was found in subjects with low cortisol levels, but no such relationship was found in subjects with high cortisol levels (Popma *et al.*, 2007). This moderating effect of cortisol yet has not been studied in prepubertal boys.

Although two studies on DHEAS have found a positive correlation between DHEAS and DBDs in children (Van Goozen *et al.*, 1998, 2000b) and one study found this relationship in children and adolescents (Dmitrieva *et al.*, 2001), one study failed to find a correlation between DHEAS and aggression in children (Constantino *et al.*, 1993).

Molecular genetics

Molecular genetics is concerned with identification of the individual genes that underlie the genetic effects. In psychiatry, the individual genes that are relevant for psychopathology are called susceptibility genes. These genes are normal allelic variations or alleles, such as in Caspi *et al.*'s study (2002) on the gene encoding MAOA, and differ from the pathogenic abnormal mutations in that they are very common and do not affect vital functions. Odds ratios of gene polymorphisms in psychiatric disorders are usually less than 2; therefore, one particular gene does not cause a specific psychiatric disorder, but instead, together with other genes and with environmental factors, they constitute part of a multifactorial causation (Rutter, 2006; Rutter *et al.*, 2006b). In general, molecular genetic studies have resulted in contradictory findings characterized by failed attempts at replication. For the genes discussed below, however, there seems to be evidence of a relation with the DBDs.

Serotonergic neurotransmission is considered to play a role in behavioural inhibition (Linnoila *et al.*, 1983; Soubrie, 1986). Therefore, genetic studies of the serotonin (5-HT) system have been conducted in individuals with aggressive behaviour. An association between a polymorphism in the promoter region (i.e. the section that regulates the transcription process) of the serotonin transporter (5-HTT) gene and aggression has been found in two studies with children (Beitchman *et al.*, 2006; Haberstick *et al.*, 2006), as well as between this polymorphism and CD in one study with adolescents (Sakai *et al.*, 2006).

Dysfunction of the dopaminergic system has been demonstrated in children and adolescents with ADHD (for reviews, see Swanson *et al.*, 2007; Wallis *et al.*, 2008). Various studies have found an association of ADHD with a specific allele of the dopamine receptor type 4 (*DRD4*) gene (e.g. LaHoste *et al.*, 1996; Swanson *et al.*, 1998). Importantly with respect to the DBDs, an association has been found between the *DRD4* gene and maternal report of problems with aggression at age 4 years (Schmidt *et al.* , 2002). Likewise, an association has been found between the *DRD4* gene and ADHD with comorbid conduct problems (Holmes *et al.*, 2002). Thus, the *DRD4* gene may also be associated with aggression and DBDs.

In the discussion of ADHD–DBD comorbidity (see Chapter 3), we noted Nadder *et al.*'s (2002) study of the substantial overlap between the genetic influences on ADHD and the genetic influences on the DBDs. It has been suggested by Thapar *et al.* (2005) that the antisocial features of ADHD are related to variations in the gene encoding catechol *O*-methyltransferase (*COMT*), which metabolizes dopamine and noradrenaline. Caspi *et al.* (2008) indeed found that heterogeneity in terms of antisocial behaviour among children with ADHD was associated with variation in the *COMT* gene. The authors of this study discuss the possible neurobiological routes by which the observed effect of *COMT* is achieved. The *COMT* gene plays a major role in modulating prefrontal cortex dopamine levels, and therefore it might be a candidate gene for modulating prefrontal EFs that are impaired in ADHD and in the DBDs (see the section on EFs later in this chapter). Alternatively, according to Caspi and colleagues, *COMT* variants may reflect a genetic predisposition that contributes to emotional dysregulation. Indeed, neuroimaging studies suggest that *COMT* alleles are related to reduced responsiveness to unpleasant stimuli, which is a characteristic of children and adolescents with DBDs (see the section on neurocircuits later in this chapter).

Besides association studies with candidate genes, some genome-wide linkage studies have been conducted in samples with individuals at high risk of substance dependence. We have already discussed Hicks *et al.*'s study (2004), which demonstrated that parents pass to their children a highly heritable general vulnerability to externalizing disorders. Therefore, genetic studies of substance abuse and dependence are particularly interesting. The three genome-wide linkage studies that have been conducted, however, have not converged on the same chromosome regions (Dick *et al.*, 2004; Stallings *et al.*, 2005; Kendler *et al.*, 2006).

Finally, Brunner *et al.* (1993) found a complete and selective deficiency of enzymatic activity of MAOA in a Dutch family with males affected by a syndrome of borderline mental retardation and impulsive aggression. In each of the affected males, a mutation was identified in the MAOA structural gene. This mutation, however, is extremely rare.

Neurotransmitters

Serotonin, dopamine and noradrenaline are important neur[o] the central nervous system. Of the three neurotransmitters, sively studied with respect to aggression and the DBDs is sero in brain serotonin levels are associated with disinhibitio (Linnoila *et al.*, 1983; Soubrie, 1986). Various measures ar serotonergic activity. These include: measurement of the principal metabolite of serotonin, 5-hydroindoleacetic acid (5-HIAA), in the cerebrospinal fluid or plasma; measurement of serotonin in whole blood; pharmacological challenges studies in which a drug or a dietary manipulation that is known to affect central nervous system serotonergic functioning is given; and measurement of serotonergic receptor activity in platelets.

According to a meta-analysis in adults, there is an inverse relationship between 5-HIAA and antisocial behaviour, with an effect size of −0.45 (Moore *et al.*, 2002). An inverse relationship between 5-HIAA and aggressive behaviour has also been found in the cerebrospinal fluid of children and adolescents with DBDs (Kruesi *et al.*, 1990) and in the plasma of children with DBDs (Van Goozen *et al.*, 1999). The results from studies investigating whole-blood serotonin in children and adolescents with CD are, however, contradictory (e.g. Rogeness *et al.*, 1982; Unis *et al.*, 1997).

Challenge studies with fenfluramine in which the prolactin response in children and adolescents was used as an indirect measure of serotonin functioning in the brain have shown mixed results (Stoff *et al.*, 1992; Halperin *et al.*, 1994, 1997; Schultz *et al.*, 2001). However, in a longitudinal study it was demonstrated that lower prolactin responsivity to fenfluramine (i.e. lower serotonergic functioning) in 9-year-old children with ADHD predicted the emergence of antisocial personality disorder in early adulthood (Flory *et al.*, 2007). Furthermore, a challenge study with sumatriptan, a selective serotonin 1B/1D receptor agonist, demonstrated that the growth hormone response was enhanced in children with ODD (Snoek *et al.*, 2002). This suggests that the sensitivity of postsynaptic serotonin 1B/1D receptors is increased, maybe secondary to a deficit in brain serotonin levels.

Platelet membranes that show similarities to serotonin pre- and postsynaptic membranes in the central nervous system have been used to measure central serotonin functioning. Various studies have shown an inverse correlation between platelet markers of serotonin function and aggression in children and adolescents with CD (e.g. Birmaher *et al.*, 1990; Blumensohn *et al.*, 1995). However, no difference in serotonin function has been found between children and adolescents with DBDs and controls (Stoff *et al.*, 1991).

Thus, there is some support for an inverse relationship between serotonin measures and aggressive behaviour in children and adolescents with DBDs, although this relationship and its origin are less clear than in adults. Studies in rhesus monkeys have shown that indices of serotonin are heritable (Higley *et al.*, 1993), but adverse environmental conditions such as peer-rearing also have been shown to be associated with serotonergic dysfunction in non-human primates (Shannon *et al.*, 2005). In addition, individuals living in areas of residence with high rates of poverty and unemployment have shown diminished serotonergic responsivity as indicated by a blunted prolactin response fluramine challenge (Manuck *et al.*, 2005). Thus, both genetic and environmental factors seem to affect the functioning of serotonin.

Noradrenaline is another important neurotransmitter in the brain. Low noradrenergic functioning results in low anxiety, decreased sensitivity to punishment (Gray, 1994) and impulsivity and intolerance to delay of gratification or delay of aversion (Pattij & Vanderschuren, 2008). To measure noradrenergic functioning, the metabolite 3-methoxy-4-hydroxyphenylglycol (MHPG) in the cerebrospinal fluid is used, as are plasma levels of dopamine-β-hydroxylase, the enzyme that converts dopamine into noradrenaline. Kruesi *et al.* (1990) found a negative correlation between MHPG in cerebrospinal fluid and aggression in children with DBDs. Similarly, studies in children and adolescents with CD have shown low plasma dopamine-β-hydroxylase (Rogeness *et al.*, 1990; Galvin *et al.*, 1991), although one study with adolescents with CD did not replicate this finding (Pliszka *et al.*, 1988). Thus, there is some evidence of decreased noradrenergic functioning in children and adolescents with DBDs.

Dopamine is involved in a large variety of psychological functions, including the regulation of attention, action generation and reward learning, and more specifically the motivation to pursue rewards by attributing incentive salience to reward-related stimuli (i.e. 'wanting' for rewards) (for a review, see Berridge, 2007). To study dopamine functioning, homovanillic acid, the metabolite of dopamine, has been used. Measuring this metabolite in the cerebrospinal fluid instead of in plasma is more appropriate.

Gray (1982) hypothesized that the dopamine system is highly responsive to signals in the environment that indicate the presence of reward. In line with this, Quay (1988) hypothesized that children and adolescents with CD are motivated by immediate gratification of needs and are likely to have high dopamine functioning. However, no correlation of homovanillic acid in cerebrospinal fluid and aggression was found in children and adolescents with DBD (Kruesi *et al.* 1990). Likewise, no correlation between homovanillic acid in plasma and conduct symptoms was found in children with CD (Rogeness *et al.*, 1987). Contrary to Quay's expectations, low homovanillic acid plasma levels have been found in children with CD (Gabel *et al.*, 1993; Van Goozen *et al.*, 1999). In conclusion, there is no evidence supporting increased dopaminergic functioning in children and adolescents with DBD. Instead, some studies suggest decreased dopaminergic functioning in these children and adolescents.

By contrast, there is clear evidence in ADHD of neural abnormality in the dopamine system (for a review, see Swanson *et al.*, 2007). Specifically, ADHD is associated with a dopamine deficit, although impaired noradrenergic functioning is also involved in ADHD (see Chapter 10). It has be₁ methylphenidate increases extrasynaptic dopamine by blocking transporter (DAT) and thus corrects an underlying dopamine d *et al.*, 1998, 2002).

Finally, MAO, as noted earlier, is an intraneuronal enzyme serotonin, noradrenaline and dopamine following reuptake fro₁ cleft. MAO activity is measured in platelets. In a longitudinal study, it was found that the co-occurrence of psychopathy-related personality traits and low-platelet MAO activity in juvenile delinquents increased the propensity to persisting criminality in adulthood (Alm *et al.*, 1996).

In conclusion, there is evidence of decreased serotonergic functioning in children and adolescents with antisocial behaviour and DBDs, as well as some evidence of decreased noradrenergic and dopaminergic functioning. Almost all studies on neurotransmitters are cross-sectional; thus, abnormalities in neurotransmitters should currently be considered to be correlates of rather than risk factors for DBD.

Neurocircuits

In the neurocircuits relevant for the DBDs, one may distinguish, on the one hand, limbic brain structures (e.g. the amygdala) involved in the processing of stimuli and, on the other hand, cortical brain structures (e.g. the orbitofrontal cortex) involved in top-down control.

The amygdala is involved in the processing of negative and positive emotional stimuli, in evaluating the environment for potential threats, and in fear conditioning resulting in avoidance learning. Findings from a functional magnetic resonance imaging (fMRI) study suggest left amygdala hyporeactivity to negative emotional stimuli in children and adolescents aged 9–15 years with CD with or without ADHD (Sterzer *et al.*, 2005). Likewise, in a study that used fMRI while children processed fearful facial expressions, children and adolescents (aged 10–17 years) with DBD with callous-unemotional traits were found to have reduced responsiveness of the amygdala in comparison to healthy controls and youth with ADHD (Marsh *et al.*, 2008). Interestingly, in this study, functional connectivity analyses demonstrated greater correlations between the amygdala and the ventromedial prefrontal cortex in healthy controls and youth with ADHD relative to those with DBDs and callous-unemotional traits. In another fMRI study, boys with conduct problems and elevated levels of callous-unemotional traits manifested lower activity of the right amygdala to fearful faces (Jones *et al.*, 2009). Thus, these studies reveal evidence of deficits in amygdala function in children and adolescents with DBDs and psychopathic or callous-unemotional traits. Importantly, a reduced recognition of sadness and fear in others may be associated with impaired empathy (Blair, 2007).

Moreover, there is some indirect evidence for deficits in amygdala function. In one study, it was shown that children with DBDs with or without ADHD had a blunted response to auditory stimuli that normally elicit a startle reflex (Van Goozen *et al.*, 2004a). Furthermore, the more delinquent the children with DBDs were, the lower the startle responses while viewing pleasant pictures. Children with comorbid ADHD were treated with methylphenidate; there were no differences between these children and the children with only DBD.

In a second study, attenuation of the eye-blink startle reflex was found both in youth with early-onset CD and in youth with adolescent-onset CD; ADHD symptoms did not affect the startle reflex, and both groups also showed impaired fear conditioning (Fairchild *et al.*, 2008). Children with psychopathic characteristics showed a selected impairment in the recognition of sad and fearful expressions (Blair *et al.*, 2001a). Likewise, children and adolescents with psychopathic traits showed reduced attention to other people's eyes, thus accounting for their problems with fear recognition; this feature is characteristic of patients with damage to the amygdala (Dadds *et al.*, 2008).

Blair (2004) suggested that dysfunction of the amygdala is associated with instrumental (or controlled, proactive) aggression, as shown by children and adolescents with psychopathic or callous-unemotional traits. The moral socialization of these children and adolescents is hypothesized to be dysfunctional, either by a lack of formative learning experiences or by impaired functioning of the neural systems, including the amygdala, mediating moral socialization. Moral socialization refers to the process by which parents and teachers reinforce behaviours that they wish to encourage and punish behaviours that they wish to discourage. Aversive conditioning, i.e. the association of a behaviour such as hitting another child with an aversive unconditioned stimulus such as the distress of the victim, is a core mechanism in moral socialization.

The amygdala is crucially implicated in aversive conditioning, and also in passive avoidance learning. The latter is also essential in moral socialization. Passive avoidance learning involves withholding from responding to particular stimuli that, if responded to, result in punishment. Children learn to avoid committing moral transgressions by either personally committing or viewing another committing a moral transgression. Thus, impaired functioning of the amygdala associated with decreased aversive stimulus reinforcement associations is thought to be characteristic of individuals with psychopathic or callous-unemotional traits (Blair, 2007).

With respect to structural deficits in the cortical brain structures, it was found in one study that prefrontal volumes in children and adolescents with early-onset CD with or without ADHD were 16% smaller than in controls, but the difference did not reach statistical significance; right temporal lobe and right temporal grey matter volumes were significantly reduced in subjects with CD compared with controls (Kruesi *et al.*, 2004).

Furthermore, reduced prefrontal grey matter volume has been shown in adult males who meet *Diagnostic and statistical manual of mental disorders*, 4th edition (DSM-IV) criteria for antisocial personality disorder when compared with healthy controls, subjects with substance dependence and psychiatric controls (Raine *et al.*, 2000). In this study, reduced autonomic activity using skin conductance and heart rate during a social stressor was also observed in subjects with antisocial personality disorder. Subjects with anti-social personality disorder who had reductions in prefrontal grey matter volume had lower skin conductance activity during stress than those without reduced prefrontal grey matter. Thus, the lower skin conductance activity (see the section on the ANS, above) in response to stress associated with poor fear conditioning, and as a result problems in socialization, may be linked to deficits in the prefrontal cortex.

It is specifically the medial prefrontal cortex (see further the orbitofrontal cortex) with its connections to the hypothalamus that can influence autonomic function in response to cortically perceived stimuli (Price, 2005). In line with this, cortical thinning in the medial prefrontal cortex was observed in violent individuals with antisocial personality disorder (Narayan *et al.*, 2007). In another study with early-onset adolescents with CD, most of whom had comorbid ADHD, reduced grey matter volumes were found in the left orbitofrontal region and bilaterally in the temporal lobes, including the amygdala and hippocampus on the left side; the mean grey matter volume was 6% smaller in the clinical group (Huebner *et al.*, 2008). Regression analyses indicated that symptoms of CD were correlated primarily with grey matter reductions in limbic brain structures, among which are the amygdala and the prefrontal areas, whereas hyperactive-impulsive symptoms were correlated with grey matter abnormalities in the frontoparietal and temporal cortices.

Finally, reduced grey matter volumes bilaterally in the anterior insula and left amygdala were found in adolescents with CD with and without ADHD (Sterzer *et al.*, 2007). Aggressive behaviour appeared to be the strongest predictor of grey matter volume in the left and right insula, whereas attention problems were the strongest predictor of grey matter volume in the left amygdala.

With respect to functional impairments, the anterior cingulate cortex, which is involved in emotion-processing and social functioning, has been studied in children and adolescents with DBDs. In an fMRI study by Stadler *et al.* (2007), children aged 9–15 years with CD viewed negative pictures and showed a deactivation in the dorsal part of the anterior cingulate cortex, i.e. the part involved in the cognitive control of emotional behaviour. The authors speculate that this abnormal suppression of neural activity might result in a failure to control emotional behaviour cognitively. Likewise, abnormal right anterior cingulate activation during the presentation of images with negative valence was shown in children and adolescents aged 9–15 years with CD (Sterzer *et al.*, 2005).

In addition, in another fMRI study, children and adolescents with CD and children and adolescents with ADHD performed an inhibition task and showed reduced activation in the posterior cingulate when compared with healthy controls; children and adolescents with CD showed reduced activation in the temporoparietal regions during failed inhibition when compared with the other groups, which did not differ in this respect (Rubia *et al.*, 2008).

Since the participants obtained feedback about their inhibition failures, the results suggest that performance monitoring networks are more dysfunctional in CD than in ADHD and healthy controls. According to the authors, this could mean that adolescents with CD care less about their mistakes than adolescents with ADHD and healthy controls, which is in line with evidence that children with DBDs are undermotivated and respond less to negative feedback than controls (Matthys *et al.*, 2004; Van Goozen *et al.*, 2004b; see the section on EFs, below).

Failed inhibition has been related by Gray (1982) to the behavioural inhibition system, involving the medial septal area, the hippocampus and the orbitofrontal cortex. Recently, the latter has been the subject of much research in individuals with antisocial behaviour and related substance use problems. The orbitofrontal and the medial prefrontal cortex, functionally considered to constitute the ventromedial prefrontal cortex, have connections with the thalamus, amygdala and striatum (Rolls, 2004). This circuit is involved in decoding and representing primary reinforcers, learning associations of stimuli to these reinforcers, and controlling and correcting reward-related and punishment-related behaviour and the related emotions (Rolls, 2004). Thus, this circuit plays a crucial role in our ability to discern the complexities of our actions and make appropriate choices (Price, 2005).

To assess orbitofrontal functioning, the Iowa Gambling Task was developed by Bechara *et al.* (1994). This decision-making task simulates real-life decisions involving reward, punishment and uncertainty of outcomes. Specifically, in this task, it is not possible to calculate the net gains and losses when making decisions; instead, one needs to develop an estimate or intuition of which choices are risky and which are profitable in the long run. Therefore, this task is supposed to assess affective or intuitive decision-making. Favouring immediate rewards despite long-term punishments, as demonstrated in impaired functioning on this task, has been shown in adults with externalizing behaviour disorders, i.e. alcohol abusers (Mazas *et al.*, 2000), cocaine abusers (Bartzokis *et al.*, 2000), opiate abusers (Petry *et al.*, 1998), violent offenders (Fishbein, 2000), pathological gamblers (Cavedini *et al.*, 2002) and young adults with psychopathic characteristics (Van Honk *et al.*, 2002). In addition, poor affective decision-making has been shown in children and adolescents with psychopathic tendencies (Blair *et al.*, 2001b), adolescents with ADHD or CD (Ernst *et al.*, 2003), and adolescents with both DBDs and substance dependence (Schutter *et al.*, 2009).

Neuroimaging studies have demonstrated which brain structures are involved in affective decision-making. Using positron emission tomography, Ernst *et al.* (2002) showed activation of the orbitofrontal and dorsolateral prefrontal cortices, anterior cingulate, insula, inferior parietal cortex and thalamus during the performance of a computerized card game in healthy subjects. Positron emission tomography only evaluates the summation of brain activity and may not highlight the anticipation of long-term consequences associated with decision-making on risks. Fukui *et al.* (2005) therefore performed an fMRI study in healthy subjects performing the task. Risk anticipation exclusively activated the medial frontal gyrus. These authors, however, remark that, as medial frontal and orbitofrontal regions are richly interconnected, it is likely that these areas comprise a neural network. Moreover, studies on the anticipatory component of decision-making have demonstrated activation of nucleus accumbens in addition to medial prefrontal and orbitofrontal activation (Breiter *et al.*, 2001; Knutson *et al.*, 2001a, 2001b).

In an fMRI study to compare brain activation during a rewarded continuous performance task that measured sustained attention as well as the effects of reward on performance, children and adolescents with CD but without ADHD showed underactivation in the right orbitofrontal cortex during the reward condition (Rubia *et al.*, 2009). This study supports the hypothesis of hyposensitivity to reward in CD (or DBDs), already discussed above (see the section on the ANS, above).

Finally, serotonin, the neurotransmitter that is considered to be involved in the inhibition of behaviour (see the section on neurotransmitters, above), appears to play a role in the functioning of the orbitofrontal cortex. Indeed, an acute dietary depletion of tryptophan, the precursor of serotonin, in healthy adults produced the same impairments in decision-making as shown by amphetamine abusers and patients with lesions of orbitofrontal cortex (Rogers *et al.*, 1999). Interestingly, it was demonstrated using a reversal learning task that serotonin is associated with a failure to inhibit responding to a previously rewarded response, resulting in cognitive inflexibility (Clarke *et al.*, 2007).

The neurocircuits involved in ADHD are relevant to discuss here because of comorbidity of ADHD with DBDs. Based on neuroimaging studies of ADHD (for reviews, see Durston, 2003; Casey & Durston, 2006; Casey *et al.*, 2007) and cognitive control theory, Nigg and Casey (2005) have proposed a model of ADHD that takes into consideration the importance of learning mechanisms in cognitive control. Cognitive control is defined as the ability to suppress inappropriate behaviours in response to contextual and temporal cues and adjust behaviour accordingly (Casey *et al.*, 2007). Nigg and Casey (2005) have distinguished three neurocircuits, each with different functions. Frontostriatal (basal ganglia) neural loops and frontocerebellar (cerebellum) neural loops operate jointly in detecting and predicting what and when important events in the environment will occur, whereas the frontoamygdala loops interact with these loops in assigning emotional significance to these events.

The detection of unpredicted rewarding or novel events has been linked to frontostriatal functioning, whereas monitoring and detecting violations in the timing of events has been linked to frontocerebellar functioning (for a discussion, see Nigg & Casey, 2005). According to Nigg and Casey (2005), these circuits provide neural mechanisms for learning about structure in the environment and detecting violations in these predictions, which are fed to the prefrontal cortex for integration with goals represented in working memory. Thus, the basal ganglia/striatum and cerebellum learn to predict and detect violations of prediction in the nature of events and in the timing of events.

When a goal-directed programme is running, the basal ganglia/striatum and cerebellum inhibit or interrupt competing thoughts and behaviours that would otherwise interfere with the prefrontally driven goal. Frontostriatal and frontocerebellar pathways thus serve to recruit top-down control when detecting changes in the environment. Their disruption in ADHD results in inefficient prefrontal recruitment to shift and maintain a behavioural set in different contexts, which is manifested as poor sustained attention, a slow response in rapid-decision contexts, difficulty in shifting from one response set to another, and an inefficient response to changing learning contexts. Dopamine is involved in forming predictions about future outcomes by detecting discrepancies between actual and expected outcomes (Schultz *et al.*, 1997). As discussed earlier, dopamine functioning is suggested to be deficient in ADHD.

The third relevant neurocircuit is the frontoamygdala circuit (Nigg & Casey, 2005). Emotional context affects the recruitment of cognitive control. Positive emotional valence or expectation of reward is related to approach, whereas negative valence or expectation of non-reward is associated with withdrawal and avoidance. Activation of the nucleus accumbens has been shown to be related to approaching a potential positive event, while activation of the amygdala is associated with avoidance of potentially unpleasant events (Nigg & Casey, 2005). In ADHD, impulsivity could result from either unregulated approach or failure to avoid potential punishment. Problems with approach have been demonstrated in ADHD, especially a preference for immediate over delayed reward (Sonuga-Barke, 2003), as well as an elevated reward threshold (Haenlin & Caul, 1987; see the section on the ANS, above); i.e. children with ADHD require higher and immediate reward in order to perform optimally.

Thus, ADHD is associated not only with abnormalities in cognitive control (see EFs, below), but also with abnormalities in delay aversion arising from disturbances in reward centres (Sonuga-Barke *et al.*, 2008). On the other hand, results of studies on insensitivity to cues for non-reward and punishment in children with ADHD are inconsistent (Luman *et al.*, 2005).

Minimal physical anomalies

Before discussing EFs that are subserved by the frontal lobes, we will briefly consider the issue of minimal physical anomalies (MPAs). These congenital malformations are considered to be indicators of a disruption of fetal development. MPAs are relatively minor physical abnormalities consisting of such features as an abnormal width between the eyes (hypertelorism), large epicanthal folds (folds of skin extending from the root of the nose to the median end of each eyebrow) and malformed ears. MPAs are thought to be a marker of fetal neural maldevelopment towards the end of the first 3 months of pregnancy. The central nervous system may be affected by the same factors that are responsible for MPAs since the development of the central nervous system is concurrent with the development of the organs that show MPAs. MPAs can be caused by environmental factors acting on the fetus such as anoxia and infection, but they may also have a genetic basis. Longitudinal studies have demonstrated that MPAs assessed at preadolescence or adolescence predict later violent delinquency (Kandel *et al.*, 1989; Arsenault *et al.*, 2000).

Executive functions

The construct of 'executive function' refers to the higher-order psychological processes involved in the control of thought, action and emotion (Séguin & Zelazo, 2005). The term 'cognitive control' is also used for this construct.

EF is not a single function but encompasses a number of different neuropsychological concepts. In young children, three components have been distinguished: inhibition, working memory and cognitive flexibility (Senn *et al.*, 2004; Garon *et al.*, 2008). In older children, a broader range of top-down cognitive abilities has been discerned, among which are planning and implementing strategies for the performance, initiation and discontinuation of actions, inhibiting habitual or prepotent responses or task-irrelevant information, performance monitoring, vigilant attention and set-switching (Castellanos *et al.*, 2006). EFs are necessary for adaptive and goal-directed behaviour, and are thought to be subserved by the frontal lobes. Specifically, the dorsolateral prefrontal cortex is thought to be associated with working memory, the orbital prefrontal cortex is thought to be associated with the ability to inhibit inappropriate actions, and the anterior cingulate gyrus is thought to be associated with emotional and cognitive control (Nigg, 2006b).

Deficits in EF have been extensively demonstrated in school-age children with ADHD (Willcutt *et al.*, 2005). Impairments in EF have also been found in children with DBDs but, according to the review by Pennington and Ozonoff (1996), these are due to the presence of comorbid ADHD. Although this has been confirmed in later studies (e.g. Oosterlaan *et al.*, 2005), the conclusion of a meta-analysis by Oosterlaan *et al.* (1998) on deficits in response inhibition, one of the EFs, in children aged 6–12 years is that these deficits are not associated uniquely with ADHD but also with DBDs. Response inhibition has been found to be specifically linked to reactive aggression rather than to proactive aggression (Ellis *et al.*, 2009).

Morgan and Lilienfeld (2000) conducted a meta-analysis including 39 studies on EF in school-age children, adolescents and adults with externalizing disorders. Overall, the average mean effect size for the groups with antisocial behaviour (criminality, delinquency, CD, psychopathy, antisocial personality disorder) was 0.62, whereas the effect size for CD was 0.36. According to Morgan and Lilienfeld (2000), one reason why the results of their study conflicted with prior results from Pennington and Ozonoff's (1996) study might be that, in the latter review, studies were included with tests for which the theoretical and empirical links to EF were unclear. On the other hand, in their descriptive review, Pennington and Ozonoff (1996) involved ADHD as a confounding factor, whereas ADHD was not included as a moderator in the meta-analysis by Morgan and Lilienfeld (2000). Finally, Morgan and Lilienfeld (2000) remark that they were unable to subdivide EF measures in terms of their associations with different brain regions such as the dorsolateral and orbitofrontal/medial cortex because of the lack of knowledge concerning the neuroanatomical substrates of most EF tasks. Thus, it might be that the overall effect size of their meta-analysis underestimates the relation between antisocial behaviour and orbitofrontal/medial dysfunction since antisocial behaviour is supposed to be mainly confined to poor functioning of the orbit-ofrontal/medial area rather than of the entire prefrontal cortex.

Indeed, dysfunctioning of the orbitofrontal and medial prefrontal networks may be a characteristic of individuals with antisocial behaviour (see the section on neurocircuits, above). Individuals with antisocial behaviour have been found to have specific EF dysfunctions when motivational processes are involved in EF tasks. The term 'hot' EF has been used for EF including motivational processes, in contrast to 'cold' EF (Zelazo & Muller, 2002). For example, response perseveration, which is the tendency to continue a response previously rewarded that is now punished, has been demonstrated in children and adolescents with DBDs (Shapiro *et al.*, 1988; Daugherty & Quay, 1991; Matthys *et al.*, 1998, 2004; Van Goozen *et al.*, 2004b) and in children with psychopathic tendencies (O'Brien & Frick, 1996). Thus, these children have difficulties in stopping their ongoing behaviour based on cues of punishment from their environment. In affective decision-making tasks such as the Iowa Gambling task, individuals with externalizing behaviour disorders continue to favour immediate rewards over long-term punishments instead of developing an estimate of which choices are risky and which are profitable in the long run (see the section on neurocircuits, above). Thus, in such tasks, these individuals seem to show that they do not learn from their experiences with punishment. However, it cannot be excluded that deficits in reward sensitivity (see the section on the autonomous nervous system, above) also play a role in the performance of children and adolescents with DBD on these tasks.

In comparison with studies on EF in school-age children and adolescents with behaviour disorders, few studies have been conducted in preschool children. Studies have found impairments in EF in 'hard-to-manage' preschoolers (i.e. preschoolers with hyperactivity and conduct problems; Hughes *et al.*, 1998), specifically poor performance in means–end thinking and planning

(Hughes *et al.*, 2000). In other studies of EF in preschoolers, the role of ADHD was taken into account more specifically. In a sample of non-clinical pre-school children, a relationship was found between deficits in response inhibition and ADHD but not conduct problems (Berlin & Bohlin, 2002). Similarly, in a population-based sample, poor EF performance on inhibition, working memory and verbal fluency tasks was associated with symptoms of ADHD but not with symptoms of ODD (Thorell & Wåhlstedt, 2006). In contrast, in a group of 4-year-old preschoolers with aggressive behaviour from a population-based sample, impairments in inhibition were found; impairments were maintained after controlling for attention problems (Raaijmakers *et al.*, 2008).

In conclusion, deficits in EF, more specifically in inhibition and especially when reward and punishment are involved, have been found in children with DBDs, and independently of ADHD. As most studies on EF in children with DBDs are cross-sectional, impairments in EF are currently to be considered to be correlates rather than risk factors.

Intelligence and language development

EFs are higher-order psychological processes that direct lower-order psychological processes such as problem-solving. Before exploring the lower-order processes, however, we should first discuss intelligence and language development in children with DBDs.

It has often been stated that low intelligence, specifically low verbal intelligence, is a characteristic of individuals with antisocial and delinquent behaviour. However, doubts have been raised over whether this also applies to children, especially when comorbidity with ADHD is controlled for. On the basis of an extensive review, Hogan (1999) concludes that the association between low intelligence and DBDs is most evident in older or delinquent subjects. Furthermore, most studies on the relation between intelligence and DBDs have not included the assessment of ADHD symptoms (Hogan, 1999). Most studies that have controlled for ADHD have demonstrated that, in contrast to children and adolescents with DBDs comorbid with ADHD, children and adolescents with DBD only did not show IQ deficits (Hogan, 1999).

Besides cross-sectional studies, only a few – albeit excellent – longitudinal studies on intelligence/language development and antisocial behaviour/delinquency/criminality have been conducted. In the Dunedin study, boys' developmental trajectories from age 3 to age 15 years were studied (Moffitt, 1990). Four groups were defined at age 13: delinquent only, ADHD only, ADHD + delinquent and non-disordered. The delinquent only boys showed no low intelligence and remained relatively free of conduct problems until they initiated delinquency at age 13. The ADHD-only boys had normal intelligence and showed only mild antisocial behaviour in middle school. The ADHD + delinquent group fared the worst on assessment of verbal intelligence. Their antisocial behaviour began before school age, escalated at school entry and persisted into adolescence.

In the Environmental Risk Longitudinal Twin Study, it was shown that low IQ was related to antisocial behaviour at age 5 years and predicted relatively higher antisocial behaviour at age 7 years when antisocial behaviour at age 5 years was controlled for; the association between IQ and antisocial behaviour among boys was larger than the same association among girls (Koenen *et al.*, 2006). Importantly, when children with ADHD were excluded, the strength of the relation between low IQ and antisocial behaviour was slightly attenuated, but the pattern of findings remained very consistent (Koenen *et al.*, 2006).

As to problems in early language development, significant correlations were found in a longitudinal study between measures of language development at 18 and 24 months, and at ages 3 and 5 on the one hand, and registered criminality in adulthood on the other (Stattin & Klackenberg-Larsson, 1993).

In conclusion, longitudinal studies offer some evidence that lower IQ, in part related to ADHD, and problems in early language development are risk factors in the development of antisocial behaviour and delinquency.

Social information-processing and social problem-solving

There is a long tradition in the study of the relationship between social cognition and social behaviour based on the premise that social cognitions are the mechanisms leading to social behaviours. Over the years, various models of social cognition have been developed, but presently the most influential one is Dodge's model (1986), which has been revised by Crick and Dodge (1994).

Social information-processing model

In this model, various social cognitive theories are integrated into theories of information-processing and cognitive problem-solving. This social information-processing model describes how children process information in order to respond appropriately or inappropriately in social settings. The set of sequential cognitive operations in the model can also be conceptualized as enduring social problem-solving skills.

Children in everyday situations are faced again and again with problems such as how to respond to situations in which the child is being disadvantaged or situations in which the child fails in a competitive game (Dodge *et al.*, 1985; Matthys *et al.*, 2001). It is assumed that children are motivated to solve these problems. For this purpose, they have at their disposal a series of cognitive skills such as defining the problem, generating possible solutions and deciding which solution will be implemented. The revised model includes six steps (Crick & Dodge, 1994):

1. encoding of cues;
2. interpretation of these cues;
3. clarification of goals;
4. response access or construction;
5. response decision;
6. behavioural enactment.

In addition, a knowledge base guides information-processing at each step. This social knowledge is derived from the child's individual experiences and is being referred to as a set of social schemas of others and self, and of social scripts. This knowledge base also consists of moral beliefs about the acceptability of aggressive behaviour (Arsenio & Lemerise, 2004). Through these schemas and social scripts, prior events and relationships influence on-line processing. We will now review studies based on social information-processing and social problem-solving.

Encoding of cues

Preceding the interpretation of the problem situation, children need to attend to cues in the environment. How much information is encoded and how accurately it is encoded may influence their behaviour. Aggressive boys have been found to base interpretations of events on fewer cues than typically developing children (Dodge & Newman, 1981). This has also been found in hyperactive-aggressive boys (Milich & Dodge, 1984), and in boys with DBDs, boys with ADHD and boys with DBDs comorbid with ADHD (Matthys *et al.*, 1999). Thus, a deficit in the encoding of the number of cues appears not to be specific for aggressive children and children with DBDs, but also occurs in children with both DBDs and ADHD, and even in children with ADHD. Further, preschool boys with aggressive behaviour have been found to selectively attend to hostile cues (Gouze, 1987).

Interpretation of cues

The interpretation of the encoded information has largely been studied from the perspective of the accuracy of the child's attributions about the motives for others' actions. However, other cognitive-affective processes are involved in interpretation as well, such as perspective-taking, i.e. inferring other people's thoughts and emotions, and empathy, i.e. feeling with others.

With respect to the interpretation of others' motives, aggressive children have been shown to have a hostile attributional bias, as they tend excessively to infer that others are acting towards them in a hostile manner (Guerra & Slaby, 1989). According to a meta-analysis on the association between hostile bias and aggressive behaviour in school-age children and adolescents, the average weighted effect size was 0.17 (Orobio de Castro *et al.*, 2002).

Misattribution of hostile intent has also been found in preschool children with ODD and conduct problems (Webster-Stratton & Lindsay, 1999). This hostile bias has been demonstrated to be increased by feelings of threat (Dodge & Somberg, 1987). Moreover, heart rate acceleration after threat appeared to be accompanied by increasing hostile attributions, whereas heart rate deceleration after threat was associated with declining hostility in attributions (Williams *et al.*, 2003).

Misinterpretation of intent may also be due to an impaired ability to attribute accidental intent in others. The latter was found in school-age children with DBDs (Kempes *et al.*, 2009). Compared with normal controls, children with DBDs less often considered that the damage they suffered was not done on purpose but was instead an accident.

Furthermore, aggressive boys have been shown to have underperceptions of their own aggressive behaviour, as well as distorted overperceptions of others' aggression (Lochman & Dodge, 1998). As a result, aggressive boys develop attributions that their peers have relative responsibility for conflict rather than assuming responsibility themselves.

Finally, children with aggressive behaviour and DBDs have inaccurate, one-sided, action-orientated perceptions of their peers, limited perspective-taking abilities and impaired empathy. Indeed, boys with DBD, when compared with normal controls, have, just like younger boys when compared with older ones, been found to perceive their peers more from an egocentric point of view and to pay less attention to their peers' inner, personal worlds (Matthys *et al.*, 1995a). Instead, they attend more to the peers' external qualities, specifically to the peers' activities with others (Matthys *et al.*, 1995a). Not only do they attend less to the inner world of their peers, but children with aggressive behaviour and externalizing symptoms have also been found to have immature abilities to accurately infer the thoughts, intentions and feelings of others (Neale, 1966; Chandler, 1973; Chandler *et al.*, 1974; Cohen *et al.*, 1985). Impaired empathy has also been found in school-age children with DBDs (De Wied *et al.*, 2005) and adolescents with CD (Cohen & Strayer, 1996).

Clarification of goals

The third step involves deciding a goal or desired outcome for the current problem situation. Lochman *et al.* (1993a) found that aggressive adolescents placed greater value on dominance and revenge social goals in comparison to their less aggressive peers, and that these dominance and revenge goals directly determined the tendencies of the aggressive adolescents to generate incompetent solutions to their social problems. It has also been demonstrated that socially adjusted children formulate goals that are likely to be relationship enhancing, whereas children with proactive aggression are more likely to prefer goals that are instrumental in nature and relatively self-enhancing (Crick & Dodge, 1996). Thus, their greater preference for instrumental goals may result in the generation of an aggressive response to the problem situation.

Response access or construction

After interpreting the problem situation and formulating a goal for the situation, children access behavioural responses from long-term memory; if the problem situation is novel, children may construct new behavioural responses.

Aggressive children have been found to show deficiencies in both the quantity and the quality of their problem-solving solutions. Aggressive boys have been found to generate fewer responses than their peers (Dodge et al., 1986). Likewise, Matthys et al. (1999) found that, when compared with normal controls, not only boys with DBDs, but also boys with ADHD and boys with both ADHD and DBDs generated fewer responses. Thus, a deficit in generating possible responses appears not to be specific for aggressive children or children with DBDs but does also occur in children with ADHD.

As to the quality of the responses generated, aggressive children have been shown to offer fewer verbal assertion solutions (Lochman & Lampron, 1986), more direct action solutions (Lochman & Lampron, 1986) and more aggressive responses following intentions that are perceived as non-hostile (Waldman, 1996). A higher frequency of aggressive solutions has also been found in preschool boys with aggressive behaviour (Gouze, 1987). Likewise, preschool children with ODD and conduct problems have been shown to generate fewer positive solutions to social problems (Webster-Stratton & Lindsay, 1999). Furthermore, children with mild intellectual abilities and externalizing behaviour problems have been found to generate more aggressive responses than children with mild intellectual disabilities but without accompanying externalizing behaviour problems (Van Nieuwenhuijzen et al., 2005). Finally, it has been shown that boys with CD produce more aggressive/ antisocial solutions in vignettes about conflicts with parents and teachers, and fewer verbal/non-aggressive solutions in peer conflicts, in comparison to boys with ODD (Dunn et al., 1997).

Response decision

The last cognitive step involves evaluation of the previously accessed responses and selection of the most positively evaluated response for enactment. A number of factors are involved in children's evaluations of responses, including the moral ('good' versus 'bad') acceptability of a response and the degree of confidence children have in their ability to enact each response (self-efficacy).

Aggressive children judge aggression to be less morally 'bad' than do other children (Deluty, 1983); by contrast, aggressive children evaluate aggressive behaviour as more acceptable (Boldizar et al, 1989). Aggressive children also are more confident in their ability to aggress than are non-aggressive children, .i.e. they are more likely than others to expect that engaging in aggression will come easily for them (Perry *et al.*, 1986). Similarly, boys with DBDs and boys with both DBDs and ADHD, but not boys with ADHD only, have been found to be more confident in their ability to enact an aggressive response when compared with normal controls (Matthys *et al.*, 1999).

Children's beliefs about the utility of aggression (Lochman & Dodge, 1994) and about their ability to successfully enact an aggressive response (Perry *et al.*, 1986) can operate to increase the likelihood of aggression being displayed, as children who hold these beliefs will be more likely also to believe that this type of behaviour will help them to achieve the desired goals, which then influences their response evaluation. It has also been shown that these beliefs about the acceptability of aggressive behaviour lead to a deviant processing of social cues, which in turn then lead to children's aggressive behaviour (Zelli *et al.*, 1999), indicating that these information-processing steps have recursive, rather than strictly linear, effects on each other.

Finally, as to response selection, Matthys *et al.* (1999) found that when boys were given the opportunity to select a response among various responses shown, boys with DBDs and boys with both DBDs and ADHD, but not boys with ADHD only, when compared with normal controls, more often selected an aggressive response and less often selected a prosocial response.

Although most studies on social information-processing are cross-sectional, some longitudinal studies that control for prior levels of aggressive behaviour support the hypothesis that impairments in social information-processing and problem-solving at prekindergarten (Weiss *et al.*, 1992), in elementary school (Zelli *et al.*, 1999) and in adolescence (Fontaine *et al.*, 2002) predict later aggressive behaviour and externalizing problems. Thus, these impairments in social information-processing and problem-solving may be considered factors that play a role in the persistence of aggressive behaviour and in the maintenance of DBDs.

Schemas

As already mentioned, schemas have been proposed to have a significant impact on the various information-processing and social problem-solving steps. Schemas are commonly regarded as patterns of thinking or beliefs that remain relatively consistent across social situations (Lochman & Lenhart, 1993) Schemas can involve children's expectations and beliefs of others (Lochman *et al.*, 2003) and of themselves, including their self-esteem and narcissism (Barry *et al.*, 2007). These latent cognitive structures are believed to promote the filtering of incoming information and can distort self and other perceptions (Fiske & Taylor, 1991). While schemas allow people to operate efficiently in their social worlds by providing prototypes for how to interpret social cues and manage social conflicts, dysfunctional schemas can perpetuate emotional and behavioural problems by negatively influencing several social information-processing steps (Lochman & Dodge, 1998).

When encoding social cues, schemas can narrow children's attention to specific facets of the social environment at the expense of other social cues (e.g. Lochman *et al.*, 1981). For example, a child with a general expectancy that others will try to dominate him may be hypervigilant to verbal and non-verbal signals about a peer's control efforts, while missing signs of the peer's friendliness or attempts to negotiate. Children's schemas can also influence the interpretation of encoded social cues, such as the tendency for a depressed or anxious child to attribute negative social events to internal, stable and global characteristics (Quiggle *et al.*, 1992; Jacobs & Joseph, 1997). Schemas can also have indirect effects on information-processing through the influence of schemas on children's expectations for their own behaviour and for others' behaviour in specific situations. Lochman & Dodge (1998) found that aggressive boys' perceptions of their own aggressive behaviour was primarily affected by their prior expectations, whereas non-aggressive boys relied more on their actual behaviour to form their perceptions.

Schemas can also play a significant role at the end stages of information-processing, as the child anticipates consequences for different problem solutions, and decides which strategy will be enacted. In this regard, social goals and outcome expectations that are consistently endorsed in social situations of a particular theme (e.g. social conflicts with peers) are often conceptualized as schemas (Rotter *et al.*, 1972; Mischel, 1990).

A central characteristic of schemas is that they typically operate at an automatic, or implicit, level, and strongly held schemas are likely to contribute to automatic, rather than deliberate, information-processing. When evaluating the social information-processing of children and adolescence, it is often useful to differentiate between more automatic versus controlled processing problems (Lazarus, 1991). Automatic processing is commonly described as occurring outside conscious awareness and is fast, effortless and unintentional. Effortful processing, on the other hand, occurs within conscious awareness and is depicted as slow, effortful and deliberate. At each stage of social information-processing, the difficulties exhibited by children and adolescents with various emotional and behavioural problems can be conceptualized as being on a continuum from relatively automatic to more controlled (Daleiden & Vasey, 1997).

While a vast majority of research with children and adolescents has focused on effortful social information-processing, studies have began examining the association between emotional problems and a more automatic processing of social stimuli. For example, trait anxiety in adults has also been associated with increased skin conductance responses to threatening pictures in comparison to neutral pictures, even when these stimuli are presented outside conscious awareness (Najstrom & Jansson, 2006). While this suggests that relatively automatic attentional biases to fear and threat cues may be associated with anxiety problems in adults, studies examining how automatic processes are related to children and adolescent anxiety, as well as other forms of psychopathology, are needed.

Anger and anger regulation

Emotions are part and parcel of social information-processing and problem-solving. Among the various emotions, anger is specifically relevant for aggressive behaviour. When affective imagery training has led to the reduction of anger in angry children, their aggressive classroom behaviour has decreased and their reports of vulnerable emotions (e.g. sadness) have increased (Garrison & Stolberg, 1983). Aggressive children may display a defensive minimization of certain emotions, such as fear and sadness, which may make them feel vulnerable (Lochman & Dodge, 1994). Anger has been found to be directly related to aggression, and this anger–aggression relationship appears to be mediated by impulsivity (Deming & Lochman, 2009). Thus, as children become more anger-aroused, they become more dysregulated, resulting in aggressive behaviour.

However, studies not always have shown more anger in aggressive children. For example, in their study of social information-processing in aggressive and depressed children, Quiggle *et al.* (1992) included affect (anger, sadness, happiness): depressed children reported more anger than controls, but aggressive children did not. It might be that some aggressive children have difficulty in experiencing anger, associated with hyporeactivity of the orbitofrontal and anterior cingulate cortex, which have been shown to be involved in the processing of angry expressions (Blair *et al.*, 1999). Besides, it is probably necessary when studying anger in aggressive children to distinguish reactive aggression and proactive aggression. Reactive, but not proactive, aggression has been shown to be accompanied by anger and heightened physiological arousal (Hubbard *et al.*, 2002).

As to anger control, it has been shown that the monitoring and regulation of one's own emotions reduces aggressiveness in aggressive boys (Orobio de Castro *et al.*, 2003), and the use of self-statements and relaxation have allowed aggressive children to better manage their reactive aggression during laboratory tasks (Phillips & Lochman, 2003).

Summary points

- Although heritability estimates of antisocial behaviour across all ages lies in the moderate range, estimates are higher in young children, in children with both antisocial behaviour and callous-unemotional traits, and probably also in children with comorbid ADHD.

- A passive gene–environment correlation occurs when the child's disruptive behaviour and the inconsistent discipline provided by the parents are correlated because they have the same origins in the parents' genotype. Parents indeed may both transmit to their child a genetic liability for disruptive behaviour and provide inconsistent discipline that is symptomatic of their genetic liability for disruptive behaviour.
- An evocative gene–environment correlation occurs when the child's disruptive behaviour and the parenting the child receives are correlated because they have common origins in the child's genotype. In other words, there is a child effect on parenting behaviour, and this child effect may be under genetic influence. Therefore, the associations found between parenting characteristics and the child's disruptive behaviour need not be causal. However, although parenting within the normal range probably does not play a causal role in the initiation of the DBDs, non-optimal parenting in the normal range may play a role in the maintenance of the DBDs.
- Gene–environment interactions occur when the effect of exposure to an environmental risk factor on the child's behaviour depends on his or her genotype. Thus, environmental risks can strongly affect children who are genetically vulnerable.
- Infants and toddlers with specific temperamental features such as irritability, restlessness and negativism are at risk for the development of DBDs, ADHD or both.
- Psychophysiological research in adolescents with antisocial behaviour suggests a lack of anticipatory fear of and reduced responsivity to punishment. Furthermore, if lower basic skin conductance level in children with aggressive behaviour and DBDs is a marker of punishment sensitivity, reduced responsiveness to negative feedback in children and adolescents with aggressive behaviour and DBDs may hinder fear conditioning and thus socialization.
- Psychophysiological research suggests reward insensitivity rather than reward hypersensitivity in children and adolescents with aggressive behaviour.
- Psychophysiological research also suggests that emotional dysregulation in children and adolescents with aggressive behaviour is associated with parasympathetic hyporeactivity.
- There is evidence for reduced basal cortisol secretion and cortisol hyporeactivity to stress in children and adolescents with DBDs, which may result in poor fear conditioning and socialization problems.
- There is some evidence of a relationship between DBDs and the genes involved in the serotonergic system, as well as in the dopaminergic system, the latter probably being related to comorbid ADHD. Likewise, there is evidence of decreased serotonergic functioning in children and adolescents with antisocial behaviour and DBDs, as well as some evidence of decreased noradrenergic and dopaminergic functioning.

- Research on neurocircuits in children and adolescents with antisocial behaviour and DBDs suggests dysfunctions of both limbic brain structures (amygdala) involved in the processing of stimuli, and cortical brain structures (prefrontal cortex) involved in top-down control. These dysfunctions result in impaired readiness of withdrawal and avoidance behaviour in potentially unrewarding or punishment contexts, impaired affective decision-making, impaired perception of fear and low empathy.
- Deficits in EF, more specifically in inhibition and especially when reward and punishment are involved, have been found in children with DBDs, and independently of ADHD.
- There is evidence that lower IQ, in part related to ADHD, and problems in early language development are risk factors in the development of antisocial behaviour and delinquency.
- Numerous deficits in social information-processing and problem-solving have been found. Children with aggressive behaviour and DBDs attend to fewer cues and to more hostile cues in social situations than their peers. They tend to misinterpret the social situation due their egocentrism and orientation toward action, their impaired perspective-taking skills and empathy, and the misattribution of hostile intentions to others. When compared with their peers, they generate few solutions to social problems, and, with respect to the quality of these solutions, they generate fewer verbal assertion solutions, more direct action solutions and more aggressive solutions. When evaluating their responses, they consider aggressive solutions as acceptable and feel confident in their ability to enact an aggressive response. As a result, they select aggressive responses to enact instead of prosocial ones.
- Research on anger in aggressive children suggests that some children have problems in controlling their rising anger, while others have problems in becoming aware of their own anger.

5

Environmental characteristics

In this chapter, important environmental correlates of children's conduct problem behaviour will be described. The chapter begins by emphasizing the utility of an ecological perspective in examining factors associated with children's behaviour and then reviews environmental correlates within several broad categories.

Environmental factors influence children's behaviour, and environmental factors moderate risk for children who are at risk because of their genes, temperament or birth complications. Contextual family factors (parents, family structure, parent psychopathology, marital conflict, parent–child attachment), parenting practices (harsh punishment, warmth, monitoring), peer factors (friendship, peer rejection, deviant peer groups), community and school factors (neighbourhood problems, school characteristics) and media factors have all been found to be associated with children's antisocial and conduct problem behaviour. Environmental factors play a role in the maintenance of the disruptive behaviour disorders (DBDs), although there is increasing evidence that environmental factors also play a uniquely important role in the initiation of the disorders through their interaction with individual factors. This chapter notes that some of these risk factors operate in a bidirectional way with children's behaviour, and that some risk factors (parenting) can mediate the effects of more general risk factors (parental depression, marital conflict).

It should be noted that few studies on environmental risk factors have controlled for genetic confounders (see the discussion of gene–environment correlations in Chapter 4). Thus, the associations between environmental risk factors and behavioural outcomes in general nevertheless shrink by at least half when controlled for genetic confounders.

Oppositional Defiant Disorder and Conduct Disorder in Childhood   By Walter Matthys and John E. Lochman
© 2010 John Wiley & Sons, Ltd.

Ecological models

Among various psychopathological disorders, conduct problems have been shown to be influenced in unusually substantial ways by the social context around the child, and the manifestations of the conduct problems directly affect persons in their social context (Moffitt & Scott, 2008). Developmental models of children's conduct problems have been heavily influenced by ecological theories of child development (Bronfenbrenner, 1995), which have suggested that children's behaviour is the result of individual characteristics (such as irritable temperament) and of social and contextual influences that radiate out around the child (Lochman *et al.*, 2005a; Lochman & Gresham, 2008).

Social contexts that are most proximal (microsystems) are those in which the child spends the most time and which are likely to have the most impact on the child's behaviour (e.g. family environment, school environment, peer groups). Children's broader environments (exosystem), such as their neighbourhoods, and the medical clinics, social agencies and recreation centres within their communities, can also impact on the children but often in an indirect way. This typically occurs because the stresses produced by these community and family forces lead to disruptions in the parents' efforts to raise and discipline their children. The ecological model also stresses the importance of understanding how these systems interact with each other (mesosystem) and how these interactions between systems also influence the children's behavioural development. For example, parents' abilities to interact in positive, proactive ways with school personnel (crossing the family and school systems) can assist children's positive behaviour.

As children develop, they can experience an accumulating and 'stacking' of risk factors within their ecology, increasing the probability of the children eventually displaying serious antisocial behaviour (Loeber, 1990). These risk factors can be conceptualized as falling within multiple categories: biological and temperamental child factors, family context, neighbourhood context, peer context and later emerging child factors involving their social cognitive processes and emotional regulation (Lochman, 2004). In this chapter's review of environmental risk factors that are related to children's conduct problems, risk factors that are biologically related will be noted first, followed by contextual factors in the family, neighbourhood and peer group, and finally by a discussion of their impact on children's developing social-cognitive and emotional regulation processes. The effects of some of these risk factors are due to their association with other environmental (such as poverty) or genetic risk factors.

Ecologically based models of risk factors have provided important conceptual frameworks for preventive and treatment interventions (Lochman, 2006). The contextual social-cognitive model (Lochman & Wells, 2002a) is one such example, and indicates that certain family and community background factors (neighbourhood problems, maternal depression, low social support, marital conflict, low socioeconomic status) have both a direct effect on children's externalizing behaviour problems and an indirect effect through their influence on key mediational processes (parenting practices, children's social cognition and emotional regulation, children's peer relations) (Lochman *et al.*, 2008b). This form of an ecological model serves as the foundation for the Coping Power programme (Lochman & Wells, 2002a), which will be described in Chapters 9 and 11.

Effect of the environment on individual biological characteristics

There are a number of environmental factors that have been found to affect children's brain and its psychological functions, resulting in subsequent aggression. These environmental factors include maternal exposure to alcohol, methadone, cocaine and severe nutritional deficiencies (Rasanen *et al.*, 1999; Delaney-Black *et al.*, 2000; Kelly *et al.*, 2000).

In a follow-up study of individuals who were prenatally exposed to severe nutritional deficiency during World War II (the Dutch Winter of Hunger of 1944–45), severe nutritional deficiency in the first or second trimester of pregnancy was associated with the development of adult antisocial personality disorder (Neugebauer *et al.*, 1999). Poor nutrition can continue to have negative effects following birth, as malnutrition at 3 years of age has been found to be associated with greater aggression at 8 years of age, externalizing problems at age 11 and more conduct disorder at age 17 (Liu *et al.*, 2004). Because the link between early malnutrition and externalizing problems at age 11 was mediated by IQ, it appears that malnutrition predisposes the child to neurocognitive deficits that in turn contribute to externalizing behaviour problems.

A mother's use of opiates and cocaine during pregnancy can have a clear effect on fetal development and can predict children's behavioural problems when they are 4 years of age (Bennett *et al.*, 2002). Maternal smoking during pregnancy has also been found to be a statistical risk predictor of children's conduct problems (Brennan *et al.*, 1999, 2003) and an earlier onset of delinquent behaviours (Wakschlag *et al.*, 2006a). Although the causal link between maternal smoking and children's conduct problems is unclear (Fergusson, 1999; Wakschlag *et al.*, 2006b), and genetic confounding can account for a large amount of the predictive effects of prenatal smoking (Maughan *et al.*, 2004), there are indications from animal research that a maternal use of substances can have direct brain effects on the fetus, and that maternal smoking can produce fetal hypoxia (Chiriboga, 2003).

Other risk factors such as birth complications and a number of biological factors discussed in Chapter 4, such as cortisol reactivity, testosterone, abnormal serotonin levels and temperament, all contribute to children's conduct problems, but only when environmental factors such as harsh parenting or low socioeconomic status are present (Dabbs & Morris, 1990; Coon *et al.*, 1992; Raine *et al.*, 1997b; Scarpa *et al.*, 1999; Arseneault *et al.*, 2002). Rather than there being main or direct effects of risk predictors, it is more commonly found that aggression is the result of interactions between child risk factors and environmental factors, encapsulated in diathesis–stress models (Masten *et al.*, 1990).

Examples of these diathesis–stress models abound in the literature on child-level risk factors. We have noted in the previous chapter how children's individual genetic risk factors, hormones and temperament predict their later conduct problems. However, these effects can clearly be moderated by environmental factors. For example, children who have a gene that expresses only low levels of the enzyme monoamine oxidase A (MAOA) have a higher rate of adolescent violent behaviour, but only when they have experienced high levels of parental maltreatment (Caspi *et al.*, 2002). In another example, in this case involving children's hormone levels, higher levels of testosterone among adolescents and higher cortisol reactivity to provocation are associated with more violent behaviour, but only when the children or adolescents live in families where they experience high levels of parental abuse or low socioeconomic status (Dabbs & Morris, 1990; Scarpa & Raine, 2000).

Similar patterns of findings have been obtained when children's temperament characteristics have been examined as child-level risk factors. Children with high levels of emotional reactivity (Scaramella & Conger, 2003), infants with a difficult temperament (Coon *et al.*, 1992) and highly active and fearful children (Colder, Lochman, & Wells, 1997) are at risk for later aggressive and conduct problem behaviour, but only when they have parents who provide poor monitoring or harsh discipline. For example, in the latter study with 64 4th- and 5th-grade boys, higher levels of aggression were evident in boys with a highly active temperament style who had received poor monitoring from their parents, and in boys who were highly fearful and who had received high levels of harsh parenting. If very active children were well supervised, their aggressive behaviours were likely to be better inhibited. If very fearful children received extremely harsh punishment, they appeared to be likely to become hypervigilant for signs of hostility from others and to then engage in more frequent aggressive behaviour. For fearful children, lower levels of harsh parenting were protective. The children's family context thus serves as a key moderator of children's underlying propensity for an antisocial outcome.

The moderating effects of the child's environment influence a variety of other biologically based risk factors as well. Birth complications, involving pre-eclampsia, umbilical cord collapse, forceps delivery and fetal hypoxia, increase the risk of later violence and life-course-persistent conduct problems among children (Brennan *et al.*, 2003), but primarily when the infants subsequently experience adverse family environments, hostile or inconsistent parenting, or maternal rejection (Raine *et al.*, 1997b; Arseneault *et al.*, 2002).

Contextual family factors

Poverty

A wide array of factors in the family can affect child aggression and conduct problems, ranging from poverty to more general stress and discord within the family. Low socioeconomic status of the family and family poverty have been found to be related to juvenile crime (Sampson & Laub, 1993), and children from families with lower incomes experience more disruptive behaviour problems (Barry *et al.*, 2005; Steiner & Dunne, 1997). Low socioeconomic status assessed as early as the preschool years has predicted teacher- and peer-rated behaviour problems at school (Dodge *et al.*, 1994). In longitudinal research, it has been found that children in persistent poverty and children in families that had moved into poverty had faster increases in antisocial behaviour (Macmillan *et al.*, 2004).

Rather than being a simple direct effect of poverty on children's aspirations and behaviour, poverty affects other family processes, especially parenting practices, which then mediate the effect of poverty (Maughan, 2001). There are several interesting examples of the mediated effects of poverty (Moffitt & Scott, 2008). Family economic stress in families in rural Iowa affected family factors such as parental depression, marital conflict and parental hostility (Conger *et al.*, 1994), and these family factors then led to higher levels of adolescent conduct problems. Family economic stress did not, however, have a direct effect on child problems. In an unusual natural experiment, Costello *et al.* (2003) found that when a casino operated by Native Americans opened in the midst of an ongoing longitudinal study, the income of the Native American families increased and their children's behaviour problems decreased. Most notably, the effect of enhanced income on children's behaviour was mediated by improvements in parent–child relationships. As family income goes down, parents become less involved with their children and become less focused on providing clear and consistent consequences for their children's behaviour.

Family structure

Research has suggested that children raised in single-parent families are more likely to display behaviour problems (Pearson, *et al.*, 1994; Vaden-Kiernan *et al.*, 1995). One reason for children living with single parents is that the parents may have recently divorced. However, epidemiological and clinical studies indicate that the principal risks to children's behavioural adjustment related to family structural changes of this type are due primarily to associated conflict between the parents rather than to separation from parent figures per se (McMahon *et al.*, 2003; Cuffe *et al.*, 2005). Besides, single mothers are more likely than married mothers to experience high levels of economic and other stress (Ali & Avison, 1997), and this enhanced stress can contribute to youths' increased problem behaviours (Grant *et al.*, 2000; Hilton & Desrochers, 2000). Time constraints due to the mother being the only care-taker may offer added difficulties in parenting the children. Children growing up with single adolescent mothers have especially increased likelihood of being aggressive (Nagin *et al.*, 1997; Spieker *et al.*, 1999), partially because the adolescent mother may not be as developmentally ready to provide child-focused responsive parenting.

Parental psychopathology

Psychiatric disorders in parents have been linked to a range of psychological disturbances in children (Stein *et al.*, 2008). Children's aggression has been linked to family background factors such as parent criminality, substance use and depression (Loeber & Stouthamer-Loeber, 1998; McCarty *et al.*, 2003; Barry *et al.*, 2005).

The presence of antisocial behaviour in parents is a major risk factor for children's antisocial behaviour (Farrington, 2005) and has specifically been partially associated with life-course-persistent (or early-onset) conduct problems in males in the Dunedin study (Odgers *et al.*, 2007a). Findings across countries have been mixed about whether parent incarceration is an additional risk predictor above and beyond parental criminality in the prediction of children's delinquency (Murray *et al.*, 2007). Indicating both genetic and environmental risks, it has been found that fewer than 10% of families in a community contribute more than half of the community's criminal offences (Farrington *et al.*, 2001). The environmental influence occurs because children can model criminal behaviour from family members, and the children are likely to be directly reinforced for criminal behaviour as well.

Research has indicated a clear relationship between maternal depression and disruptive behaviour problems in children (Klein *et al.*, 1997a). Depression is the most common psychiatric disorder among mothers and has a point prevalence of 8% (Weissman *et al.*, 1988). Mothers experiencing higher levels of depression consistently report more externalizing symptomatology in their children, particularly attention problems, hyperactivity, defiance, aggression and delinquency (e.g. Spieker *et al.*, 1999). Although maternal depression contributes to child aggression over time, bidirectional effects are evident, as evidenced by findings that a difficult infant temperament elicits a higher risk of depression in mothers (Murray *et al.*, 1996). Because there have been concerns about whether these effects are merely due to the depressed mothers having a more pessimistic and distorted view of their children, research has examined other sources of information about children's behaviour as well. Fathers have corroborated depressed mothers' reports of child behavioural problems (Cicchetti *et al.*, 1998), and teachers have reported more antisocial and aggressive behaviours and poorer academic performance in children with mothers who have recovered from depression (Wright *et al.*, 2000).

In an effort to examine whether the negative effects of maternal depression were merely the result of correlated family risk factors, the relation between maternal distress and children's disruptive behaviours was found to be evident over and above the influence of socioeconomic status and stress that families experienced (Barry *et al.*, 2005). In this sample of families with 215 preadolescents, both maternal depression and maternal anxiety/somatization predicted attention problems and aggressive behaviour in their children, even after controlling for the other environmental factors.

Marital conflict

The amount of marital aggression a child witnesses is inversely proportional to that child's adjustment (Grych *et al.*, 2000), and has moderate effects on children's behavioural disturbances according to meta-analyses (Kitzmann *et al.*, 2003; Wolfe *et al.*, 2003). Starting as early as the preschool years, marital conflict is likely to cause disruptions in parenting, and these disruptions contribute to children's high levels of stress and consequent aggression (Dadds & Powell, 1992). Both boys and girls from homes in which marital conflict is high are especially vulnerable to externalizing problems such as aggression and conduct disorder even after controlling for age and family socioeconomic status (Dadds & Powell, 1992). Marital conflict contributes to young children's aggressive behaviour in both school and home settings (Erath *et al.*, 2006).

Marital conflict often occurs within a variety of other indicators of violence within the family (Jones, 2008), with violence occurring between multiple family members (Krueger *et al.*, 1998). Sixty per cent of families with significantly violent parents have violence occurring between the parents in both directions and between each parent and each child (Slep & O'Leary, 2005).

Parent–child attachment

Attachment theory (Bowlby, 1971) describes a biobehavioural system that accounts for the parental protection of young children. An important aspect of good attachment in the first year of life is that parents are responsive to infants' distress (Goldberg *et al.*, 1999). In subsequent years, positive attachments facilitate children's development of mental representations of the child's significant others. In non-human research, separation from maternal figures can produce enduring neurobiological changes (Caldji *et al.*, 2000).

There are mixed results on whether insecure parent–child attachments (avoidant, ambivalent, controlling) are related to children's aggressive behaviour (Shaw & Vondra, 1995; Vondra *et al.*, 2001). Ambivalent and controlling attachment, using the Strange Situations Test, predicted changes in children's disruptive behaviours (Moss *et al.*, 2006) in one study. However, in another study, insecure attachment was related to a diagnosis of oppositional defiant disorder in preschool boys, but was unable to predict the seriousness of conduct problems at follow-up (Speltz *et al.*, 1999). It appears that insecure attachment can better predict conduct problems when higher-risk samples are examined (Van IJzendoorn *et al.*, 1999; Moffitt & Scott, 2008).

Summary of family contextual factors

All of these family risk factors intercorrelate, especially with socioeconomic status (Luthar, 1999). These broad family risk factors can in some cases influence child behaviour through their effect on parenting processes, as will be discussed in the next section.

Parenting practices

Deficient parenting practices can interact with children's escalating oppositional behaviour to create coercive cycles of behaviour between parents and children, and thus serve as one of the important aetiological factors in developing and maintaining young children's aggressive behaviours (Patterson *et al.*, 1992; see also Chapter 8). Robust research often involving a direct observation of parent–child interactions in the home and laboratory settings over the past four decades have found an array of parenting processes linked to children's aggression (e.g. Patterson *et al.*, 1992; Shaw *et al.*, 1994; Reid *et al.*, 2002), including:

- non-responsive parenting at age 1 year, with pacing and consistency of parent responses not meeting children's needs;
- coercive, escalating cycles of harsh parental nattering and child non-compliance, starting in the toddler years, especially for children with difficult temperaments;
- harsh, inconsistent discipline;
- unclear directions and commands;
- lack of warmth and involvement;
- lack of parental supervision and monitoring as children approach adolescence.

If there is differential parenting, with harsher parenting being provided to one child compared with another in the family, that child is likely to become increasingly disruptive over time (Caspi *et al.*, 2004).

Harsh punishment

Stormshak *et al.* (2000) found that parents' punitive discipline – defined in their study as verbally aggressive parenting behaviours – and spanking predicted children's disruptive behaviour. Weiss *et al.* (1992) also found that ratings of the severity of parental discipline were positively correlated with teacher ratings of aggression and behaviour problems. In addition to higher aggression ratings, children experiencing harsh discipline practices exhibited poorer social information-processing even when controlling for the possible effects of socioeconomic status, marital discord and child temperament. Part of the stability and continuity of aggressive behaviour may come not from ongoing effects of harsh parenting itself, but instead from the child's development of social cognitive distortions and deficiencies as a result of harsh parenting. The child's social cognitive difficulties may then lead to an ongoing maintenance of aggressive behaviour (Lochman, 2003).

The self-maintaining effects of aggressive behaviour were also found by Maughan *et al.* (1995). Using a sample that included a high-risk subsample of parents receiving psychiatric services as well as a general subsample from London, UK, Maughan *et al.* found that, for males in particular, harsh parenting produced conduct problems, which in turn led to a persistence of the problems and to the onset of new problems in adulthood. Once harsh parenting has contributed to the escalating cycle of aggressive behaviour in a child, the child's later movement towards more severe conduct problems and substance use may be more the result of continuity in the behaviour itself, rather than the effects of ongoing harsh parenting (Lochman, 2003).

Parental physical aggression, such as spanking and more punitive discipline styles, have been associated with oppositional and aggressive behaviour in both boys and girls, but these relations are more apparent in some ethnic groups (white American children) than in others (African-American children) (Deater-Deckard *et al.*, 1996). Although spanking and milder punishment does seem to be related to children's aggressive behaviour with certain types of children, the link between parental physical abuse and children's aggressive behaviour is more consistent across groups of children (Hill, 2002) and can produce long-lasting, although modest, effects on children's behaviour across the years (Widom, 1997). Using a sample of over 1000 British 5-year-old twins, Jaffee *et al.* (2004a) found that physical maltreatment predicted new and future antisocial outcomes in the children, in a direct dose–response manner, and that these effects remained even when controlled for the parents' histories of antisocial behaviour and for any genetic transmission of risks.

Parental warmth

Maternal affection has been related to lower levels of youth antisocial behaviour (Brook *et al.*, 1983), and positive parenting (positive reinforcement, acceptance, responsiveness, synchrony, approval, guidance) has been found to be negatively related to child behaviour problems (e.g. Smith *et al.*, 2000). Stormshak *et al.* (2000) found that low parental warmth/involvement predicted children's oppositional behaviours. Supportive parenting has also been found to buffer against some known risk factors of poor adjustment such as single-parent households and low socioeconomic status (Pettit *et al.*, 1997). Parental warmth and involvement may also serve an especially important role as a buffer, or protective factor, in the context of more forceful and demanding forms of parenting behaviours (Lochman, 2003).

Research on positive parenting behaviours supports the bidirectional nature of the relationship between this form of parenting and children's behaviour (Kandel & Wu, 1995). In a longitudinal study of 208 mothers and children, who were interviewed twice over a 6-year interval, parental reports of positive (closeness to children, close supervision) and negative parenting (punitive discipline) and of children's behaviour (aggression, control problems, positive relations with the parent, being well adjusted) were collected. Negative parenting was found to reinforce negative behaviour in children more than positive parenting was able to reduce children's negative behaviour. Most importantly, negative behaviour in children was found to evoke significant decreases in positive reinforcing behaviours by parents as well as small increases in negative parenting. In this regard, negative childhood behaviour was found to have more effects on parental behaviour than did positive childhood behaviour.

Monitoring and supervision

One of the strongest links between parenting practices and substance abuse involves poor parental monitoring. Monitoring, which involves knowing where children are and who they are with, may be distinguished from supervision, which typically involves controlling a young child's behaviour in the presence of the parent. Thus supervision, in this sense, is more related to behaviour management, involving attention, tracking and structuring (Dishion & McMahon, 1998). Monitoring involves an adequate awareness of children's behaviour, even when the children are not physically in the parent's presence. High levels of parental monitoring can insulate children from drug and alcohol use and a broad range of other antisocial behaviours (Snyder *et al.*, 1986; Steinberg, 1987).

Poor parental monitoring has also been associated with aggression in preadolescent children, as well as with later adolescent antisocial behaviour. Haapasalo and Tremblay (1994) found that boys who fought more often with their peers reported having less supervision and more punishment than boys who did not fight. Interestingly, the boys who fought reported having more rules than the boys who did not fight, suggesting the possibility that parents of aggressive boys may have numerous strict rules that are difficult to follow.

According to the Oregon Social Learning Center model (e.g. Dishion *et al.*, 1988), ineffective parental monitoring and harsh parenting lead to poor social skills and aversive behaviour among children, which in turn leads to association with deviant peer groups and to drug and alcohol use. Fletcher *et al.* (1995) examined the joint influence of parental monitoring and peer drug use on substance use. High-school students provided self-report information about parental monitoring, substance use and their closest friends at two annual assessments. Cross-sectional analyses indicated that parental monitoring was negatively associated with levels of substance use for boys and girls. Longitudinal analyses indicated that high levels of parental monitoring discouraged boys and girls from beginning to use drugs, encouraged boys to lessen their involvement with drugs when they were already heavily involved, and finally encouraged girls to move from experimentation to non-use. However, parental monitoring did not affect boys' movement from experimentation to heavier use or non-use over time; instead, boys moved towards the levels of substance use reported by their immediate friends. Thus, for transitions from the experimenting stage, both parental monitoring and peer groups influenced changes for girls. For boys, the peer group was critical.

Mutual parent–child influences

As noted from Kandel and Wu's (1995) findings on parental warmth (see above), the relationship between parenting and child behaviour is complex, with some evidence supporting parenting influences on child behaviour, and other evidence supporting child behaviour as an influence on parenting. Although decades of research have examined bidirectional parental influences on child behaviour and child influences on parenting, surprisingly little research has examined mutual influences (Kuczynski, 2003).

Vuchinich *et al.* (1992) examined the mutual influence of parental discipline (i.e. consistency, strictness, power assertion, aversiveness) and antisocial behaviour in a longitudinal study. They tested cross-lagged paths and reciprocal causal paths within school grades. The cross-lagged paths (i.e. 4th-grade parenting predicting 6th-grade child behaviour and vice versa) were not statistically significant, suggesting no support for prospective reciprocal relations. However, when examining mutual influences within grade (i.e. 6th-grade parenting predicting 6th-grade child behaviour and vice versa), a reciprocal relationship between parental discipline and boys' antisocial behaviour was found in the 6th grade, such that higher levels of good discipline practices elicited lower levels of antisocial behaviour and lower levels of antisocial behaviour elicited higher levels of good discipline practices.

In a further study of mutual parent–child effects with a sample of 122 boys, Fite *et al.* (2006) examined the bidirectional relationship between parenting and boys' externalizing behaviour and the stability of parenting and boys' externalizing behaviour from 4th to 8th grade. Boys' behaviour was found to influence poor parental monitoring in the 5th and 6th grades and inconsistent discipline above and beyond prior levels of parenting at all grade levels assessed. None of the parenting behaviours was found to influence boys' behaviour at any grade level, suggesting that, after taking into account the stability of boys' externalizing behaviour, boys' externalizing behaviour is independent of parenting behaviour from 4th to 8th grade in this community-recruited high-risk sample. In addition, patterns of stability for poor parental monitoring and child behaviour suggested that 6th grade was a transitional point for the children as well as the parents. Stability of child behaviour decreased from 5th to the 6th grade, and stability of parental monitoring decreased from 5th to 6th and 6th to 7th grades. These sets of results indicate the important effects of children's behaviour on their parents, especially as children approach adolescence, and suggest that the maximal period of parental influence on children's behaviour is in the preschool and early childhood years.

Parenting as a mediator between family risk factors and child behaviour

As noted in the section above on background family characteristics, the effects of those risk factors on children's behaviour may be indirect, and may in particular be mediated through effects on parenting practices. There are clear indications that disruptions in parenting may account for the effects of maternal depression and marital conflict.

Barry *et al.* (2009) examined inconsistent discipline as a mediator in the association between maternal distress and child aggression and attention problems. The participants were 215 boys, ranging in age from 9 to 12 years, and their mothers. The mothers provided self-report data on socioeconomic status, parenting stress, distress (depression and anxiety/somatization) and use of parenting practices. They also rated their sons' levels of aggression and attention problems. Of five parenting practices measured, inconsistent discipline was most clearly related to the maternal and child variables of interest. Regression analyses indicated that inconsistent discipline partially mediated the relation between maternal distress and child aggression, when controlling for socioeconomic status and stress, whereas the mediating role of inconsistent discipline in the association between maternal distress and attention problems was less clear. The different pattern for attention problems, which also includes non-disruptive behaviours, suggests that this mediation may be specific to certain types of child behaviour.

In studies of marital conflict, the effects of interparental hostility on children's adjustment have been found to be indirect, as marital hostility can cause greater parental emotional unavailability and in turn lead to child adjustment problems (Sturge-Apple *et al.*, 2006). With regard to children's aggression as a particular outcome, Erath *et al.* (2006) examined aggressive marital conflict and child aggressive-disruptive behaviour at home and school in a cross-sectional study of 360 kindergarten children. Direct pathways linking aggressive marital conflict to child aggressive-disruptive behaviour at home and at school were identified, along with a partially mediated pathway that found the relationship between aggressive marital conflict and child aggressive-disruptive behaviour at home to be mediated by maternal harsh punishment. Maternal harsh punishment accounted for 40% of the variance linking aggressive marital conflict with child aggressive-disruptive behaviour at home.

Parenting has also served to mediate the effects of marital conflict in longitudinal research, thus more clearly demonstrating the temporal ordering of these factors. Baden *et al.*, 2009) examined data across 3 years for 74 4th- and 5th-grade at-risk aggressive boys who had been living in two-parent households. Marital conflict was assessed in the first year, inconsistent parenting was assessed in the next year, and children's aggressive behaviour was assessed in the following year. The results indicated that marital or cohabitating couples who were embroiled in verbally and physically aggressive conflict behaved in increasingly hostile ways towards their children. This parental hostility – expressed in both verbally and physically aggressive ways – was subsequently linked to increased levels of children's aggressive behaviour. The pathway connecting marital conflict and children's aggression could be explained by aggressive parenting tactics.

These results are consistent with the spillover hypothesis, in which negative affect and aggressive behaviour from the marital relationship influence the parent–child relationship, contributing to irritable and harsh parental reactions to child misbehaviour (Erel & Burman, 1995).

Contextual peer factors

Children with DBDs can have highly conflictual relations with their peers. In a direct observation study, boys with DBD and normal control boys played separately with the same unaffected peer (Matthys *et al.*, 1995b). It was shown that boys with a DBD had more difficulties than normal controls in neutralizing incipient conflicts in that they reacted to antisocial behaviour on the part of the normal peer with less prosocial and less neutral behaviour than did the control boys (Matthys *et al.*, 1995b). In addition, children with a DBD have been found to react to both antisocial behaviour and prosocial behaviour with more antisocial behaviour in interaction with other children with a DBD than in interaction with normal peers (Matthys *et al.*, 1995c). These interactional styles are related to how these children with a DBD are accepted by their peers.

Friendships

Two central aspects of children's peer relations that have been linked to their adjustment are their friendships and the degree to which they are accepted or actively rejected by their peer group. Peer friendships can be defined when children have reciprocated best friend nominations, as they independently identify each other as one of their best friends. Children's abilities to form friendships has proven to be a protective factor when the children are experiencing other family-based stressors and risk factors. Children who had reciprocated best friends or high-quality friendships were less affected by being maltreated by their parents (Bolger *et al.*, 1998). Having close friends buffered these children from some of the negative effects of maltreatment on their self-esteem. Similarly, harsh, punitive and hostile family environments predicted children's later victimization by peers, but only when they had a low number of friendships (Schwartz *et al.*, 2000).

Peer rejection

A peer factor that has been more firmly linked to the development and maintenance of aggressive behaviour is peer rejection. Children with disruptive behaviours are at risk of being rejected, or actively disliked, by their peers (Cillessen *et al.*, 1992; Bierman, 2004; Pardini *et al.*, 2006). Similar to the bidirectional relations evident between the degree of parental positive involvement with their children and children's aggressive behaviour over time (Bry *et al.*, 1999), children's aggressive behaviour and their rejection by their peers reciprocally affect each other (Conduct Problems Prevention Research Group, 2004b). The combination of being aggressive and rejected greatly enhances children's risk of later antisocial behaviour. Coie *et al.* (1992) found that 3rd-grade children who were rejected by their classmates and who were also perceived to be aggressive by their peers had three times the risk rate of having problematic adjustment in middle school according to teacher, parent and self-reports.

Childhood aggressive behaviour and peer rejection assessed in elementary schools can additively and independently predict serious antisocial behaviour such as delinquency rates even later, in high school (Lochman & Wayland, 1994). Aggressive children who are also socially rejected tend to exhibit more severe behaviour problems than children who are either aggressive only or rejected only. Bierman and Wargo (1995) found that aggressive-rejected children had more problematic longitudinal outcomes than did aggressive-nonrejected or rejected-nonaggressive children, and Miller-Johnson *et al.* (2002) found that aggressive behaviour and peer rejection at the beginning of elementary school both independently predicted later poor adjustment.

This early predictive role for rejection and aggression continues to be apparent even through middle-to-late adolescence as adolescents develop through adolescence. In general, early childhood aggression appears to predict a wider range of adolescent offending, and of involvement in deviant peer groups, than does rejection alone (Coie *et al.*, 1995b; Miller-Johnson *et al.*, 1999a). However, the combination of aggression and rejection in 3rd grade has predicted both serious and non-serious offending through the high-school years for boys, and this has been especially evident in predicting felony assault (Miller-Johnson, 1999a). These predictors have a less robust capacity to predict adolescent girls' antisocial behaviour, although earlier peer rejection does predict minor assault offences by adolescent girls, and aggression emerges as a primary predictor of juvenile child-bearing and arrests in girls (Coie et al., 1995b; Miller-Johnson et al., 1999a, 1999b).

Moderators of social rejection effects: gender and race

Despite the compelling nature of these findings, race and gender may moderate the relation between peer rejection and negative adolescent outcomes. With regard to gender, it was noted earlier that peer rejection can predict serious delinquency in boys, but it can fail to do so with girls (Miller-Johnson et al., 1999a).

With regard to race, Lochman and Wayland (1994) found that peer rejection ratings of African-American children within a mixed-race classroom did not predict subsequent externalizing problems in adolescence, whereas peer rejection ratings of Caucasian children were associated with future disruptive behaviours. This latter finding may be related to the effects of being in the majority or minority race when sociometric data are collected (Jackson et al., 2006).

Some research suggests that peer nominations are influenced by superficial characteristics, such as race (Coie et al., 1990; Kistner et al., 1993), and that the behaviours associated with negative peer evaluations depend on the classroom context (Wright et al., 1986; Boivin et al., 1995; Stormshak et al., 1999). Research from the perspective of person–environment congruency (Wright et al., 1986; Livert & Hughes, 2002; Rhodes et al., 2004) suggests that child race effects may depend on the racial make-up of the classroom and the concomitant shifts in behavioural norms that might occur with different racial compositions. Out-group bias is evident in children as young as 5 years of age. As they grow, children are more likely to evaluate similar behaviours more negatively for out-group than in-group members (Abrams et al., 2003).

The effect of race moderation of peer status is not fully understood because African-American children rarely hold a classroom majority and teachers' race has rarely been investigated. To explore these effects, Jackson et al. (2006) conducted research from the perspective of person–environment congruency which suggested that child race effects depended on the race composition of the class and the larger society's beliefs about race. Sociometric nominations were obtained from 1268 5th-graders (53% African-American) enrolled in 57 classrooms (3–95% African-American students). Fifty per cent of the teachers were African-American. For each of the five sociometric measures – social preference, like most, like least, leaders and fights – black children's ratings improved as a function of their increased representation in the classroom.

Considered in isolation from the findings for white children, the results for black children support the theories of in-group bias and Wagner's (1996) opportunity and threat effects. As black children became more numerous in their classrooms, their social interactions with classmates might have increased, resulting in more positive peer nominations. When their representation in the classroom was low, black children might have been more socially isolated because of feelings of intimidation in the dominant racial group, resulting in fewer nominations. Ratings for white children appeared to be less sensitive to classroom race composition. These findings suggest that white children might be buffered from the effects of being a classroom minority by their relatively greater presence and dominance in the larger community.

The effects of teacher's race were weaker, but the one significant finding evidenced a pattern similar to the effects of racial composition in the classroom. Black children received more nominations for leader when their classrooms were headed by black as opposed to white teachers. However, white children's ratings stayed above those of black children even when the teacher was black, indicating that these findings cannot simply be explained by teachers' favouritism toward same-race children. In summary, results indicated that ratings for African-American children were more sensitive to classroom race composition than ratings for white children. Teachers' race thus influenced leader nominations.

Children's perceptions of their social status

Aggressive children who are rejected by their peers are a diverse group (Parker & Asher, 1987; Pardini *et al.*, 2006), with some children having perceptions of their social status that converge with peer ratings and others overestimating their peer acceptance (Salmivalli *et al.*, 1999; Hughes *et al.*, 2001; Baumeister *et al.*, 2003). Aggressive children who are disliked by their peers but hold a positive perception of their own social acceptance may have more severe externalizing problems than children who are disliked by their peers and describe their own social acceptance as poor (Diener & Milich, 1997). Some children who are disliked by their peers but report positive views of their social status have been found to exhibit more externalizing problems (e.g. aggression, delinquency) and engage in more bullying behaviour than children who hold views of their social acceptance that are more concordant with peer reports (Edens *et al.*, 1999; Salmivalli *et al.*, 1999; Hughes *et al.*, 2001). Thus, those aggressive-disruptive children who are both disliked and hold high perceptions of their social acceptance may be at the greatest risk of negative behavioural outcomes.

However, other researchers have suggested that there may also be some advantages related to overperceiving one's own social standing with peers (Bjorklund & Green, 1992; Hughes *et al.*, 1997). For example, inflated self-perceptions are linked to externalizing problems but are unrelated to internalizing symptoms in the absence of deviant behaviour (Gresham *et al.*, 1998). There is also substantial evidence indicating that positive self-perceptions, whether inflated or in line with others' assessments, are related to greater levels of happiness (Baumeister *et al.*, 2003). Youth who inflate their social status may ignore or exclude information viewed as damaging to defend against feelings of loneliness or recover from emotional trauma (Webster-Stratton & Lindsay, 1999). Thus, high self-perceptions of one's own social standing may keep aggressive-disruptive children who are rejected by their peers from developing significant internalizing problems (e.g. Bjorklund & Green, 1992).

A different pattern of children's distorted perceptions of their social acceptance involves social status deflation, in which children who are relatively well liked by their peers tend to rate their own social standing as poorer than it is. Social status deflation is often associated with more internalizing symptomatology and a depressogenic attributional style (Panak & Garber, 1992; Cole *et al.*, 1999; McGrath & Repetti, 2002). Children with depressive and externalizing problems tend to deflate their social standing (Rudolph & Clark, 2001). Thus, aggressive-disruptive youth who tend to underestimate their social status are likely to have internalizing problems, and their disruptive behaviour problems may be related to a constellation of problems associated with mood disturbances in children.

To explore both inflated and deflated perceptions of social status, Pardini *et al.* (2006) collected sociometric and self-perception data on 245 at-risk aggressive children in 17 schools. After controlling for the overlap between acceptance by peers and self-perceived social acceptance, children who reported higher levels of self-perceived social acceptance exhibited higher levels of peer-rated fighting at school. Among children with higher levels of social standing among their peers, self-perceived social acceptance was negatively related to parent-reported oppositional defiant behaviour and conduct problems (i.e. better self-perceptions were related to lower levels of problem behaviours). In addition, children who perceived their social acceptance in a positive light had the lowest levels of self-reported emotional dysregulation and parent-reported affective problems, regardless of their acceptance by their peers. This is consistent with suggestions that children who hold a positive view of their social acceptance despite being rejected by their peers may not be at increased risk of internalizing problems (Bjorklund & Green, 1992). Taken together, these findings are intriguing because they suggest that children with deflated self-perceptions of their social acceptance have higher levels of externalizing problems at home, even if there are well liked by their peers, while inflated self-perceptions are related in a positive way to children's aggression at school.

Deviant peer groups

As children with conduct problems enter adolescence, they tend to associate with deviant peers. Peer influences to increase antisocial behaviour are primarily apparent in the adolescent developmental stage (Warr, 2002), and adolescents' problem behaviour is often embedded in their involvement in their peer groups (Dishion *et al.*, 1999). As youth begin to spend increasing amounts of time in a deviant peer group, they are exposed to frequent negative referent models, reinforcement of negative attitudes and behaviours, and peer pressure to engage in increasingly antisocial behaviour. Highly antisocial dyads have been found to reinforce each others' delinquent talk more than low antisocial dyads (Dishion *et al.*, 1994).

Research over the past 60 years has indicated a strong association between children's antisocial behaviour and that of their peers (Sutherland, 1939; Arnold & Hughes, 1999). When adolescents enter a deviant peer group, they often increase their rates of school truancy and drop-out, placing themselves in even more contact with each other, which leads directly to increased rates of delinquency (Coie *et al.*, 1995b; Lochman, 2003). Children's association with deviant peers in adolescence becomes one of the strongest proximal risk predictors for a growth in subsequent delinquency (Patterson, 1993; Tremblay *et al.*, 1995; Miller-Johnson *et al.*, 1999a). Moderately aggressive boys have been found to be most susceptible to the negative effects of aggressive friends (Vitaro *et al.*, 1997). Deviant peers can influence a range of antisocial behaviours because exposure to high levels of peer drug abuse within the deviant peer groups is also associated with high levels of concurrent drug use by adolescents (Dishion *et al.*, 1988) and with escalating drug use over time (Wills *et al.*, 1996). The relationship between childhood conduct problems and adolescent delinquency is at least partially mediated by deviant peer group affiliation (Vitaro *et al.*, 1999).

Several studies have noted the causal effects of deviant peers on adolescents' behaviour. Dishion and Andrews (1995) randomly assigned high-risk young adolescents to one of four conditions varying in terms of whether the youth received 12 youth-only sessions, their parents received 12 parent-only sessions, the youths and the parents both received combined intervention, or the youths and parents received no intervention. All three of the Adolescent Transition Program intervention cells had some positive effects at post-intervention assessment, and the conditions providing youth intervention produced reductions in negative family interactions and a good acquisition of the concepts presented in the intervention. However, by the time of a 1-year follow-up, the youth who had received youth sessions had higher rates of tobacco use and of teacher-rated delinquent behaviours than did the control children, and these iatrogenic effects were evident even if the parents had also received intervention in the combined condition. At a 3-year follow-up, the teen intervention conditions continued to have more tobacco use and delinquency (Poulin *et al.*, 2001). Analyses of the iatrogenic group conditions revealed that subtle dynamics of deviancy training during unstructured transitions in the groups predicted a growth in self-reported smoking and a growth in teacher ratings of delinquency (Dishion *et al.*, 2001). The effect of the deviant peer group on individuals' behaviour is also evident in social contextual research on gang involvement. Youths' rates of violent delinquent behaviour have been found to sharply increase when they become involved in gangs and to decline when they leave the gangs (Thornberry & Krohn, 1997).

It is believed that many of these teens have been continually rejected from more prosocial peer groups because they lack appropriate social skills and, as a result, turn to antisocial cliques as their only means of social support (Miller-Johnson *et al.*, 1999). As a result of poor social competence and active social rejection by their peers (often because of highly aggressive, noxious behaviour directed toward these peers), children and adolescents may gravitate to a deviant peer group in early adolescence (Coie, 1990; Lochman, 2003). These socially rejected and disliked youth still typically have social goals that place a substantial value on affiliating with their peers (Lochman *et al.*, 1993a), and they begin to spend time with the only type of peer group that will usually accept them, namely peers who are similarly socially rejected and antisocial (Cairns *et al.*, 1988; Coie *et al.*, 1992, 1995b). The tendency for aggressive children to associate with one another increases the probability that their aggressive behaviours will be maintained and/or will escalate due to modelling effects and the reinforcement of deviant behaviours (e.g. Dishion *et al.*, 1995).

Deviant peer groups, peer rejection and subtypes of aggression

The last paragraph suggests that being rejected by one's peers may be one reason for adolescents' movement to deviant peer groups. However, there may be different paths to deviant peer group involvement for different types of youth, and one important distinction may be whether they primarily display proactive or reactive aggressive behaviour.

Prior research has examined the impact of proactive and reactive aggression on peer relations and long-term outcomes (Fite *et al.*, 2007). There are mixed findings about the peer relations of proactively aggressive children. Some studies suggest that proactively aggressive children are more negatively evaluated by their peers over time (Dodge & Coie, 1987; Poulin & Boivin, 1999). Other studies suggest, however, that proactive aggression is associated with having a good sense of humour and leadership qualities in childhood (Dodge & Coie, 1987; Price & Dodge, 1989; Poulin & Boivin, 2000a) and high levels of popularity in adolescence (Prinstein & Cillessen, 2003). Finally, other research suggests that proactively aggressive children tend to associate with other proactively aggressive children (Poulin & Boivin, 2000b), and thus their deviant peer groups might not include many rejected, proactive aggressive children. Thus, overall, proactively aggressive children may have some difficulties in peer relations, but they are often positively evaluated by their peers and are not socially isolated.

The pattern of peer relation problems has been found to be more consistent in prior research. Reactively aggressive children are not liked by their peers at any age (e.g. Dodge & Coie, 1987; Price & Dodge, 1989; Prinstein & Cilessen, 2003). More specifically, reactively aggressive children exhibit social skills deficits (Day *et al.*, 1992), are negatively evaluated by their peers (Dodge *et al.*, 1997; Prinstein & Cilessen, 2003), report low levels of friendship satisfaction and are unlikely to be selected as best friends (Poulin & Boivin, 1999). Thus, reactive aggression appears to be associated with more severe deficits in peer relations than proactive aggression.

In a direct test of whether different pathways of peer relations exist for youth with higher levels of reactive versus proactive aggressive behaviour, Fite *et al.* (2007) tested 126 at-risk aggressive children in a longitudinal study. The subtypes of aggressive behaviour and children's peer acceptance were assessed in 5th grade, involvement with deviant peers was assessed in 8th grade, and substance use was assessed in 9th grade. Analyses examined whether proactive and/or reactive aggression was related to substance use (alcohol, tobacco, marijuana). In addition, the study examined whether peer rejection and peer delinquency mediated the relationship between these two dimensions of aggression and substance use. Findings suggested that proactive aggression was directly associated with tobacco use and indirectly associated with alcohol and marijuana use through peer delinquency. Children who had been proactively aggressive in 5th grade gravitated to deviant peer associations by 8th grade, and the changes in their alcohol and marijuana use by 9th grade were predicted by their deviant peer involvement.

Reactive aggression was marginally significantly positively associated with alcohol use through a complex mediational chain, such that 5th-grade reactive aggression was associated with 5th-grade low peer acceptance, which was in turn a marginally significant predictor of 8th-grade peer delinquency and subsequent 9th-grade alcohol use. Furthermore, reactive aggression was protective of substance use after accounting for peer acceptance, such that reactive aggression was negatively associated with peer delinquency and subsequent alcohol and marijuana use. Thus, reactive aggression may be both a risk and a protective factor for different individuals. Reactively aggressive individuals who are not chronically rejected by their peers may avoid delinquent peers and substance use because they are hypervigilant to threatening and punishing cues (e.g. Dodge, 1991; Dodge *et al.*, 1997). That is, reactively aggressive individuals may be avoiding the potentially negative consequences associated with delinquency and substance use.

When the first initiation of substance use between 4th and 9th grades, rather than actual use, was examined, similar patterns of peer influence occurred, although there were variations according to the substance initiated (Fite *et al.*, 2008). Survival analyses were conducted with the same sample as in the prior study, and proactive aggressive behaviour predicted children's involvement with deviant peers, and then with the initiation of marijuana and tobacco initiation. Alcohol initiation was only directly predicted by higher levels of proactive aggression, suggesting that the presence of deviant peers does not have an important effect on the initiation of alcohol use. In contrast, higher levels of reactive aggressive behaviour led to early marijuana and tobacco initiation only when reactively aggressive youth were disliked by their peers and then gravitated to peers who were engaged in delinquent behaviour.

Contextual community and school factors

Neighbourhood problems

In addition to family interaction problems, peer rejection and involvement in deviant peer groups, neighbourhood and school environments have also been found to be risk factors for aggression and delinquency over and above the variance accounted for by family characteristics (Kupersmidt et al., 1995). Deprived neighbourhoods are characterized by high unemployment rates, dense public housing, social isolation and crime and violence (Jenkins, 2008), and have been found to account for 5% of the variance in teacher-reported emotional and conduct problems (Boyle & Lipman, 2002).

An exposure to neighbourhood violence increases children's aggressive behaviours (e.g. Colder et al., 2000; Guerra et al., 2003) and their beliefs about aggression (Guerra et al., 2003), and begins to have heightened effects on the development of antisocial behaviour during the middle childhood, preadolescent years (Ingoldsby & Shaw, 2002). Children in deprived neighbourhoods are exposed to high rates of violence – 17% of youth in urban Chicago neighbourhoods reported that their family members had been robbed or attacked, and 16% had seen someone shot or killed in the prior year (Gorman-Smith & Tolan, 1998) – and this level of exposure led to an increase in the adolescents' disruptive behaviour over the following year.

Neighbourhood problems also have effects on parenting behaviours (Pinderhughes et al., 2001; Gutman et al., 2005) by failing to support parents in their efforts to rear their children (Moffitt & Scott, 2008). Problematic neighbourhoods also have a direct impact on children's aggressive, antisocial behaviours (Schwab-Stone et al., 1995; Greenberg et al., 1999) above and beyond the effects of poor parenting practices. An early onset of aggression and violence has been associated with neighbourhood disorganization and poverty partly because children who live in lower socioeconomic status and disorganized neighbourhoods are not well supervised, engage in more risk-taking behaviours and experience the deviant social influences that are apparent in problematic crime-ridden neighbourhoods.

It is plausible that community-level problems may have more influence on one subtype of aggressive behaviour than another (Fite et al., 2009). Reactive aggression is believed to develop from children experiencing abuse and punitive discipline that leads to hypervigilance to threat cues (Dodge, 1991; Vitaro *et al.*, 2006). In contrast, proactive aggression is believed to develop from an exposure to and endorsement of aggressive behaviour (Dodge, 1991; Vitaro *et al.*, 2006). Disadvantaged neighbourhoods can have greater levels of violence and aggression in the streets (e.g. Markowitz, 2003), and these neighbourhoods may serve as a modelling mechanism for aggression, leading to increases in proactively aggressive behaviour. Thus, neighbourhood disadvantage may be more strongly related to proactive than reactive aggression.

To examine this question, Fite *et al.* (2009) identified 22 neighbourhood census tracts of 126 children, with analyses taking into account how children were aggregated into neighbourhoods. Consistent with expectation, neighbourhood disadvantage (characterized by factors such as high unemployment and a high density of housing) was a unique predictor of proactive, and not reactive, aggression when also taking into account the stability of the aggression and the variance associated with reactive aggression, gender and race. Thus, neighbourhood-level risk factors have most effect on proactive aggression, which is the form of aggression most clearly predictive of later delinquency and substance use.

School characteristics

Schools can further exacerbate children's conduct problems through the frustration they experience from academic demands and from the additional peer influences on their behaviour. School and classroom characteristics can broadly reflect the sociodemographic characteristics of schools along with aspects of the classroom environments. Thomas *et al.* (2009) explored how school-level factors can add to child-level risk factors in predicting child behaviour. Child characteristics and vulnerabilities (aggressive-disruptive behaviour at home, attention problems) accounted for most (approximately 74%) of the variance explained in children's level of aggression at school for 1st-grade students in four communities, but school factors (particularly low-quality classroom contexts) acted as cumulative risk factors, significantly increasing the children's risk of aggressive-disruptive problems in school. These results of natural factors in classrooms and schools extend results from experimental studies suggesting that classroom contexts characterized by disapproving teachers and disengaged students undermine the effectiveness of the classroom learning environment and elicit and reinforce disruptive behaviour.

Research has also examined the effects of the social behaviour of students in classrooms as predictors of individual child behaviour. Adaptive behaviours such as task orientation and prosocial interactions are more likely to increase if the classroom holds many students who exhibit high levels of these behaviours and who reinforce them in others. Similarly, classrooms with a high number of students with poor academic or deviant social skills are likely to perpetuate these maladaptive behaviours (Barth *et al.*, 2004). Thus, the aggregate of individual child characteristics in a class provides an important determinant of classroom environment and individual behaviour.

Previous research on the effects of classmates primarily addressed 'ability grouping'. Research had indicated that the achievement gap between children tracked in the lower and upper ability groups increased over time, and that being tracked in the lower ability group had adverse effects on self-concept (Dornbusch *et al.*, 1996). In contrast, there are only a limited number of studies on 'social grouping' or on how the social make-up of classrooms influences children's behaviour.

In support of the person–group similarity model that could account for group processes, Wright *et al.* (1986) reported that withdrawal and aggression were only related to the peer acceptance of 10-year-old boys when these were relatively uncommon characteristics in the social group. Similarly, Boivin *et al.* (1995) and Stormshak *et al.* (1999) found that individual levels of reactive aggression and withdrawal were related to poor social status in 1st and 3rd grade only when they were relatively rare behaviours for the peer group as a whole. When each of these behaviours was more prevalent in the classroom, it became less associated with low social status.

Across a 6-year longitudinal period, Kellam *et al.* (1998) found that classroom environment could account for changes in children's behaviour. They found that highly aggressive 1st-grade boys in highly aggressive classrooms had an increased likelihood of maintaining their level of aggression in 6th grade compared with comparable aggressive children placed in non-aggressive 1st-grade classrooms. Similarly, Thomas *et al.* (2006) followed a longitudinal sample of 4907 children and examined demographic factors associated with an exposure to high-aggression classrooms, including school context factors (school size, student poverty levels, rural versus urban location) and child ethnicity (African-American, European-American). The developmental impact of different temporal patterns of exposure (e.g. primacy, recency, chronicity) to high-aggression classrooms was evaluated on child aggression.

In this study, analyses revealed that African-American children attending large, urban schools that served socioeconomically disadvantaged students were more likely than other students to be exposed to high-aggression classroom contexts. Hierarchical regressions demonstrated cumulative effects for temporal exposure whereby children with multiple years of exposure showed higher levels of aggressive behaviour after 3 years than children with less recent and less chronic exposure, controlling for initial levels of aggression. The implications for developmental research and preventive interventions were discussed.

Stearns *et al.* (2008) also explored these classroom effects at the beginning of elementary school using normative data from the Fast Track study, and investigating the effects of peer social context and child characteristics on the growth of teacher-rated reports of behaviour problems relating to authority acceptance across grades 1, 2 and 3. Three hundred and sixty children (51% male, 46% African-American) and their classmates were assessed in each grade by teacher ratings using the revised Teacher Observation of Child Adaptation (TOCA-R) questionnaire. Children's growth in behaviour problems relating to acceptance of authority across time was partially attributable to the level of disruptive behaviour in the classroom peer context into which they were placed. Peer-context influences, however, were strongest among same-gender peers. Findings held for both boys and girls, both European-American and African-American children, and non-deviant, marginally deviant and highly deviant children. Findings suggest that children learn and follow behavioural norms displayed by their same-gender peers within the classroom.

To examine the effects of other classroom characteristics on student behaviour, and to examine these effects at a later preadolescent point, when the children are at the end of elementary school, 378 children were assessed in 65 classrooms in 17 schools, and their individual and classroom-level sociometric ratings and school-level characteristics were tested in three-level hierarchical linear models (Barth *et al.*, 2004). Student aggression, poor peer relations and poor academic focus were significantly predicted by classroom-level environment measures of these same three constructs (using the composite scores of the students in each of the classrooms). In contrast, school environment, as measured by achievement test scores and the percentage of children in the school who received free or subsidised lunches because of their low family income, was a relatively weaker predictor of behaviour. The fact that similar patterns emerged for both the 4th- and 5th-grade time points provided additional confidence for the conclusion that the characteristics of students in a classroom have a substantial effect on child behaviour during the year they are in that classroom. If a child is in a classroom that has a high density of other aggressive children, this increases the probability of a given student becoming more aggressive. Similar to research on academic ability grouping and small-group clinical interventions (Dishion *et al.*, 1999), these findings suggest that putting behaviourally similar children together in a group may be beneficial when the group members are collectively highly competent, but can otherwise have deleterious effects.

Media factors

Children's exposure to aggressive and violent content on television, in video game playing and through violent song lyrics have all been linked to children's aggressive behaviour. Huesmann *et al.* (2003) followed up 557 children who had been originally assessed at ages 6–10 years, and found that exposure to television violence in childhood predicted the young adults' rates of arrest and prosecution for criminal acts. This relationship between television violence and subsequent antisocial behaviour in this long-term longitudinal study was especially apparent when the child had identified with the aggressive television character.

Video game play, including an involvement with highly violent video games, is quite common among youth. Anderson and Dill (2000) found that laboratory-based video game play was associated with their aggressive behaviour in their daily life. Violent video game play may be a more harmful risk factor than violent television because video games are interactive, are very engaging and require the player to identify with the aggressor.

Other forms of media may also be linked to aggressive behaviour, although the causal evidence for this is not yet clear. However, Anderson *et al.* (2003) have found that songs with violent lyrics increased aggression-related thoughts and emotions in older adolescents.

Environmental factors affecting social information-processing

Based on children's temperaments and biological dispositions, and on their contextual experiences arising from their family, peers and community, they begin to form stable patterns of processing social information (Dodge *et al.*, 2002) and of regulating their emotions (see Chapter 4). Children's exposure to their social environments is likely to help shape their social information-processing style (their likelihood of having hostile attributional biases, of thinking of competent solutions to their social problems, of anticipating positive or negative consequences for their aggressive and prosocial behaviours) and to have a profound effect on their schemas, which inform their social information-processing (Lochman *et al.*, 2006a, 2008e).

Summary points

- Environmental factors such as maternal alcohol use, severe nutritional deficiencies and birth complications are risk factors for later behaviour problems.
- Environmental factors such as harsh parenting and family poverty can amplify children's genetic risk factors; if a child with a genetic risk factor (such as a polymorphism of the MAOA gene) does not experience certain social environmental risk factors, he or she is not as likely to display serious violent behaviour.
- Contextual family risk factors that are associated with children's aggression include family poverty, single parenting, parental criminality and depression, marital conflict and weak parent–child attachment.

- The effects of maternal depression and maternal conflict on children's aggressive behaviour are at least partially mediated through the parents' more inconsistent and harsh parenting that spills over from the marital conflict or parental depression.
- Problematic parenting practices that are especially associated with children's aggressive behaviour include harsh punishment, inconsistent discipline, lack of warmth and positive attention, and poor monitoring.
- The relationship between parents' parenting practices and their children's behaviour is bidirectional, with poor discipline predicting increases in children's behaviour, and high levels of children's problem behaviour predicting a deterioration in parenting practices.
- Peer factors that can contribute to the development and maintenance of children's aggressive behaviour are low-quality friendships, high levels of peer rejection and involvement in deviant peer groups.
- The peer-related mediating factors contributing to early substance use differ for children with primarily reactive versus primarily proactive aggression, with deviant peer groups being a critically important mediating factor for both groups of children, and peer rejection being a specific mediator for reactive-aggressive children. Reactive aggressive children become more rejected by their peers, and this increases their risk of substance use.
- Broader exosystem environmental risk factors, such as neighbourhood problems and high densities of aggressive children in the classroom, are predictive of an increase in children's aggressive behaviours.

6

Clinical assessment

The clinical assessment of a child can be considered to be a decision-making process in which the clinician assesses the presence (or not) of one or more psychiatric disorders, considers the underlying aetiology and plans treatment. We will describe this decision-making process in eight steps:

- the collection of written information from the parents;
- the initial interview with the parents and the child;
- the formulation of a hypothesis on possible diagnoses and comorbidities;
- the clinical interview and observation of the child;
- the completion of additional assessments, if necessary;
- the administration of a *Diagnostic and statistical manual of mental disorders*, 4th edition, text revision (DSM-IV-TR)-orientated interview with the parents (and the older child separately);
- the integration of all available information in view of a multiaxial diagnosis and diagnostic formulation including considerations about aetiology, and the decision of a treatment plan;
- the discussion of the diagnosis and treatment plan with the parents.

First, however, we will discuss some general issues.

General issues

The clinical assessment of a child results in three decisions. First, the clinician decides whether the child's behavioural problems are severe enough to qualify as a disruptive behaviour disorder (DBD) and whether one or more comorbid disorders may be diagnosed. This first step in the assessment procedure results in one or more DSM-IV-TR axis I diagnoses. Second, the clinician tries to

Oppositional Defiant Disorder and Conduct Disorder in Childhood   By Walter Matthys and John E. Lochman
© 2010 John Wiley & Sons, Ltd.

understand the factors involved in the development of the disorder. This is included in a diagnostic formulation. Third, the clinician proposes to the parents a treatment plan resulting from the diagnosis and the considerations about aetiology.

Let us first discuss issues related to the establishment of a DBD. Although most psychopathological phenomena in children can best be regarded as quantitative variations, many clinical decisions have to be categorical. Deciding whether a child has an oppositional defiant disorder (ODD), a conduct disorder (CD) and one or more comorbid disorders is based on whether the description of the child's symptoms meets the criteria for one of these diagnostic categories. Thus, the child either suffers, or does not suffer, one or more disorders. This decision concerning DSM-IV-TR axis I is needed for practical purposes: for whether treatment or special education is indicated and for whether resources for these and other purposes (e.g. social services) should be made available.

Although the distinction between normative misbehaviour and problematic behaviour is crucial in all children, specific attention to this issue is required in preschool children. Non-compliance, temper loss and physical aggression are that common in early childhood that they may be called normative misbehaviours (Wakschlag *et al.*, 2007). Thus, a distinction needs to be made between normative non-compliance and clinically significant non-compliance or oppositionality (Wakschlag & Danis, 2004). Normative non-compliance reflects a child's self-assertion and may therefore be called assertive non-compliance. It is short lived and is elicited by the desire to do something autonomously. In contrast, oppositional behaviour is less responsive to ignoring the misbehaviour or providing distractions, and thus is intransigent.

Likewise, with respect to difficulty recovering from negative affect after frustration, a distinction needs to be made between normative tantrums that are brief in duration and clinically relevant tantrums that are easily elicited, are long in duration (10 minutes or more), are associated with aggressive and destructive behaviour, and require substantial adult support to calm the child down (Wakschlag & Danis, 2004). Finally, in contrast to normative aggressive misbehaviour, clinically relevant physical aggression occurs more frequently, is proactive (with the aim of deliberately being cruel to another person) as well as reactive, has more varied manifestations (biting, scratching, pulling hair) and is also directed towards adults (Wakschlag & Danis, 2004) when physical aggression is a symptom of CD.

The dichotomy between normality and pathology that characterizes classification systems does not, however, preclude a dimensional approach. It is important to assess the severity of the disorder and to make decisions about the intensity of treatment. The relative frequency and severity of symptoms are also important when planning targeted prevention programmes. An assessment of severity can be made by counting the number of symptoms.

Thus, a child with seven symptoms of ODD in general needs a more intensive intervention than a child with four symptoms. However, severity may also be assessed by using standardized rating scales that will be discussed later.

Related to severity is the issue of impairment. According to DSM-IV-TR, symptoms need to cause a clinically significant impairment of social, academic or occupational functioning before a child qualifies for a psychiatric disorder. Thus, it is insufficient for the clinician to check whether a child fulfils four criteria of ODD or three criteria of CD in order to diagnose a child with ODD or CD. On axis V of DSM-IV-TR, the clinician uses the Global Assessment of Functioning (GAF) to rate the individual's overall level of functioning. This level of psychological, social and occupational functioning is to be considered on a hypothetical continuum of mental health–illness from 1 to 100 (American Psychiatric Association, 2000). Below we give the description of the most relevant areas of impairment with respect to the DBDs.

- The range of scores between 61 and 70 corresponds to 'mild symptoms ... OR some difficulty in social, occupational, or school functioning (e.g. occasional truancy or theft within the household), but generally functioning pretty well, has some meaningful interpersonal relationships'.
- The range of scores between 51 and 60 corresponds with 'moderate symptoms ... OR moderate difficulty in social, occupational, or school functioning (e.g. few friends, conflicts with peers or co-workers)'.
- The range of scores between 41 and 50 corresponds with 'serious symptoms ... OR any serious impairment in social, occupational, or school functioning (e.g. no friends, ...)'.
- The range of scores between 31 and 40 corresponds with 'some impairment in reality testing or communication ... OR major impairment in several areas, such as work or school, family relations, judgment, thinking, or mood (e.g. ... child frequently beats up younger children, is defiant at home, and is failing at school)'.

There is a relationship between the level of overall functioning and the presence of a psychiatric disorder. On the Children's Global Assessment Scale (C-GAS), a measure similar to the GAF, the level of overall functioning in disordered children and adolescents in general is lower than 70 or 65 (Shaffer et al., 1983; Bird et al., 1987). Thus, one should not consider a child who fulfils the symptom criteria of ODD, CD or attention deficit/hyperactivity disorder (ADHD) without any impairment as suffering from these disorders. In line with this, when impairment in functioning is not taken into account, prevalence rates of psychiatric disorders in children and adolescents are much higher (Bird et al., 1990). The assessment of the level of overall functioning is also important with respect to the choice of treatment. For example, medication in most preschool children with ADHD (and a comorbid DBD) is not indicated as a first step in treatment, but it may be appropriate in those preschool children with severe impairment because of a high frequency of accidents and injuries.

An important diagnostic concern occurs when a child's GAF or C-GAS score is 65 or lower but when the child does not qualify for ODD or CD because he or she only fulfils three symptoms of ODD or two symptoms of CD. Such a child may be considered to function at a subclinical level. In many countries, this child would be excluded from any intervention, whereas behavioural management training (see Chapter 8) might be helpful in preventing the development of ODD or CD. It would be inappropriate to withhold such a child and his or her family from an indicated preventive intervention since it has been shown that children with three (or even two) symptoms of ODD plus impairment are very similar to those with four or more symptoms in terms of outcome 1 year later (Angold & Costello, 1996). Thus, in our view, the inclusion of subclinical (subthreshold or borderline clinical) functioning in the DSM-V/*International classification of diseases*, 11th revision (ICD-11) should be considered to be an indicator leading to prevention services for DBDs, especially in preschool children.

The multiaxial system DSM-IV-TR has three more axes besides axes I and V, i.e. axis II (Personality disorders and mental retardation), axis III (General medical conditions) and axis IV (Psychosocial and environmental problems). Thus, DSM-IV-TR gives a succinct summary of the essential features of a child and his or her parents. However, this is not enough to draw conclusions about the treatment needed for this particular child. In contrast, a diagnostic formulation also includes a hypothesis about causal processes and a hypothesis about therapeutic interventions (Rutter & Taylor, 2008). With respect to causal processes, a distinction needs to be made between factors involved in the initiation and factors involved in the maintenance of the disorder. To make hypotheses that can productively assist with planning therapeutic interventions, we should distinguish proximal from distal risk factors, and modifiable from stable factors. Thus, for the planning of treatment, we should focus mainly on the factors that play a role in the maintenance of the disorder and are modifiable and proximal.

As already discussed in Chapter 3, our present knowledge does not allow us to clearly identify the specific causal processes underlying the disorder in each child. In some children, factors that probably have played a role in the causation, such as very low birth weight, may be identified, but it would not be realistic to aim at a complete understanding of the causation of the disorder in each child. Thus, the issue for the clinician is how extensive the assessment should be in order to generate a hypothesis on the aetiology in the child that is good enough for a rational treatment plan. In this context, acknowledging the large number of children who are referred for the assessment and treatment of DBDs and ADHD due to the high prevalence of these disorders, we should avoid long waiting lists caused by unnecessarily lengthy assessments. We therefore advocate an assessment that is, on one the one hand, 'good enough' for a satisfactory understanding of the aetiological factors involved in the development of the disorder in this particular child but, on the other hand, is not unnecessary detailed. In the assessment, it is essential to identify factors that are associated with the maintenance of the disorder, such as the child's borderline intellectual functioning or inappropriate parental skills, and that have consequences for the treatment and education of the child.

An overview of the assessment procedure

In the assessment, data are collected that the clinician needs in order to make decisions with respect to the five DSM-IV-TR axes, to generate hypotheses about aetiology and to propose a treatment plan to the parents and children. With respect to axis I diagnosis there is a risk of idiosyncratic decision-making if the clinician uses only so-called open or clinical interviews, as the clinician may focus on a particular set of symptoms and fail to explore the full range of psychopathology. The unreliability of clinical methods has led to the development of structured interviews and rating scales for research purposes.

Although structured or semi-structured interviews are to be preferred to clinical interviews because of their proven reliability and validity, the current use of (semi-)structured interviews in everyday clinical practice is often not feasible because specific training is needed to administer these interviews appropriately. Monitoring of the appropriate ongoing administration of clinical interviews is also needed. In addition, not all rating scales can be easily used in clinical practice, because only a limited number have been standardized and thus have clinical cut-off points. In the description of the assessment procedure we therefore discuss both (semi-)structured interviews, clinical interviews and (standardized) rating scales, leaving open to the clinician the decision on which methods are feasible in his or her clinical setting. Moreover, we suggest a strategy using multiple methods to collect information from multiple informants (parents, teacher, child) in terms of various steps to be made over time.

Eight decision-making steps may be followed:

1. After the child has been referred, parents are asked to give *written information* on the child and family prior to the first visit to the clinic, including completing a comprehensive standardized rating scale.
2. The assessment starts with an *initial interview with the parents and child*. The clinician clarifies questions about the referral and is sensitive to the parents' concerns. When parents feel valued, it is easier for them to participate in the structured part of the assessment. Important information is gathered on the child's development, his or her problem behaviour and the family. Parent–child interactions are also observed.

3. Based on this information and scores on one of the comprehensive standardized rating scales, the clinician generates a differential diagnosis, i.e. *a hypothesis on possible diagnoses and comorbidities.*
4. This hypothesis helps the clinician to decide which issues he or she needs to focus on in the *clinical interview and observation of the child.*
5. An evaluation is made of whether *additional assessments* are needed in view of a full understanding of the case, such as a cognitive or neuropsychological assessment, contact with the school or observation at school.
6. In view of a categorical diagnosis, the clinician administers a *DSM-IV-TR-orientated interview with the parents (and with the older child separately).* Preceding this interview, the parents are given the opportunity to provide additional information on issues that were difficult to discuss in the initial interview in the presence of the child.
7. The clinician needs to integrate all the information available in view of the *multiaxial diagnosis and diagnostic formulation, including considerations about aetiology, and the decision of a treatment plan.*
8. The clinician has a *discussion of the diagnosis and treatment plan with the parents.*

The identification of these various steps in the decision-making process does not mean that we are in favour of an assessment procedure that takes many weeks to conduct. In contrast, as already discussed, we are in favour of a succinct assessment procedure. Thus, steps 2–6 can even be made in 1 day, including some additional assessments (e.g. cognitive and neuropsychological assessment); however, more time would be needed to collect other additional information, such as from observation at school.

Written information

To save time and to actively involve the parents in the assessment procedure, it is appropriate to send the parents both a questionnaire and a comprehensive standardized rating scale to be completed by them and the child's teacher or, in case of young children, the professional daycare-giver. Also, relevant reports from previous medical assessments, from the school and from previous psychological and educational evaluations may be sent by either the parents or the referring agent. This information is used later in the open interview with the parents.

Questionnaire

Below is an overview of the items that may be included in the questionnaire.

Child information
- Pregnancy: duration, complications, illnesses, use of medication and substances (e.g. alcohol, nicotine, cannabis).
- Birth: gestational age, type of delivery, the newborn's weight and length, state at birth, Apgar scores, subsequent neonatal course.
- Previous spontaneous abortions.
- Developmental milestones: motor (gross motor, fine motor), language and communication, play, toilet-training.
- Medical history: medical conditions, injuries, hospitalizations, current medications.
- Age at which the behavioural problems were first observed.
- Possible treatments for the behavioural problems and their success or failure.
- Life events: removal, divorce.
- School: type (regular, special), current grade, marks (reading, spelling, writing, language, arithmetic), grade retention.

Family information
- Siblings: date of birth, type of school (regular, special) and current grade, in care or have been in care.
- Parents: birth date, profession, educational level.
- Family history: medical conditions among family members; ADHD, alcohol/drug abuse and delinquency among parents and grandparents.

Comprehensive rating scales

It is often appropriate to use one of the comprehensive standardized rating scales (Verhulst & Van der Ende, 2008). Such rating scales assess a number of areas of adjustment rather than a single domain of behaviour. Moreover, because they have been standardized using large normative samples, the referred child's ratings on a given scale can be compared with those of typically developing children. Thus, scores give a quick view on whether the child functions within the clinical or normal range of various domains.

Both parents and teachers are useful as informants. Low levels of agreement between different informants do not invalidate the reports of any of them (Verhulst & Van der Ende, 2008). The different views of parents and teachers on the child's problems result not only because of different standards and different levels of professionalism, but also because children behave differently at home and at school.

ASEBA. The ASEBA family of instruments (Achenbach System of Empirically Based Assessment; Achenbach & Rescorla, 2000, 2001) is widely used and has been standardized in many countries. For young children, there is a 100-item version to be completed by parents (Child Behavior Checklist [CBCL/1.5–5]) and care-givers/teachers (Caregiver/Teacher Report Form [C-TRF/1.5–5]) of children aged 1½–5 years (Achenbach & Rescorla, 2000). For elementary school children and adolescents, there is a 112-item version to be completed by the parents (CBCL/6–18) and teachers (TRF/6–18) of children aged 6–18 years; for youth of 11–18 years, there is also the Youth Self-Report (YSR) (Achenbach & Rescorla, 2001).

The ASEBA instruments yield Total, Internalizing and Externalizing broad-band scales and narrow-band scales. The CBCL/1.5–5 Externalizing broad-band scale comprises the narrow-band scales for Aggressive Behavior and Attention Problems, whereas the CBCL/6–18 Externalizing scale comprises Aggressive Behavior and Rule-breaking Behavior. Attention Problems is not part of the Externalizing Scale in the CBCL/6-18, whereas it is in the CBCL/1.5–5. This also holds true for the care-giver/teacher versions. The CBCL/1.5–5 Internalizing broad-band scale comprises the narrow-band scales Emotionally Reactive, Anxious/Depressed and Somatic Complaints, whereas the CBCL/6–18 Internalizing scale comprises Anxious/Depressed, Withdrawn/Depressed and Somatic Complaints. This also holds true for the teacher versions.

Strengths and Difficulties Questionnaire. A much briefer comprehensive scale is the Strengths and Difficulties Questionnaire (SDQ; Goodman, 1997). The SDQ has been studied less extensively than ASEBA, but the number of studies in various countries is increasing (see the Special Issue of *European Child and Adolescent Psychiatry*, Vol. 13, Supplement 2, 2004). The SDQ consists of 25 items. There are various forms: for the parents and teachers of 3- and 4-year-olds, 4–10-year-olds and 11–17-year-olds, and for self-completion by 11–17-year-olds; these forms can be downloaded free of charge from www.sdqinfo.com.

The SDQ asks about 25 attributes, 10 of which would generally be thought of as strengths (e.g. Generally obedient, usually does what adults request; Thinks things out before acting), 14 items of which would generally be thought of as difficulties (e.g. Often has tempers tantrums or hot tempers; Restless, overactive, cannot stay still for long) and 1 of which is neutral. The SDQ yields five scales: the Hyperactivity, Emotional Symptoms, Conduct Problems, Peer Problems and Prosocial scales. Norms for Britain, the USA, Australia, Finland, Sweden and Germany can be found on the website.

Behavior Assessment System for Children. The Behavior Assessment System for Children Second Edition (BASC-2; Reynolds & Kamphaus, 2004) assesses a wide range of adjustment difficulties in children and adolescents aged 2 to 21. The BASC has forms for parent, teacher and child (ages 8–21). It has been standardized for the USA.

Besides two conduct problem domains (Aggression and Conduct Problems), many other domains are assessed as well: Adaptability, Anxiety, Attention Problems, Atypicality, Depression, Hyperactivity, Leadership, Learning problems, Functional Communication, Social Skills, Somatization, Study Skills, Withdrawal, Activities of Daily Living, Attitude to School, Attitude to Teachers,

Interpersonal Relations, Locus of Control, Relations with Parents, Self-esteem, Self-reliance, Sensation-Seeking, Sense of Inadequacy, and Social Stress.

Conners' Rating Scales. The Revised Conners' Rating Scales (CRS-R; Conners, 1997) have a primary emphasis on externalizing problems. The CRS-R has forms for parent (CPRS-R), teacher (CTRS-R) and adolescent (CASS). Each measure has a short version (including oppositional and hyperactivity scales) and a long version. The parent and teacher versions are intended for use with children aged 3–17 years.

Initial interview with the parents and child

Building a rapport and empathizing with the parents' feelings is part of the process of the initial clinical interview. The clinician may start with an interview in which he or she asks about the parents' main reasons for referral, their concerns, whether they suspect a specific diagnosis, what they think is the cause of the behaviour problem and how they think the problem may be treated. Similarly, parents are typically worried and want to express their concerns about the future of their child. Some parents have strong negative feelings about their child, while others feel the need to also stress their child's positive characteristics.

The clinician needs to be sensitive from the outset to possible biases of the parents. Various biases with respect to psychiatric disorders and specifically ODD and CD can exist. For example, DBDs are often thought to be the result of bad parenting and inevitably result in criminality or drug abuse. It is important to clarify that, in clinical psychology and psychiatry, and in medicine in general, causation is most often to be considered in a probabilistic rather than a deterministic way. Thus, if we do diagnose a disorder in the child, we will try to identify factors that have increased the risk in the child of developing the disorder, but we will not be able to find the only factor that caused the disorder.

Moreover, we will also pay attention to the strengths of the child and the family. In other words, we will also assess the protective and promotive factors in the child and his or her environment, such as the child's well-developed motor skills or sense of humour and the parent's mutual support in parenting. Furthermore, at the end of the initial interview, it is important to give parents the opportunity to provide additional information. Parents may feel that no attention has been paid to important issues. Some parents feel embarrassed that attention has one-sidedly been focused on their child's problems. The parents of young children especially feel the need to stress the strengths of their child, such as his or her cheerfulness or enthusiasm.

Using the written information the parents have sent to the clinic, the interview starts with a clarification about who initiated the referral, the reasons for referral, why the referral was made at this point, the parents' concerns and their assumptions with respect to the diagnosis and treatment. Additional information is, when needed, obtained on the pregnancy, birth, medical history and developmental milestones.

In-depth information is obtained on the onset and the development of the referral and behaviour problems over time. Specifically, the clinician asks at what age the various behavioural problems first occurred (e.g. defiant behaviour, losing temper, difficulty sustaining attention), in which settings they were seen (home, school, neighbourhood, sports club) and in interaction with which individuals they were observed (parents, other adults in the family, other adults outside the family, teachers, siblings, peers). For each behaviour, the course over the years is discussed, as is whether the behavioural problem still occurs, in terms of frequency, interactions with which individuals and consequences for overall functioning (position in the peer group, friendship relations, academic achievement), i.e. impairment.

In this context, it is important also to gather information on the child's current social functioning, i.e. his or her social and communication skills (to enter a group of peers who are already playing together, to ask to play with another child, to compete with other children) and social problem-solving skills (to appropriately interpret social situations, to adequately take the perspective of the other person and infer his or her thoughts and feelings, to feel with the other person). Likewise, the child's characteristic responses to the parent's management of his or her misbehaviour is asked for, i.e. the child's sensitivity to cues of punishment, as well as the child's responses to the parents' praise or reward of the child's appropriate behaviours, as there is evidence that DBDs are characterized by a decreased sensitivity to punishment and reward.

In line with a discussion of the reasons for referral and the current problems, information on prior care and contacts with health, mental health and educational professionals is gathered. One may then also ask for the parents' thoughts about the diagnosis and about the treatment needed.

Information is gathered on the parents and the wider family. However, it is not feasible to obtain additional information on possible psychiatric disorders and other problems in the parents or other family members (ADHD, substance abuse or dependence, delinquency, mood disorders, personality disorders) in the presence of the child. Therefore, this information is obtained when talking with the parents separately at the DSM-IV-TR interview with the parents. Spontaneous information given by the parents assists in evaluating the parental relationship, the support they receive from friends, neighbours and the extended family, and their parenting skills (consistency, amount of praise, punishing techniques, supervision). However, if needed, specific questions related to parental style should be asked. One may ask parents to describe situations that have resulted in the child being disciplined. The parents then may be asked about how they handled the situation, how the child reacted and how the situation was resolved. Moreover, in this initial interview, the clinician may observe how the parents support each other.

During this initial meeting, it is appropriate also to involve the child. For younger children, toys and play materials are made available. The clinician thus has the opportunity to observe how the parents present their reasons for referral and their concerns in the child's presence, how the child responds to this, whether the parents encourage the child to express his or her views, whether they spontaneously mention the child's strengths, and how they manage the behaviour problems the child manifests. Likewise, the clinician has the opportunity to observe the child. Although in general, in child psychiatry and clinical psychology, it is true that many symptoms cannot be observed during the assessment, this specifically applies to children with DBDs. Indeed, one does not often observe physical aggression, but milder symptoms such as deliberately annoying the parents while they talk with the clinician or blaming others for the child's misbehaviours that are discussed may occur even during the initial interview.

Hypothesis on possible diagnoses and comorbidities

Based on the information gathered, the clinician generates a differential diagnosis. The issue is not only which possible psychiatric diagnoses should be taken into consideration with this child, but also which disorders may co-occur. This differential diagnosis is to be considered a clinical hypothesis that needs further testing in the next steps of the assessment.

Besides ODD and CD, the following diagnostic categories should be considered as the first diagnosis when a child presents with symptoms of disruptive behaviour, hyperactivity, impulsivity and attention problems:

- *ADHD:* mild forms of oppositional and aggressive behaviours frequently occur as associated features.
- *Pervasive Developmental Disorder* (Autistic Disorder, Asperger's Disorder, Pervasive Disorder Not Otherwise Specified): disruptive behaviours such as aggression, impulsivity and hyperactivity frequently occur as associated features.
- *Communication Disorder* (Expressive and Mixed Receptive-Expressive Language Disorders): disruptive behaviours may occur as a result of problems in communicating the child's needs and goals, and in understanding complex social situations.
- *Adjustment Disorder with Disturbance of Conduct or with Mixed Disturbance of Emotions and Conduct:* conduct problems such as in the DBDs develop in response to an identifiable psychosocial stressor.
- *Parent–Child Relational Problem:* although not a psychiatric disorder, this category is used to indicate a pattern of interaction between parent and child

(e.g. parental overprotection and disruptive behaviour in the child) associated with an impairment in individual or family functioning; it is therefore a focus of clinical attention.

- *Dysthymic Disorder:* in children depressed mood may manifest as irritability and related disruptive behaviour.
- *Reactive Attachment Disorder, Disinhibited Type:* the indiscriminate sociability or lack of selectivity in the choice of attachment figures may suggest problems in inhibition, such as in ADHD and the DBDs.
- *Bipolar Disorder, Manic Episode:* rages or explosive outbursts may characterize a specific type of bipolar disorder in children and adolescents (Carlson, 2007).

Other disorders that co-occur with the DBDs should also be considered. Special attention should be given to the Learning Disorders (Reading, Mathematics and Written Expression). Since there is much evidence that the co-occurrence of learning disorders with the DBDs is largely attributable to the presence of comorbid ADHD (for a review of studies, see Hinshaw, 1992), the clinician should be specifically attentive to learning disorders in children with DBDs comorbid with ADHD. With respect to both learning and communication disorders, it should be noted that developmental delays in, say, reading or language might not be severe enough to diagnose as a clear disorder, but are nevertheless important to acknowledge and to include in the clinician's understanding of the child's dysfunctioning. Reading problems may lead to disruptive behaviour as a result of the frustration and marginalization engendered by school failure. Likewise, language problems specifically in preschool children may lead to disruptive behaviour as a result of difficulties in understanding the rules and requests made by adults, in understanding complex social interactions with peers and in communicating the child's needs.

Below we give the list of comorbid disorders to be considered. Note that if symptoms of ODD occur exclusively during the course of a mood disorder such as dysthymic disorder, the diagnosis of ODD should not be given. In contrast, DSM-IV-TR allows the co-occurrence of CD and mood disorders.

- ADHD;
- Dysthymic Disorder;
- Separation Anxiety Disorder, Generalized Anxiety Disorder;
- Reading Disorder, Mathematics Disorder, Disorder of Written Expression;
- Expressive Language Disorder, Mixed Receptive-Expressive Language Disorder;
- Developmental Coordination Disorder;
- Borderline Intellectual Functioning (IQ in the range 71–84) and Mild Mental Retardation (IQ in the range 50–70).

Note that Borderline Intellectual Functioning and Mild Mental Retardation are coded on axis II.

Interview and observation of the child

The clinical interview and observation of the child are needed for several purposes: for the exclusion of other disorders such as a pervasive developmental disorder or dysthymic disorder, for the identification of comorbid disorders such as ADHD and separation anxiety disorder, for the assessment of personality characteristics such as callous-unemotional traits, for the observation of characteristic symptoms of DBDs such as being touchy or blaming others for one's own mistakes or misbehaviour, and for the observation of characteristic cognitions of DBDs such as hostile attributions of intent. Importantly, the child is also given the opportunity to express his or her views on (and concerns about) family members.

In general, observational methods are appropriate for the assessment of preschool children, whereas a mixture of observation and interview is appropriate for children over 6 years of age. A number of highly structured observational methods and interviews have been developed for research purposes. These methods are difficult to use in clinic settings since specific training is needed to administer them, as is ongoing monitoring of administration.

A structured observation assessment has been developed for the clinical assessment of preschool children (i.e. the Disruptive Behavior Diagnostic Observation Schedule [DB-DOS]; Wakschlag *et al.*, 2008a, 2008b). The DB-DOS is a highly structured method that allows the child's behaviour to unfold during a variety of challenging and pleasurable activities or tasks. These tasks, lasting approximately 5 minutes, tap into compliance, frustration, social interaction and internalization of rules. The DB-DOS is composed of three interactional modules or contexts: one parent–child module and two examiner modules (Wakschlag & Danis, 2004). When compared with the examiner module, the parent–child interaction context creates a more familiar situation for the child and thus facilitates the occurrence of problem behaviour. This module also provides an opportunity to observe parenting skills. In the parent module, the parent is normally responsive to the child's behaviour, but a waiting task is included in which the child needs to look at a picture book while the parent completes a questionnaire. In the first examiner module, the examiner is normally responsive to child behaviour; this is the examiner active support module. Then, within the context of minimal support, the child is observed while working independently, with the examiner being busy doing her or his own work. Some characteristics of the DB-DOS may be used in everyday clinical practice by including an observation of parent–child interaction, a variety of tasks and a changing gradation of responsiveness.

With children aged over 6, one may chat without playing, but observation of the child while playing may give additional information. Open questions are preferred to closed questions as they offer the chance to provide a wide range of answers, while closed questions call for one or a limited set of answers (Angold, 2002). Importantly, one should not rush into difficult topics (such as the reason for the referral) but instead focus initially on neutral or pleasant topics in order to engage the child (Goodman & Scott, 2005). Thus, one may start with questions about the name of the child's school, what grade the child is in and what he or she likes doing at school. One may then go on with more difficult questions such as how he or she gets along with the teacher and whether he or she has friends in class. In this way, issues known to be problematic for the child are explored. The various topics to be discussed are: the school; friends; hobbies, activities and clubs; relationships with parents, siblings and other family members; anxieties, worries; self-esteem; mood; defiant behaviour; aggression; and antisocial behaviour.

When observing and clinically interviewing the child, the clinician can attend to the features of disorders (including pervasive developmental disorders) other than the DBDs and ADHD. Instead of describing the assessment of the child in general, we here pay attention only to features that are characteristic of the DBDs and ADHD.

- *hyperactivity:* fidgets, restless, leaves the seat, runs about, talks excessively;
- *impulsivity:* blurts out answers before question has been completed, has difficulty waiting turn during a competitive game, interrupts the clinician;
- *attention:* is easily distractible by noises outside the room, has difficulty sustaining attention during play activity or while talking;
- *oppositional behaviours:* refuses to comply with the parent's or clinician's requests and persists in this behaviour;
- *hostile behaviours:* blames others for his or her mistakes when these are discussed; deliberately annoys parents while he or she is asked to wait;
- *emotional dysregulation:* is touchy or loses temper while performing a task that is frustrating for the child;
- *negative mood:* is annoyed, miserable and grouchy;
- *threatening:* verbal aggression with threat to harm;
- *physical aggression towards objects:* rough handling of toys, slapping, banging;
- *rule-breaking:* touching of prohibited objects;
- *lack of problem awareness and distress:* does not acknowledge behavioural problems or minimizes the severity and negative consequences of these behaviours (e.g. peer rejection) and his or her responsibility for these behaviours;
- *low sensitivity to negative cues:* is not sensitive to negative feedback or threats of punishment, is careless about mistakes, shows a lack of fear in situations that normally elicit fear, has a high pain threshold (does not cry when hurt);

- *low sensitivity to praise:* is unresponsive when praised;
- *callous-unemotional traits:* lack of empathy (does not feel concern for family members when they are ill or did hurt), lack of guilt, callous use of others for one's own gain;
- shows *fewer negative emotions* such as disappointment and sadness;
- *narcissistic traits:* arrogant, requires excessive admiration, expects automatic compliance with his or her expectations (entitlement);
- *deficient social information-processing:* attribution of hostile intent to others, impaired perspective-taking, generation of aggressive responses to social problems, thoughts about aggressive solutions (that they are acceptable, feeling of confidence in their ability to enact them);
- *deficient conscience:* standards and norms are in line with those generally accepted in society but these are not internalized enough, i.e. the child needs an adult's prompts; these standards and norms are not used because of impulsivity in responding; standards and norms are deviant from those generally accepted in society.

For children from 9 years onwards, structured interviews may be used. These are child versions of the structured interviews with parents to be discussed in the paragraph on interviews with parents. These structured interviews are DSM-orientated and generate a DSM-IV-TR diagnosis for most but not all disorders. A specific assessment procedure has been developed for the diagnosis of a Pervasive Developmental Disorder (Autism Diagnostic Observation Schedule [ADOS]; Lord *et al.*, 2000).

Physical examination and additional investigations vary largely from patient to patient and depend on whether medical information (from a paediatrician, physiotherapist, speech therapist and/or child neurologist) is already available at referral. Most children referred for psychiatric or clinical psychological assessment have already been physically examined. In all patients, attention should be paid to signs of neglect of abuse, to minimal physical anomalies or dysmorphic features, and to motor behaviour (gait disturbance, clumsiness) suggestive of a developmental coordination disorder (Baird & Gringras, 2008). It is advised always to measure the child's height, weight and head circumference. A basic neurological examination is indicated in children with a history of seizures, developmental delay, abnormal gait, not using both hands well, dysmorphic features or skin signs of a neurocutaneous disorder (Bailey, 2002; Goodman & Scott, 2005). If an abnormality is found, the child should be referred to a paediatrician or a child neurologist. If visual or hearing problems are suspected, the child should probably be referred to an appropriate clinic.

Additional assessments

A number of additional assessments and rating scales may be used. Some of these assessment procedures, such as cognitive assessment, are standardized, but others have been developed for research purposes and do not have clinical cut-off points.

Doubts about a child's overall cognitive developmental level and language development may arise during the assessment process, possibly on the basis of teacher reports or because of low scores on standardized testing of academic achievement. Psychological testing using a standardized assessment of intellectual ability (IQ) is then indicated. The results of a test of intelligence or the need to get more insight into possible deficits in executive functioning may lead to additional neuropsychological testing (attention, memory, visuospatial skills, executive functioning) and speech–language assessment (Charman *et al.*, 2008).

In addition, the clinician may feel the need to have a more differentiated insight into the variety of the disruptive symptoms. For the assessment of callous-unemotional or psychopathic traits, various rating scales have been developed for children, among which are the Antisocial Process Screening Device (APSD; Frick & Hare, 2001) and the Child Psychopathy Scale (CPS; Lynam, 1997). For the distinction between proactive and reactive aggression, Dodge and Coie (1987) developed a teacher rating scale. Other rating scales are the Parent-rating scale of Reactive and Proactive Aggression (PRPA; Kempes *et al.*, 2006) and the teacher report Instrument for Reactive and Proactive Aggression (IRPA; Polman *et al.*, 2009). To assess social skills, the clinician may use the Social Skills Rating Scale (SSRS; Gresham & Elliott, 1990). To identify the specific social situations that are problematic for the child, the Taxonomy of Problem Situations (TOPS) may be used (Dodge *et al.*, 1985; Matthys *et al.*, 2001).

The clinician may want to have a more specific insight into parents' parenting skills. To assess parenting skills, various instruments are available: the Alabama Parenting Questionnaire (APQ; Frick, 1991) and the Parenting Practices Interview (PPI; Webster-Stratton *et al.*, 2001; www.incredibleyears.com). To measure care-giver stress, the Parenting Stress Index (Abidin, 1990) may be used.

If there is a discrepancy between scores on rating scales completed by teachers and parents' reports of the child's problem behaviour at school, contact with the school is useful, and observation at school may be needed. Nock and Kurtz (2005) have developed clinical procedures including not only the observation of the child's behaviour, but also a description of school and classroom context and the collaboration with teachers and school psychologists.

To determine whether the symptoms result in impairment, overall impairment may be assessed using the C-GAS (Shaffer *et al.*, 1983). Likewise, to assess the impact of the behaviour problems on the functioning of the family the Impact on the Family Scale (IFS; Sheeber & Johnson, 1992) may be used.

DSM-IV-TR-orientated interview with the parents or child

To confirm a DSM-IV-TR diagnosis, the criteria of various disorders need to be checked. Information from parents is crucial as the criteria of DSM-IV-TR are described in terms of behaviours that occur in everyday life. Children from the age of 9 on can in general also accurately report on their emotional and behavioural problems, although the test–retest reliability of psychiatric disorders including ODD is somewhat lower when highly structured interviews are administered to children rather than to parents (Jensen *et al.*, 1995). Importantly, preceding the check of the criteria of psychiatric disorders with the parents, the clinician gives the parents an opportunity to provide additional information on important issues they have not discussed in the initial interview, such as the presence of their own problems.

As already discussed, structured diagnostic methods have been developed for use in research contexts. Although these methods are to be preferred to open, non-structured clinical interviews, most institutions do not have the resources for the training and ongoing monitoring of administration of these methods. A distinction is made among the structured interviews with parents (and children) between respondent-based interviews and interviewer-based interviews. Respondent-based interviews such as the Diagnostic Schedule for Children (DISC; Shaffer *et al.*, 2000) do not allow any interpretation of the parent's or child's response. The wording of questions is predetermined, and the range of responses is limited. This highly structured interview is also called a lay interview as no in-depth knowledge of psychopathology is needed to administer the interview. One other respondent-based interview is the Diagnostic Interview Schedule for Children and Adolescents (DICA; Reich, 2000).

By contrast, interviewer-based interviews such as the Kiddie-Schedule for Affective Disorders and Schizophrenia (K-SADS; Ambrosini, 2000) leave the interviewer free to ask whatever questions are needed to elicit from the child the information needed for the interviewer to decide whether the particular criterion is or is not present. Therefore, only experienced clinicians can administer these types of interview. The Child and Adolescent Psychiatric Assessment (CAPA; Angold & Costello, 2000) is another interviewer-based interview. For preschool children, the Kiddie Disruptive Behavior Disorders Schedule (K-DBDS; Keenan *et al.*, 2007) has been developed for the assessment of the DBDs and ADHD; this is an adaptation of the disruptive behaviour module of the K-SADS with additional questions about the frequency, duration and contexts of symptoms. For the assessment of almost all disorders, the Preschool Age Psychiatric Assessment (PAPA; Egger *et al.*, 2006) has been developed, which is an adaptation of the CAPA. Importantly, all these interviews do not cover the pervasive developmental disorders. To diagnose the latter, one may use the Autism Diagnostic Interview – Revised (ADI; Lord *et al.*, 1994).

In everyday clinical practice, clinicians use non-structured, open interviews. It is extremely important to carefully check each criterion separately with the parents by asking for specific examples of behaviours corresponding to the relevant criterion. One of the issues here is the frequency of the behaviours ('the child often argues, loses temper etc.') in each criterion. Clinicians would often like to have some empirical information about the frequency at which behaviour should be considered a symptom instead of relying on their own judgement. On the basis of empirical data in a general population of 9–13-year-old children, Angold and Costello (1996) have suggested frequency cut-off points for clinical use. The following behaviours should occur at least four times a week in order to be considered a symptom: angry or resentful, and deliberately annoys others. The following behaviours should occur at least twice a week in order to be considered a symptom: touchy or easily annoyed; loses temper; argues with adults; defies or refuses adults' requests. The following behaviours should have occurred at all during the last 3 months: spiteful and vindictive; blames others for his or her mistakes. For preschool children, such cut-off points are presently being developed.

Multiaxial diagnosis, diagnostic formulation, and the treatment plan

Multiaxial diagnosis

How should clinicians proceed in obtaining a final DSM-IV-TR diagnosis? Based on the information available, the clinician needs to decide whether the referred child qualifies for an axis I DSM-IV-TR diagnosis or not. For this, it is necessary to integrate the information from different sources (standardized questionnaires, interview and observation of the child, the DSM-IV-TR interview with the parents or child) at the level of each criterion or symptom, decide whether the criterion is being met and record this. In this respect, it should be noted that, while considering standardized questionnaires, one should not only look at whether the scores on the scales (e.g. the broad-band or narrow-band scales of the ASEBA) fall within the clinical domain, but also check at the level of items whether behaviours (or symptoms, criteria) are scored in terms of clearly present or not.

One issue is what to do with disagreement between informants. According to Angold (2002), the simple rule of regarding a symptom as being present if any informant reports it usually suffices well enough. Thus, it is suggested to 'ignore' the source and add up all positive symptoms from any source. Although this rule seems attractive because of its simplicity, biases may occur in reporting symptoms on the part of teachers because of school characteristics and on the part of parents because of personality characteristics, psychiatric disorders or personal interests. In cases of disagreement between informants, we suggest that the clinician interpret this discrepancy and make a decision on whether or not the specific symptom should be considered to be present.

With respect to disagreement between informants, we pay attention to two frequent misunderstandings. First, in order to diagnose ODD, the symptoms need not be present in two settings: symptoms are 'almost invariable present in the home setting, but may not be evident at school or in the community' (American Psychiatric Association, 2000, p. 92). Second, with respect to ADHD, a frequent misunderstanding is that at least six symptoms need to be present in both settings. According to DSM-IV-TR, however, although '[behavioural] manifestations usually appear in multiple contexts ... some impairment must be at least present in at least two settings' (American Psychiatric Association, 2000, p. 79). Thus, some impairment in at least two settings is obligatory, whereas symptoms may occasionally be observable only in one setting (American Academy of Child and Adolescent Psychiatry, 2007).

One specific problem still needs to be discussed. If a child has scores within the clinical range on standardized rating scales and also has a number of clinical meaningful characteristics but still does not fulfil the DSM-IV-TR criteria for either ODD or CD (Rowe *et al.*, 2005), a diagnosis may be made. For example, he or she may have three symptoms of ODD and one symptom of CD while having an overall level of functioning of 60. In line with the results of this evaluation, one might diagnose such children with a Disruptive Behaviour Disorder Not Otherwise Specified. A precondition for such a diagnosis is an overall functioning of 65 or below. Thus, Disruptive Behaviour Disorder Not Otherwise Specified may be given as a diagnosis in cases of: 3 symptoms of ODD and at least 1 symptom of CD, 2 symptoms of ODD and at least 2 symptoms of CD, or 2 symptoms of CD and at least 1 symptom of ODD. When, however, the child fulfils three symptoms of ODD without any symptom of CD or two symptoms of CD without any symptom of ODD, then, as already discussed in the section on general issues, above, the child is functioning at a subclinical level and should not be diagnosed with ODD or CD.

According to DSM-IV-TR, if more than one diagnosis is present, the clinician should indicate the principal diagnosis by listing it the first. It is, however, acknowledged that determining which diagnosis is the principal one is somewhat arbitrary. Furthermore, with respect to axis II, it is not usual to diagnose a child below the age of 13 years with a personality disorder. However, characteristics of narcissism in boys or of a borderline personality disorder in girls can sometimes be identified. Although no diagnosis is then given, one may in these instances note narcissistic or borderline personality features on axis II. Furthermore, axis II is used for reporting Borderline Intellectual functioning (IQ in the range 71–84) and Mild Mental Retardation (IQ in the range 50–70).

Diagnostic formulation

Besides a DSM-IV-TR diagnosis on all five axes, a diagnostic formulation or case formulation is needed in which a hypothesis is included about the risk and protective factors that play a role in the development of the disorders. Although our understanding of the aetiology of DBD is increasing, the application of this knowledge at the level of the individual child and his or her family is still limited. Some risk factors can be identified during the assessment, including maternal nicotine use during pregnancy, hereditary factors, a delay in language development, inappropriate parenting skills and parental disharmony. But even then it remains unclear to what extent these factors have played a role in the causation of the disorder(s) in this particular child. Therefore, clinicians should be extremely cautious in explaining the parents why the disorder(s) have developed in their child. Instead, a more general framework about aetiology may be explained.

In this framework, a distinction is made between factors that may have played a role in the initiation of the disorder(s) and factors that probably play a role in the maintenance of the disorder(s). The factors that play a role in the maintenance of the disorder(s) will be the targets of interventions, while the factors that have played a role in the initiation of the disorder(s) many years ago will not. Thus, in the case formulation, in the report of the assessment and in the discussion of the assessment with the parents, priority is placed on the factors that maintain the disorder(s) above the factors that may have played a role in the initiation of the disorders, as the former factors will lead to the intervention(s) that are proposed to the parents and the child.

Finally, strengths in the child (e.g. acknowledgement of misbehaviour), in the parents (e.g. agreement about managing the child's misbehaviour) and in the school (e.g. good cooperation with the parents) should be acknowledged as they are also important for treatment.

Treatment plan

In the next chapters, the three evidence-based intervention methods, and their combination, are discussed: behavioural parent training (see Chapter 8), cognitive-behavioural therapy for the child (see Chapter 9) and pharmacotherapy (see Chapter 10). Here we give an outline of the decision the clinician needs to make with respect to the selection of interventions dependent on the age of the child (preschool-age or school-age child or early adolescent), the presence of ADHD and the level of severity of the symptoms and impairment.

In preschool children with DBDs with ADHD comorbidity or symptoms of ADHD, behavioural parent training is given as a first step. Pharmacotherapy is added when the effect of behavioural parent training is insufficient. The combination of behavioural parent training and pharmacotherapy may also be indicated from the start in preschool children with severe symptoms and severe social impairment. In preschool children with DBDs but without ADHD comorbidity or symptoms of ADHD, the treatment consists of behavioural parent training.

In school-age children and early adolescents with DBDs with ADHD comorbidity or symptoms of ADHD, the combination of pharmacotherapy and behavioural parent training is indicated. Cognitive-behavioural therapy may be added either when the symptoms and impairment are severe or when the effect of behavioural parent training is insufficient. In school-aged children and early adolescents with DBDs but without ADHD comorbidity or symptoms of ADHD, one may start with behavioural parent training and add cognitive-behavioural therapy when the symptoms and impairment are severe or when the effect of behavioural parent training is insufficient. When children do not respond to these methods and still manifest severe physical aggression, pharmacotherapy with one of the antipsychotic medications is indicated for a limited time.

School interventions often are needed in view of the management of disruptive behaviour and improving underachievement. Most children can be treated in outpatient settings or by school-based mental health clinicians. However, when the combination of the above-mentioned methods is not effective because of the severity of the disorder(s) or when there are severe barriers to attendance at and adherence to outpatient treatment, day treatment or inpatient/residential treatment is indicated. These settings, when compared with the outpatient setting, offer more opportunities to integrate the various interventions discussed above, also giving the child more opportunities to practise behavioural and cognitive skills in milieu therapy.

Discussion of the diagnosis and treatment plan with the parents

The diagnosis and the proposed treatment plan are discussed with the parents and child. Information that parents may have gathered from the media, especially from the Internet, may become part of this discussion. This information sometimes engenders extremely negative biases about ODD and CD. Parents, for example, may assume that negative outcomes such as delinquency and substance use disorders are to be considered as an inescapable future for their child. DBDs are still thought to be the result only of bad parenting, while the active role the child plays in the onset of DBDs is often ignored. Thus, it is necessary to give accurate general information on our present knowledge on the aetiology and outcome of the DBDs.

When discussing the factors that might have played a role in the development of the disorder(s), it is more important to focus on the child, family and other environmental factors that probably play a role in the maintenance of the disorder(s), as these will be the targets of intervention, than to focus on the factors that have probably played a role in the initiation of the disorder(s). Thus, it should be clarified that an indication for behavioural parent training (see Chapter 8) does not imply that inappropriate parenting actually did cause the onset of DBD; instead, it is discussed in terms of an improvement in the parents' skills changing the behaviour of their child as inappropriate parenting is likely to maintain the child's misbehaviours. Similarly, deviant social cognitions have probably not caused the onset of the disorders(s) but have developed over the years and have thus come to play a role in the maintenance of the disorder(s). Cognitive-behavioural therapy (see Chapter 9) targets these deviant social cognitions, and improvement in these skills are likely to result in behavioural change.

When discussing specific treatment methods with the parents and child, clinicians should be prepared to encounter barriers. Some parents of children with DBD may not accept that the parents themselves should invest in treatment (behavioural parent training) while the child is left out of treatment. To motivate parents, the distinction may be made between ordinary parenting that is 'good enough' for 'normal children' and the additional qualities of parenting (e.g. the use of mild punishment procedures, stress management in the parents; see Chapter 8) that are needed for children with DBDs. Participating in a behavioural parent training programme is easier for the parents of older children to accept when the child also is involved in the treatment (cognitive-behavioural therapy).

Thus, the parents' and the child's engagement in treatment, and their motivation to attend and adhere to treatment, are important issues to assess when the proposed treatment plan is discussed. In response to this concern, a Parent Participation Enhancement Intervention has been developed and evaluated (Nock & Kazdin, 2005). It consists of three brief (5–15-minute) additional interventions composed of motivational enhancement techniques to be included in the therapy sessions. It has been shown that parents who received this intervention had greater treatment motivation, attended more sessions and showed a greater adherence to treatment (Nock & Kazdin, 2005).

Finally, when discussing with the parents the outcome of the disorder(s) in their child, clinicians should be reluctant to give a prognosis as so many factors are involved in the outcome. Instead, the various factors involved in the outcome may be discussed, as may the need to target these factors (e.g. supervision, appropriate education).

Summary points

- The clinical assessment of a child can be considered to be a decision-making process in which the clinician assesses for the presence (or otherwise) of one or more psychiatric disorders, considers the underlying aetiology and plans treatment.
- In order to avoid errors in diagnosing children due to possible biases on the part of the clinician, it is crucial to systematically collect information and make decisions accordingly; therefore, in the diagnostic decision-making process we distinguish eight steps.
  1. the collection of written information from the parents;

2. the initial interview with the parents and the child;
3. the formulation of a hypothesis on possible diagnoses and comorbidities;
4. the clinical interview and observation of the child;
5. the completion of additional assessments, if necessary;
6. the administration of a DSM-IV-TR-orientated interview with the parents (and the older child separately);
7. the integration of all available information in view of a multiaxial diagnosis and diagnostic formulation, including considerations about aetiology, and the decision on a treatment plan;
8. the discussion of the diagnosis and treatment plan with the parents.

- Although the distinction between normative misbehaviour and problematic behaviour is crucial in all children, specific attention to this issue is required in preschool children.
- Besides a consideration of psychopathology from the point of view of categorization, it is important to assess the severity of the disorder(s) and the impairment in social and academic functioning of the child in view of decisions about the intensity of intervention.
- Subclinical levels of functioning (three symptoms of ODD, two symptoms of CD) are to be considered as an indicator leading to prevention services for the DBDs, especially in preschool children.
- While our understanding of the aetiology of DBDs is growing, it is currently not realistic to aim at a complete understanding of the causation of the disorder in each child, especially with respect to the initiation of the disorder. We therefore advocate an assessment that is, on the one hand, 'good enough' for a satisfactory understanding of the aetiological factors involved in the development of the disorder in this particular child but is, on the other hand, not unnecessarily detailed. With respect to causal processes, a distinction needs to be made between factors involved in the initiation and factors involved in the maintenance of the disorder. To make hypotheses that can productively assist with planning therapeutic interventions, we should distinguish proximal from distal risk factors, and modifiable from stable factors. Thus, for planning treatment, we should mainly focus on the factors that play a role in the maintenance of the disorder and are modifiable and proximal.
- From the start of the assessment onwards, the clinician needs to be sensitive to possible biases on the part of the parents with regard to the aetiology and outcome of the DBDs.
- When generating a hypothesis on the diagnosis in a child referred for disruptive behaviour, the clinician should consider not only diagnoses other than ODD or CD such as Pervasive Developmental Disorder or Dysthymic Disorder, but also comorbid diagnoses such as ADHD, Learning Disorders and Borderline Intelligence.
- When, in view of a DSM-IV-TR diagnosis, it is not feasible to use a (semi-) structured interview, it is extremely important to carefully check each

criterion of the disorder(s) separately with the parents by asking for specific examples of behaviours corresponding to the relevant criterion.

- In cases of disagreement between the informants (parents, teachers, child) on the occurrence of symptoms, the clinician needs to interpret this discrepancy and make a decision on whether the specific symptom should or should not be considered to be present.

- A child may be diagnosed with Disruptive Behaviour Not Otherwise Specified in cases of: 3 symptoms of ODD and at least 1 symptom of CD, 2 symptoms of ODD and at least 2 symptoms of CD, or 2 symptoms of CD and at least 1 symptom of ODD. A precondition, however, for such a diagnosis is an overall functioning of 65 or below.

- Besides a DSM-IV-TR diagnosis, a case formulation or diagnostic formulation is needed in which a hypothesis is included about the risk and protective factors that play a role in the development of the disorders. Although our understanding of the aetiology of DBD is increasing, the application of this knowledge at the level of the individual child and his or her family is still limited. Therefore, clinicians should be extremely cautious in explaining to the parents why the disorder(s) have developed in their child. Instead, a more general framework about aetiology may be explained. In the case formulation, in the report of the assessment and in the discussion of the assessment with the parents, priority is placed on the factors that maintain the disorder(s) above the factors that may have played a role in the initiation of the disorders as the former factors will lead to the intervention(s) that are proposed to the parents and child.

- In preschool children with DBDs with ADHD comorbidity or symptoms of ADHD, behavioural parent training is given as a first step. Pharmacotherapy is added when the effect of behavioural parent training is insufficient. The combination of behavioural parent training and pharmacotherapy may also be indicated from the start in preschool children with severe symptoms and severe social impairment. In preschool children with DBDs but without ADHD comorbidity or symptoms of ADHD, the treatment consists of behavioural parent training.

- In school-age children and early adolescents with DBDs with ADHD comorbidity or symptoms of ADHD, a combination of pharmacotherapy and behavioural parent training is indicated. Cognitive-behavioural therapy may be added either when the symptoms and impairment are severe or when the effect of behavioural parent training is insufficient. In school-aged children and early adolescents with DBDs but without ADHD comorbidity or symptoms of ADHD, one may start with behavioural parent training and add cognitive-behavioural therapy when the symptoms and impairment are severe or when the effect of behavioural parent training is insufficient. When children do not respond to these methods and still manifest severe physical aggression, pharmacotherapy with one of the antipsychotic medications is indicated for a limited time.

7

Intervention and intervention development

This chapter discusses how treatment and prevention exist on a continuum, and how some interventions may be used for both purposes. Developmental models that describe the evolution of specific childhood disorders are very important in identifying active mechanisms that contribute to the development and maintenance of the disorders, and that can be the target of intervention. We will also discuss the criteria for determining whether interventions are evidence based, and describe the distinction between efficacy, effectiveness and dissemination research. Finally, the chapter will describe how moderation and mediation are examined in intervention research.

The intervention continuum

In a book that has a focus on the treatment of conduct problems in children, it is useful to consider the relationship between treatment and prevention for several reasons. First, the treatment of a given childhood problem (e.g. overt aggressive behaviour) might lead to the prevention of a later associated problem (e.g. marijuana use) that would have existed on that child's developmental pathway (Zonnevylle-Bender *et al.*, 2007). Second, successful prevention approaches can reduce the incidence of diagnosed disruptive disorders in high-risk children (e.g. Conduct Problems Prevention Research Group, 2007), thus reducing the need for costly treatment services for some of these youth. Third, because the active mechanisms contributing to problem behaviour are the same or similar, some interventions may be used both in targeted prevention (with at-risk individuals, who are on a pathway for disorder) and in treatment (with children diagnosed with oppositional defiant disorder [ODD] or conduct disorder), and we will find that to be the case.

Oppositional Defiant Disorder and Conduct Disorder in Childhood   By Walter Matthys and
John E. Lochman
© 2010 John Wiley & Sons, Ltd.

In 1994, the Institute of Medicine (IOM) provided a new conceptualization of treatment and prevention approaches that indicated how they exist as a continuum of services rather than as discrete and qualitatively separate endeavours (Mrazek & Haggerty, 1994). The IOM conceptualized three classes of service – prevention (universal, selective, indicated), treatment (case identification, standard treatment) and maintenance (compliance with long-term care, aftercare) – and emphasized how certain forms of each blended into the next category. Thus, a targeted form of prevention for at-risk individuals (indicated prevention) was not conceptually far removed from efforts to identify identifiable and diagnosable cases in the treatment category, although the families of the children referred for treatment might have had more stress and related risk factors (Angold *et al.*, 2000).

The treatment and maintenance categories of services in the IOM continuum are self-evident, but the specific forms of prevention that are identified require further clarification because we will encounter those later in this book. Universal preventive interventions target entire groups or populations (e.g. all 3rd-graders at an elementary school) and are designed to address specific developmental risk factors, without attempting to discern which youths are at elevated risk. In contrast, selective prevention programmes are delivered to individuals who are considered to be at risk because they have certain group-level risk factors (e.g. the children of alcoholic parents), and indicated preventive interventions target individual children who are already showing behaviours associated with the disorder but who are not yet in the diagnosable range (e.g. 3rd-graders who score in the at-risk range on a measure of classroom behaviour problems). Thus, targeted preventive interventions (selective and indicated) differ from universal preventive interventions because of the population served (Weisz *et al.*, 2005).

Universal and targeted prevention approaches each offer advantages and disadvantages (Lochman *et al.*, 2009a). Because universal programmes typically include positive skill-building strategies that promote well-being, they are seen as beneficial for all and may be more readily accepted and less stigmatizing than other levels of intervention (Greenberg *et al.*, 2001). However, such programmes may not provide a sufficient duration or intensity to alter the developmental trajectory of children who are already at significant risk, and universal prevention programmes have been criticised for devoting some resources to a portion of the population without problems.

A central advantage of targeted preventive interventions is that they direct resources toward the individuals in greatest need (Offord, 1996). Targeted preventive interventions typically require a screening process to identify at-risk youth. Thus, the potential disadvantages of targeted approaches are that children or families may feel labelled or resist intervention because they did not actively seek it out themselves, and that the success of the programme is dependent on the accuracy of the screening methods. Although teacher and parent screening of at-risk aggressive elementary school children has been found to have adequate enough levels of sensitivity and specificity for use with targeted preventions, false-positive rates can approach 50% (Hill *et al.*, 2004). Thus, nearly half of the children identified as being at risk, at least in the early elementary school years, may not be.

Exemplars of both types of prevention programme – universal and targeted – have been shown to have a lasting positive impact on children's social and emotional development (e.g. Greenberg *et al.*, 2000; Kutash *et al.*, 2006). The wide-scale dissemination of these evidence-based prevention programmes, similar to the efforts to disseminate evidence-based treatment programmes, is a priority.

Developmental models and intervention development

How should new interventions for children with conduct problems be optimally developed? Developmental models can serve as the foundation for new interventions by identifying the active mechanisms, which can be the targets of the intervention (Lochman, 2006; Lochman & Gresham, 2008; Lochman *et al.*, 2008a). Chapters 4 and 5 reviewed risk factors and active mechanisms contributing to disruptive behaviour disorders (DBDs) in children, and Chapters 8–11 will indicate how those active mechanisms have led to interventions for these children. Therapeutic innovations are more likely to occur when theory is emphasized in treatment research (Jensen, 1999). Thus, interventions should be rooted in clear, well-articulated models for the development and maintenance of particular problems behaviours (Conduct Problems Prevention Research Group, 1992).

The conceptual developmental model can indicate how certain characteristics of the child and the child's social context can influence the child's behaviour and adjustment, and how these influences can vary over time. This developmental aspect of the conceptual foundations for interventions has often been deficient, but intervention research in recent years has begun to be more focused on developmental trajectories leading up to the expression of the particular form of psychopathology to be addressed (Lochman & Gresham, 2008).

As an example of the use of research findings to form a contextual social-cognitive developmental model that serves as the basis of the Coping Power programme (Lochman & Wells, 2002a), empirically identified risk factors that have predicted children's antisocial behaviour were examined (Hawkins *et al.*, 1992; Coie & Dodge, 1998; Loeber & Farrington, 2001; Pennington, 2002). These risk factors could be conceptualized as falling within several categories that have been discussed in previous chapters: biological child factors, family context, neighbourhood context, peer context and later-emerging child factors involving their social cognitive processes and emotional regulation. As noted in Chapters 4 and 5, child and environmental characteristics associated with a disorder can be conceptualized as a correlate or a risk factor in the development of the disorder, or as a factor in the maintenance of the disorder. By carefully considering the active mechanisms that contribute to the DBDs, a clear conceptual model can then have several key effects on intervention research and intervention application by:

- serving as the framework for the *development of intervention goals and activities* that target multiple active mechanisms contributing to the development of the disorder (e.g. role-play and game-like tasks designed to amplify anger management, or to promote parents' more consistent use of positive consequences for appropriate behaviour);
- permitting the *testing of the theory* underlying the intervention, through mediational analyses;
- permitting the *individualization of the actual implementation of the intervention* in a rigorous, non-haphazard manner, when children are assessed and identified to have certain, but not all, of the identified deficits in the conceptual model (Lochman & Gresham, 2008). For example, if a particular aggressive child does not have attributional biases, the intervention should focus on the problem-solving deficits that do exist, and intervention activities addressing attributional biases should be de-emphasized.

The conceptual, assessment and intervention models should all be well integrated. Issues related to how the developmental models can underlie intervention development and the individualization of intervention are further explored in the next sections.

Intervention development

If contextual factors have clear direct effects on children's outcomes, those parental and peer contextual factors that are malleable, and are potentially able to be influenced by an intervention, should be considered as intervention targets (Lochman, 2007). An intervention model should reflect the developmental model that describes the emergence of the problem behaviour (Conduct Problems Prevention Research Group, 1992). If certain parenting practices are key aspects of the model describing the development of conduct problems, components addressing those parenting practices should logically be included in the intervention. Consistent with this premise, multicomponent interventions that include behavioural parent training directed at improving parenting skills, and child training directed at their social problem-solving skills, may be especially powerful; multicomponent interventions for children with conduct problems will be explored in Chapter 11.

Because children's peers and their classroom environment are contextual effects that influence children's behavioural problems, one implication of a developmental model for the DBDs is that a broader universal intervention directed at whole classrooms can be appropriate as a stand-alone preventive intervention or as an adjunct to other more intense interventions. Classroom-wide preventive interventions can lead to notable changes in children's interpersonal relations and behaviour in the classroom as a whole (Conduct Problems Prevention Research Group, 1999b), and can reduce the likelihood of substance use in high-risk children (Lochman & Wells, 2002b). In conjunction with treatment or targeted preventive interventions directed at high-risk children, classroom-wide interventions can assist these children's improvements in school behaviour at later follow-ups (Lochman & Wells, 2002b). The combination of targeted and universal interventions can be particularly powerful because:

- as the targeted intervention produces social and behavioural changes in the high-risk child, those changes can produce positive radiating effects on the surrounding children's behaviour (Allen *et al.*, 1976; Kelly, 1971);
- the classroom intervention can affect the peer groups' social behaviours in positive ways, creating a less toxic, more accepting peer environment for the targeted high-risk child;
- the targeted and universal programmes can have additive effects on the behaviour of the high-risk child through repeated exposure and practice on key intervention concepts.

Contextual factors as predictors of individuals' need for, and response to, intervention components

At the intervention research level, the researcher can determine whether certain baseline risk characteristics predict which children will have better or worse outcomes on the defined outcome, and hence whether these variables predict intervention effects (Lochman, 2007). At the clinical level, the clinician can be engaged in a somewhat analogous task of determining which specific risk factors are present in a particular case, and hence whether even a structured intervention should be adapted to a degree to emphasize the areas of particular risk for that case.

The literature on family context risk factors as potential predictors of intervention outcome is relatively mixed (Kazdin, 1995), as children of depressed mothers and single parents have been found to have a poorer response to intervention in some studies (e.g. McMahon *et al.*, 1981; Dumas & Albin, 1986; Webster-Stratton & Hammond, 1997) but not in others (Dumas & Wahler, 1983; Webster-Stratton, 1985; Holden *et al.*, 1990). Similarly, children living in families with low socioeconomic status and socioeconomic disadvantage have not benefited as much from intervention in some studies (Webster-Stratton, 1985; Dumas & Albin, 1986; Holden *et al.*, 1990) although not in others (Serketich & Dumas, 1996).

These results indicate that specific parental and family context risk factors are important to assess as potential predictors of intervention outcome, but that the particular risk predictors may vary from one intervention programme to another, depending on the format and characteristics of the intervention. In addition, a certain risk predictor, such as maternal depression, can predict a lack of intervention responsivity on certain outcomes, such as teacher ratings of school behaviour, but not on other outcomes within the same intervention, such as parent ratings of children's aggression (Conduct Problems Prevention Research Group, 2002b).

When a clinical intervention is delivered to a specific child, the absence of certain risk factors in the general developmental model can lead to appropriate adaptations to the delivery of the intervention programme. For example, if, counter to the general model of risk factors for DBD, a given family had a lack of family stressors and parent psychopathology and a lack of hostile attributional biases in the child, intervention delivery could de-emphasize the stress management portions of a parent training programme, and de-emphasize the attribution-retraining portions of a child cognitive-behavioural intervention.

Evidence-based interventions

There have been a number of advances over the past 10–15 years in the development and implementation of evidence-based practices for children's and adolescents' emotional and behavioural difficulties (Lonigan *et al.*, 1998; Stoiber & Kratochwill, 2000; Kazdin & Weisz, 2003; Walker *et al.*, 2004), including ODD and conduct disorder (Brestan & Eyberg, 1998; Eyberg *et al.*, 2008). In this book, we will discuss a number of interventions that have had at least some degree of empirical support.

There has been debate concerning the level of evidence necessary for determining whether particular interventions are effective with specific problems (Gresham & Lochman, 2008). Barlow (1996) suggested that there are increasing pressures from outside agencies such as managed care, governmental agencies, funding agencies and professional organizations to demonstrate the efficacy and effectiveness of interventions with children and adolescents, which has led to proliferating lists of evidence-based treatments. Unfortunately, the lists do not agree completely on which interventions should be listed. In the following sections, we will briefly discuss several issues that are important for determining and interpreting the level of empirical support for a given intervention. For a fuller discussion of these issues, see Gresham and Lochman (2008).

Determining evidence-based interventions

Empirical support

Evidence-based interventions (EBIs) have empirical support that is based on appropriate experimental design features using either group or single-case experimental designs. Studies using group experimental designs should randomly assign participants to experimental and control conditions to have the strongest evidence-based support because this procedure provides statistically unbiased estimates of treatment effects. When extraordinary conditions exist, and randomization is not possible, a matched-control design can provide some preliminary indication of intervention effects. Studies using single-case experimental designs must use designs that adequately control for threats to internal validity (e.g. multiple baseline, withdrawal or multi-element designs).

Although these requirements appear clear, variations exist across lists of evidence-based treatments because different groups make different decisions about some of the criteria for empirical support. What if one treatment programme does not do better than another with the core symptoms of a disorder (e.g. non-compliant behaviour, for ODD) but does a better job of influencing ancillary dependent measures (improved social skills)? In studies using multiple outcome measures, it is unclear what standard should be used to judge whether or not a treatment has adequate empirical support. Should studies be required to produce significant changes on the majority of outcome measures (>50%), on a primary outcome measure or on all outcome measures?

Other possible conundrums are that a treatment may produce significant changes on associated characteristics for a behavioural disorder but no changes on the core features of the disorder, or that a treatment may produce changes immediately after the conclusion of treatment (immediate post-test) but not at 6-month, 1-year or 2-year follow-up. Would that be an empirically supported treatment? The answer to this latter question might be 'yes' and 'no'. Yes, it would be an evidence-based short-term treatment, and no, it would not be an evidence-based long-term treatment. Although lists of evidence-based treatments are important resources, clinicians and researchers examining these must clearly do so with a careful and critical eye.

Statistical significance and clinical significance
Statistical significance deals with issues of reliability of change and group differences, as well as the magnitude of effects expressed as effect sizes (Gresham & Lochman, 2008). The behavioural and social sciences (unlike the physical and biological sciences) use units of measurement that are arbitrary and which are placed on different scales of measurement. To correct for this, researchers often convert mean scores into standardized units of measurement so that the effects of various studies are placed on comparable scales of measurement.

The most common statistical conversion is to express group mean differences as effect sizes or a standardized mean difference using Cohen's *d* (Cohen, 1988). Cohen (1988) provided guidelines for interpreting effect sizes as small (0.2), medium (0.5) and large (0.8). Effect sizes can provide an estimate of an intervention's effects even when the sample size, and associated statistical power, are limited. Power is a function of four variables: (1) sample size, (2) significance level, (3) effect size, and (4) power level (Cohen, 1992). A power analysis specifies the required sample size (N) that is required to obtain a given level of significance (α) for a given effect size (small, medium, large) at a given power level (typically 0.80). Many studies in both psychology and education produce either non-significant or weak effects because of low statistical power (Maxwell, 2004).

Whereas statistical significance deals with the reliability of change based on group differences, clinical significance involves the determination of whether the quantity and quality of behaviour change make a socially important difference in an individual's functioning. Kazdin (2003) defined clinical significance in terms of whether an intervention made a real, genuine, palpable, practical or noticeable difference in everyday life to the individual and the people with whom that person interacted.

Kazdin (2003) reviewed several indices of clinical significance, each of which has strengths and weaknesses. Perhaps the most common index of clinical significance is the amount or degree of behaviour change. The amount of behaviour change can be operationalized in several ways. First, one can calculate the absolute level of behaviour change without reference to a normative sample. Kazdin (2003) suggested three ways of doing this: (1) calculating the amount of change from pre treatment to post treatment (e.g. a change of 2 standard deviations), (2) determining whether the individual continues to meet the classification criteria for a psychiatric diagnosis, and (3) a complete elimination of behavioural difficulties, although the latter is usually not realistic with DBDs.

Another method of demonstrating clinical significance is comparing an individual's scores to normative criteria before and after treatment. An intervention that moves an individual's score at pretest from the 98th percentile (+2 standard deviations above the mean) on a problem behaviour measure to the 55th percentile at post-test would be considered clinically significant. Pelham *et al.* (1998) used this logic in their review of the attention deficit/ hyperactivity disorder (ADHD) intervention literature and showed that, even after treatment (medication or psychosocial), individuals were still functioning 1 standard deviation above the mean (84th percentile) on behavioural measures of ADHD.

Efficacy, effectiveness and dissemination of interventions

An important distinction one has to make in evaluating EBIs is between efficacy research and effectiveness research (Weisz *et al.*, 1995; Kazdin, 2000; Gresham & Lochman, 2008). Efficacy research involves measurable behavioural or symptom reduction and increased adaptive functioning demonstrated under tightly controlled experimental conditions. Efficacy studies emphasize the replication of research studies so that other researchers can conduct similar studies in similar settings with similar participants to validate treatment effects (Nathan *et al.*, 2000).

This emphasis on replication requires the use of appropriate control groups against which the experimental conditions can be compared. As such, random assignment to experimental and control groups becomes a critically important methodological component of efficacy studies. The randomized clinical trial, in which participants are randomly assigned to treatment and control or comparison groups (e.g. no treatment, waiting list, placebo), represents the prototypical efficacy study (Nathan *et al.*, 2000). Efficacy studies typically use participants who are homogenous on a particular diagnostic category (e.g. ODD) and use therapists who are well trained in the delivery of the intervention procedures.

Efficacy research is concerned with the internal validity of experimental designs: was the intervention responsible for changes in the outcome measures rather than this being due to extraneous factors? Shadish *et al.* (2002) discuss a number of potential threats to the internal validity of research studies. These include history, maturation, instrumentation, statistical regression, selection biases, attrition and the interaction of selection biases with other threats to internal validity (e.g. selection × maturation or statistical regression × attrition).

Effectiveness research refers to the clinical or educational utility of a particular intervention in the natural environment or in 'real-world' settings such as schools, homes and the community. Randomization to experimental and control conditions is also an important component of effectiveness studies; however, the focus is on the generality of findings (external validity) rather than on tight experimental control (internal validity). A number of control condition options exist in experimental efficacy and effectiveness research. These include no-treatment controls, placebo controls, alternative treatment controls (care-as-usual) and delayed treatment (waiting list) controls (see Gresham & Lochman, 2008, for a further discussion of the types of control condition and the advantages of randomized designs). The major limitation of a waiting list control condition is that the long-term effects of history, maturation, repeated testing and other influences cannot be evaluated (Kazdin, 1992, 2000).

Effectiveness studies typically use treatment agents who may not be highly trained in a particular treatment protocol and utilize participants who may have not been rigorously diagnosed for a particular disorder or who may be comorbid for several psychological disorders (Nathan *et al.*, 2000). A third form of intervention research, dissemination research, moves even further into the 'real world', beyond effectiveness research, by providing training to clinicians but then having no control over how they implement the programme in their own settings (clinics, residential units, community agencies, schools).

Effectiveness research focuses on the external validity of research designs: will the findings of the study generalize to other participants and across other settings not included in the study? Sample characteristics may limit the generalizability of research findings to other samples that may differ on key variables (an effectiveness study with only white children and families will have limited generalization to African-American and Latino families). Another major threat to the external validity of research studies is *multiple treatment interference*, which refers to interpreting the results of a particular treatment within the context of other treatments (Kazdin, 1992). Naturally occurring treatments can obscure treatment versus control differences, by causing an underestimate of intervention effects (if individuals in the control condition receive some evidence-based treatments from other sources; Weisz *et al.*, 2006) or an overestimate of intervention effects (if the intervention is delivered in settings that are rich in other intense collateral services).

Mediators and moderators of EBIs

An important consideration in evaluating the effects of interventions is the specification of those variables that moderate treatment effects and those variables that mediate treatment effects (Gresham & Lochman, 2008). Moderator variables are those variables that affect the relationship between two variables such that the level of one variable (the moderator) affects the level or value of another variable (the criterion or outcome variable) (Holmbeck, 1997). Baron and Kenny (1986) defined a moderator variable as a qualitative or quantitative variable that changes the strength or direction of a relationship between a predictor variable and a criterion variable. Moderator variables can be qualitative or nominal (e.g. age, sex, race, diagnostic category) and/or quantitative or interval (e.g. IQ, level of depression, verbal skills). Mediator variables specify how or the mechanism by which a given effect occurs (Holmbeck, 1997). Baron and Kenny (1986) characterize mediator variables as generative mechanisms through which focal independent variables influence or thereby 'cause' changes in a dependent variable.

A number of variables have been shown in the child psychotherapy literature to moderate effects or outcomes. For example, Weisz *et al.*'s (1995) meta-analysis found that age, sex and age-by-sex interaction moderated treatment effects on various outcome measures. In terms of mediator variables, it has been demonstrated that intervention-produced improvements in effective parenting and reductions in inconsistent discipline mediate or 'cause' the reduction of antisocial behaviour in children (Lochman & Wells, 2002a; DeGarmo *et al.*, 2004).

Intervention research is ideally a programmatic set of studies in which researchers proceed from pilot testing and controlled studies of basic intervention effects to increasingly refined studies of the mechanisms of action and studies of moderator effects (Lochman, 2006). Intervention science accumulates information over time using rigorous experimental designs and involves 'model-building', leading to revisions in the model. An often-neglected role of intervention research is to provide tests of the theory that is the basis for the intervention (Koretz, 1991; Cicchetti & Toth, 1992). Intervention research has a unique capacity to test causal mechanisms and to examine the malleability of elements of the developmental model (Kellam & Rebok, 1992). Mediating processes can be tested, with the mediators being proximal targets of intervention, for outcomes such as drug use and delinquency.

As an example from our Coping Power research, we have found that aggressive children who receive the intervention have had lower rates of delinquent behaviour, lower substance use rates and reduced conduct problems at school across two separate samples at 1-year follow-up (Lochman & Wells, 2003, 2004). To determine whether changes in targeted processes did in fact mediate the children's reduced risk for these problem behaviours, path analyses were conducted that included a set of potential mediators (children's hostile attributions, children's outcome expectations for their aggressive behaviour, children's person perception abilities, children's locus of control, inconsistent parental discipline). When changes from baseline to post intervention in these targeted processes were included in the path analytic models with a sample of 183 aggressive boys, the improvements in these processes were found to produce the improvements at the 1-year follow-up in delinquency, substance abuse and school problems (Lochman & Wells, 2002a). Thus, these analyses provided a test for the developmental model, and the findings support a portion of the underlying model for the Coping Power intervention.

Summary points

- Targeted prevention interventions are used with at-risk children, and universal prevention interventions are used to enhance the functioning of everyone within a population.
- Some interventions are used both for targeted prevention programmes for children showing early signs of disorder and for the treatment of already diagnosed children.
- Developmental models can serve as the foundation for new interventions by identifying the active mechanisms, which can be the targets of the intervention.
- Efficacy research involves testing intervention effects under tightly controlled experimental conditions, while effectiveness research refers to the clinical or educational utility of a particular intervention in the natural environment or in 'real-world' settings such as schools, homes and the community.
- A moderator variable is a qualitative or quantitative variable that changes the strength or direction of a relationship between a predictor variable and a criterion variable.
- Mediator variables are the mechanisms that account for the effect of distal variables, including an intervention, on later outcomes.

8

Behavioural parent training

Behavioural parent training is a psychotherapeutic intervention that aims to alter maladaptive parent–child interactions by training parents to use behavioural techniques to decrease children's disruptive behaviours and to increase socially appropriate behaviours. We first present the theoretical background of behavioural parent training and then discuss behavioural techniques related to the principles of operant learning theory. Over the years, many behavioural parent training programmes have been developed. Before describing what makes some of these programmes specific, we present general characteristics of behavioural parent training.

Theoretical background

Behavioural parent training is a psychotherapeutic method in which parents, either individually or in a group, are trained to change the behaviour of their children using social learning techniques. These techniques are based on operant conditioning, the learning theory according to which behaviour (B) develops and can be altered by focusing on its antecedents (A) and its consequences (C) (Kazdin, 2005). In addition, in some behavioural parent training programmes, observational learning is also crucial. According to this learning theory, one learns by observing another individual (a model) engage in behaviour without performing the behaviour oneself. Children indeed learn aggressive behaviour by observing others (Bandura, 1973). Likewise, parents learn appropriate parenting skills by observing other parents, the therapist or models from videotapes in behavioural parenting training group sessions. Thus, both the theory of operant learning and the theory of observational learning describe how inappropriate behaviours develop and how they can be altered.

Oppositional Defiant Disorder and Conduct Disorder in Childhood   By Walter Matthys and John E. Lochman
© 2010 John Wiley & Sons, Ltd.

Operant conditioning focuses on the contingencies of reinforcement, i.e. the relationships between behaviours and the environmental events that influence the behaviours (Kazdin, 2005). Among these environmental events, the significance of the various consequences (C) that may follow the behaviours seem to be more obvious than the significance of the antecedents (A). It is now self-evident that praising following child's compliance is likely to increase the occurrence of compliance in the future and that ignoring following whining will probably decrease whining. However, antecedents of behaviour (A) are important as well.

Prompts and setting events may be distinguished as specific types of antecedent (A) (Kazdin, 2005). Prompts are specific antecedents that directly facilitate the performance of behaviour. For example, one command that is clear and given politely is likely to be more successful than a series of commands, especially in children with comorbid attention deficit/hyperactivity disorder (ADHD) who may have problems in processing complex information. On the other hand, setting events 'set the stage' and influence behaviour. For example, a noisy room will affect the homework of a child with attention problems. Besides external events, internal states also are considered to be setting events as they affect behaviour as well. An irritable mood, for example, following a fight with a sibling will affect obeying a command given by a parent.

Behaviours (B) that parents want to develop in their children are called target behaviours. It is crucial for parents both to specify which behaviour they want to target and to evaluate over the treatment whether their goal has been achieved. Providing antecedents, such as appropriately given commands, or consequences, such as praise, may be sufficient to increase the specific behaviour when the individual child has the target behaviour in his or her repertoire. However, if the behaviour is not part of the child's repertoire, shaping can be used to reinforce approximations of the target behaviour. For example, praising the first movement to comply in a persistently non-complying child is likely to increase compliance.

Consequences (C) will alter a particular behaviour when given contingent upon performance. Four types of consequence may be distinguished: positive reinforcement, negative reinforcement, punishment and extinction. Positive reinforcers are events that are presented after a behavioural response has been performed and that increase the likelihood of the behaviour they follow. Two categories of positive reinforcer may be distinguished (Kazdin, 2005). Unconditioned or primary positive reinforcers such as sweets are reinforcing without requiring special learning. Conditioned or secondary reinforcers such as praise acquire reinforcing properties by being paired with events that are already reinforcing, such as food or physical touch. Some conditioned reinforcers such as money or tokens (points or stars) are associated with many other reinforcers. These are called generalized conditioned reinforcers because they can be exchanged for a variety of reinforcing events, known as back-up reinforcers (Kazdin, 2005).

While the techniques based on positive reinforcement are the most important ones in behavioural parent training, the principle of negative reinforcement is essential to understanding how disruptive behaviours develop. Here,
the ground-breaking work of Patterson and colleagues in Oregon needs to be
discussed (Patterson, 1982; Patterson *et al.*, 1992; Reid *et al.*, 2002). On the
basis of numerous studies of meticulous direct observations of child–parent
interactions in the home, Patterson and colleagues described the coercion
mechanism, a sequence of interactions based on negative reinforcement. The
sequence starts with a parent acting aversively towards the child, for example
scolding the child for not doing his homework. The boy may react aversively
to this, by replying insolently, and the mother gives in. As the boy's reaction
'worked', it is more likely to occur again in future exchanges.

According to the principle of negative reinforcement, any behaviour that
terminates an aversive condition is likely to increase in frequency in the
future. Thus, children with disruptive behaviours are inadvertently rewarded
for their disruptive interactions. Importantly, the coercion process may start
in toddlers and probably even in infants. Individual temperamental characteristics such as negativism and irritability (see Chapter 4) probably play an
important role in explaining the early beginnings of the coercive process
(Patterson, 2002). Although the parent's understanding of negative reinforcement in everyday interactions is an important issue in behavioural parent
training, negative reinforcement is not used to alter behaviour.

While positive as well as negative reinforcement refers to an increase in the
likelihood of response when that response is immediately followed by consequences, punishment and extinction decrease the possibility of a response.
There are two types of punishment. In the first type, an aversive consequence
such as slapping and giving harsh reprimands is presented after a response.
The second type is the removal of a positive consequence such as losing
privileges after a response.

In extinction, a consequence that was previously provided no longer
follows the behaviour, resulting in a decrease in the likelihood of the behaviour in the future. For example, ignoring the child's whining will reduce the
child's inappropriate behaviour if the parent had previously been attending
to the whining.

Behavioural techniques

In behavioural parent training, the behavioural techniques that increase the
likelihood of behaviour, i.e. those based on positive reinforcement, are much
more important than the behavioural techniques that decrease the likelihood
of behaviour, i.e. those based on punishment and extinction. There are several
types of reinforcer: food, social reinforcers (e.g. praise and physical contact),

privileges and activities, and tokens. Kazdin (2005) discusses the conditions for the effective application of reinforcers. For a reinforcer to be effective, the reinforcer should be liked by the child (quality), and the reinforcer should be provided only when the behaviour occurs (contingency), immediately after the behaviour occurs (immediacy) and every time the behaviour occurs (continuously). Social reinforcers are always available and therefore can be easily administered, but it is not easy for the parents to administer them consistently and for the therapist to monitor their use. Tokens such as stars, coins and points also can be readily used. A token economy, i.e. a reinforcement system based on tokens in which tokens are backed up by other reinforcers such as privileges and activities, makes the contingencies explicit and is easier for the therapist to monitor (Kazdin, 2005).

For a behaviour to be reinforced, it needs to be part of the child's behavioural repertoire and ready to be performed. Prompts such as instructions and showing how to do something help children to initiate the behaviour that they have in their repertoire so it can be reinforced. In terms of the A B C scheme, prompts are antecedents (A) needed for a behaviour (B) to be performed and then be reinforced (C). But it may also be that the child does not have the behaviour (B) in his or her repertoire. The behaviour, then, can be developed gradually by reinforcing parts of the behaviour; this is called shaping.

These reinforcement techniques not only effectively increase the amount of appropriate behaviours, but also decrease the amount of inappropriate behaviours. This seems counterintuitive as one is inclined to use punishment techniques in order to reduce inappropriate behaviours. However, one may reinforce appropriate behaviours such as cooperative play with siblings or compliance towards parents that are 'positive opposites' of inappropriate behaviours such as fighting or defiant behaviour (Kazdin, 2005). Much practice is needed for parents to think consistently in terms of positive opposites, i.e. to find out and reinforce the opposites of the behaviours they want to suppress.

It is crucial to use mainly positive reinforcement and only rarely use punishment. In general, as children adapt to punishment, the punishing consequence may lose its effectiveness, which results in an escalation of punishment (Kazdin, 2005). Moreover, there is evidence that children with disruptive behaviour disorders (DBDs), especially those with callous-unemotional traits, are less sensitive to punishment (see Chapter 4). Thus, the parents of children with DBDs are at increased risk of getting caught in an escalating cycle of punishment.

However, the clinician should also anticipate that children with DBDs may be less sensitive to rewards than typically developing children, and that those with comorbid ADHD have both an elevated reward threshold and a preference for immediate reward (see Chapter 4). Thus, in children with DBDs, and maybe even more in those with comorbid ADHD, the praise and tangible rewards should be given with more emphasis than is usually given in typically developing children; the issue of immediacy applies to all children.

Although positive reinforcement is the main focus of behavioural parent training, punishment techniques are important in the treatment of DBDs for two reasons (Kazdin, 2005). First, mild punishment procedures may be added to positive reinforcement of positive opposites to complement a reinforcement programme. Second, instead of the harsh, frequent and inconsistent punishment practices that the parents of children with DBDs often use, parents should learn mild punishment techniques. Although spanking, slapping or hitting a child may result in an immediate decrease of inappropriate behaviour, it is not clear whether these punishment techniques are effective over time (Benjet & Kazdin, 2003). Instead, the effectiveness of much milder punishment techniques has been established.

A mild punishment technique that parents learn to use in behavioural parent training is time out, which is an abbreviation of 'time out from reinforcement'. This procedure is much more difficult to use than it seems at first sight. The child sits in a special chair in the room or goes to a special place in the home for a few minutes contingent on the inappropriate behaviour that he or she has shown. Various issues need to be discussed and skills need to be practised with the parents, such as how to cope with a child who resists going to the time out chair or the time out place, and how to cope with a child who leaves his or her time out chair or place before the end of time out. Importantly, after the completion of time out, parents are inclined to discuss with the child his or her misbehaviour preceding the time out. However, in this way, they again pay attention to and thus reinforce the inappropriate behaviour while the essential characteristic of 'time out from reinforcement' is not to reinforce inappropriate behaviour.

Response cost, i.e. the loss of a positive reinforcer, is another mild punishment technique. It is used in the context of a token economy and consists of the removal of a token. Before using response cost, it is made clear to the child which misbehaviours will result in a loss of tokens. In contrast to time out, conflicting parent–child interactions are avoided when using response cost as the child is not required to do something (Kazdin, 2005). The use of response cost in the context of a token economy in young children is more problematic as they may have difficulty in combining the positive reinforcement of appropriate behaviour with the response cost of misbehaviour together in one programme. Loss of a privilege, for example TV time, also is an example of response cost.

A third technique specifically useful to eliminate low-rate inappropriate behaviours is the completion of some activity such as a chore that the child must perform as restitution.

Finally, one important technique based on extinction is ignoring; this is used to decrease mild inappropriate behaviours that have been reinforced by merely providing attention.

General characteristics of programmes and effectiveness

The goal of behaviour parent training is to change the child's referral problems by improving the parents' skills that affect parent–child interactions. Typically, programmes consist of a series of sessions each of which covers a specific operant conditioning principle and related procedures. Thus, programmes start with sessions on positive reinforcement and the use of praise and tokens, whereas later sessions focus on extinction and ignoring, mild punishment and the use of time out, and response cost and loss of privileges.

Because practising the parenting skills at home is essential in behavioural parent training, sessions begin by reviewing the parents' experiences with the skills covered the previous week. A new principle and related procedures are then presented. The skills are practised using role-play (i.e. with other parents or with the therapist playing the role of the child) and in vivo practice (i.e. with the child), with the therapist giving support, feedback and modelling. Finally, assignments to practise the skills at home are discussed. Between sessions, the therapist is available to the parents to address problems in implementing the skills at home. Moreover, when the programme is delivered in a group format, parents may support each other between sessions.

Research on the effectiveness of behavioural parent training is extensive. Numerous studies on the effectiveness of behavioural parent training have been conducted. In a meta-analysis of behavioural parent training and cognitive-behavioural therapy (see Chapter 9) for children and adolescents with antisocial behaviour, the mean effect size of behavioural parent training was 0.47 and that of cognitive-behavioural therapy 0.35 (McCart *et al.*, 2006). When comparisons were made involving children in the 6–12 years age range, the effect size for behavioural parent training (0.45) was significantly higher than that for cognitive-behavioural therapy (0.23), probably because children in this age range are dependent on their parents and are only beginning to develop the more abstract cognitive skills that are part of cognitive behaviour therapy (McCart *et al.*, 2006).

One important limitation in research on behavioural parent training is that the mediating role of improving parental skills on the decrease of child's problem behaviour has been insufficiently studied (Kazdin & Nock, 2003). Indeed, although some studies have demonstrated associations between an improvement in parental skills and a decrease in children's problem behaviour, most studies (e.g. Gardner *et al.*, 2006) have examined these changes at the same time. However, in order to demonstrate that the improvement of parenting skills did indeed cause the decrease of problem behaviour, the former must be assessed prior to the latter (Kazdin & Nock, 2003). In one study, the sequential pattern of changes was demonstrated, i.e. increases in effective parenting predicted a reduction in child behaviour problems (DeGarmo *et al.*, 2004). One other issue that has been neglected is the inclusion of neurobiological factors as moderators of effectiveness while it has been demonstrated that some of these factors play a role in the maintenance of DBDs (see Chapter 4).

Examples of programmes

We will now briefly describe examples of behavioural parent training programmes that have an evidence base for their effectiveness. In the overview, we do not categorize programmes as well established, probably efficacious and possibly efficacious. Instead, we specify the characteristics of each programme and mention important studies of the evidence of effectiveness.

Parent Management Training Oregon

Based on their extensive research on parent–child interactions, on the coercion theory they developed and on the demonstration of the role of specific inept child-rearing practices that contribute to aggressive behaviour in children, Patterson and colleagues have developed Parent Management Training Oregon (PMTO; Patterson *et al.*, 1975). PMTO is the first behavioural parent training programme that has been thoroughly studied. PMTO was originally developed for the treatment of referred children aged 3 to 13 years with antisocial behaviour. Families are seen individually for weekly sessions. In one study, the average treatment period was 17 hours (Patterson *et al.*, 1982). The content of the sessions largely corresponds to the description given in the previous section. To teach parents the principles and related procedures, reading material is used (e.g. Patterson, 1976).

The effectiveness of PMTO has been demonstrated both as a treatment method with referred children (Patterson *et al.*, 1982) and in group format as a preventive method with recently separated mothers (DeGarmo *et al.*, 2004).

Parent Management Training

Kazdin's (2005) Parent Management Training (PMT) programme for children aged 2 to 14 years also is delivered individually: group treatment was considered to be too diluted for the children's degree of problem behaviour and the degree of parent dysfunction among the families to be treated. The core treatment is 12 sessions, each session lasting between 45 and 60 minutes. Between sessions, the therapist calls the parents to provide support for the practising of parenting skills at home. There is an ongoing evaluation of child and parent progress, using role-play and contact sessions in which the parent and child are seen together. Optional sessions are added to work on areas where the skills are still poor before moving to the next theme. The essential characteristics of the content have been described earlier in the chapter. The description of the manual is detailed, and it contains handouts, charts and aides for parents (Kazdin, 2005).

The effectiveness of PMT has been demonstrated also in combination with children's Problem Solving Skills Training (Kazdin *et al.*, 1992; see also Chapter 11).

Parent–Child Interaction Therapy

Parent–Child Interaction Therapy (PCIT) is a programme developed for the treatment of young children with DBDs (ages 2–7 years; Brinkmeyer & Eyberg, 2003). PCIT is given on an individual basis. In comparison with other programmes, two essential characteristics of PCIT are the participation of both the child and the parent in all the sessions, and coaching by the therapist while the parent is playing with the child. If a one-way mirror is available, the coaching is done using a 'bug in the ear'; if not, the therapist coaches the parent in a low voice while next to the parent. Thus, the therapist shapes the parent's behaviour using prompts, reinforcement and corrective statements.

Families meet for weekly 1-hour sessions for an average of 12–16 sessions. PCIT has two segments: child-directed interaction and parent-directed interaction. In the child-directed interaction part, the therapist teaches the parents skills to foster attachment and relations such as praising the child's behaviour, reflecting the child's statements, imitating the child's play, describing the child's play and using enthusiasm. In the parent-directed interaction part, parenting skills such as giving clear instructions and giving time out are taught.

PCIT is highly individualized. At the beginning of the session, parent–child interaction is observed in order to decide which skills to work on during the session. In line with this, there is no limit in the number of sessions. Instead, treatment is performance based and continues until the parents express confidence in their ability to manage their child's behaviour.

Numerous studies that have examined the effectiveness of PCIT are included in a meta-analysis by Thomas and Zimmer-Gembeck (2007). When compared with using a waiting list, medium and large effects were found favouring PCIT in terms of the mother's and father's reports of their child's negative behaviour.

Incredible Years

Incredible Years has been developed for the treatment DBDs in young children (2–8 years of age) (Webster-Stratton, 2001, 2002; Webster-Stratton & Reid, 2003). The programme consists of separate complementary modules that have been developed for parents, teachers and children. Here, we discuss the two-parent modules: the initial module, BASIC, consisting of 12–14 sessions (Webster-Stratton, 2001), and ADVANCE, consisting of 8 sessions (Webster-Stratton, 2002).

Incredible Years is delivered in a group format and includes the use of videotapes and a book on parenting skills (Webster-Stratton, 2005a). A collaborative relationship is developed between the therapist and the parents. The group format enables parents to support each other during the sessions and to serve as 'buddies', helping each other to complete home assignments between sessions. The use of a book enables parents to prepare for sessions by reading a chapter on the skills that are the topic of the particular session, avoiding a didactic approach, which may result in parental resistance. Videotapes of real-life parent–child, child–child and parent–parent interactions elicit group discussions on specific problem behaviours and how to handle them. Following the videotapes, the therapists ask open questions to elicit discussions and problem-solving by the parents. Therapists thus avoid giving direct answers and advice as an expert. Instead, a collaborative relationship is established in which the therapist's and the parents' knowledge, strengths and perspectives are equally utilized.

In each session (2 hours per session), 8–12 parents participate. BASIC starts with 'How to play with your child'. Parents learn to follow the child's lead, to pace at the child's level, to praise and encourage the child's ideas and creativity, and to use descriptive comments instead of asking questions. The programme then focuses on the appropriate use of praise. In addition to the basic skills of praising children, parents learn to praise their child in front of other people (e.g. the mother praises the child in the father's presence), and they learn to praise themselves and to model self-praise. With regard to a token economy, it is stressed that the parents of young children need to make the programme simple and fun, avoid mixing rewards and punishment, and gradually to replace tokens with social approval. In the sessions on limit setting, parents learn to make commands short, positive and polite. Thus, 'stop' and 'don't' commands ('Don't shout') should be avoided and replaced by 'do' commands ('Speak softly').

Finally, skills to handle inappropriate behaviours are taught. In these sessions, parents learn to consistently ignore mild inappropriate behaviours by moving away from the child, avoiding eye contact and discussion, and returning attention to the child as soon as the misbehaviour stops. Parents also learn to use time out appropriately. They learn to explain the time out procedure to the child, to practise time out with the child, to be polite and calm when sending the child to time out, to ignore the child while in time out, to use loss of privileges for not going to time out, and to give the child the opportunity to behave appropriately after time out.

ADVANCE focuses on communication skills such as listening, speaking up and avoiding mixed messages. Furthermore, parents learn to manage upsetting thoughts and manage stress through personal time out. They finally learn problem-solving in various steps, for both themselves and their child.

Evidence for the effectiveness of Incredible Years BASIC as a treatment method has been shown in studies conducted not only by the developer in the USA (Webster-Stratton & Hammond, 1997; Webster-Stratton *et al.*, 2004), but also by other researchers in other countries (Taylor *et al.*, 1998; Scott *et al.*, 2001; Gardner *et al.*, 2006; Larsson *et al.*, 2009). The effectiveness of Incredible Years as an indicated prevention has been established in Head Start classrooms (Webster-Stratton, 1998), in Sure Start areas in Wales (UK; Hutchings *et al.*, 2007) and in children with one incarcerated family member (Brotman *et al.*, 2005).

Positive Parenting Program

The Positive Parenting Program (Triple P) incorporates five levels of intervention targeting children and adolescents with varying degrees of severity of dysfunction (Sanders *et al.*, 2003). Thus, the programme focuses on preventing DBDs as well as providing treatment to children and adolescents who already have DBDs. The content of Triple P is similar to the programmes described earlier.

Universal Triple P (Level 1) is a media-based (television and newspaper) parent information campaign. Selected Triple P (Level 2) is a one- or two-session intervention delivered by primary healthcare providers for parents with concerns about mild behavioural problems. Primary Care Triple P (Level 3) is a four-session intervention, also delivered by primary healthcare providers. Parents learn parenting skills to manage moderately severe behavioural problems. Standard Triple P (Level 4) has different variants, including individual, group and self-directed options. The programme is delivered by mental health providers, consists of up to 12 sessions and targets the parents of children with severe behaviour problems. Finally, Enhanced Triple P (Level 5) is an individually tailored programme of 11 sessions for parents with child behaviour problems and family dysfunction (parent depression or marital problems).

A series of studies has examined the effectiveness of the various levels of intervention. These studies have been included in a meta-analysis by Nowak and Heinrichs (2008). The overall effect size for parenting and child problem behaviour ranged between 0.35 and 0.48, this range corresponding with the range found in another meta-analysis (Thomas & Zimmer-Gembeck, 2007). Furthermore, Levels 4 and 5 have been found to be superior to Levels 1–3 in improving parenting and child problem behaviour (Thomas & Zimmer-Gembeck, 2007), consistent with other research that has found larger effects in treatment contexts than in preventive contexts.

Summary points

- The theory of operant learning and the theory of observational learning describe how inappropriate behaviours develop and how they can be altered.
- The principle of negative reinforcement is essential to understand how disruptive behaviours develop and are maintained. According to this

principle, any behaviour that terminates an aversive condition is likely to increase in frequency in the future. Thus, children with disruptive behaviours are inadvertently rewarded for their disruptive interactions.

- In behavioural parent training, the behavioural techniques that increase the likelihood of a behaviour, i.e. those based on positive reinforcement, are much more important than the behavioural techniques that decrease the likelihood of a behaviour, i.e. those based on punishment and extinction.
- For a reinforcer to be effective, the reinforcer should be liked by the child (quality) and be provided only when the behaviour occurs (contingency), immediately after the behaviour occurs (immediacy) and every time the behaviour occurs (continuously).
- Social reinforcers are always available and can therefore be easily administered, but it is not at all easy for the parents to administer them consistently and for the therapist to monitor their use. A token economy, i.e. a reinforcement system based on tokens in which tokens are backed up by other reinforcers such as privileges and activities, makes the contingencies explicit and is easier for the therapist to monitor.
- Positive reinforcement is effective not only to increase the amount of appropriate behaviours, but also to decrease the amount of inappropriate behaviours. This seems counterintuitive as one is inclined to use punishment techniques in order to reduce inappropriate behaviours. However, one may reinforce appropriate behaviours that are the 'positive opposites' of inappropriate behaviours.
- The issue of using mainly positive reinforcement and only exceptionally using punishment is crucial. In general, as children adapt to punishment, the punishing consequence may lose its effectiveness, which results in an escalation of punishment. Moreover, there is evidence that children with DBDs, especially those with callous-unemotional traits, are less sensitive to punishment. Thus, the parents of children with DBDs are at increased risk of getting caught in an escalating cycle of punishment.
- With the use of positive reinforcement such as praise, one should take into consideration the fact that children with DBDs may be less sensitive to rewards than typically developing children, and that those with comorbid ADHD may have both an elevated reward threshold and a preference for immediate reward. Thus, in children with DBDs, and maybe even more so in those with comorbid ADHD, the praise and tangible rewards should be given with more emphasis than is usually given for typically developing children.
- Punishment techniques are an important topic in behavioural parent training for two reasons. First, besides the positive reinforcement of positive opposites, mild punishment procedures may be added to complement a reinforcement programme. Second, instead of the harsh, frequent and inconsistent punishment practices that the parents of children with DBD often use, parents should learn mild punishment techniques such as time out and loss of privileges.

9

Cognitive-behavioural therapy

This chapter first describes the history of cognitive-behavioural therapy (CBT), including its application with children with conduct problems. Common and central clinical aspects of CBT programmes for conduct problem children are discussed, and examples of research-based CBT programmes for these children are described. The programmes are grouped by age (preschool to early elementary school, late elementary school, early adolescence) and include classroom prevention programmes as well as treatment programmes. Brief summaries of findings from interventional research are presented.

Roots in observational learning, social learning and developmental theories

As its name implies, 'cognitive-behavioural therapy' focuses on children's cognitions and on their behaviour (as well as on other characteristics such as emotions, as described later in this chapter). Current CBTs with children have important roots in the social learning theories and developmental theories that were being proposed in the 1950s, 60s and 70s (Lochman & Pardini, 2008). Bandura's research on observational learning has been particularly influential (Bandura, 1973).

Observation learning theory stresses the important role of cognitions by highlighting that a child's observations of real-life models and symbolic models could influence the child's subjective perceptions of how rewards and punishments were contingent on their behaviours and on the child's decision-making processes. To acquire new behaviours through modelling, a child must pay attention to a model (e.g. a peer entering a soccer game on the playground), cognitively retain and remember relevant aspects of the model's

Oppositional Defiant Disorder and Conduct Disorder in Childhood   By Walter Matthys and
John E. Lochman
© 2010 John Wiley & Sons, Ltd.

behaviour, enact the behaviour that has been observed, and then be reinforced for the reproduced behaviour. Viewing models can also affect the rate at which children emit behaviours, as similar sequences of cognitions and behaviours can also account for how children reproduce (or perform) already existing behaviours within their behavioural repertoire.

Based on early research, it was apparent that children tended to imitate aggressive behaviour when they observed a model being reinforced for aggression, and were less likely to imitate aggressive behaviour when they observed a model being punished for aggression (Bandura *et al.*, 1963). Subsequent studies demonstrated that observational learning could be used to promote children's abilities to seek delayed rather than immediate gratification (Bandura & Mischel, 1965). These observational research studies provided early evidence that modelling could be used to influence children's cognitions and promote positive behavioural change.

Other important research about how individuals' cognitions could guide their behaviour came from the social learning theories of Julian Rotter (Rotter *et al.*, 1972) and his student, Walter Mischel (Mischel, 1973). Rotter had proposed a theory predicting how individuals' expectancies for receiving rewards and their acquired perceived reinforcement values could jointly determine their behaviour. A series of elegant laboratory studies supported this theory and found that expectancies could be generalized (e.g. internal or external locus of control) or specific to the situation, and that generalized, cross-situational expectancies were derived from an individuals' accumulation of situation-specific expectancies.

Mischel (1973) integrated the work of Bandura and Rotter with experimental research on cognitive processing and symbolic mental representations (Neisser, 1967) in an attempt to explain the complex and dynamic interactions between children and their environment. Mischel's theory predicted that individuals' behavioural reactions to environmental stimuli were affected by their encoding strategies, outcome expectancies and values, behavioural regulation systems and planning abilities. Environmental characteristics were believed to influence future behaviour in so far as they changed an individual's cognitive perceptions at these various stages or levels.

Based on Bandura's notion of reciprocal determinism, Mischel (1973) also theorized that children's overt behaviour could produce changes in the environment and modify their social stimuli (e.g. a teacher's behaviour towards them). As a result, children were viewed as active participants in their social environment, with the ability to influence social exchanges and reinforcement contingencies, as well as be influenced by them (Lochman & Pardini, 2008).

Developmental psychologists were focusing on related cognitions and behaviours during this time. Piaget described children as developing an increasingly sophisticated set of mental representations and logical structures in order to master their own behaviour and the environment (for a review, see Thomas, 1996). According to Piaget, children initially perceived the world through simple cause-and-effect relationships driven by their own overt actions. However, children quickly learned to represent objects and events using symbols (e.g. words and mental imagery) and then began performing logical operations on these symbols to represent cause-and-effect relations in the real world, helping to facilitate behavioural planning and effortful self-control (Lochman & Pardini, 2008).

In the early 1960s, Vygotsky (1962) hypothesized from a different perspective that children's words could direct their mental operations, and that these mental operations in turn controlled children's problem-solving behaviour (Smith *et al.*, 2005). Similarly, Luria (1961) proposed that children go through three developmental stages as they voluntarily initiate or inhibit their own behaviour: (1) relying on other- (usually a parent) directed control, (2) controlling their behaviour through their overt speech, and (3) controlling their behaviour through inner, or covert, speech. Thus, these developmental theorists emphasized the connection between cognitions and behaviour, and specifically how cognitive operations are involved in the development of self-control. Their theories had important effects on early cognitive-behavioural therapists, such as Donald Meichenbaum, who began working on enhancing children's self-control.

Early forms of CBT and theories with children

Expanding traditional conditioning paradigms with a multidimensional approach that included covert processes (i.e. cognition), Meichenbaum (1977) described the verbal self-regulation of behaviour as talking to oneself to guide problem-solving or behaviour. In 1971, Meichenbaum and Goodman found that a combination of modelling and self-instructional training was successful in decreasing children's impulsive behaviour. The programme taught children to control their own behaviour by modelling self-control verbalizations and instructed children on how to engage in private self-speech while performing sustained-attention tasks. Findings suggested that impulsive children who underwent this treatment improved their ability to use private self-speech to orient their attention and think carefully when making important decisions.

Kendall and Braswell (1982) developed a more comprehensive cognitive therapy that taught impulsive children the general steps to problem-solving and how to use internalized coping statements to deal with frustration and failures when engaged in goal-directed behaviours. Children who received this intervention were shown to have better school compliance at a 10-week follow-up than children who received behavioural training alone.

Along with Meichenbaum, Mahoney (1974) argued that a strict reliance on operant and classical conditioning fell short of adequately predicting or explaining complex patterns of human behaviour such as impulsivity or aggression, and that ignoring the vital role of cognition resulted in techniques that temporarily altered behaviour but did not teach useful strategies or result in positive long-term outcomes. Thus, the internalization of self-statements was considered fundamental to developing self-control. Conversely, deficient or maladaptive self-statements were seen to contribute significantly to child-hood behaviour problems, including aggression.

While relatively simplistic, these early CBT studies demonstrated that chil-dren could be taught cognitive strategies to help improve their behavioural functioning (Lochman & Pardini, 2008). It is worth noting from a clinical perspective that modelling self-control strategies (Bandura, 1986) continues to be a vital component of CBT. In the course of sessions, clinicians can 'think out loud' as they talk about how they might handle their own emotions (par-ticularly those that could lead to aggressive acts), analyse a situation, choose a course of action and/or evaluate the outcome of their behaviour. Their explanations of the cognitive strategies they use and their metacognitive awareness of those strategies can serve as a powerful model for their child clients to emulate (Smith *et al.*, 2005).

Other researchers began to explore whether deficits in social problem-solving contributed to children's aggressive behaviour (see D'Zurilla & Goldfried, 1971; Spivack & Shure, 1974; Spivack *et al.*, 1976; D'Zurilla & Nezu, 1980). They defined effective problem-solving as a cognitive-behavioural process that (1) enables the generation of a variety of alternative responses when faced with a problem, and (2) increases the probability of evaluating consequences to implement the most appropriate choice (Smith *et al.*, 2005). Spivack and Shure's (1974) early research demonstrated that social problem-solving training could be used effectively with children and their parents, and social problem-solving training became a key element of behaviourally orien-tated community psychology interventions that began to be delivered preven-tively to children in school settings (Allen *et al.*, 1976).

Based on clinical work with low-income aggressive children that began in the late 1970s, Lochman *et al.* (1981) developed an anger arousal model, and an accompanying Anger Control program, that incorporated both the self-instruction training methods from Meichenbaum and the social prob-lem-solving training methods from Shure and Spivack. Aggressive children were seen as having two primary areas of cognitive difficulty in this anger arousal model. First, the children had to accurately perceive and interpret the problematic social situations they encountered (aggressive children had cognitive distortions at this step and were expected to have misperceptions and accompanying anger arousal), and then the children had to go through a problem-solving sequence that involved thinking of possible solutions to the problem, considering the anticipated consequences of the solutions and then picking an optimal solution (aggressive children showing deficiencies in the number and types of solution that they could generate).

A more comprehensive social information processing model was subsequently developed by Dodge (1993; Crick & Dodge, 1994) and it has been extremely influential in the development of a variety of cognitive-behavioural interventions with children and adolescents. The model explicitly describes the 'online' cognitive processing steps that occur when children are engaged in social interactions, and includes a focus on encoding and interpreting social information, identifying one's goals in a problem situation, generating possible solutions to the problem, making a decision about which solution to enact and then enacting the solution (see Chapter 4 for a description of the social information-processing deficits of aggressive children). Children who are able to develop skills at each stage of social-cognitive processing may be able, theoretically at least, to execute these skills in guiding their behaviour in a variety of settings, independent of adult control. Cognitive-behavioural strategies may thus offer a degree of self-control not provided by strictly behavioural approaches.

Contemporary CBT

CBT is based on the premise that thoughts, emotions and behaviours are reciprocally linked and that changing one of these will necessarily result in changes in the others (Gresham & Lochman, 2008). These reciprocal relationships between thoughts, emotions and behaviours serve as the fundamental basis of all CBTs. Kendall (2000) has suggested that CBTs for child and adolescent problems need to emphasize both the influence of external contingencies (e.g. reinforcement and punishment) and the child's internal information-processing style to resolve children's adjustment difficulties. In a cognitive-behavioural approach, cognitions, emotions, perceptions and information-processing style all play a central role in the development and remediation of behavioural and adjustment difficulties.

In contrast to purely cognitive therapies, interventions that are cognitive-behavioural in nature (like the ones used with children with conduct problems) are likely to incorporate techniques based on basic behavioural principles when appropriate (Lochman & Pardini, 2008). For example, cognitive-behavioural interventions for young children with conduct problems often teach parents and teachers how to use the behavioural principles of reinforcement, extinction and shaping to change children's behaviour (Brestan & Eyberg, 1998). It is also important to note that contemporary cognitive-behavioural interventions often have multiple components, including parent training interventions; these multicomponent interventions for children's conduct problems will be discussed in Chapter 11. However, all cognitive-behavioural interventions seek to integrate these strategies into an overarching treatment model that emphasizes the influence of both cognitive factors and behavioural contingencies in the development of problematic emotions and behaviours.

The cognitive-behavioural approach encompasses a variety of specific strategies for remediating significant behaviour problems. Problem-solving, self-instructional training (SIT), attribution retraining, relaxation training and verbal mediation have all been used effectively to improve behaviour (cf. Hughes, 1988; Kaplan, 1995). Intervention typically involves teaching children to identify internal and external 'triggers' that cue their behaviour and to use internal stimuli such as self-statements, problem-solving and visualization to control their behaviour. Kendall has noted that cognitive-behavioural techniques use rewards, modelling, role-plays and self-evaluation, and incorporate behaviour therapy (e.g. modelling, feedback and reinforcement) and cognitive mediation (e.g. think-alouds) to build a new 'coping template' (Kendall, 1993).

The largest application of CBT to child and adolescent psychopathology has focused on the treatment of conduct problems (e.g. aggression, defiance, oppositional behaviours and rule-breaking) (Lochman & Pardini, 2008). While cognitive-behavioural therapies for conduct problems differ based on the developmental level of the target population (e.g. preschool children versus adolescents) and the severity of the behaviour problems being targeted (e.g. treatment for DBDs versus preventive intervention for minor aggressive behaviour), common elements pervade most empirically supported cognitive-behavioural approaches.

As a result, typical cognitive-behavioural intervention elements for treating conduct problems in youth will be described, using the child component of the Coping Power programme as an example (Lochman, 2006; Lochman et al., 2008c), followed by empirical evidence supporting the efficacy of a set of cognitive-behavioural interventions with various populations. The Coping Power child component is a more extended and comprehensive version of the earlier Anger Coping programme (Lochman *et al.*, 1981) for aggressive children. The two overarching goals for the Anger Coping cognitive-behavioural programme are, first, to assist children in finding ways to cope with the intense surge of physiological arousal and anger that they experience immediately after a provocation or frustration, and second, to assist children in retrieving from memory an array of possible competent strategies that they could use to adaptively resolve the frustrating problem or conflict that they are experiencing.

Behavioural and personal goals

In the sessions, children are asked to generate rules for the behaviour in sessions and to identify long-term and short-term goals for themselves. These goals lead to specific behavioural goals that children commit themselves to achieving during the subsequent week, using goal sheets. It is useful to solicit a menu of potential goals (graded by level of likely difficulty) from teachers and parents prior to programme. These behavioural goals should be clearly observable, and the initial goals should be of moderate difficulty to assist children in having successful experiences in the early stages of goal attainment. Each child's goals are monitored on a daily basis by the teacher or parent, and the child earns points based on their success. Prior research with the Anger Coping programme had demonstrated that the inclusion of behavioural goal-setting procedures, with adult monitoring and reinforcement, determined whether children's behavioural improvement would transfer into classroom settings, according to independent observers (Lochman *et al.*, 1984).

Organizational and study skills

Relatively early in the intervention, there are several sessions on adjusting to the organizational and study skills required for adequate school progress. Children identify useful and less useful study skills (e.g. developing a plan for a long-term project versus studying in a noisy living room). These sessions particularly address how these organizational and study skills will become even more important in middle school. Children work in conjunction with their parents to create a homework contract that specifies when and where homework will be done, and whether there are contingencies for homework completion.

Awareness of arousal and anger

Two sessions concentrate on children's emotional reactions in various problematic situations, especially focusing on their experience of anger in response to provocation or frustration. Children learn to identify cognitive, behavioural and physiological indicators of each emotion. The focus is on increased self-awareness of one's own emotions, as well as a more accurate perception of other people's emotions. Using an anger thermometer, children are assisted to identify the different levels of anger they may experience (e.g. rage, irritation, annoyance) and the different types of problem that trigger these different levels of anger. The anger thermometer is then used throughout the intervention. For example, when children begin to use the problem-solving process, it is best done initially with problems that are in the low-to-moderate level of anger, so that children can better learn the skills and so that they are more likely to be successful.

Anger management and self-regulation

This focus on self-awareness of the physiological and behavioural signs of anger then leads to a major unit in the Coping Power intervention on methods for anger management. Children are introduced to the use of coping self-statements, distraction techniques and brief deep-breathing relaxation methods as a means to handle the arousal associated with anger without resorting to aggression.

The use of coping self-statements is a central focus of this part of the programme, and is meant to disrupt children's reflexive aggressive responses and to facilitate a more adaptive problem-solving process. The coping statements are initially spoken out loud, but the goal is for these self-statements to go 'underground' and become internalized thoughts to assist with self-control, consistent with the research by Luria (1961) and Vygotsky (1962). Children are reinforced for creating a personal repertoire of coping self-statements that are meaningful to them and that they can use in real-life situations.

A series of activities designed to be progressively more realistic are used to assist children in trying out these methods in vivo in the sessions. Children first try to screen out distractions from their peers during simple memory and building tasks, and then use the anger management skills during puppet role-plays, finally using the skills during taunting tasks with peers. It is important for leaders to model these skills at each stage of these tasks and to proactively coach children in their use of these skills during the taunting tasks. These activities are based on the assumption that children must learn how to handle the surge in arousal and anger in response to a perceived provocation before they can successfully begin to use problem-solving strategies. Parents and teachers are often taught to cue and assist the child in using anger management strategies at home and at school, and are instructed in how to reinforce the successful implementation of these skills.

Perspective-taking, problem identification and attribution retraining

Three perspective-taking sessions introduce the first part of the problem-solving model, known as Problem Identification, Choices, Consequences (PICC). Like all of these units, children first are presented with a set of game-like tasks that are meant to be enjoyable and that permit the clinician to present the main points of the unit. These initial tasks are followed by activities that are more challenging and are more related to the difficulties that the children experience. Role-playing and discussion activities are used to illustrate how hard it often is to accurately understand another person's intentions in a problem situation, and there is a primary emphasis on retraining the hostile attributional bias that many aggressive children have. Although the main focus of these activities is on peer situations, aggressive children also often misperceive teachers' intentions. Thus, a teacher interview has been designed to address the perceived unfairness and harshness of teachers.

Social problem-solving skills

The unit of the intervention with the largest number of sessions involves the steps and the use of the PICC problem-solving model. As children learn to define the problems that they encounter in precise behavioural terms, they also indicate their degree of anger activation in the situation and identify their goal in the situation. Clinicians shape the goal to be as positive as possible (e.g. what the child wants to achieve in the situation rather than wanting to get back at a presumed provocateur), and the brainstorming of solutions is directed towards this goal rather than towards the problem per se. Brainstorming discussions, as well as hands-on activities and the use of PICC forms, are used to introduce the range of choices, or possible solutions, that children have in most social problem situations, and then to introduce the range of consequences that result from these various choices. The children then use the consequences they have brainstormed to decide on a 'winning' solution. The exercises also address how children's social goals and their use of impulsive, automatic processing can impair their problem-solving skills. The PICC model is then used on children's own problems.

A particularly useful way to generate children's active involvement in learning problem-solving is to have the children create a videotape of a problem situation with several possible 'winning' solutions. Because they typically look forward to this task, the video-taping activity tends to maintain children's motivation in the programme, even among these high-risk children. Later problem-solving sessions address how the PICC model could be used in common problem situations with teachers, siblings and peers. The peer sessions focus on the difficulties many of these children experience with successfully joining in with the ongoing activities of their peers, and in negotiating with their peers during disagreements.

Peer pressure and involvement with non-deviant peers

The latter sessions primarily address issues related to peer pressure and children's involvement in deviant peer groups. These sessions focus on children's awareness of peer pressure to participate in drug use, and in various peer pressure coping strategies, using videotapes and role-plays. The dangers that can be evident in children's neighbourhoods are addressed by having children complete neighbourhood surveys, emphasizing dangers that can lead to peer pressure to engage in deviant behaviour or that can lead to violence. These sessions also assist children in thinking about where they stand in existing peer groups in their schools and their neighborhoods, and how they can become progressively more involved with less deviant groups of peers.

Examples of intervention programmes for conduct problem behaviour

In the following sections, we will present information about a set of intervention programmes that have been used with children with conduct problems (for greater detail, see Smith *et al.*, 2005; Lochman, 2006, 2003; Lochman *et al.*, 2006b, 2009b). The section is organized into three age periods (preschool and early elementary school years, late elementary school years, early adolescence in the middle school years). Within each age range, programmes are organized into those which are universal prevention programmes (typically delivered in the school setting) and those which have been used as treatments for diagnosed disruptive behaviour disorders (DBDs) or as targeted prevention programmes for those at-risk children who are beginning to display the early stages of the disorder. Although all of these programmes have some degree of empirical support, the degree of evidence for their ability to reduce conduct problems varies.

Intervention in preschool and early childhood

Universal prevention programmes

Good Behavior Game
The Good Behavior Game was created by Barrish and colleagues (1969). The prevention focuses on increasing children's acceptance of authority and rules within the school classroom, and is based on operant conditioning (see Chapter 8). The Good Behavior Game is taught to children and is not a curriculum-based intervention (Barrish *et al.*, 1969; Embry, 2002).

Children in the classroom are divided into teams, and a scoreboard is kept to indicate which teams have accrued the fewest 'fouls' (a foul being a rule that is broken). Rewards are given to the team with the fewest fouls, and smaller rewards are given to teams that have earned a number of fouls below an established threshold (Embry, 2002). In several studies comparing the effects of the Good Behavior Game and another intervention designed to increase family and school communication and partnership, the Good Behavior Game yielded the strongest results for the reduction of aggressive behaviour, poor achievement and shy behaviours (Ialongo *et al.*, 1999; Embry, 2002).

Promoting Alternative Thinking Strategies
The Promoting Alternative Thinking Strategies (PATHS) programme is an example of a universal prevention programme that seeks to promote general social-emotional competencies and cognitive skill-building in elementary school children (Greenberg & Kusché, 2006). Greenberg and colleagues train teachers to use PATHS to instruct children in emotion awareness, emotional regulation and social problem-solving skills (Kusché & Greenberg, 1994). Although the PATHS curriculum has been implemented primarily with children in regular education classrooms, it has also been used with children with special needs (e.g. behaviourally at-risk or deaf children). Overall, the results

at 1- and 2-year follow-ups have indicated that children receiving the PATHS intervention were better at understanding emotions, better at problem-solving and reported decreases in conduct problems and impulsivity compared with children in a control group (Greenberg *et al.*, 2001, 2006).

Second Step Program

The primary goal of the Second Step Program is to prevent impulsive and aggressive behaviour by teaching social competence and thus increasing prosocial behaviour. Skill areas targeted are anger management, empathy and impulse control. Exercises that encourage generalization are built into each session (Grossman *et al.*, 1997). Outcome research for the elementary school programme has indicated increased knowledge and improved skills in anger management, impulse control, empathy, social problem-solving and conflict resolution. Comparisons of intervention versus control schools indicated that the schools did not differ significantly on parent and teacher behaviour ratings scales. However, behavioural observations did yield a decrease in physical aggression immediately following the universal intervention and at a 6-month follow-up. In addition, increases in prosocial behaviour were noted through behavioural observations (Grossman *et al.*, 1997). Smaller-scale studies comparing one intervention school and one control school have found significant increases in teacher-rated social competence and decreases in teacher-rated antisocial behaviour at the intervention school (Taub, 2001).

Treatment and targeted prevention programmes

Dinosaur School – child training

This programme was initially developed as part of a larger preventive intervention designed to examine the relative and additive effectiveness of parent training and child training for 4–7-year-olds with early-onset conduct problems (Webster-Stratton & Hammond, 1997). The child component, which is referred to as 'Dinosaur School', addresses issues that young children with conduct problems frequently face: social skills problems, an inability to emotionally empathize or engage in perspective-taking, effective conflict resolution and dealing with feelings of loneliness, stress and anger.

An analysis of treatment groups revealed that the child training led to a significant reduction in the number of conduct problems reported in the home and increases in social problem-solving skills in comparison to controls (Webster-Stratton & Hammond, 1997). Moreover, at 1-year follow-up, nearly two-thirds of the children in the child treatment group had parent ratings of behavioural problems in the normal rather than clinically significant range. The Dinosaur School has been examined as one component within the multicomponent Incredible Years programme (see Chapter 11).

Intervention in later childhood

Universal prevention programmes

Seattle Social Development Project (SSDP)

The SSDP is a universal prevention designed to reduce aggression by creating a positive school environment. This prevention programme has been predominantly used for public elementary schools serving high-crime areas of Seattle, Washington state, USA. The SSDP includes training for teachers to increase the use of non-punitive classroom behavioural management such as positive reinforcement, and more recent versions of the intervention have also included parent training and child problem-solving and social skills training (Hawkins *et al.*, 1999; Berryhill & Prinz, 2003).

Longitudinal research conducted with the SSDP has found significant prevention or reductions of alcohol use (Hawkins *et al.*, 1999; Lonczak *et al.*, 2001), reductions in delinquency, a lower frequency of sexual intercourse and number of sexual partners, and decreased reports of pregnancy for females and causing pregnancy for males (Hawkins *et al.*, 1999). In addition, students receiving the prevention reported more positive feelings and commitment to school compared with the control groups, improved academic achievement and less student-reported school misbehaviour (Hawkins *et al.*, 1999).

Positive Behavior Supports

A fairly new, but rapidly growing, approach to the universal promotion of students' positive social and academic functioning is the school-wide application of Positive Behavior Support (PBS, also known as Positive Behavior Interventions and Supports; Sugai & Horner, 2002). The PBS approach has an established record of reducing challenging behaviours in children with developmental and intellectual disabilities, and research is beginning to emerge supporting the effectiveness of PBS as a school-wide preventive intervention to reduce the incidence of problem behaviours and increase student learning. An example of a school-wide or universal application of PBS is the 'teaching recess', in which workshops are held for the entire school, including staff and students, outlining positive behavioural expectations for break-times. Following such an intervention, recess-related office referrals were found to decrease by 80% (Todd *et al.*, 2002).

Bullying Prevention Program

The Bullying Prevention Program was a nationwide universal preventive intervention conducted in Norway. The programme's objectives include reducing the acceptance of bullying among children and school staff and improving school supervision and deterrence of bullying through instilling awareness with booklets, providing suggestions for preventing bullying, initiating classroom meetings and using videos (Berryhill & Prinz, 2003; Olweus, 1993). Results from the 42 elementary and middle schools in Norway showed at least a 50% decrease in bullying and decreased reports of delinquency including vandalism, fighting, intoxication, theft and truancy. Impressively, the results indicated even greater positive effects at a 2-year follow-up compared with a 1-year follow-up (Olweus, 1992; Greenberg *et al.*, 2001).

Child Development Project (CDP)
The CDP's main objective is to increase children's respect and responsibility within the auspice of creating a caring school community (Lewis *et al.*, 2003). Some of the components include cooperative learning where students are encouraged to work together (rather than compete), non-punitive discipline, reading activities, cross-grade 'buddies' activities where older and younger students are paired together to complete activities, parent activities for home use, and community-building activities, which involve all the students, parents, teachers and staff working together within a school (Berryhill & Prinz, 2003; Lewis *et al.*, 2003).

Overall, the results indicate that students in schools that had a high fidelity of curriculum implementation had increases in personal, social and ethical values and attitudes relative to control schools and schools that did not implement the curriculum with a high degree of fidelity (Solomon *et al.*, 2000). Three- and 4-year follow-ups of schools with a high degree of programme fidelity had reductions in many measures of substance use and delinquency compared with control schools (Solomon *et al.*, 2000; Berryhill & Prinz, 2003).

Treatment and targeted prevention programmes

Problem Solving Skills Training
Problem Solving Skills Training (PSST) is probably one of the most extensively researched cognitive-behavioural treatments for antisocial behaviour in childhood (Kazdin *et al.*, 1987). The programme itself focuses on teaching and reinforcing prosocial problem-solving skills among children with disruptive behaviour disorders in order to promote their ability to effectively manage potentially volatile interpersonal situations. Research examining the PSST programme has indicated that it is superior to non-directive relationship therapy and control conditions in reducing global measures of externalizing and internalizing problems, including aggression, and increasing social activities and overall school adjustment among psychiatric impatient children (Kazdin *et al.*, 1987).

A subsequent study also revealed that the addition of an in vivo practice component to PSST can help to improve children's social and behavioural functioning at school, but this effect was found only post treatment and not at 1-year follow-up. Despite this finding, both the original and the modified PSST were more effective in reducing disruptive behaviours and increasing prosocial activities both at home and in school in comparison to non-directive behaviour therapy, and these effects remained at 1-year follow-up (Kazdin *et al.*, 1989). The effectiveness of PSST in reducing children's reports of aggression and delinquency was also evident in a subsequent study in which PSST was one component in a large intervention (Kazdin *et al.*, 1992; see Chapter 11).

Anger Coping programme
The Anger Coping programme was developed as a targeted prevention programme for at-risk aggressive children, but it has been used in clinical settings as well. The programme a structured manual outlining each of the programme's activities (Lochman *et al.*, 1999; Larson & Lochman, 2002) and consists of 18 weekly sessions. The programme was delivered in small school-based groups in the intervention research studies but has been used in individually based interventions.

Initial promising pilot research had found that aggressive children receiving the Anger Coping programme in school settings had reductions in teacher-rated aggression (Lochman *et al.*, 1981). Subsequent studies that randomly assigned aggressive children to Anger Coping or to control or alternate intervention conditions (two lists were created based on rank orderings from teachers' aggression ratings, and the lists were randomly assigned to intervention or to control) found that aggressive children had lower rates of aggressive-disruptive off-task classroom behaviour according to independent observers, had lower parent- and teacher-rated aggressive behaviour, and had higher rates of perceived social competence or self-esteem (Lochman *et al.*, 1984, 1989; Lochman & Curry, 1986). When an adaptation of the Anger Coping programme was used with aggressive-rejected boys, similar reductions in problem behaviours were evident (Lochman *et al.*, 1993b).

Examination of the longer-term preventive effects of the programme have shown indicators of maintenance of gains and preventive effects but have also found that some other behavioural gains were not maintained (Lochman, 1992). Compared with untreated controls and non-aggressive boys, programme participants had higher levels of self-esteem, lower rates of irrelevant solutions to problems on a problem-solving measure and lower rates of alcohol, marijuana and other drug use at a follow-up 3 years after the intervention. On these follow-up measures, the programme participants were functioning in a range comparable to the non-aggressive boys, indicating a preventive effect for substance use and a relative normalization of self-esteem and social problem-solving skills.

Intervention in early adolescence

Universal prevention programmes

Life Skills Training

The Life Skills Training Programme is an example of a universal prevention programme designed to prevent substance abuse in adolescents (Botvin & Griffin, 2004). The programme was developed for middle-school students. It is implemented across 15 class periods during the first year of middle school (11–14 years of age), with supplemental booster sessions during the following 2 years. Cognitive-behavioural skills training techniques are used to teach students personal self-management skills, social skills and drug resistance skills. The programme has been shown to be highly effective in reducing alcohol, tobacco, marijuana and polydrug use in a series of randomized controlled efficacy trials and in two effectiveness studies. Evaluation results support the long-term effectiveness of the programme as well as its generalizability to diverse geographical, socioeconomic and racial/ethnic groups.

Responding in Peaceful and Positive Ways

Responding in Peaceful and Positive Ways (RIPP) interventionists teach middle-school adolescents problem-solving steps, better communication skills and achievement techniques to aid in the promotion of non-violence. The original RIPP programme is used with 6th-grade students (a mean age of 11 years; Farrell *et al.*, 2001), and a newer version was developed for 7th-grade students (a mean age of 12; Farrell *et al.*, 2003). Teens are encouraged to internalize these skills through repetition and mentally rehearsing problem-solving steps, experiential learning and didactic teaching (Farrell *et al.*, 2001).

Results show that teens in the RIPP intervention had decreases in school punishment for engaging in violent acts, including fewer suspensions, compared with teens in the control groups. Gender differences were found as boys maintained fewer suspensions compared with the control group 1 year later, whereas girls did not maintain a significantly different number of suspensions compared with controls. Adolescents in the RIPP programme also indicated that they used peer mediation more frequently than controls. Overall, students who had the highest rates of disruptive behaviours prior to receiving the prevention achieved the greatest benefit from RIPP (Farrell *et al.*, 2001, 2003).

Positive Youth Development

Positive Youth Development (PYD) is a universal preventive intervention created to increase adolescents' personal and social competence during the 6th and 7th grades (ages 11–14). Sessions specifically cover topics including stress management, self-esteem, problem-solving, substances and health information, assertiveness and social networks (Caplan *et al.*, 1992). Studies comparing RIPP with control groups found that teens receiving the intervention improved in positively solving conflicts, impulse control and popularity according to teacher ratings. Teens in the RIPP groups also reported increases in the use of problem-solving, and decreases in the intent to use substances and alcohol (Caplan *et al.*, 1992; Greenberg *et al.*, 2003).

School Transitional Environment Project
The School Transitional Environment Project (STEP) targets adolescents' adaptation skills during transitional stages such as the transition from elementary to middle school, and the transition from middle school to high school. One of the main components of STEP is reorganizing the school social system, including creating smaller class sizes and maintaining a consistent set of peers. STEP also restructures the home-room teacher's role by encouraging the teacher to be the main communicator between the parents and the school, and overall teacher support is increased (Felner *et al.*, 2001).

A long-term follow-up of middle-school and high-school students receiving STEP indicate a 50% reduction in drop-out rates and significant increases in school achievement and attendance (Felner *et al.*, 1993). In particular, when fidelity to treatment methods are high, STEP has been found to incite a 'whole-school' change in which socioemotional, behavioural and academic difficulties, developmental competency and adaptation are all significantly improved compared with control groups (Felner *et al.*, 1993, 2001).

Treatment and targeted prevention programmes

The Art of Self-control
This cognitive and behaviourally oriented group (and individual) adolescent control programme is described in a session-by-session format in Feindler and Ecton (1986). The group programme consists of 12 sessions lasting from 45 to 90 minutes once weekly in outpatient settings and twice weekly in residential treatment settings. The groups typically consist of 8–12 members, and the leaders may come from a variety of settings, (e.g. child care workers, counsellors, nurses, probation officers, psychiatrists, psychologists, social workers, teachers or even involved parents). This programme uses SIT and provides training in relaxation, self-instruction, the use of coping statements, assertiveness, self-monitoring of anger and conflictual situations, and problem-solving.

Outcome research for this programme has indicated reductions in aggressive and disruptive behaviour and improvements in problem-solving abilities, social skills, cognitive reflectivity and adult-rated impulsivity and self-control (Feindler & Ecton, 1986). The populations examined included adolescents who had experienced fairly extreme or chronic histories of aggression (e.g. adolescents at an in-school junior high-school programme for multisuspended and delinquent youth, adolescents at an inpatient psychiatric facility).

This programme also has been adapted for use primarily with incarcerated adolescents. This adaptation, called Anger Control Training, is part of a larger programme (Aggression Replacement Training) aimed to help reduce adolescent aggression. A detailed description of this programme (in a session-by-session format) can be found in Goldstein and Glick (1994).

Summary points

- Historical antecedents of CBT include the clinical and research work of Bandura on observational learning, and of Rotter and Mischel on cognitive expectancies for reward outcomes.
- The developmental psychologists Luria and Vugotsky described how children's guiding self-statements go 'underground' as they develop and become thoughts that guide their behaviour.
- In part, CBT attempts to establish these 'underground' inhibitory self-statements.
- Key elements of most CBT programmes include a focus on children's behavioural goals, emotional awareness and self-regulation, perspective-taking and attribution retraining, social problem-solving skill training and avoidance of deviant peer processes.
- Some effective universal prevention programmes have been used to train teachers to provide clear consequences for behaviour (e.g. the Good Behavior Game) and to stimulate children's social-emotional development (e.g. PATHS).
- Social problem-solving is a key aspect of most evidence-based CBT programmes for conduct problem children (e.g. PSST and Anger Coping), and is typically delivered through discussion, role-play, homework exercises and the creation of therapeutic products such as videos.

10

Pharmacotherapy

Although this chapter on pharmacotherapy is briefer than the chapters on psychotherapeutic interventions, this does not imply that pharmacological treatment is less important. On the contrary, the treatment of disruptive behaviour disorders (DBDs) increasingly includes pharmacotherapy. The number of psychotherapeutic interventions, however, is much larger than the number of medications that have been proven to be efficacious in children with DBDs.

We will first discuss some general issues on pharmacological treatment in children with DBDs. Then we will present research on the use of psychostimulants, specifically methylphenidate, to reduce symptoms of attention deficit/hyperactivity disorder (ADHD) and disruptive symptoms in children with DBD and comorbid ADHD, and in children with DBD and symptoms of ADHD. Other agents then are discussed, for example atomoxetine, atypical neuroleptics and mood stabilizers, which may be used in children with both disorders and in children with DBD only.

General issues

Although there is no licensed medication for the treatment of the DBDs, pharmacotherapy has in recent years become an important part of treatment of the DBDs. On the one hand, we have increased our knowledge about the effectiveness and adverse effects of medications for the treatment of DBDs, and about the underlying neurobiological mechanisms indicating how drugs work. On the other hand, however, there remain concerns about the safety of medication on the developing brain.

Among the principles of medication management in the DBDs, the first one is thus that pharmacotherapy should only be considered when strictly

Oppositional Defiant Disorder and Conduct Disorder in Childhood   By Walter Matthys and
John E. Lochman
© 2010 John Wiley & Sons, Ltd.

necessary. Specifically, psychopharmacological treatment is not indicated in mild forms of DBDs with or without ADHD since there are concerns about the long-term effects of medications on brain development in children (see, for example, Volkow & Insel, 2003). However, withholding medication from a child while he or she is suffering from a severe DBD with or without ADHD is also inappropriate as the negative consequences for both the child and his or her environment may be huge. These sequelae can include the negative impact of persistent criticism and harsh punishment on the child's emotions and cognitions, and the risk of a number of negative outcomes such as child abuse, school drop-out, substance use disorders, delinquency, depression and personality disorders. Symptoms in children with DBD can have a negative impact on siblings, peers, parents and teachers. Thus, the clinician, together with the parents, needs to make a balanced decision between decreasing the risk of negative short-term and long-term outcomes against the uncertainty about the possible but not clearly documented long-term effects of medication on brain development.

Second, pharmacotherapy never should be the only treatment method; instead, pharmacotherapy should be one of the multiple components of treatment. The clinician hopes that the addition of medication to behavioural parent training (see Chapter 8) and cognitive-behavioural therapy (see Chapter 9) will result in a greater effect of these methods. Thus, the improvement in parental skills may have a larger impact on the child's disruptive behaviour when the child attends better to parental instructions due to medication. Similarly, medications that support the child's weakly developed inhibitory capabilities may increase the child's opportunities to actually use in everyday life the cognitive skills that he or she has learned in cognitive-behavioural therapy. Unfortunately, interactions between mechanisms targeted by psychotherapeutic methods and targeted by pharmacotherapy have not yet been examined.

Third, the clinician should start a medication trial only after an assessment of the child and his family has been completed (see Chapter 6). Thus, it is crucial to know whether the child has been diagnosed not only with a DBD, but also with comorbid ADHD or has a large number of ADHD symptoms. More evidence-based medications are available for the pharmacotherapy of ADHD than of DBDs.

Fourth, the target behaviours and associated impairment in social and academic functioning need to be defined. These target behaviours should be considered as part of one of the DBDs, one of the subtypes of ADHD or both. For example, impulsive, reactive aggression may be part of oppositional defiant disorder (ODD). However, a mild form of reactive aggression may be part of the ADHD hyperactive/impulsive type as well. When present in a severe form, reactive aggression may be indicative of comorbid conduct disorder (CD) and ADHD or of CD alone. The evaluation of the effects of medication should be done within the context of the child's disorder(s), as different medications and higher doses may be needed to affect the targeted behaviours.

Finally, it is important to assess the effect of medication on target behaviours and to assess the side-effects. As a result, a medication should first be introduced as a single intervention and not together with another treatment method or an adaptation of another treatment method. Various outcome tools such as the revised Conners' Rating Scales (CRS-R; Conners, 1997; see Chapter 6) and the Swanson Nolan and Pelham-IV (SNAP-IV; Swanson, 1995) are available to assess the effectiveness of a medication.

Psychostimulants

As already discussed in Chapter 5, the frontostriatal, frontocerebellar and frontoamygdalar circuits are dysfunctional in children with ADHD. Dopamine is one of the important neurotransmitters involved in these neurocircuits, and dopaminergic function is impaired in children with ADHD. Methylphenidate, the most frequently used psychostimulant in the pharmacological treatment of ADHD, blocks the dopamine transporter. This indirect dopamine agonistic effect may be critical for its therapeutic effects (Volkow *et al.*, 1998, 2002). In addition, methylphenidate also blocks the noradrenaline (norepinephrine) transporter, and there is increasing awareness that this property of methylphenidate contributes to its therapeutic effects in ADHD (Biederman & Spencer, 1999; Arnsten, 2006). Thus, by stimulating dopaminergic and noradrenergic neurotransmission, psychostimulant drugs may enhance the functions of the above-mentioned circuits, resulting in improved inhibition and working memory.

A large number of studies have documented robust effects of methylphenidate and other psychostimulants such as dextroamphetamine on the core symptoms of ADHD. Methylphenidate is the first-choice medication, but if methylphenidate is not efficacious, dexamphetamine is an alternative. According to a meta-analysis conducted in 1983, the mean effect size of methylphenidate in school-age children with ADHD is 0.98 (Ottenbacher & Cooper, 1983). The efficacy of methylphenidate in preschool children with ADHD has been demonstrated in the Preschool ADHD Treatment Study (PATS; Greenhill *et al.*, 2006). The presence of ODD as a comorbid disorder has not affected the efficacy of methylphenidate on ADHD symptoms in preschoolers with ADHD (Ghuman *et al.*, 2007) or in school-age children with ADHD (Jensen *et al.*, 2001a). The effect sizes in preschool children who have ADHD and low comorbidity (e.g. only ODD) are similar to the effect sizes in school-age children (Ghuman *et al.*, 2007).

The effect of psychostimulants on disruptive behaviours has been examined in a number of studies and in one meta-analysis. In an important study on the effect of methylphenidate on disruptive behaviours, 6 of 38 children had disruptive symptoms but no symptoms of inattention and hyperactivity, 9 of 38 children had symptoms of inattention and hyperactivity but no disruptive symptoms, and 23 children had both disruptive symptoms and symptoms of inattention and hyperactivity (Taylor *et al.*, 1987). Methylphenidate was an effective treatment for many children with disruptive behaviour. In this study, hyperactivity was the predictor of the effectiveness of methylphenidate. Specifically, it was hyperactivity rather than defiance that predicted the degree to which defiance was reduced. Interestingly, the diagnosis of ADHD did not predict outcome. This study suggests that methylphenidate is indicated in children with DBDs and ADHD symptoms, even when a formal diagnosis of ADHD is not given. In contrast, as suggested by the authors, children with DBDs with none of the features of inattention and hyperactivity are unlikely to respond well to methylphenidate. In conclusion, this study demonstrates that psychostimulants affect disruptive behaviour in children with symptoms of ADHD but without a formal diagnosis of ADHD.

The effectiveness of methylphenidate in the treatment of children with ADHD comorbid with DBDs was also demonstrated in the Multimodal Treatment Study of Children with ADHD (MTA) (Jensen *et al.*, 2001a). In this study, school-age children with ADHD and comorbid disorders (ODD/CD, anxiety disorders or both) were treated with methylphenidate, behavioural treatment, a combination of both or community care. Children with ADHD only and children with ADHD comorbid with ODD/CD responded well to methylphenidate and did not differ in their response to methylphenidate either in terms of inattentive, hyperactive-impulsive symptoms or in terms of oppositional/aggressive symptoms. However, children with ADHD and both ODD/CD and anxiety disorders responded best to the combination of methylphenidate and behaviour therapy.

Connor *et al.* (2002) have conducted a meta-analysis of the effect size for psychostimulants on overt and covert aggression-related behaviours in children and adolescents with ADHD. In 24 of the 28 studies reviewed, ADHD was the primary diagnosis; of the 24 studies in which ADHD was the primary disorder, 17 studies had CD or ODD as a comorbid diagnosis. In two studies CD was the primary diagnosis with ADHD as comorbid disorder, and in two studies mental retardation was the primary diagnosis with ADHD and CD as comorbid disorders. The overall weighted mean effect size was 0.84 for overt aggression and 0.69 for covert aggression. However, in studies in which ADHD was the primary diagnosis, an increased prevalence of either ODD or CD led to diminished effect sizes for overt aggression. Thus, although psychostimulants affected aggression in children with ADHD, ODD and CD appeared to moderate the effect.

There is one well-conducted study on the efficacy of methylphenidate in children and adolescents with CD; two-thirds of the children and adolescents also met the criteria for ADHD (Klein *et al.*, 1997b). Methylphenidate was shown to reduce antisocial behaviour. This effect was independent of the severity of the children's initial ADHD symptoms, which is contrary to the findings of the study by Taylor *et al.* (1987). Thus, Klein *et al.*'s study shows an independent influence of methylphenidate on antisocial behaviour. The authors propose that the effect of methylphenidate on antisocial behaviour in children and adolescents with CD is the result of their enhanced impulse control.

Based on these studies, we conclude that psychostimulants reduce DBD symptoms in children with DBDs comorbid with ADHD, as well as in children with DBDs and symptoms of ADHD. In algorithms, it is sometimes proposed that psychostimulants be used only in children with DBDs comorbid with ADHD (Kutcher *et al.*, 2004). However, the studies discussed above suggest that psychostimulants may decrease disruptive behaviours even in children with a high number of ADHD symptoms who do not qualify for a formal diagnosis of ADHD. Therefore we suggest that a trial with psychostimulants is also appropriate in children with DBDs and at least four symptoms of one of the subtypes of ADHD. The mechanisms of this treatment effect are, however, unclear. It may be that the effect of psychostimulants on disruptive behaviour is mediated by the enhancement of functioning of not only the neurocircuits affected in ADHD, but also the neurocircuits affected in DBDs.

Methylphenidate can be given in a fast-release form (acting for 3–4 hours) and in slow-release/long-acting forms (acting for up to 10–12 hours or 6–8 hours), with the latter being increasingly used in clinical practice. There is also a long-acting formulation of mixed amphetamine salts (see Banaschewski *et al.*, 2006). The studies on methylphenidate discussed above were on the efficacy of the short-release form of methylphenidate. However, the effect of long-acting methylphenidate on ODD/CD symptoms in children and adolescents with ADHD has also been demonstrated in a study in which almost two-thirds of the sample with ADHD were diagnosed with ODD or CD (Sinzig *et al.*, 2007).

Methylphenidate has adverse effects such as difficulty falling asleep, a decrease in appetite and an increase in irritability; the latter often temporary. There are probably more adverse effects in preschooler children than in school-age children (Wigal *et al.*, 2006). Since the mean optimal dose for preschoolers is slightly lower than that for school-age children (Greenhill *et al.*, 2006), starting with lower doses of methylphenidate may improve tolerability in preschooler children (Greenhill *et al.*, 2008). Finally, there is now clear evidence of an increased risk of growth retardation in both school-age children and preschoolers, perhaps as a result of increased dopamine levels reaching the pituitary (Wigal *et al.*, 2006; Swanson *et al.*, 2007).

Atomoxetine

When psychostimulants are not effective with a specific child, or when there are severe adverse effects such as tics, a serious decrease in appetite or sleep problems, atomoxetine is the second-choice medication for treatment.

Atomoxetine is a noradrenaline transporter inhibitor; its therapeutic effects are thought to be mediated by augmenting noradrenergic and, indirectly, dopaminergic neurotransmission in the prefrontal cortex (Bymaster *et al.*, 2002).

A number of studies have shown the efficacy of atomoxetine in the treatment of ADHD. For example, in children and adolescents with ADHD (of whom one in five had comorbid ODD), the effect size on the primary outcome measure of once-daily administration of atomoxetine was 0.71 (Michelson *et al.*, 2002). However, studies have shown inconsistent effects of atomoxetine on DBD symptoms in children who have ADHD and comorbid DBDs. In one study in which 39% of children and adolescents with ADHD were diagnosed with comorbid ODD, not only was there an improvement in both ADHD and ODD symptoms, but also treatment response was similar in youth with and without ODD (Newcorn *et al.*, 2005). Thus, as noted by the authors, ODD does not adversely affect the treatment of ADHD with medication, consistent with the conclusions from the MTA study. Indeed, medication treatment targeting ADHD also leads to an improvement in ODD. Of note, the reduction in ODD symptoms was highly related to the magnitude of the ADHD response, which is consistent with results of Taylor *et al.*'s (1987) study on psychostimulants. In contrast, in a study involving children with both ADHD and ODD, atomoxetine did not reduce the severity of ODD symptoms, whereas it was effective for the treatment of ADHD (Kaplan *et al.*, 2004).

As ADHD is typically treated over extended periods, studies have examined the long-term efficacy of atomoxetine treatment. In one study in which 43% of the children and adolescents were diagnosed with ODD, atomoxetine was superior to placebo in maintaining a response for the ensuing 9 months in children who responded well to initial treatment (Michelson *et al.*, 2004). Indeed, compared with patients in the placebo group, atomoxetine-treated patients had lesser symptoms of ADHD, lower oppositional behaviour and superior psychosocial functioning after 9 months. It was also shown that comorbid ODD did not alter the rate of relapse in ADHD symptoms and psychosocial functioning (Hazell *et al.*, 2006).

Finally, the efficacy of atomoxetine was examined in a pilot study with 5- and 6-year-old children with ADHD (Kratochvil *et al.*, 2007). Half of the children were also diagnosed with ODD. In this open-label study, atomoxetine was effective for reducing ADHD symptoms.

In conclusion, atomoxetine is efficacious in the treatment of ADHD, even in children who have comorbid ODD, and there is evidence that atomoxetine also leads to an improvement in ODD.

Atypical antipsychotics

Antipsychotics such as haloperidol have been shown to reduce aggression in hospitalized children with CD (e.g. Campbell *et al.*, 1984). However, extrapyramidal symptoms including acute dystonic reactions and parkinsonism are clear adverse effects of haloperidol. Therefore, the efficacy and adverse effects of atypical neuroleptics such as risperidone have been investigated. Risperidone blocks dopamine as well as serotonin receptors.

A large number of studies have been conducted on the short-term and long-term efficacy of risperidone. For example, in a small study, the short-term effect of risperidone was demonstrated to be superior to that of placebo in ameliorating aggression in children and adolescents with CD (Findling *et al.*, 2000). Likewise, risperidone appeared to be effective in reducing aggression in a study of children with subaverage intelligence and DBDs (Snyder *et al.*, 2002) and in a study of adolescents with subaverage intelligence and severe aggression (Buitelaar *et al.*, 2001). However, treatment with risperidone is compromised with adversive effects. Therefore, studies on long-term efficacy and safety are crucial.

In a study in which risperidone treatment lasted for 48 months, there were no extrapyramidal symptoms and no cases of tardive dyskinesia (Findling *et al.*, 2004). However, weight gain occurred in one of five children. In another treatment study with children and adolescents with ODD, weight initially increased but then plateaued over a 6-month maintenance period (Reyes *et al.*, 2006). The subjects in this study were also involved in a further 1-year extension follow-up (Haas *et al.*, 2008). No subject developed tardive dyskinesia, and weight gain was reported in 4.3% of the subjects. Prolactin levels tended to increase with risperidone, although this effect diminished with prolonged use. There were no relevant changes in glucose or lipid metabolism.

Nevertheless, there remain concerns about risks of diabetes, dyslipidaemia and sexual side-effects related to hyperprolactinaemia, such as amenorrhoea and breast symptoms (enlargement, pain, galactorrhoea) (Correll, 2008). Therefore, laboratory assessments should be used to monitor these side-effects (Correll, 2008).

There are other atypical antipsychotics such as quetiapine for which there is preliminary evidence of efficacy in children with DBDs (Findling *et al.*, 2006). Finally, in clinical practice, atypical antipsychotics are sometimes combined with a psychostimulant (Findling *et al.*, 2007).

In conclusion, although the efficacy of atypical antipsychotics in the treatment of DBDs has been clearly demonstrated, concerns about the long-term effect on the brain (Andersen *et al.*, 2002) suggest that these agents should only be used for a limited time period.

Other medications

When the above-mentioned medications are not effective in a particular child, other agents with less clear evidence of efficacy have been used. Lithium, a mood stabilizer used to treat mania, has antiaggressive properties, probably mediated by its effects on serotonergic activity in the brain. Various studies have shown the efficacy of lithium in reducing aggression in children and adolescents with CD (Campbell *et al.*, 1984, 1995; Malone *et al.*, 2000), although one study failed to demonstrate an efficacy of lithium in adolescents with CD (Rifkin *et al.*, 1997). Typically, these studies have been conducted with hospitalized patients, as close blood monitoring is necessary during treatment.

Clonidine is an adrenergic agonist that has proven to be efficacious in the treatment of ADHD. In a meta-analysis, it was shown that the effect size of clonidine wais 0.58 on symptoms of ADHD (Connor *et al.*, 1999). Thus, clonidine appears to be less effective than psychostimulants and atomoxetine. Moreover, clonidine treatment is associated with a high prevalence of side-effects, including sedation and irritability. A study has also examined whether the addition of clonidine to ongoing psychostimulant therapy in children and adolescents with ADHD and either ODD or CD would result in a decrease of hyperactivity and conduct problems (Hazell & Stuart, 2003). It appeared that the combination of psychostimulants and clonidine reduced conduct symptoms but not hyperactivity symptoms.

Valproate is an anticonvulsant that is used in the treatment of bipolar disorder. It has also been shown to be an efficacious treatment for explosive temper and mood lability in children and adolescents with DBDs (Donovan *et al.*, 2000).

Summary points

- Pharmacotherapy is never the only method used to treat children with DBDs.
- Psychostimulants are efficacious in reducing DBD symptoms in children with DBDs comorbid with ADHD, as well as in children with DBDs and symptoms of ADHD.
- A trial with psychostimulants is appropriate in children with DBDs and comorbid ADHD and in children with DBDs who also have at least four symptoms of ADHD but do not qualify for a formal diagnosis of ADHD.
- Atomoxetine is efficacious in the treatment of ADHD, even in children who have comorbid ODD, and there is evidence that atomoxetine also leads to an improvement in ODD.
- Risperidone is effective in reducing aggression in children with DBDs, but treatment with risperidone is compromised by adverse effects and there are concerns about the effect of this and other atypical antipsychotics on the developing brain of children. Therefore these agents should be used only for a limited time period.
- Other medications for which there is some evidence of an effect are lithium, clonidine in addition to psychostimulants, and valproate.

11

Multicomponent intervention

In this chapter, we will discuss multicomponent interventions for children with conduct problems, describing the rationale for these programmes and providing relevant example programmes for developmental periods of childhood through early adolescence.

Need for multiple components

Hawkins *et al.* (1992) suggested that a promising line for intervention research lay in testing interventions that targeted multiple early risk factors for antisocial behaviour. In one series of studies, Kazdin and his colleagues (Kazdin *et al.*, 1987, 1992) combined behavioural parent training with cognitive problem-solving skills training for preadolescents to reduce antisocial behaviour in children. The combined intervention was more effective than either parent training or problem-solving skills training alone in placing a greater proportion of children within the range of normal functioning. These results were maintained at a 1-year follow-up. In general, multicomponent programmes are more effective than programmes that provide intervention only to the child with disruptive behaviour problems (for a detailed discussion, see Lochman, 2009b).

Multicomponent interventions are not restricted to those which use parent-focused programmes and child-focused programmes, but they could also include a focus on a broad range of community-level risk factors. Pentz and colleagues (Pentz *et al.*, 1989; Johnson *et al.*, 1990) developed a multicomponent programme including a 10-session school programme emphasizing drug use resistance skills for children in grade 6 or 7. It included homework sessions with children and parents, the training of parents in positive parent–child communication skills, the training of community leaders and mass media

Oppositional Defiant Disorder and Conduct Disorder in Childhood   By Walter Matthys and
John E. Lochman
© 2010 John Wiley & Sons, Ltd.

coverage. Randomly assigned control schools received only the latter two components. Three years after their involvement, children in the programme had reduced prevalence rates of monthly cigarette smoking and marijuana use. These results were obtained for both high-risk and low-risk children.

Multicomponent programmes can be as important in settings with intensive treatment, such as residential, inpatient and day-treatment settings, as in the more commonly considered outpatient and school settings. The various evidence-based methods for working with children and their families can be used together to integrate and strengthen the learning processes that residential treatment and day treatment can foster (Matthys, 1997).

It is important to consider that multicomponent interventions can involve the combination of psychopharmacotherapy and psychosocial treatments. The Multimodal Treatment Study of Children with ADHD (MTA) is a useful example of this type of multicomponent study involving children with attention deficit/hyperactivity disorder (ADHD; Jensen *et al*, 2001b). Children with ADHD in the MTA study were randomly assigned to medication management, to behavioural treatment (parent training, a summer treatment programme, a behavioural classroom aide or teacher consultation), to a combination of the two treatments or to community care. The combination treatment did not add to the effect of medication alone in influencing ADHD symptoms. However, the combination of treatments did produce a small advantage over medication in reducing children's oppositional behaviour (Jensen *et al.*, 2001b), and produced significant improvements in positive and constructive parenting, in comparison to medication and community care (Wells *et al.*, 2006).

Although the results of these and other multicomponent studies are encouraging, that is not always the case. In a programme that included parent and youth components, Dishion and Andrews (1995) raised troubling concerns about possible iatrogenic effects of child-focused group interventions. Adolescents in 6th–8th grades and their parents were randomly assigned to parent focus only, teen focus only, combined parent and teen focus and a control condition for self-directed change. These four groups were also compared to a quasi-experimental control group that was not randomly assigned. Interventions involved 12 weekly 90-minute sessions. Both the children's and the parents' interventions produced reductions in coercive behaviour by children and parents during observed parent–child interactions. However, the parent-only intervention produced short-term behavioural improvements at school (which faded at the 1-year follow-up) while the teen-only intervention produced higher levels of tobacco use and higher teacher-rated behaviour problems by the 1-year follow-up. The teen-only intervention appeared to produce this iatrogenic effect through peer reinforcement of deviant talk during group sessions. These findings were sobering, and suggest that adopting a strategy of 'more is better' is not always productive.

Because of these marked differences in findings, research needs to continue to explore whether, and under which conditions, childhood interventions can augment parental intervention. The ongoing multicomponent studies, such as the Coping Power programme (Lochman & Wells, 1996) and the Fast Track Program (Conduct Problems Prevention Research Group, 1992), which are discussed below, may be useful in generating hypotheses about how the composition, timing and content of childhood intervention programmes may affect outcomes.

Parallel to the structure of Chapter 9, we will in this section of the chapter present information about a set of intervention programmes that have been used with children with conduct problems (Lochman, 2003, 2006; Smith *et al.*, 2005; Lochman *et al.*, 2006b, 2009b). The section is organized into three age periods (preschool and early elementary school years, late elementary school years, early adolescence in the middle-school and early high-school years). Although some of the multicomponent intervention programmes have universal prevention components, there are few multicomponent programmes that focus solely on universal prevention. Thus, with the exception of the Linking the Interests of Families and Teachers (LIFT) programme (Reid & Eddy, 2002) for use throughout the elementary school years, this chapter will primarily address programmes that have been used as treatments for diagnosed disruptive behaviour disorders or as targeted prevention programmes for those at-risk children who are beginning to display the early stages of the disorder (see Chapter 7 for a description of targeted prevention programmes).

Intervention in early childhood

Universal prevention programmes

Linking the interests of families and teachers
The LIFT programme is an example of a multicomponent universal preventive intervention designed to prevent conduct problems (Reid & Eddy, 2002). The programme begins in 1st grade and covers the entire elementary school period. LIFT targets elementary-age schoolchildren and their families who are living in high-risk neighbourhoods. LIFT is a 10-week intervention that includes:

- parent training in consistent limit-setting, effective discipline practices and an active involvement in children's school and social activities;
- a 20-session classroom-based social skills programme designed to increase children's social problem-solving skills and to help children resist negative peer groups;
- a behavioural programme to reduce playground aggression based on the Good Behavior Game (Embry & Straatemeier, 2001);

- systematic communication between teachers and parents regarding school work and classroom behaviour, via a telephone and answering machine installed in each classroom.

In a randomized trial with 671 families, significant improvements in family problem-solving and playground aggression were found following intervention. Children in the intervention group were also significantly less likely to have been arrested by the police and to be using alcohol 30 months following the intervention during the middle-school years. However, differences were not found between the two groups in terms of the frequency and onset of using other substances such as tobacco or marijuana (Reid & Eddy, 2002; Eddy *et al.*, 2003).

Treatment and targeted prevention programmes

The montreal delinquency prevention program
This 2-year intervention consisted of a parent-training component based on the programmes developed by the Oregon Social Learning Center (Patterson, 1982) and a child component consisting of social skills and self-control training that took place in the 2nd and 3rd grades (Tremblay *et al.*, 1996). At a follow-up when the boys were 12 years of age, boys who received the intervention were less likely to have serious adjustment problems in school (Tremblay *et al.*, 1992) and antisocial friends (Vitaro & Tremblay, 1994), and they reported fewer instances of trespassing and stealing (McCord *et al.*, 1994) than untreated boys. Moreover, during adolescence, individuals who received the treatment were less likely to be involved in gangs (Tremblay *et al.*, 1996) and reported lower levels of delinquency and substance use (Tremblay *et al.*, 1995) than the untreated controls.

Since many of these treatment effects emerged at age 12 and remained stable up until the age of 15, the results of this preventive intervention provide substantial evidence that early multicomponent interventions in the elementary school years can produce effects that last throughout adolescence. It should be noted that these effects are for parent and child training combined, making it difficult to interpret the unique effect that the child-centred cognitive-behavioural component or the parent training component had on treatment gains.

Incredible Years
The Incredible Years Training Series was originally developed as a parent training intervention for the treatment of DBDs in young children (see Chapter 8). The series also includes a child training programme, Dinosaur School (see Chapter 9), and a teacher component (Webster-Stratton, 2005b). The teacher curriculum includes strategies for strengthening home–school connections, improving teachers' classroom management skills, fostering

teachers' use of effective discipline strategies, reinforcing prosocial child behaviours, and increasing teachers' ability to teach and reinforce social-emotional skills in the classroom. The Incredible Years Training Series has also been adapted for use as a targeted prevention programme.

Research findings regarding the effectiveness of the Incredible Years child, parent and teacher training interventions alone and in combination have been impressively replicated across multiple samples. As noted in Chapter 8, the parent training component has repeatedly been shown to produce significant reductions in child conduct problems at home and school, decreases in negative parenting and increases in positive parenting in comparison to waiting-list control conditions (Webster-Stratton, 1984; Webster-Stratton & Hammond, 1997; Webster-Stratton *et al.*, 1988, 2004). In addition, evidence suggests that overall improvements in children's behaviour problems as the result of the parenting intervention can still be seen at 3-year follow-up (Webster-Stratton, 1990).

As noted in Chapter 9, the Incredible Years child intervention has also been shown to produce significant reductions in the amount of conduct problems children exhibit at home and school, as well as to produce increases in social problem-solving skills in comparison to waiting-list control conditions (Webster-Stratton & Hammond, 1997; Webster-Stratton *et al.*, 2004). There is also evidence indicating that, at 1-year follow-up, approximately two-thirds of children who participated in the intervention had parent ratings of behavioural problems in the normal rather than clinically significant range (Webster-Stratton & Hammond, 1997).

Although the combination of child and parent training proved superior to each of the component pieces, this finding indicates that cognitive-behavioural treatments directed at young children can be effective in reducing disruptive behaviour problems and could potentially be used when parents are unwilling or unable to participate in treatment. Multicomponent versions of the programme have been shown to have the strongest outcome effects in randomized controlled trials (Reid *et al.*, 2007).

Fast Track

The Fast Track Program (Conduct Problems Prevention Research Group, 1992) is a multisite, comprehensive, long-lasting prevention programme that is specifically targeted towards high-risk children who are displaying early-onset disruptive behaviours in kindergarten. Following the kindergarten screening by teachers, the high-risk children who had been randomly assigned to the intervention began receiving social skills training, tutoring, peer-pairing activities with non-risk peers, and teacher-administered, classroom-wide social competence training in 1st grade. The latter programme – Promoting Alternative Thinking Strategies (PATHS; Kusché & Greenberg, 1994) – served to provide universal prevention as well as to reinforce positive concepts and skills with the high-risk children in the classroom. For elementary school children, the intervention emphasizes understanding and communicating emotions, self-control and problem-solving steps. The parents of the high-risk children participated in parent groups, in parent–child activities and in home visits. These developmentally guided interventions continued with the high-risk children through the elementary school grades. Adolescent-phase interventions continued with high-risk children through the 10th grade to attempt to prevent an array of adolescent problem behaviours, including substance abuse, conduct disorder and delinquency.

The outcome effects of Fast Track indicate significant intervention effects on peer ratings of aggression and disruptive behaviour, and on ratings of classroom atmosphere. In addition, at the end of 1st grade, moderate positive social effects were reported on children's social, emotional and academic skills (Conduct Problems Prevention Research Group, 1999a). Many of these effects on children's behaviours and social cognitive processes were maintained at the end of 3rd grade (Conduct Problems Prevention Research Group, 2002a), and up to the end of elementary school, through 4th and 5th grades (Conduct Problems Prevention Research Group, 2004a). In later years, the intervention effect has been moderated by child factors. For example, Fast Track was found to reduce children's likelihood of receiving a diagnosis of conduct disorder or oppositional defiant disorder relative to children in the control group, but only for the highest-risk youth (Conduct Problems Prevention Research Group, 2007).

Family Check-Up

The Family Check-Up was recently adapted for application as an indicated preventive intervention for the parents of young toddlers (i.e. between 1 and 2 years old) who have socioeconomic, family and/or child risk factors for future conduct problems (Shaw *et al.*, 2006). The Family Check-Up is a brief, three-session intervention based on motivational interviewing techniques. The intervention typically includes an initial contact session, a session devoted to assessing child and family functioning and parent–child interactions, and a feedback session focused on supporting existing parenting strengths, exploring parents' willingness to change problematic parenting behaviours and identifying needed family services.

In a recent randomized trial of the Family Check-Up, families were offered up to six additional follow-up sessions to address parenting practices, other family management issues and contextual concerns (e.g. marital adjustment, housing, vocational training). At a 2-year follow-up, significantly greater maternal involvement and reduced child disruptive behaviour were observed among families in the intervention condition. Of particular note, this brief intervention was effective in reducing disruptive behaviour among a group of children positive for two risk factors for persistence of early conduct problems: initially high levels of inhibition and maternal depressed mood. These findings provide preliminary support for the efficacy of the Family Check-Up for preventing early starting conduct problems among young toddlers who are already at risk.

Intervention in later childhood

Treatment and targeted prevention programmes

Problem Solving Skills Training plus Parent Management Training
The full PSST + PMT programme has a component addressing parent training and a component addressing prosocial problem-solving skills among children with disruptive behaviour disorders (see Chapter 9 for further description of the PSST child component and its outcomes). This programme is targeted at school-age antisocial children between 7 and 13 years old. Children attend 25 weekly sessions lasting approximately 50 minutes each (Kazdin *et al.*, 1992). PSST emphasizes the daily interpersonal situations that children face and specifically focuses on individual interpersonal deficits. Techniques such as role-playing, reinforcement, modelling and feedback are all utilized to teach and reward effective problem-solving skills. Children are also given tasks called super-solvers that allow them to practise techniques from the sessions outside the group, with other people. Parent participation is a large component of the training, and parents attend their own training as well as watch the child sessions, serve as a co-leader and supervise the child's use of the new skills at home (Kazdin *et al.*, 1992).

Outcome studies suggest that PSST significantly reduces antisocial behaviour during 1-year follow-up periods. Although PSST has been found to do better than parent management training at increasing children's social competence at school and reducing self-reports of aggression and delinquency, a combination of both treatments is optimal for most outcomes (Kazdin *et al.*, 1992). The combination of PSST with an increased parent-focused intervention was found to have the greatest improvements in statistical and clinical significance, compared wit the PSST or parent-focused interventions alone (Kazdin *et al.*, 1992). This accumulation of evidence suggests that PSST + PMT is an effective and long-lasting treatment for antisocial behaviour in children.

Coping Power programme
The Coping Power programme described was derived from earlier research on an Anger Coping program (Lochman, 1992; Larson & Lochman, 2002). Coping Power is a comprehensive, multicomponent intervention programme that is based on the contextual social-cognitive model of risk for youth violence (Lochman & Wells, 2002a). Coping Power draws upon many of the cognitive and behavioural techniques of well-established parent training programmes while also incorporating techniques that target malleable child-level

social-cognitive risk factors for externalizing behaviour problems (Lochman *et al.*, 2008b). Coping Power includes a 34-session child component and a coordinated 16-session parent component, both of which are designed to be delivered over a 16–18-month period of time. Session-by-session treatment manuals and workbooks are available for both the child and parent components (Lochman *et al.*, 2008c, 2008d; Wells *et al.*, 2008a, 2008b). A teacher curriculum is also available and is typically administered during in-service teacher workshops.

The Coping Power programme can be implemented by mental health professionals in clinical practice settings or by school guidance counsellors and related school personnel. Coping Power was originally designed to be implemented with 4th–6th-grade children but has been successfully adapted for younger and older children. It has also been successfully adapted for other languages (e.g. Dutch, Spanish) and cultures. An abbreviated version was recently developed that can be readily completed in one academic year (24 child sessions and 10 parent sessions), and a promising version of the programme that can be delivered individually rather than in groups is currently being evaluated.

The content of the child sessions was described in Chapter 9. In addition to new content for each session, several activities are repeated at the beginning and end of each child group session. Sessions begin with a review of each child's behavioural goal from the previous week and end with the selection of a goal for the following week. At the beginning of each session, the children are also asked to recall one of the main topics discussed or skills learned during the previous session. The goal of this activity is to foster children's recall and generalization of skills from week to week. At the end of each group meeting, the children are asked to give positive feedback to one another and are given an opportunity make purchases from a menu of reinforcers (e.g. walkie-talkies, a mini indoor basketball set, markers and lip gloss) using points earned for meeting personal behaviour goals, following group rules and positive participation. During each session, role-plays, structured activities and homework assignments are also used to facilitate transfer of skills to outside the group setting.

The parent component of Coping Power addresses the behavioural parenting skills described in Chapter 8, including an emphasis on increasing parents' positive reinforcement and attention to children's positive behaviours, ignoring minor disruptive behaviours, providing clear instructions and rules, providing consistent and contingent discipline for negative child behaviours (including the use of time out, work chores and removal of privileges), and increasing the monitoring and supervision of children's out-of-home behaviour. Sessions also address stress management for the parents and enhancement of family communication skills. In addition to these 'standard' parent training skills, parents in the Coping Power programme also learn skills that support the social-cognitive and problem-solving skills their children are learning in the Coping Power child groups. Parent and child groups are scheduled such that parent skills are introduced at the same time as the respective child skills are introduced, so that parents and children can work together at home on what they are learning. For example, parents learn to set up homework support structures and to reinforce organizational skills at the same time that children are learning study skills and organization in the Coping Power child group.

In an initial efficacy study of the Coping Power programme, Lochman and Wells (2002a, 2004) randomly assigned 183 aggressive boys (60% African-American and 40% white non-Hispanic) to one of three conditions: a cognitive-behavioural Coping Power child component, combined Coping Power child and behavioural parent training components and an untreated cell. The two intervention conditions took place during the 4th and 5th or 5th and 6th grades, and the intervention lasted for 1.5 school years. Screening of risk status took place in 11 elementary schools and was based on a multiple-gating approach using teacher and parent ratings of children's aggressive behaviour. The at-risk boys were in the top 20% according to teacher ratings of their classrooms.

Analyses of outcomes at the time of the 1-year follow-up indicated that the intervention cells (child component only, child plus parent components) had produced reductions in children's self-reported delinquent behaviour as well as in parent-reported alcohol and marijuana use by the child, and improvements in teacher-rated functioning at school during the follow-up year, in comparison to the high-risk control condition (Lochman & Wells, 2004). Results indicated that the effects of the Coping Power intervention in terms of lower rates of parent-rated substance use and of delinquent behaviour at the 1-year follow-up, in comparison to the control cell, were most apparent for the children and parents who received the full Coping Power programme with child and parent components. In contrast, boys' teacher-rated behavioural improvements in school during the follow-up year appeared to be primarily influenced by the Coping Power child component.

Mediation analyses, using path analytic techniques, indicated that the intervention effect for both of the intervention cells on the delinquency, parent-reported substance use and teacher-rated improvement outcomes at the 1-year follow-up were mediated by intervention-produced improvements in children's internal locus of control, their perceptions of their parents' consistency, children's attributional biases, person perception and the children's expectations that aggression would not work for them (Lochman & Wells, 2002a).

Given these positive findings from the prior efficacy study, the next research questions examined whether Coping Power has similar positive effects in other settings and with personnel who are more equivalent to typical school and agency staff. Several types of effectiveness and dissemination study have been conducted with Coping Power, indicating intervention effects on children's aggressive behaviour and problem-solving skills among aggressive deaf children in a residential setting (Lochman *et al.*, 2001b), and on the overt aggression of children with oppositional defiant disorder or conduct disorder in Dutch outpatient clinics in comparison to care-as-usual children (van de Wiel *et al.*, 2007).

A long-term follow-up analyses of this sample, 4 years after the end of the intervention, indicated that the Dutch version of Coping Power (Utrecht Coping Power Program [UCPP]) had preventive effects by reducing adolescent use of marijuana and cigarettes in the children in UCPP programme in comparison to the care-as-usual children, although long-term effects were not found for alcohol use. These rates of substance use of the children in the UCPP were within the range expected for typically developing Dutch adolescents (Zonneyville-Bender *et al.*, 2007). Analyses of the cost-effectiveness of UCPP found that the Coping Power programme produced reductions in children's conduct problems at the end of the intervention for 49% less cost than the care-as-usual condition (van de Wiel *et al.*, 2003).

In a larger-sample effectiveness study, the effects of the Coping Power programme (the combined child and parent components) as an indicated preventive intervention directed at high-risk children were examined along with the effects of a universal, classroom-level preventive intervention (Lochman & Wells, 2002b). A total of 245 male and female aggressive 4th-grade students were randomly assigned to one of four conditions. Children were selected from 17 elementary schools, and the study had a greater proportion of schools from inner-city, high-poverty schools than was the case for the prior efficacy study. Intervention began in the fall of the 5th-grade year, and was delivered by personnel more equivalent to counsellors and social workers in school settings, with higher case loads and less opportunity for home visits.

At post intervention, the three intervention conditions (Coping Power alone, Coping Power plus classroom intervention, classroom intervention alone) produced lower rates of substance use than did the control cell (Lochman & Wells, 2002b). Children who received both interventions displayed improvements in their social competence with their peers, and their teachers rated these children as having the greatest increases in problem-solving and anger-coping skills. The Coping Power programme also produced reductions in parent-rated and teacher-rated proactive aggressive behaviour, and increases in teacher-rated behavioural improvement. A 1-year follow-up of this sample replicated the findings of the prior efficacy study. Children in the Coping Power programme were found to have lower rates of self-reported substance use and delinquency, and lower levels of teacher-rated aggressive social behaviour at school, in comparison to the control children (Lochman & Wells, 2003).

Intervention in early adolescence

Treatment programmes

More comprehensive family- and community-based treatments are often needed when multiple risk factors are present in early adolescence (e.g. child maltreatment, marital discord, parental psychopathology, poverty, exposure to neighbourhood violence) and for early adolescents with serious behaviour problems. Although the following programmes have been largely researched with adolescents, the samples have included children as young as 10 for Multisystemic Therapy (MST; e.g. Huey *et al.*, 2005), and as young as 12 for Multidimensional Treatment Foster Care (MTFC; Eddy *et al.*, 2004). A related foster parent-training intervention has been used with children in the 5–12-year age range (Price *et al.*, 2008). Thus, these programmes have clear relevance for children and early adolescents.

Multisystemic therapy

MST is an intensive family- and community-based treatment programme that has been implemented with chronic and violent juvenile offenders, substance-abusing juvenile offenders, adolescent sexual offenders, youths in psychiatric crisis (i.e. homicidal, suicidal, psychotic) and maltreating families (Henggeler & Lee, 2003). MST is an individualized intervention that focuses on the interaction between adolescents and the multiple environmental systems that influence their antisocial behaviour, including their peers, family, school and community (Henggler *et al.*, 1992).

Strategies for changing the adolescent's behaviour are developed in close collaboration with family members by identifying the major environmental drivers that help to maintain the adolescent's deviant behaviour. Services are delivered in the family's natural environment and can include a variety of treatment approaches such as parent training, family therapy, school consultation, marital therapy and individual therapy. Although the techniques used within these treatment strategies can vary, many of them are either behavioural or cognitive-behavioural in nature (e.g. contingency management and behavioural contracting). Clinicians are guided by a set of nine MST principles that include concepts such as focusing on systems strengths, delivering developmentally appropriate treatment and improving effective family functioning. Throughout the intervention, clinician adherence to these treatment principles is closely monitored through weekly consultation with MST experts.

Evaluations of the effectiveness of MST with chronic and violent juvenile offenders have produced promising results. Several investigations have shown that families who receive MST report lower levels of adolescent behaviour problems and improvements in family functioning after treatment in comparison to alternative treatment conditions (Henggeler *et al.*, 1992; Borduin *et al.*, 1995). In the first randomized clinical trail, MST was compared with treatment-as-usual with a sample of 84 serious juvenile offenders. Juveniles in the MST condition had significantly fewer arrests (mean 0.87 versus 1.52) and weeks of incarceration (mean 5.8 versus 16.2) at a 59-week follow-up (Henggeler *et al.*, 1992), and showed reduced recidivism at a 2-year follow-up in comparison to youths receiving treatment as usual.

Results from a subsequent extensive evaluation of MST found lower recidivism rates in juvenile offenders assigned to MST in comparison to youths who completed individual counselling at 4-year follow-up (Borduin *et al.*, 1995). Among those offenders who did recidivate, those assigned to MST had a lower number of total arrests and were charged with less serious offenses in comparison to youths assigned to individual counselling.

Multidimensional Treatment Foster Care

The Oregon MTFC programme is a comprehensive and systemic intervention designed to treat adolescent juvenile offenders in non-restrictive, family-style, community-based settings (Chamberlain & Smith, 2003). MTFC is an alternative to traditional group-care settings for antisocial youth who are removed from the care of their parents or guardians. MTFC temporarily places antisocial youth with a community-based foster family where contingencies governing the youth's behaviour are systematically modified through consultation with a comprehensive treatment team (Fisher & Chamberlain, 2000). As the youth's behaviour improves, a gradual transition is made from the MTFC setting back to their parent or guardian's home. Each foster family is assigned a behavioural support specialist, youth therapist, family therapist, consulting psychiatrist, parent daily report caller and case manager/clinical team manager to assist with programme implementation.

Foster parents, who are informally screened for programme participation, engage in a 20-hour preservice training that provides an overview of the treatment model and teaches techniques for monitoring and modifying adolescent behaviour. Adolescents are able to earn privileges within the foster home by following a daily programme of scheduled activities and fulfilling behavioural expectations. The youth's biological parents or guardians assist in the treatment-planning, engage in family therapy to learn effective parenting skills and begin applying their newly learned skills during short home visits. As the family's functioning improves, the visits are extended until complete reunification occurs. Family therapists continue to follow the case for 1–3 months following reunification to assist in the successful resolution of problems that arise.

Research on the effectiveness of MTFC has provided encouraging results. An early version of MTFC was compared with placement in community-based group care facilities for adjudicated delinquent adolescents using a matched control design (Chamberlain & Reid, 1998). Results from this investigation indicated that juveniles in the MTFC condition were more likely than group-care youth to complete their placement and had fewer days of incarceration 2 years following treatment. Another matched control design involving younger abused boys in the juvenile justice system revealed that youth in MTFC had significantly fewer arrests, fewer self-report criminal activities and fewer days of incarceration 1 year following treatment in comparison to group-care controls (Fisher & Chamberlain, 2000). At 2 year post-discharge, boys in the MTFC programme reported using drugs less often than group-care controls.

A subsequent randomized clinical trail compared MTFC with placement in community-based group-care facilities with 79 adolescent boys, many of whom had been previously charged with several serious criminal offences and had a history of running away from previous placements (Eddy & Chamberlain, 2000). In comparison to group care, boys in the MTFC condition were more likely to complete their programme and spent 60% fewer days incarcerated a year following their referral to the programme. MTFC boys also had a fewer number of criminal referrals and reported lower levels of serious and violent crimes in comparison to boys in group care 1 year after programme completion.

Summary points

- In general, multicomponent programmes are more effective than programmes that provide intervention only to the child or to the parent.
- Multicomponent interventions can involve a combination of psychopharmacotherapy and psychosocial treatments; the MTA is a useful example of this type of multicomponent approach with children who have ADHD.
- There are few multicomponent programmes that focus solely on universal prevention, with the exception of the LIFT programme for use throughout the elementary school years.
- The multicomponent programmes typically involve parent intervention and child intervention components (e.g. Fast Track, Incredible Years, PSST + PMT and Coping Power), and the full multicomponent interventions have produced better outcomes than single components.
- An exception has been research reporting that some group interventions for adolescent-age youth have produced iatrogenic effects through deviancy training within group sessions.

Factors that influence intervention delivery and outcomes

This chapter will overview key factors that influence how evidence-based interventions for children with disruptive behaviour disorders are disseminated into real-world settings. Dissemination factors that influence outcomes include those at the programme level (degree of adaptation of the programme, use of booster sessions, applications to settings other than those planned), at the client level (parental engagement, comorbidity, ethnic and community context), at the intervention group level (group composition), at the level of the relationship between the clinician and the child and/or parent (therapeutic alliance), at the level of clinicians and their practice settings (clinician personality, organizational characteristics, intensity of training) and at the level of cost-effectiveness.

Dissemination to real-world settings

In this book, we have examined how a relatively broad set of risk factors are related to children's aggressive and disruptive behaviours, and have examined how a menu of evidence-based intervention strategies and programmes has been developed to work with these children and their parents. In this final chapter, we wish to address the basic question of whether this can make a difference to the real-world clinical and preventive care of these children. After the efficacy and effectiveness of an intervention have been established, an important next step is the dissemination of the programme for 'real-world' implementation (Lochman et al., 2009b).

Psychotherapy with children and adolescents has traditionally been a field in which many empirically unsupported approaches have been used (Roberts et al., 2003), typical community-based care has had consistently poor

Oppositional Defiant Disorder and Conduct Disorder in Childhood   By Walter Matthys and
John E. Lochman
© 2010 John Wiley & Sons, Ltd.

outcomes (Bickman, 2002) and the use of evidence-based programmes (EBPs) has remained infrequent in treatment settings (Addis & Krasnow, 2000; Henderson *et al.*, 2006). Until recently, there was a scarcity of evidence-based research on child interventions (Rubenstein, 2003). However, support for their implementation is increasing through recommendations and mandates of funders, national associations and national- and state-level legislation (Bickman, 2002; Hawley & Weisz, 2002; Glisson & Schoenwald, 2005). As EBPs move from carefully controlled research studies to clinical practice, there is a need to identify the factors that might promote or interfere with their successful dissemination, and a growing body of research has examined this topic.

Research can assist with this process of understanding how to disseminate interventions (Schoenwald & Hoagwood, 2001; Lochman, 2006). For example, outcomes for evidence-based interventions may not be as strong when disseminated to real-world settings (schools, clinics, community agencies) (Lochman, 2001). In addition, a variation in implementation effects across sites can be more important than average effect sizes across sites, and can lead to a greater understanding of the factors that can moderate intervention effects in the real world (Raudenbush & Willms, 1991). Thus, the challenges that exist in disseminating evidence-based interventions can shape and sharpen our understanding of the dissemination process, of the interventions being disseminated and of their developmental models.

Critical issues that may need to be answered during dissemination, and that are addressed in this chapter, occur:

- at the intervention programme level: How much adaptation is all right? Are booster sessions needed? Can a programme developed in one type of setting be used broadly in clinics, private practice, schools, residential treatment and inpatient settings, and juvenile justice settings?;
- at the client level: How can limited parental engagement be addressed, both clinically and in terms of research effects? How should comorbidity be handled? Will ethnicity and community context make a difference in terms of programme implementation and outcomes? Can children's interest in technology and Internet use be harnessed to enhance child engagement?;
- at an intervention group level: When interventions are delivered to groups of youth with disruptive behaviour problems, do concerns about deviancy training exist and how should they be addressed?;
- at the level of the relationship between the clinician and the child and/or the parent: What impact does the therapeutic alliance have on outcomes?;
- at the level of the clinicians and their practice settings: Do therapists' skills, attitudes and personalities make a difference to how they implement programmes? Do the organizational characteristics of the practice setting make a difference in the implementation of programmes? Does the level of intensity of training provided to clinicians have an effect on outcomes?;

- at the level of cost-effectiveness and public health significance of the intervention efforts: What are the costs to society of stable antisocial behaviour, and are there indications that these programmes may be cost-effective?

At the intervention programme level

How much adaptation is all right?

Manuals developed for intervention studies during efficacy and effectiveness trials have the benefits of supporting the integrity of the intervention and of promoting the transportability of the programme as the broader dissemination of a programme begins. By specifically delineating the programme's key features, manuals increase the likelihood that future replications of the programme will yield effects similar to those of intervention trials (Kendall & Chu, 2000).

These benefits not withstanding, practising clinicians have raised concerns about the use of manual-based treatments in 'real-world' clinical work (Addis *et al.*, 1999). Criticisms involve beliefs that manuals have a limited focus on one therapeutic perspective, de-emphasize common factors such as positive engagement and the therapeutic alliance, do not attend to client-specific characteristics (including comorbidity), may prolong treatment due to the required adherence to a linear, invariant protocol, and may limit therapists' ability to use their clinical judgement during treatment sessions (Kendall & Beidas, 2007).

Although intervention developers may often insist on a complete adherence to protocols, innovations inevitably occur as development proceeds (Berwick, 2003), including adjustments made to programme materials to address participants' educational developmental and motivational levels (Lochman & Pardini, 2008). Innovative interventions often need to be adapted to the realities of intervening with children in applied settings (Stirman *et al.*, 2004). When exporting interventions from research laboratories to clinical practice settings, refinements should likely be made to fit clinic conditions (Weisz *et al.*, 1995) and to make strategies appropriate for the target audiences.

The creative, flexible use of manual-based interventions can permit an individualization of intervention, increase the likely transportability of the intervention to new settings and reduce clinicians' resistance to new programmes (Kendall *et al.*, 1998). As long as rigid adherence to manuals is avoided (Henry, 1998), clinicians may not regard a manual as a 'required cookie-cutter approach' (Kendall, 2002). Thus, manuals derived from intervention research may not be expected to be followed word for word in applied practice, but could instead provide a *guide* for core skills and concepts to be covered (Connor-Smith & Weisz, 2003). As Kendall and Beidas (2007) have proposed, evidence-based, manual-based treatments can be designed to promote 'flexibility within fidelity', allowing practitioners to use their clinical judgement to individualize an EBP for a given client while retaining the critical features of the programme.

Despite the likelihood of programmes being adapted over time, and the possibility that the rigid, inflexible use of manuals may lead to a less effective outcome when interventions are disseminated to applied settings, little research has examined the effects of programme adaptations. Only two studies, both addressing internalizing conditions, have directly addressed this issue with child interventions. Harnett and Dadds (2004) found that the facilitators' degree of deviation from session activities was not significantly associated with programme outcomes, in either a positive or a negative direction.

Kendall and Chu (2000) asked therapists who had used a structured evidence-based cognitive-behavioural intervention manual with 148 children (aged 9–13 years) who had primary anxiety disorders what kinds of adaptations they made to interventions. The study found that the therapists' ratings of the flexible adaptation of intervention activities were not related to intervention outcome. It appears that the combination of requiring strict adherence to session goals while permitting careful flexibility in adapting specific activities meant to address the session goals can lead to a successful implementation of programmes in 'real-world' settings.

Our own dissemination efforts with the Coping Power programme have indicated that clinicians appreciate the opportunity to adapt the programme content to suit case-specific needs (Boxmeyer *et al.*, 2008 Lochman *et al.*, 2009b). For example, clinicians might supplement the session content with favourite activities from their clinical repertoire (e.g. adding a 'feelings bingo' game to the component on emotional awareness), or may adapt activities to better match client characteristics (e.g. conducting role-plays rather than discussions for children demonstrating symptoms of attention deficit/hyperactivity disorder). To make Coping Power relevant for younger children or developmentally delayed children, activities may have to be more concrete, highly engaging and briefly presented, and make frequent use of stimulating books, puppets and arts-and-crafts activities. Coping Power includes several activities that are completely individualized for each participant or group of participants, including making a video to reinforce problem-solving skills and creating a pictorial representation of specific peer groups in the child's school or community. It is important to note that flexible adaptations such as these do not include omissions of programme content or radical departures from the protocol, which would instead be considered a lack of adherence and would be expected to detract from the effectiveness of an EBP.

Are booster sessions needed?

The current intervention literature indicates that one of the greatest difficulties with interventions for children with disruptive behaviour problems is that the children's improved changes in behaviour tend to erode over time (e.g. McMahon & Wells, 1998). This is partly because the children remain in the same peer, family and neighbourhood settings following intervention, and these may have contributed to or maintained the child's baseline level of problems. Thus, gains are not positively reinforced, and others, such as teachers, still expect that the perpetrator of the formerly aggressive behaviour will continue to behave in antisocial ways.

One solution to this problem has been to consider the use of booster interventions, which have been found to assist in maintaining intervention effects (Bry *et al.*, 1999). In research on the Anger Coping programme, Lochman (1992) found that earlier intervention-produced reductions in children's disruptive off-task behaviour in school settings were maintained at a 3-year follow-up only for aggressive children who had received a booster intervention. However, although use of booster sessions with conduct problem children can make intuitive sense, there is very little research to guide clinical practice in this area.

Can a programme developed in one type of setting be used broadly in clinics, private practice, schools, residential treatment and inpatient settings, and juvenile justice settings?

A practical problem that many practitioners encounter is that it is not clear whether a programme developed, tested and found to be effective in one setting (e.g. an outpatient clinic) can be meaningfully used in another setting (e.g. a residential centre or inpatient unit). For example, the Anger Coping programme (Larson & Lochman, 2002) was originally developed in school-based settings, and that method of intervention delivery had certain clear advantages. These advantages included:

- an opportunity for early screening, early intervention and prevention with children with emerging disruptive behaviour disorders;
- an opportunity to work on children's interpersonal behaviour problems within one of the settings where many of these problems occurred;
- a ready and easy opportunity to consult with children's teachers on a regular basis, thus extending the 'reach' of the intervention by direct contingencies for children's behaviour in the classrooms and by reinforcing teachers' skills in facilitating the development of children's social-cognitive skills;
- the inclusion of school personnel such as school counsellors and school psychologists as co-leaders, thus increasing the likelihood that the intervention would be accepted by other staff within the school setting and that the intervention would be maintained over time;
- often higher attendance rates for children in their groups than would be the case if children were being seen in an outpatient setting.

However, we later found that the structure for the Anger Coping programme could be easily used in outpatient settings as well, and this had certain other advantages, including: (1) the inclusion of parents into parent groups that met at the same time as the child groups; (2) an extension of group meeting time, sometimes to 90 minutes, permitting more intensive work within the group sessions; and (3) opportunities to provide the Anger Coping programme as part of an integrated treatment plan, which could include medication and other psychosocial treatments for comorbid conditions such as ADHD and anxiety disorders.

Similar advantages occur when children are in a residential or inpatient setting. The Anger Coping programme appears to be an appropriate component treatment in these settings, and sessions can be offered in a more dense way by meeting several times a week or even daily (Lochman *et al.*, 1992, 2001). Research on other social problem-solving interventions has demonstrated the efficacy of these forms of cognitive-behavioural intervention with inpatient and outpatient children (Kazdin *et al.*, 1987, 1992).

At the client level

How can limited parental engagement be addressed, both clinically and in terms of research effects?

Most EBPs for children with conduct problems include a strong focus on the parents. Outcome research studies conducted to determine the effectiveness of such programmes are performed under relatively ideal conditions, in which, compared with the typical treatment setting, more resources are available, therapists have smaller case loads and parents are often more motivated to participate. Unfortunately, it appears that, even with substantial efforts to promote attendance, many parents will not join intervention groups (e.g. Reid *et al.*, 1999), raising concerns for the transportability of these programmes into typical resource-strapped intervention settings (Lochman *et al.*, 2009b).

Dissemination research investigating parent involvement in EBPs is needed to provide empirically based recommendations for promoting attendance and engagement. Until this obstacle can be effectively addressed, problems with parent engagement will remain a significant challenge in the dissemination of EBPs for children. Anecdotal reports from our own dissemination efforts have yielded several low-cost strategies for encouraging attendance at parent meetings, including flexible scheduling that accommodates parents' work and family obligations, providing personalized reminders of meetings (telephone calls and notes), facilitating pot-luck meals at meetings and planning a child presentation (e.g. a skit illustrating programme concepts) during a parent meeting.

The most effective strategy for promoting parent attendance we have encountered came from an elementary school guidance counsellor who achieved near-100% parent participation for her group of nine students. In addition to the strategies suggested above, this counsellor reported that she developed positive relationships with all of the students' parents through telephone calls and emphasized the children's positive attributes during parent meetings (e.g. by starting each meeting by asking each parent to brag about his or her child). Efforts to disseminate EBPs might find that promoting clinicians' relationship-building strategies might offer a cost-effective way to address parent engagement issues.

Limited parent attendance at sessions also can dramatically affect the power of testing intervention effects in treatment research studies. In a study comparing several alternative analytical methods for addressing the dosage of parent attendance in behavioural parent training sessions in a new abbreviated form of Coping Power (Lochman *et al.*, 2006a), the type of analytical method used affected the interpretation of the programme's efficacy. Using traditional and rigorous intention-to-treat (ITT) analyses, this intervention, an abbreviated form of the Coping Power programme, tended to produce reductions in teachers' ratings of children's externalizing behaviour problems at post-intervention assessments, but the effect only approached conventional levels of statistical significance.

ITT analyses provide a strong and clear test of whether participants who are randomized to an intervention differ from randomly assigned controls at the close of the intervention. However, because those who have been randomly assigned may not participate in an intervention at equal rates, the ITT provides a conservative, and potentially erroneously low, estimate of the actual effects of an intervention. Instead, when parents' compliance with the parent component of the intervention was modelled using propensity scores and complier average causal effect (CACE) analyses, the intervention was found to produced statistically significant reductions in children's teacher-rated externalizing behaviour among those who complied with the intervention. The results indicated the utility of both the propensity score approach and the CACE approach to address participant attendance and compliance, as statistical adjuncts to traditional ITT analyses.

Propensity analyses using the greedy matching technique appear to be a particularly useful method for controlling for differential levels of parent attendance in interventions. Propensity score approaches match individuals who are estimated to be similar according to a defined set of baseline characteristics and make no assumptions about the equivalence of non-compliant participants across the intervention and control groups on the outcome variable.

How should comorbidity be handled?

Structured manual-based cognitive-behavioural therapy (CBT) may ignore the complexities of individual cases and neglect the individual, idiographic nature of each client (Henry, 1998; Herschell *et al.*, 2004). Thus, the manual may be targeted at the average client with the particular disorder being addressed, but it may not permit a focus on comorbid problems or on individuals with extremely serious versions of the disorder (Weisz *et al.*, 1995). Future intervention development and research should examine how best to integrate existing programmes for discrete disorders (e.g. integrating an intervention for children's anxiety disorders with an intervention for their conduct problem behaviour for intensely reactive aggressive children who display both externalizing and internalizing pathology) to treat comorbid youth. This focus will include how to integrate medication with psychosocial intervention elements, as illustrated by multicomponent interventions for ADHD (Jensen *et al.*, 2001b).

Will ethnicity and community context make a difference in terms of programme implementation and outcomes?

Interventions must be delivered in ways that make them relevant and appropriate for the varying types of population that can be found in urban, suburban and rural settings. Children's cultural experiences lead them to develop social schemas that guide their behaviour (Lochman *et al.*, 2008e), and to develop forms of ethnic identity that can directly affect their aggressive behaviour (Holmes & Lochman, 2009).

Lochman *et al.* (2000) noted that the effects of a cognitive-behavioural intervention such as the Anger Coping programme could be limited by certain cultural constraints. Within African-American, low-income populations, children's abilities to accept and use non-aggressive strategies to solve problems may be limited by their parents' modelling of physical aggression through their greater use of corporal punishment, and by their parents' direct advice to retaliate when confronted by certain types of threatening situation. These parental responses can often be the result of the parents' desire to protect their children within a threatening, violent environment in a low-income community. Intervention may need to explicitly advocate the use of 'code-switching' among these African-American youth (Lochman *et al.*, 2000), so that children can acquire a different code of behaviour depending on the environment they are in (e.g. a violent, crime-ridden neighborhood versus a relatively orderly school).

Can children's interest in technology and internet use be harnessed to enhance child engagement?

Individuals pay more attention to and learn more deeply from multimedia presentations than from verbal-only messages, resulting in greater problem-solving transfer (Walma van der Molen & van der Voort, 2000; Lieberman,

2001; Eveland *et al.*, 2002; Mayer, 2003). Children and adolescents indicate that their preferred method of learning involves interactive multimedia (Lieberman, 2001). Multimedia programmes can foster deep-level cognitive processing and thus offer two benefits: (1) increased intrinsic motivation for learning; and (2) favourable learning outcomes, such as a greater recall of material and a deeper conceptual understanding (Kennedy, 2004). Increased motivation to work on a task, stimulated by the interactivity of a media presentation, can produce more effortful and deliberate cognitive processing (Sanbonmatsu & Fazio, 1990) as well as reductions in biases and distortions in cognitive processing (Amodio *et al.*, 2003).

Given this evidence and the popularity of computers and video games among children and adolescents (Vorderer & Ritterfeld, 2003), it is not surprising that electronic media have become a popular modality for violence prevention interventions. Children and adolescents indicate that their preferred method of learning involves interactive multimedia platforms (Lieberman, 2001). Multimedia programmes have been developed to prevent youth violence. One such programme, SMART Talk (Students Managing Anger and Resolution Together) aims to teach middle-school students anger management and conflict resolution skills through a similar set of computer-based activities. While no significant changes in the frequency of aggressive behaviour were found in a randomized controlled study of SMART Talk, significant effects were observed on several mediating factors associated with violence. In particular, students in the intervention condition were less likely to value violence as a solution to conflict, were more likely to report intentions to use non-violent strategies, and reported more self-awareness about their response to anger in conflict situations than did students in the control group (Bosworth *et al.*, 2000).

While the role of video materials in enhancing intervention outcomes has received limited attention in the area of youth conduct problems, an early study yielded findings consistent with those from other target populations. McClure and colleagues (1978) compared four methods of teaching elementary students social problem-solving skills: (1) no treatment control; (2) video modelling tapes; (3) video modelling tapes plus discussion exercises; and (4) video modelling tapes plus role-play exercises. Outcome analyses revealed that the students who received the combined video modelling and role-play or discussion interventions generated a significantly greater number of solutions and more effective solutions on a problem-solving outcome measure than students in the control or video modelling-only conditions. Additional findings suggest that students in the combined video modelling and role-play intervention condition were most likely to transfer effective problem-solving skills to real-life social interactions with their peers.

In current ongoing research, Lochman and colleagues are developing brief and humorous animated cartoons that illustrate key concepts in the Coping

Power programme, and they plan to test directly whether using cartoons in sessions significantly adds to the effectiveness of the intervention.

At an intervention group level

When interventions are delivered to groups of youth with disruptive behaviour problems, do concerns about deviancy training exist and how should they be addressed?

Before widespread dissemination of evidence-based CBT interventions occurs, it is critical to understand who the interventions successfully influence, and whether there are intervention characteristics that can produce iatrogenic effects or subgroups of youth who are vulnerable to the iatrogenic effects of a given intervention programme. Within the field of youth violence prevention, a critical such concern that has arisen is the potential iatrogenic effect due to working with antisocial children in group formats where they may escalate, rather than reduce, their behaviour problems (Lochman & Pardini, 2008).

In one of the seminal articles on this form of iatrogenic effects, Dishion and Andrews (1995) found that youth who had received youth intervention sessions had higher rates of tobacco use and of teacher-rated delinquent behaviours than did the control children, and these iatrogenic effects were evident even if the parents had also received intervention in the combined condition. At a 3-year follow-up, the teen intervention conditions continued to show more tobacco use and delinquency (Poulin *et al.*, 2001).

A recent meta-analysis by Weiss *et al.* (2005) concludes that the risk for iatrogenic effects may currently be overstated. Weiss *et al.* updated their prior treatment meta-analysis datasets with new studies, and found that there was no overall difference in effect size for group versus individual treatment (a group effect size of 0.79 and an individual effect size of 0.68). However, groups tended to have worse effects as children approached adolescence, consistent with prior concerns that group iatrogenic effects may be most noticeable as children move into early adolescence. This meta-analysis suggests that the iatrogenic effects of group interventions are not universal effects, and suggests that it is critically important to further research the potential iatrogenic effects of group interventions at key developmental points.

In addition to developmental issues, children's characteristics and the therapists' behaviours may play a key role in whether deviancy training emerges in CBT groups. Particularly important child characteristics that might exacerbate the deviancy training effects are callous-unemotional traits, effortful control and status among peers. Effortful control, described as a tendency to be cautious and controlling of one's personal behaviour, has been shown to be a relevant factor in the initiation of substance abuse among high-risk boys (Pardini *et al.*, 2004). In regard to peer relations, peer victimization has been found to relate to substance abuse, aggression and delinquent behaviours (Sullivan *et al.*, 2006), as well as school adjustment problems (Graham *et al.*, 2006) in early adolescence. Peer rejection in elementary school has consistently been found to predict negative adolescent outcomes such as school failure, criminality and early-onset substance abuse (Kellam *et al.*, 1980; Brook *et al.*, 1986; Coie, 1990; Hawkins *et al.*, 1992).

At the stage of composing a group, we have found that the likelihood of creating a productive group increases when the children selected have the kinds of problem-solving deficits that are the focus of the Anger Coping and the Coping Power programmes, when some group members can serve as solid peer models for how to enact more competent, verbal assertion and negotiation strategies, and when group members have at least a minimal level of motivation to work on their anger management difficulties. During the course of group sessions, we attempt to enhance a positive group process by including positive feedback from all group members at the end of group sessions, and we include group-wide contingencies for earning group reinforcements, which thus promote cooperative behaviour among the group members. In addition, we encourage the group to plan prosocial group activities that can positively impact on others outside the group (e.g. creating drug prevention posters that focus on handling peer pressure and that can be mounted in their school).

When disagreements and conflicts develop between group members during sessions, these can be opportunities to directly model and reinforce the social-cognitive skills that are the focus of these cognitive-behavioural interventions, including finding ways to cool down, listening to the other person's point of view, getting a better understanding of the perspective of their peers, and using verbal assertion and negotiation skills under controlled conditions, while the group leaders provide coaching.

Carefully managed and supervised groups may avoid iatrogenic effects (Dishion & Dodge, 2006). The ability of the adult group leaders to manage and structure peer interactions can assist in redirecting or stopping peers' reinforcement of deviant behaviours. For example, high levels of useful group structure can be evident in leaders' tight time schedules that do not permit opportunities for deviant talk, while leaders who provide little structure and permit a free discussion of all ideas can instead stimulate deviant peer contagion (Dishion *et al.*, 2006). Leader behaviours considered to be important for the successful implementation of groups include behaviour management strategies (attention to rules, use of rewards and punishments) and specific teaching strategies (praise for cooperative behaviours, reviews of activities, the introduction of activities, the discussion of skills. directions for activities) (Letendre & Davis, 2004). The deviancy effects may be substantially reduced or eliminated if the group leaders exercise adequate control over deviancy training behaviours in the group sessions.

At the level of the relationship between the clinician and the child or the parent

What impact does the therapeutic alliance have on outcomes?

Historically, the therapeutic relationship has been viewed as a key change mechanism in child psychotherapy (Shirk & Karver, 2003). At the present time, most child psychologists and psychiatrists report in surveys that they believe therapeutic alliance and other non-specific processes remain critical for change in child treatment (Kazdin *et al.*, 1990; Chu *et al*, 2004). Therapeutic alliance has been conceptualized (Chu *et al.*, 2004): (1) as a means to an end, such as the working alliance in psychoanalytic therapy; (2) as a necessary and sufficient mechanism for therapeutic change, as in play therapy and client-centred therapy; or (3) in CBT, with the therapist serving as an active 'coach', with an emphasis on a collaborative process. Thus, therapeutic alliance is assumed to be necessary but not sufficient in contemporary evidence-based CBTs. A therapeutic alliance may be especially important in child intervention because children do not initiate treatment. The affiliative bond between the client and therapist and the agreement of and involvement in intervention tasks may be key in child interventions.

There is minimal research to date, but a meta-analysis (Shirk & Karver, 2003) and literature review (Green, 2006) indicate:

- a small but significant effect for therapeutic alliance (0.21), with a somewhat greater effect for externalizing (0.30) than internalizing (0.10) problems;
- that measures of therapeutic alliance taken late in treatment are more strongly associated with outcome than are measures taken early in treatment;
- that there has been little support for the predictive effect of therapeutic alliance.

However, recent research has found that a positive alliance between parents and therapists in parent management training for antisocial children predicted improvements in parenting practices (Kazdin & Whitley, 2006), and that a positive child–therapist alliance predicted improvements in children's behaviour (Kazdin *et al.*, 2006). To address a lack of examination of therapeutic alliance in group forms of CBT, Lochman *et al.* (2005b) examined therapeutic alliance in a sample of 80 children screened as being in the top 30% of children according to 4th-grade teachers. The children received the Coping Power group CBT programme. Findings indicated that the children's baseline behaviour problems predicted poor therapeutic alliances, and weak therapeutic alliances were related to higher levels of children's problem behaviours at the end of intervention. However, therapeutic alliance was not a very good predictor of change in children's externalizing behaviour during intervention, suggesting that therapeutic alliance was not the primary mechanism accounting for CBT effects in group interventions with children.

At the level of the clinicians and their practice settings

Do therapists' skills, attitudes and personalities make a difference to how they implement programmes?

Clinicians charged with the actual implementation of a given programme may facilitate or impede the programme's success, depending on their attitudes and behaviours. Clinicians' implementation efforts are related to their perceptions of a new programme (Schmidt & Taylor, 2002; Stirman *et al.*, 2004), and fostering favourable attitudes appears to be critical in effective dissemination. Clinician resistance to EBPs may present a significant obstacle to dissemination efforts and may have its basis in concerns such as the degree of appropriateness or flexibility of a given intervention (Stirman *et al.*, 2004). Practitioners also need to be convinced that a new EBP offers advantages over their established practices (Stirman *et al.*, 2004).

Other factors proposed to relate to practitioners' abilities to effectively implement EBPs include their level of confidence, self-efficacy, prior experience, perceived barriers to implementation and familiarity with the intervention and its theoretical model (Turner & Sanders, 2006). Cynicism about organizational change, which may develop after exposure to unsuccessful change efforts, also appears to affect practitioners' openness to new programmes and their willingness or ability to implement new programmes effectively (Wanous *et al.*, 1994).

Clinicians' openness to new programmes appears to be influenced by the characteristics of 'change agents', a group that includes trainers and interagency proponents of the new programme (Stirman *et al.*, 2004). In fact, Schmidt and Taylor (2002) found that the credibility and personal characteristics of the change agents were some of the most powerful influences on practitioners' adoption of new practices. Experts also recommend that practitioner attitudes be addressed early in the training process, as clinicians' feelings and beliefs about new programmes can affect their receptiveness and implementation (Gotham, 2006). Clinicians' attitudes and beliefs can also be addressed less formally throughout the training process, with trainers taking a proactive role in eliciting a discussion of practitioner concerns (e.g. that EBPs are rigid and ineffective) and providing education on the flexibility and demonstrated benefits of EBPs (e.g. Stirman *et al.*, 2004).

The clinician's ability to identify social problems or negative group process issues is essential in group interventions (Lochman *et al.*, 2006). For example, when the child or any group member (if using a group format) begins discussing a current social problem that has recently happened, clinicians can respond by immediately shifting their agenda for the session to the presented problem, rather than rigidly sticking to the planned activities for the session. The clinician can thus take advantage of the naturally presented opportunity to model and reinforce problem-solving skills. It is critical that clinicians are mindful of the overall objectives of the programme so that the clinicians' flexible responses to children's problems and to group process issues can still have a direct impact on the targeted social-cognitive difficulties of aggressive children.

Do the organizational characteristics of the practice setting make a difference in the implementation of programmes?

New interventions and programmes need organizational support to be adequately implemented (Forman, 1995; Berwick, 2003; Henggeler & Lee, 2003). One of the central influences within Rogers' (1995) model of the diffusion of innovations involves characteristics of the social system in which the innovation will be embedded, including how decisions are made to adopt innovations and the organizational norms of the setting. The social environment of the organization, and the relationships between individuals in the work setting, are critical characteristics of the organization and are evident in the patterns of leadership, control, autonomy and communication among workers and supervisors (Pfeffer, 1983; O'Reilly, 1991; Porras & Robertson, 1992; Mowday & Sutton, 1993; Turnipseed, 1994; Wilpert, 1995; Weich & Quinn, 1999). The work environment can be conceptualized as having certain systematic characteristics (Trickett & Moos, 1973; Moos, 1974, 2002), consisting of a relationship dimension (involvement, peer cohesion, staff support), a personal growth and development dimension (autonomy, task orientation, work pressure) and a system maintenance and change dimension (clarity, control, innovation, physical comfort).

In regard to the dissemination of programmes, research suggests that new programmes are disseminated more quickly within a hierarchical structure in which the decision to implement an EBP is made solely by administrators in a top-down manner; however, dissemination efforts made under such conditions are less successfully maintained than those made in more collaborative circumstances (Henggeler *et al.*, 2002). Sustainability of new programmes is also influenced by organizations' turnover rates for clinicians and administrators (Schmidt & Taylor, 2002).

Individual staff members who perceive their school climate as negative have been found to have more burn-out (McClure, 1980), while a positive perceived school climate has been associated with the successful implementation of new practices in schools (Bulach & Malone, 1994). Collegiality, shared authority among colleagues and positive leadership by principals have been shown to be relevant factors in facilitating positive changes and improvements in schools, which might include the addition of EBPs into the curriculum

(Peterson, 1997). Other school-level factors that may have an impact on the implementation of EBPs include school size, the ethnic composition of schools, the socioeconomic level of the student body and school-wide aggression levels among students (Kellam *et al.*, 1998; Barth *et al.*, 2004). Although these particular factors may not be readily amenable to change, their identification can help to inform issues related to programme implementation, such as the need for ongoing consultation and support.

Does the level of intensity of training provided to clinicians have an effect on outcomes?

Characteristics of the training process have the potential to influence the implementation of a programme and, through this mechanism, can impact on outcomes (Henggeler *et al.*, 1997). Many agencies and systems provide training to staff members through 1- or 2-day workshops, and while this arrangement may be efficient and economical, it does not appear to be adequately effective. For example, in a study investigating the effectiveness of three different types of training in CBT procedures, Sholomskas *et al.* (2005) found that training workshops alone, in the absence of other techniques and supports, were not effective in establishing clinician competency. However, when workshops were followed by continuing supports such as ongoing supervision, expert consultation and the provision of feedback on cases, competence and adherence to the EBP protocol could be improved (e.g. Stirman *et al.*, 2004).

Although rarely examined in the intervention literature, the degree of intensity of training can be anticipated to affect intervention outcomes. Henggeler and colleagues (1998) have advocated that Multisystemic Therapy (MST) can have a maximal impact only when training is both intense (5-day initial training), ongoing (weekly supervision by MST-trained supervisors) and carefully specified. With sufficient intensity, training can achieve its primary purpose of enabling high levels of adherence to the intervention protocol and producing high levels of intervention integrity (Henggeler *et al.*, 1998). For example, adherence to MST intervention principles has been found to be an important predictor of key outcomes of criminal activity, incarceration and psychiatric symptoms for adolescents receiving MST (Henggeler *et al.*, 1998).

An example of training, clinician and organizational characteristics in dissemination

A National Institute of Drug Abuse-funded study of dissemination of the Coping Power prevention programme has been implemented in a field trial in 57 schools within five school districts in the USA. This field trial is examining whether the Coping Power prevention programme can be usefully taken 'to scale' and delivered in an effective manner by existing staff in a range of urban school sites within Tuscaloosa, Alabama and the Birmingham, Alabama metropolitan area. In this field study, existing school staff members (school counsellors) have been trained to use the Coping Power programme with high-risk children at the time of transition to middle school.

In this study of the school-based violence prevention programme, we used a teacher-rating approach to screen the at-risk students who were eligible for the indicated intervention (Lochman & the Conduct Problems Prevention Research Group, 1995; Hill *et al.*, 2004). Using a similar screening system, we have found screening scores to be valid and stable over time, and have found subsequent aggressive behaviour problems to be primarily predicted by teacher ratings of conduct problems (collected as an initial first gate in the screening process), with parent ratings of conduct problems (collected as the second gate in the screening process) adding only 3% of the variance in predicting to outcomes (Hill *et al.*, 2004; Lochman and the Conduct Problems Prevention Research Group, 1995). Thus, in this study, we used a teacher rating screen. Our prior research has found aggressive samples selected in a similar manner to have significantly higher parent and teacher ratings of aggressiveness (as expected), more observed off-task behaviour in the classroom, more social-cognitive difficulties associated with aggressive behaviour and a higher risk of later violence, delinquency and substance use compared with non-aggressive samples (e.g. Lochman & Dodge, 1994).

During screening, 3rd-grade teachers were asked in the spring of the year to rate how reactively and proactively aggressive all of the children in their classes were, using a six-item scale. Based on these ratings, we determined the 30% of most aggressive children across all classes. Across two cohorts, 3,774 children were screened. Consent was obtained for 531 of these participants (79% of those contacted), and they were assessed at baseline. Sixty-five per cent were male. Eighty-four per cent were African-American, 14% were Caucasian, and 2% were of other race/ethnicity. Retention was 95% at post-intervention assessment 2 years after the baseline assessment. The field trial randomly assigned counsellors in 57 elementary schools to one of three conditions: Coping Power – Intensive Training for Counselors (CP-IT), Coping Power – Basic Training for Counselors (CP-BT) or a care-as-usual comparison. Nineteen schools were in each condition, with 183 children in CP-BT, 168 children in CP-IT and 180 in the control group. The Coping Power programme was delivered during the 4th- and 5th-grade years.

Counsellors in both conditions for training of the Coping Power programme attended a 3-day initial workshop training in the autumn prior to the beginning of the intervention, and participated in monthly ongoing training sessions (2 hours) in which the trainers provided concrete training for upcoming sessions, debriefed previous sessions and problem-solved about the barriers and difficulties involved in the implementation of the programme. The counsellors in the CP-IT condition had two additional training elements.

First, individualized problem-solving related to barriers and difficulties in the implementation of the programme was available only to school site intervention staff in the CP-IT condition through a technical assistance component. This component included access by the implementation staff to an email account in which they could raise implementation concerns and problems and through which they could receive trainers' responses; it also included a telephone 'hotline' in which trainers were available for telephone consultation about these same concerns. Second, research staff coded the audiotapes of child and parent group sessions in terms of completion of objectives and quality of implementation.

A first set of research questions involved whether the counsellor and school characteristics were related to the implementation of the Coping Power programme. Indicators of quality of implementation (quality of engagement by counsellors with children in child groups and with parents in parent groups, rated from audiotapes of the sessions) and programme delivery (as indicated by the proportion of sessions' objectives completed and by the number of sessions scheduled) have been examined using research assistants' ratings of the session audiotapes (Lochman *et al.*, 2009c). Two broad categories of predictive factor – school-level characteristics and individual interventionist characteristics – were explored in this study. Counsellors' agreeableness and conscientiousness were positively associated with facets of the implementation process, including the number of sessions scheduled and the quality of engagement with the children and parents. Counsellors who were cynical about organizational change and who were in schools that had rigid managerial control and little autonomy for school professional staff were less likely to implement the programme with high quality. Counsellor characteristics and school climate characteristics were both linked to the counsellors' ability to implement the intervention with a high level of quality.

In hierarchical linear modelling analyses, the intensity of training provided to counsellors has been found to have a notable impact on outcomes, with children of intensively trained counsellors having significant lower levels of externalizing behaviour relative to control children according to parent, teacher and youth ratings (Lochman *et al.*, 2009d). Children who had worked with intensively trained counsellors also had better social and academic skills at school and improved social cognitive abilities. Children who received intervention from basically trained counsellors did not demonstrate behavioural improvement. Significant behavioural improvements occurred only when the Coping Power training was provided in an intensive way, with immediate feedback to counsellors from audiotapes of the sessions.

We have collected information about the sustained use of Coping Power 1 year after completion of training for the first cohort of counsellors. Eighty-three per cent of the counsellors continued to use at least portions of the child component of Coping Power in the next year, with the greatest use of components addressing goal-setting, peer relationships, organizational and study skills, and emotional awareness and management. Counsellors had found it more difficult to get parents to attend parent sessions during the field trial, and the counsellors had lower rates of sustained use of the parent component of Coping Power, with 55% of counsellors using at least some portion of the parent programme. Overall, it appears that counsellors are generally sustaining the use of most of the child component of the programme, with some adaptation, providing policy-level support for the importance and utility of training regular school counsellors in these procedures (Boxmeyer *et al.*, 2008).

At the level of cost-effectiveness and public health significance of the intervention efforts

What are the costs to society of stable antisocial behaviour, and are there indications that these programmes may be cost-effective?

Based on our understanding of the course of development of children with disruptive behaviour problems, we know that there are a group of children whose conduct problems begin early in childhood (Shaw *et al.*, 2003), whose behaviour is often associated with genetic factors operating in combination with environmental experiences (Rutter, 2008), and who have stable or escalating levels of antisocial and violent behaviour through adolescence (Moffitt, 1993; Lacourse *et al.*, 2003). As noted in Chapter 2, these children can be described as 'early starters' or as 'life-course-persistent'. Longitudinal research indicates that this pattern of aggressive, antisocial behaviour is likely to continue into adulthood for some of these individuals (Roisman *et al.*, 2004).

In a 10-year follow-up, when two subsamples of participants were either 22–29 years of age (the household sample) or 29–34 years of age (the sample from juvenile institutions), Cernkovich and Giordano (2001) found that somewhat different predictors of antisocial behaviour emerged in young adulthood for the two subsamples. If youth in the normative household survey sample were able to establish stronger social bonds with others in their young adulthood years, their likelihood of continuing their antisocial behaviour was reduced. However, for youth in both groups, their adolescent levels of antisocial behaviour were predictive of their adult antisocial behaviour, supporting the critical importance of a latent trait that governs the antisocial behaviour of these individuals. It appears that these latent traits are established early in life and are relatively impervious to change (Cerkovich & Giordano, 2001), especially for youth who have already had to be institutionalized for their delinquency as juveniles.

Thus, there is a relatively small group of children who do not grow out of their serious antisocial and criminal behaviour in adolescence, but who continue their involvement in serious and persistent antisocial behaviour well beyond this time. These youth create an enormous cost to society because of their chronic antisocial behaviour and its consequences. Cohen (2005) has estimated the life-course cost of each career criminal to be over US$2 million. Among high-risk kindergarten-age children, the children with most conduct problems have been shown to increase their conduct problems exponentially over time, and are most at risk for meeting the criteria for a diagnosis of conduct disorder (CD; Conduct Problems Prevention Research Group, 2009). Thus, these especially problematic young children represent the 'power few' and are the children ultimately most likely to cause society the greatest amount of harm and to create the largest costs to society (Sherman, 2007; Conduct Problems Prevention Research Group, 2009).

The intransigence of this behavioural pattern underscores the clear importance of intervention with these children and their families. And we have seen in this book, various interventions have been demonstrated to have significant effects on the behaviours of some of these children after intervention and at longer-term follow-up assessments. However, are these intervention effects cost-effective? Are the amounts of funds required for the type of intensive, comprehensive and multicomponent interventions needed to have an effect with early-onset behavioural problems really worth it? Research needs to be conducted with the variety of interventions described in the previous chapters, but initial results are encouraging. Even expensive interventions may still be cost-effective, but the intervention must target a population that is particularly costly to society when left untreated, such as early starters for CD. For example, analyses of the costs of the multiyear Fast Track intervention and its effects on diagnoses of CD indicate that the intervention is cost-effective for the highest-risk children (Foster *et al.*, 2006). A condition such as CD (and the subsequent violent behaviour that often results from it) creates enormous public costs and is a cost-effective focus for these evidence-based interventions.

Summary points

- Outcomes for evidence-based interventions may not be as strong when disseminated to real-world settings (schools, clinics, community agencies).
- Evidence-based, manual-based treatments can be designed to promote 'flexibility within fidelity', allowing practitioners to use their clinical judgment to individualize an EBP for a given client, while retaining the critical features of the programme.
- Although the use of booster sessions for children with conduct problems can make intuitive sense, there is very little research to guide clinical practice in this area.
- Even with substantial efforts to promote attendance, many parents will not engage in intervention, raising concerns for the transportability of these EBPs.

- In intervention research, both the propensity score approach and the CACE approach can be used to address participant attendance and compliance, as statistical adjuncts to traditional ITT analyses.
- Given the popularity of computers and video games among children and adolescents, it is not surprising that electronic media have become a popular new modality for interventions to prevent violence.
- Carefully managed and supervised groups may avoid iatrogenic effects; the group leaders' abilities to manage and structure peer interactions can assist in redirecting or stopping peers' reinforcement of deviant behaviours.
- There has been limited support to date for the assumption that greater therapeutic alliance will predict better outcomes.
- Dissemination of programmes into real-world settings can be affected by the personality characteristics of the clinicians, by the organizational climate of the practice settings, and by the level of intensity of training provided to clinicians.

References

Abidin, R. R. (1990). *Parenting Stress Index-manual* (3rd ed.). Charlottesville, VA: Pediatric Psychology Press.

Abrams, D., Rutland, A., Cameron, L. & Marques, J. M. (2003). The development of subjective group dynamics: When in-group bias gets specific. *British Journal of Developmental Psychology, 21*, 155–176.

Achenbach, T. M. (1974). *Developmental psychopathology*. New York: Ronald Press.

Achenbach, T. M. (1991). *Manual for the Child Behavior Checklist 4–18 and 1991 profile*. Burlington, VT: University of Vermont Department of Psychiatry.

Achenbach, T. M. & Edelbrock, C. S. (1978). The classification of child psychopathology: A review and analysis of empirical efforts. *Psychological Bulletin, 85*, 1275–1301.

Achenbach, T. M. & Rescorla, L.A. (2000). *Manual for the ASEBA Preschool Forms and Profiles*. Burlington, VT: University of Vermont.

Achenbach, T. M. & Rescorla, L.A. (2001). *Manual for the ASEBA School Age Forms and Profiles*. Burlington, VT: University of Vermont.

Addis, M. E. & Krasnow, A. D. (2000). A national survey of practicing psychologists' attitudes toward psychotherapy treatment manuals. *Journal of Consulting and Clinical Psychology, 68*, 331–339.

Addis, M. E., Wade, W. A. & Hatgis, C. (1999). Barriers to dissemination of evidence-based practices: Addressing practitioners' concerns about manual-based psychotherapies. *Clinical Psychology: Science and Practice, 6*, 430–441.

Aguilar, B., Sroufe, L. A., Egeland, B. & Carlson, E. (2000). Distinguishing the early-onset/persistent and adolescence-onset antisocial behavior types: From birth to 16 years. *Development and Psychopathology, 12*, 109–132.

Ali, J. & Avison, W. R. (1997). Employment transitions and psychological distress: the contrasting experiences of single and married mothers. *Journal of Health and Social Behavior, 38*, 345–362.

Allen, G., Chinsky, J., Larcen, S., Lochman, J. & Selinger, H. (1976). *Community psychology and the schools: A behaviorally oriented multilevel preventive approach*. New York: Wiley.

Alm, P. O., af Klinteberg, B., Humble, K. *et al.* (1996). Psychopathy, platelet MAO activity and criminality among former juvenile delinquents. *Acta Psychiatrica Scandinavica, 94*, 105–111.

Ambrosini, P. J. (2000). Historical development and present status of the schedule for affective disorders and schizophrenia for school-age children (K-SADS). *Journal of the American Academy of Child and Adolescent Psychiatry, 39*, 49–58.

Oppositional Defiant Disorder and Conduct Disorder in Childhood   By Walter Matthys and John E. Lochman
© 2010 John Wiley & Sons, Ltd.

American Academy of Child and Adolescent Psychiatry (2007). Practice parameters for the assessment and treatment of children with attention deficit hyperactivity disorder. *Journal of the American Academy of Child and Adolescent Psychiatry, 46,* 894–921.

American Psychiatric Association (1994). *Diagnostic and statistical manual of mental disorders* (4th ed.) (DSM-IV). Washington DC: American Psychiatric Association.

American Psychiatric Association (2000). *Diagnostic and statistical manual of mental disorders* (4th ed., Text revision) (DSM-IV-TR). Washington DC: American Psychiatric Association.

Amodio, D. M., Harmon-Jones, E. & Devine, P. G. (2003). Individual differences in the activation and control of affective race bias as assessed by startle eyeblink response and self-report. *Journal of Personality and Social Psychology, 84,* 738–753.

Andersen, C., Hamer, R. M., Lawler, C. P., Mailman, R. B. & Lieberman, J. A. (2002). Striatal volume changes in the rat following long-term administration of typical and atypical antipsychotic drugs. *Neuropsychopharmacology, 27,* 143–151.

Anderson, C. A. & Dill, K. E. (2000). Video games and aggressive thoughts, feelings, and behavior in the laboratory and in life. *Journal of Personality and Social Psychology, 78,* 772–790.

Anderson, C. A., Carnagey, N. & Eubanks, J. (2003). Exposure to violent media: The effects of songs with violent lyrics on aggressive thoughts and feelings. *Journal of Personality and Social Psychology, 84,* 960–971.

Angold, A. (2002). Diagnostic interviews with parents and children. In M. Rutter & E. Taylor (Eds.), *Child and adolescent psychiatry* (pp. 32–51). Oxford: Blackwell.

Angold, A. & Costello, E. J. (1996). Towards establishing an empirical basis for the diagnosis of oppositional defiant disorder. *Journal of the American Academy of Child and Adolescent Psychiatry, 35,* 1205–1212.

Angold, A. & Costello, E. J. (2000). The Child and Adolescent Psychiatric Assessment (CAPA). *Journal of the American Academy of Child and Adolescent Psychiatry, 39,* 39–48.

Angold, A., Costello, J. E. & Erkanli, A. (1999). Comorbidity. *Journal of Child Psychology and Psychiatry, 40,* 57–87.

Angold, A., Costello, J. E., Burns, B. J., Erkanli, A. & Farmer, E. M. Z. (2000). Effectiveness of nonresidential specialty mental health services for children and adolescents in the 'real world'. *Journal of the American Academy of Child and Adolescent Psychiatry, 39,* 154–160.

Arnold, M. E. & Hughes, J. N. (1999). First do no harm: Adverse effects of grouping deviant youth for skills training. *Journal of School Psychology, 37,* 99–115.

Arnsten, A. F. (2006). Fundamentals of attention-deficit/hyperactivity disorder: circuits and pathways. *Journal of Clinical Psychiatry, 67* (Supplement 8), 7–12.

Arsenault, L., Tremblay, R. E., Boulerice, B., Seguin, J. R. & Saucier, J.-F. (2000). Minor physical anomalies and family adversity as risk factors for violent delinquency in adolescence. *American Journal of Psychiatry, 157,* 917–923.

Arseneault, L., Tremblay, R. E., Boulerice, B. & Saucier, J. F. (2002). Obstetric complications and adolescent violent behaviors: Testing two developmental pathways. *Child Development, 73,* 496–508.

Arsenault, L., Moffitt, T. E., Caspi, A. *et al.* (2003). Strong genetic effects on cross-situational antisocial behaviour among 5-year old children according to mothers, teachers, examiner-observers, and twin-reports. *Journal of Child Psychology and Psychiatry, 44,* 832–848.

Arsenio, W. F. & Lemerise, E. A. (2004). Aggression and moral development: Integrating social information processing and moral domain models. *Child Development, 75,* 987–1002.

Baden, R., Lochman, J. E. & Wells, K. C. (2009). Effects of marital conflict and aggressive parenting on boys' aggressive behavior (under review).

Bailey, A. (2002). Physical examination and medical investigations. In M. Rutter & E. Taylor (Eds.) *Rutter's Child and adolescent psychiatry* (5th ed., pp. 141–160). Malden, MA: Blackwell.

Baird, G. & Gringras, P. (2008). Physical examination and medical investigation. In M. Rutter & E. Taylor (Eds.) *Rutter's Child and adolescent psychiatry* (5th ed., pp. 317–335). Malden, MA: Blackwell.

Banaschewski, T., Coghill, D., Santosh, P. *et al.* (2006). Long acting medications for the hyperkinetic disorders: A systematic review and European treatment guide. *European Child and Adolescent Psychiatry, 15*, 476–495.

Bandura, A. (1973). *Aggression: A social learning analysis.* Englewood Cliffs, NJ: Prentice-Hall.

Bandura, A. (1986). *Social foundations of thought and action: A social cognitive theory.* Upper Saddle, NJ: Prentice-Hall.

Bandura, A. & Mischel, W. (1965). Modification of self-imposed delay of gratification through exposure to live and symbolic models. *Journal of Personality and Social Psychology, 2*, 698–705.

Bandura, A., Ross, D. & Ross, S. A. (1963). Vicarious reinforcement and imitative social learning. *Journal of Abnormal and Social Psychology, 67*, 601–607.

Barlow, D. (1996). Health care policy, psychotherapy research, and the future of psychotherapy. *American Psychologist, 51*, 1050–1058.

Baron, R. & Kenny, D. (1986). The moderator-mediator variable distinction in social psychology research: Conceptual, strategic, and statistical considerations. *Journal of Personality and Social Psychology, 51*, 1173–1182.

Barrish, H. H., Saunders, M. & Wolf, M. M. (1969). Good behavior game: Effects of individual contingencies for group consequences on disruptive behavior in a classroom. *Journal of Applied Behavior Analysis, 2*, 119–124.

Barry, T. D., Dunlap, S. T., Cotton, S. J., Lochman, J. E. & Wells, K. C. (2005). The influence of maternal stress and distress on disruptive behavior problems in children. *Journal of the American Academy of Child and Adolescent Psychiatry, 44*, 265–273.

Barry, T. D., Thompson, A., Barry, C. T., Lochman, J. E., Adler, K. & Hill, K. (2007). The importance of narcissism in predicting proactive and reactive aggression in moderately high and high aggressive children. *Aggressive Behavior, 33*, 185–197.

Barry, T. D., Barry, C. T., Deming, A. M. & Lochman, J. E. (2008). Stability of psychopathic characteristics in childhood: The influence of social relationships. *Criminal Justice and Behavior, 35*, 243–262.

Barry, T. D., Dunlap, S., Lochman, J. E. & Wells, K. C. (2009) Inconsistent discipline as a mediator between maternal distress and aggression in boys. *Child and Family Behavior Therapy, 31*, 1–19.

Barth, J. M., Dunlap, S. T., Dane, H., Lochman, J. E. & Wells, K. C. (2004). Classroom environment influences on aggression, peer relations, and academic focus. *Journal of School Psychology, 42*, 115–133.

Bartzokis, G., Lu, P. H., Beckson, M. *et al.* (2000). Abstinence from cocaine reduces high-risk response on a gambling task. *Neuropsychopharmacology, 22*, 102–103.

Baumeister, R. F., Campbell, J. D., Krueger, J. I. & Vohs, K. D. (2003). Does high self-esteem cause better performance, interpersonal success, happiness, or healthier lifestyles? *Science in the Public Interest, 4*, 1–44.

Baxter, L. R., Jr, Schwartz, J. M., Bergman, K. S. *et al.* (1992). Caudate glucose metabolic rate changes with both drug and behavior therapy for obsessive-compulsive disorder. *Archives of General Psychiatry, 49*, 681–689.

Beauchaine, T. P. (2001). Vagal tone, development, and Gray's motivational theory: Toward an integrated model of autonomic nervous system functioning in psychopathology. *Development and Psychopathology, 13*, 183–214.

Beauchaine, T. P., Gatzke-Kopp, L. & Mead, H. K. (2007). Polyvagal theory and developmental psychopathology: emotion dysregulation and conduct problems from preschool to adolescence. *Biological Psychology, 74*, 174–184.

Beauchaine, T. P, Hong, J. & Marsh, P. (2008). Sex differences in autonomic correlates of conduct problems and aggression. *Journal of the American Academy of Child and Adolescent Psychiatry, 47*, 788–796.

Bechara, A., Damasio, A.R., Damasio, H. & Anderson, S.W. (1994). Insensitivity to future consequences following damage to human prefrontal cortex. *Cognition, 50*, 7–15.

Beitchman, J. H., Baldassarra, L., Mik, H. *et al.* (2006). *American Journal of Psychiatry, 163*, 1103–1105.

Bell, R. Q. (1968). A reinterpretation of the direction of effects in studies of socialization. *Psychological Review, 75*, 81–95.

Benjet, C. & Kazdin, A. E. (2003). Spanking children: the controversies, findings, and new directions. *Clinical Psychology Review, 23*, 197–224.

Bennett, D. S., Bendersky, M. & Lewis, M. (2002). Children's intellectual and emotional-behavioral adjustment at 4 years as a function of cocaine exposure, maternal characteristics, and environmental risk. *Developmental Psychology, 38*, 648–658.

Berlin, L. & Bohlin, G. (2002). Response inhibition, hyperactivity, and conduct problems among preschool children. *Journal of Clinical Child Psychology, 31*, 242–251.

Berridge, K. C. (2007). The debate over dopamine's role in reward: the case for incentive salience. *Psychopharmacology, 191*, 391–431.

Berryhill, J. C. & Prinz, R. J. (2003). Environmental interventions to enhance student adjustment: implications for prevention. *Prevention Science, 4*, 65–87.

Berwick, D. M. (2003). Disseminating innovations in health care. *Journal of the American Medical Association, 289*, 1969–1975.

Bickman, L. (2002). The death of treatment as usual: An excellent first step on a long road. *Clinical Psychology: Science and Practice, 9*, 195–199.

Biederman, J. & Spencer, T. (1999). Attention-deficit/hyperactivity disorder (ADHD) as a noradrenergic disorder. *Biological Psychiatry, 46*, 1234–1242.

Bierman, K. L. (2004). *Peer rejection: Developmental processes and intervention strategies.* New York: Guilford Press.

Bierman, K. L. & Wargo, J. B. (1995). Predicting the longitudinal course associated with aggressive-rejected, aggressive (nonrejected), and rejected (nonaggressive) status. *Development and Psychopathology, 7*, 669–682.

Bierman, K. L., Smoot, D. L. & Aumiller, K. (1993). Characteristics of aggressive-rejected, aggressive (nonrejected), and rejected (nonaggressive) boys. *Child Development, 64*, 139–151.

Bird, H. R., Canino, G., Rubio-Stipec, M. & Ribera, J. C. (1987). Further measures of the psychometric properties of the Children's Global Assessment Scale. *Archives of General Psychiatry, 40*, 1228–1241.

Bird, H. R., Yager, T. J., Staghezza, B., Gould, M. S., Canino, G. & Rubio-Stipec, M. (1990). Impairment in the epidemiological measurement of childhood psychopathology in the community. *Journal of the American Academy of Child and Adolescent Psychiatry, 29*, 796–803.

Birmaher, B., Stanley, M., Greenhill, L., Twomey, J., Gavrilescu, A. & Rabinovich, H. (1990). Platelet imipramine binding in children and adolescents with impulsive behavior. *Journal of the American Academy of Child and Adolescent Psychiatry, 29*, 914–918.

Bjorklund, D. F. & Green, B. L. (1992). The adaptive nature of cognitive immaturity. *American Psychologist, 47*, 46–54.

Blair, R. J. R. (2004). The roles of orbital frontal cortex in the modulation of antisocial behaviour. *Brain and Cognition, 55*, 198–208.

Blair, R. J. R. (2007). Dysfunctions of medial and lateral orbitofrontal cortex in psychopathy. *Annals of the New York Academy of Sciences, 1121*, 461–479.

Blair, R. J. R., Morris, J. S., Frith, C. D., Perrett, D. I. & Dolan, R. J. (1999). Dissociated neural responses to facial expressions of sadness and anger. *Brain, 122*, 883–893.

Blair, R. J. R., Colledge, E., Murray, L. & Mitchell, D. G. V. (2001a). A selective impairment in the processing of sad and fearful expressions in children with psychopathic tendencies. *Journal of Abnormal Child Psychology, 29*, 491–498.

Blair, R. J. R., Colledge, E. & Mitchell, D. G. V. (2001b). Somatic markers and response reversal: Is there orbitofrontal cortex dysfunction in boys with psychopathic tendencies? *Journal of Abnormal Child Psychology, 29*, 499–511.

Blumensohn, R., Ratzoni, G., Weizman, A. *et al.* (1995). Reduction in serotonin $5HT_2$ receptor binding on platelets of delinquent adolescents. *Psychopharmacology, 118*, 354–356.

Bohnert, A. M., Crnic, K. A. & Lim, K. G. (2003). Emotional competence and aggressive behavior in school-age children. *Journal of Abnormal Child Psychology, 31*, 79–91.

Boivin, M., Dodge, K. A. & Coie, J. D. (1995). Individual-group behavioral similarity and peer status in experimental play groups of boys: The social misfit revisited. *Journal of Personality and Social Psychology, 69*, 269–279.

Boldizar, J. P., Perry, D. G. & Perry, L. C. (1989). Outcome values and aggression. *Child Development, 60*, 571–579.

Bolger, K. E., Patterson, C. J. & Kupersmidt, J. B. (1998). Peer relationships and self esteem among children who have been maltreated. *Child Development, 69*, 1171–1179.

Bongers, I. L., Koot, H. M., Van der Ende, J. & Verhulst, F. C. (2003). The normative development of child and adolescent problem behavior. *Journal of Abnormal Psychology, 112*, 179–192.

Bongers, I. L., Koot, H. M., Van der Ende, J. & Verhulst, F. C. (2004). Developmental trajectories of externalizing behaviors in childhood and adolescence. *Child Development, 75*, 1523–1537.

Borduin, C. M., Mann, B. J., Cone, L. T. *et al.* (1995). Multisystemic treatment of serious juvenile offenders: Long-term prevention of criminality and violence. *Journal of Consulting and Clinical Psychology, 63*, 569–578.

Bosworth, K., Espelage, D. & DuBay, T. (2000). Preliminary evaluation of a multimedia violence prevention program for adolescents. *American Journal of Health Behavior, 24*, 268–280.

Botvin, G. J. & Griffin, K. W. (2004). Life Skills Training: Empirical findings and future directions. *Journal of Primary Prevention, 25*, 211–232.

Bowlby, J. (1971). *Attachment and loss* (Vol. 1). *Attachment*. London: Hogarth Press.

Boxmeyer, C. L., Lochman, J. E., Powell, N. R., Windle, M. & Wells, K. (2008). School counselors' implementation of Coping Power in a dissemination field trial: Delineating the range of flexibility within fidelity. *Report on Emotional and Behavioral Disorders in Youth, 8*, 79–95.

Boyle, M. H. & Lipman, E. L. (2002). Do places matter? Socioeconomic disadvantage and behavioral problems of children in Canada. *Journal of Consulting and Clinical Psychology, 70*, 378–389.

Breiter, H. C., Aharon, I., Kahneman, D., Dale, A. & Shizgal, P. (2001). Functional imaging of neural responses to expectancy and experience of monetary gains and losses. *Neuron, 30*, 619–639.

Brennan, P. A., Grekin, E. R. & Mednick, S. A. (1999). Maternal smoking during pregnancy and adult male criminal outcomes. *Archives of General Psychiatry, 56*, 215–219.

Brennan, P. A., Grekin, E. R. & Mednick, S. A. (2003). Prenatal and perinatal influences on conduct disorder and serious delinquency. In B. Lahey, T. E. Moffitt &

A. Caspi (Eds.), *Causes of conduct disorder and delinquency* (pp. 319–344). New York: Guilford Press.

Brestan, E. & Eyberg, S. (1998). Effective psychosocial treatments for conduct-disordered children and adolescents: 29 years, 82 studies, and 5,272 kids. *Journal of Clinical Child Psychology, 27,* 180–189.

Brinkmeyer, M. Y. & Eyberg, S. M. (2003). Parent–child interaction therapy for oppositional children. In A. E. Kazdin & J. R. Weisz (Eds.), *Evidence-based psychotherapies for children and adolescents* (pp. 204–223). New York: Guilford Press.

Bronfenbrenner, U. (1995). Developmental ecology through space and time: A future perspective. In Moen, P., Elder, G. H. & Luescher, K. (eds). *Examining lives in context: Perspectives on the ecology of human development* (pp. 619–647). Washington, DC: American Psychiatric Association.

Brook, J. S., Whiteman, M., & Gordon, A. S. (1983). Stages of drug abuse in adolescence: Personality, peer, and family correlates. *Developmental Psychology, 19,* 269–277.

Brook, J. S., Gordon, A. S., Whiteman, M. & Cohen, P. (1986). Some models and mechanisms for explaining the impact of maternal and adolescent characteristics on adolescent stage of drug use. *Developmental Psychology, 22,* 460–467.

Brotman, L. M., Gouley, K. K., Chesir-Teran, D., Dennis, T. & Klein, R. G. (2005). Prevention for preschoolers at high risk for conduct problems: Immediate outcomes on parenting practices and child social competence. *Journal of Clinical Child and Adolescent Psychology, 34,* 724–734.

Brotman, L. M., Gouley, K. K., Huang, K. Y., Kamboukos, D., Fratto, C. & Pine, D. S. (2007). Effects of a psychosocial family-based preventive intervention on cortisol response at a social challenge in preschoolers at high risk for antisocial behaviour. *Archives of General Psychiatry, 64,* 1172–1179.

Brumfield, B. D. & Roberts, M. W. (1998). A comparison of two measurements of child compliance with normal preschool children. *Journal of Clinical Child Psychology, 27,* 109–116.

Brunner, H. G., Nelen, M., Breakefield, X. O., Ropers, H. H. & van Oost, B. A. (1993). Abnormal behavior associated with a point mutation in the structural gene for monoamine oxidase A. *Science, 262,* 578–580.

Bry, B. H., Catalano, R. F., Kumpfer, K., Lochman, J. E. & Szapocznik, J. (1999). Scientific findings from family prevention intervention research. In R. Ashery (Ed.), *Family-based prevention interventions* (pp. 103–129). Rockville, MD: National Institute of Drug Abuse.

Buitelaar, J. K., van der Gaag, R. J., Cohen-Kettenis, P. & Melman, C. T. M. (2001). A randomized controlled trial of risperidone in the treatment of aggression in hospitalized adolescents with subaverage cognitive abilities. *Journal of Clinical Psychiatry, 62,* 239–248.

Bulach, C. & Malone, B. (1994). The relationship of school climate to the implementation of school reform. *ERS Spectrum, 12,* 3–8.

Buss, K. A. & Kiel, E. J. (2004). Comparison of sadness, anger, and fear facial expressions when toddlers look at their mothers. *Child Development, 75,* 1761–1773.

Bymaster, F. P., Katner, J., Nelson, D. L. *et al.* (2002). Atomoxetine increases extracellular levels of norepinephrine and dopamine in prefrontal cortex of rat: a potential mechanism for efficacy in attention deficit/hyperactivity disorder. *Neuropsychopharmacology, 27,* 699–711.

Cadoret, R. J., Yates, W. R., Troughton, E., Woodworth, G. & Stewart, M. A. S. (1995). Genetic–environmental interaction in the genesis of aggressivity and conduct disorders. *Archives of General Psychiatry, 52,* 916–924.

Cairns, R. B., Cairns, B. D., Neckerman, H. J., Gest, S. D. & Gariepy, J. L. (1988). Social networks and aggressive behavior: Peer support or peer rejection? *Developmental Psychology, 24,* 815–823.

Caldji, C., Francis, D., Sharma, S., Plotsky, P. M. & Meaney, M. J. (2000). The effects of early rearing environment on the development of GABAA and central benzodiazepine receptor levels and novelty-induced fearfulness in the rat. *Neuropsychopharmacology*, *22*, 219–229.

Campbell, M., Small, A. M., Green, W. H., Jennings, S. J., Perry, R., Bennett, W. G. & Anderson, L. (1984). Behavioral efficacy of haloperidol and lithium carbonate. *Archives of General Psychiatry*, *41*, 650–656.

Campbell, M., Adams, P. B., Small, A. M. *et al.* (1995). Lithium in hospitalized aggressive children with conduct disorder: a double-blind and placebo-controlled study. *Journal of the American Academy of Child and Adolescent Psychiatry*, *34*, 445–453.

Caplan, M., Weissberg, R. P., Grober, J. S., Sivo, P. J., Grady, K. & Jacoby, C. (1992). Social competence promotion with inner-city and suburban young adolescents: Effects on social adjustment and alcohol use. *Journal of Consulting and Clinical Psychology*, *60*, 56–63.

Carlson, G. A. (2007). Who are the children with severe mood dysregulation, a.k.a. "rages"? *American Journal of Psychiatry*, *164*, 1140–1142.

Casey, B. J. & Durston, S. (2006). From behavior to cognition to the brain and back: What have we learned from functional imaging studies of attention deficit hyperactivity disorder?

Casey, B. J., Nigg, J. T. & Durston, S. (2007). New potential leads in the biology and treatment of attention deficit-hyperactivity disorder. *Current Opinion in Neurology*, *20*, 119–124.

Caspi, A. & Moffitt, T. E. (2006). Gene–environment interactions in psychiatry: Joining forces with neuroscience. *Nature Review Neurosciences*, *7*, 583–590.

Caspi, A., Henry, B., McGee, R. O., Moffitt, T. E. & Silva, P. A. (1995). Temperamental origins of child and adolescent behavior problems: From age three to age fifteen. *Child Development*, *66*, 55–68.

Caspi, A., McClay, J., Moffitt, T. *et al.* (2002). Role of genotype in the cycle of violence in maltreated children. *Science*, *297*, 851–854.

Caspi, A., Moffitt, T. E., Morgan, J. *et al.* (2004). Maternal expressed emotion predicts children's antisocial behavior problems: Using monozygotic-twin differences to identify environmental effects on behavioral development. *Developmental Psychology*, *40*, 149–161.

Caspi, A., Langley, K., Milne, B. *et al.* (2008). A replicated molecular genetic basis for subtyping antisocial behavior in children with attention-deficit/hyperactivity disorder. *Archives of General Psychiatry*, *65*, 203–210.

Castellanos, F. X., Sonuga-Barke, E. J. S., Milham, M. P. & Tannock, R. (2006). Characterizing cognition in ADHD: beyond executive functions. *Trends in Cognitive Sciences*, *10*, 117–123.

Cavedini, P., Riboldi, G., Keller, R., D'Annucci, A. & Bellodi, L. (2002). Frontal lobe dysfunction in pathological gamblers. *Biological Psychiatry*, *51*, 434–441.

Cernkovich, S. A. & Giordano, P. C. (2001). Stability and change in antisocial behaviour: The transition from adolescence to early adulthood. *Criminology*, *39*, 371–410.

Chamberlain, P. & Reid, J. B. (1998). Comparison of two community alternatives to incarceration for chronic juvenile offenders. *Journal of Consulting and Clinical Psychology*, *66*, 624–633.

Chamberlain, P. & Smith, D. K. (2003). Antisocial behavior in children and adolescents: The Oregon Multidimensional Treatment Foster Care Model. In A. E. Kazdin & J. R. Weisz (Eds.), *Evidence-based psychotherapies for children and adolescents* (pp. 282–300). New York: Guilford Press.

Chandler, M. (1973). Egocentrism and antisocial behaviour: The assessment and training of social perspective-taking skills. *Developmental Psychology*, *9*, 326–332.

Chandler, M., Greenspan, S. & Barenboim, C. (1974). Assessment and training of role-taking and referential communication skills in institutionalized emotionally disturbed children. *Developmental Psychology, 10,* 546–553.

Charman, T., Hood, J. & Howlin, P. (2008). Psychological assessment in a clinical context. In M. Rutter & E. Taylor (Eds.) *Rutter's Child and adolescent psychiatry* (5th ed., pp. 299–316). Malden, MA: Blackwell.

Chiriboga, C. A. (2003). Fetal alcohol and drug effects. *Neurologist, 9,* 267–279.

Chu, B. C., Choudhury, M. S., Shortt, A. L., Pncus, D. B., Creed, T. A. & Kendall, P. C. (2004). Alliance, technology, and outcome in the treatment of anxious youth. *Cognitive and Behavioral Practice, 11,* 44–55.

Cicchetti, D. & Toth, S. L. (1992). The role of developmental theory in prevention and intervention. *Development and Psychopathology, 4,* 489–493.

Cicchetti, D., Rogosch, F. A. & Toth, S. L. (1998). Maternal depressive disorder and contextual risk: Contributions to the development of attachment insecurity and behavior problems in toddlerhood. *Development and Psychopathology, 10,* 283–300.

Cillessen, A. H., Van IJzendoorn, H. W., Van Lieshout, C. F. & Hartup, W. W. (1992). Heterogeneity among peer-rejected boys: Subtypes and stabilities. *Child Development, 63,* 893–905.

Clanton, N. R. & Lochman, J. E. (2009). Psychophysiological correlates of aggressive behavior in children: An examination of differences between recovery responses. Poster presented at the annual meeting of the International Neurological Society, Atlanta, Georgia, February.

Clanton, N. R., Lochman, J. E., Barth, J. M., Williams, S. C. & Wells, K. C. (2009). Childhood psychophysiological correlates of adolescent delinquency and aggression. *Journal of the American Academy of Child and Adolescent Psychiatry* (under review).

Clarke, H. F., Walker, S. C., Dalley, J. W., Robbins, T. & Roberts, A. C. (2007). Cognitive flexibility after prefrontal serotonin depletion is behaviourally and neurochemically specific. *Cerebral Cortex, 17,* 18–27.

Cleckley, H. (1976). *The mask of insanity* (5th ed.). St. Louis: Mosby.

Cohen, D. & Strayer, J. (1996). Empathy in conduct-disordered and comparison youth. *Developmental Psychology, 32,* 988–998.

Cohen, J. (1988). *Statistical power analysis for the behavioral sciences* (2nd ed.). Hillsdale, NJ: Lawrence Erlbaum.

Cohen, J. (1992). A power primer. *Psychological Bulletin, 112,* 155–159.

Cohen, M. A. (2005). *The costs of crime and justice.* New York: Routledge.

Cohen, N., Kershner, J. & Wehrspann, W. (1985). Characteristics of social cognition in children with different symptom patterns. *Journal of Applied Developmental Psychology, 6,* 277–290.

Coie, J. D. (1990). Towards a theory of peer rejection. In S. R. Asher & J. D. Coie. (Eds.). *Peer rejection in childhood* (pp. 365–398). New York: Cambridge University Press.

Coie, J. D. & Dodge, K. A. (1998). Aggression and antisocial behavior. In N. Eisenberg & W. Damon (Series Eds.). *Handbook of child psychology* (Vol. 3), *Social, emotional and personality development* (5th ed., pp. 779–862). New York: Wiley.

Coie, J. D., Dodge, K. A. & Kupersmidt, J. B. (1990). Peer group behavior and social status. In A. Steven & J. D. Coie (Eds.), *Peer rejection in childhood* (pp. 17–59), New York: Cambridge University Press.

Coie, J. D., Lochman, J. E., Terry, R. & Hyman, C. (1992). Predicting early adolescent disorders from childhood aggression and peer rejection. *Journal of Consulting and Clinical Psychology, 60,* 783–792.

Coie, J. D., Terry, R., Lenox, K., Lochman, J. E. & Hyman, C. (1995a). Childhood peer rejection and aggression as predictors of stable patterns of adolescent disorder. *Development and Psychopathology, 7,* 697–713.

Coie, J. D., Terry, R., Zakriski, A. & Lochman, J. (1995b). Early adolescent social influences on delinquent behavior. In J. McCord (Ed.), *Coercion and punishment in long-term perspectives* (pp. 229–244). Cambridge: Cambridge University Press.

Colder, C. R., Lochman, J. E. & Wells, K. C. (1997). The moderating effects of children's fear and activity level on relations between parenting practices and childhood symptomatology. *Journal of Abnormal Child Psychology, 25,* 251–263.

Colder, C. R., Mott, J., Levy, S. & Flay, B. (2000). The relation of perceived neighborhood danger to childhood aggression: A test of mediating mechanisms. *American Journal of Community Psychology, 28,* 83–103.

Cole, D. A., Martin, J. M., Peeke, L. G., Seroczynski, A. D. & Fier, J. (1999). Children's over- and underestimation of academic competence: A longitudinal study of gender differences, depression, and anxiety. *Child Development, 70,* 459–473.

Conduct Problems Prevention Research Group (1992). A developmental and clinical model for the prevention of conduct disorder: the Fast Track Program. *Development and Psychopathology, 4,* 509–527.

Conduct Problems Prevention Research Group (1999a). Initial impact of the Fast Track prevention trial for conduct problems: I. The high-risk sample. *Journal of Consulting and Clinical Psychology, 67,* 631–647.

Conduct Problems Prevention Research Group (1999b). Initial impact of the Fast Track prevention trial for conduct problems. II. Classroom effects. *Journal of Consulting and Clinical Psychology, 67,* 648–657.

Conduct Problems Prevention Research Group (2002a). Evaluation of the first three years of the Fast Track prevention trial with children at high risk of adolescent conduct problems. *Journal of Abnormal Child Psychology, 30,* 19–35.

Conduct Problems Prevention Research Group (2002b). Predictor variables associated with positive Fast Track outcomes at the end of third grade. *Journal of Abnormal Child Psychology, 30,* 37–52.

Conduct Problems Prevention Research Group (2004a). The effects of the Fast Track program on serious problem outcomes at the end of elementary school. *Journal of Clinical Child and Adolescent Psychology, 33,* 650–661.

Conduct Problems Prevention Research Group (2004b). The Fast Track experiment: Translating the developmental model into a prevention design. In J. B. Kupersmidt & K. A. Dodge (Eds.), *Children's peer relations: From development to intervention* (pp. 181–208). Washington, DC: American Psychological Association.

Conduct Problems Prevention Research Group (2007). The Fast Track randomized controlled trial to prevent externalizing psychiatric disorders: Findings from grade 3 to 9. *Journal of the American Academy of Child and Adolescent Psychiatry, 46,* 1250–1262.

Conduct Problems Prevention Research Group (2009). Fast Track intervention effects on youth arrests and delinquency (under review).

Conger, R. D., Ge, X., Elder, G. H., Lorenz, F. O. & Simmons, R. L. (1994). Economic stress, coercive family process and developmental problems of adolescents. *Child Development, 65,* 541–561.

Conners, C. K. (1997). *Conners' Rating Scales-Revised: Technical manual.* North Tonawanda, NY: Multi-Health Systems.

Connor, D. F. (2002). *Aggression and antisocial behaviour in children and adolescents: Research and treatment.* New York: Guilford Press.

Connor, D. F., Fletcher, K. E. & Swanson, J. M. (1999). A meta-analysis of clonidine for symptoms of attention deficit hyperactivity disorder. *Journal of the American Academy of Child and Adolescent Psychiatry, 38,* 1551–1559.

Connor, D. F., Glatt, S., Lopez, I., Jackson, D. & Melloni, R. (2002). Psychopharmacology and Aggression. I. A Meta analysis of stimulant effects on overt-covert aggression-related behaviors in ADHD. *Journal of the American Academy of Child and Adolescent Psychiatry, 41,* 253–261.

Connor-Smith, J. K. & Weisz, J. R. (2003). Applying treatment outcome research in clinical practice: Techniques for adapting interventions to the real world. *Child and Adolescent Mental Health, 8,* 3–10.

Constantino, J. N., Grosz, D., Saenger, P., Chandler, D. W., Nandi, R. & Earls, F. J. (1993). Testosterone and aggression in children. *Journal of the American Academy of Child and Adolescent Psychiatry, 32,* 1217–1222.

Coon, H., Carey, G., Corley, R. & Fulker, D. W. (1992). Identifying children in the Colorado adoption project at risk for conduct disorder. *Journal of the American Academy of Child and Adolescent Psychiatry, 31,* 503–511.

Correll, C. U. (2008). Antipsychotic use in children and adolescents: Minimizing adverse effects to maximize outcomes. *Journal of the American Academy of Child and Adolescent Psychiatry, 47,* 9–20.

Costello, E. J., Compton, S. N., Keeler, G. & Arnold, A. (2003). Relationships between poverty and psychopathology: A natural experiment. *Journal of the American Medical Association, 290,* 2023–2029.

Crick, N. R. & Dodge, K. A. (1994). A review and reformulation of social information-processing mechanisms in children's social adjustment. *Psychological Bulletin, 115,* 74–101.

Crick, N. R. & Dodge, K. A. (1996). Social information-processing mechanisms in reactive and proactive aggression. *Child Development, 67,* 993–1002.

Crick, N. R. & Grotpeter, J. K. (1995). Relational aggression, gender, and social-psychological adjustment. *Child Development, 66,* 710–722.

Crider, A., Kremen, W. S. & Xian, H. (2004). Stability, consistency, and heritability of electrodermal response lability in middle-aged male twins. *Psychophysiology, 41,* 501–509.

Crone, E. A., Jennings, J. R. & Van der Molen, M. W. (2003). Sensitivity to interference and response contingencies in attention-deficit/hyperactivity disorder. *Journal of Child Psychology and Psychiatry, 44,* 214–226.

Crowell, S., Beauchaine, T. P., Gatzke-Kopp, L., Sylvers, P., Mead, H. & Chipman-Chacon, J. (2006). Autonomic correlates of attention-deficit/hyperactivity disorder and oppositional defiant disorder in preschool children. *Journal of Abnormal Psychology, 115,* 174–178.

Cuffe, S. P., McKeown, R. E., Addy, C. L. & Garrison, C. Z. (2005). Family and psychosocial risk factors in a longitudinal epidemiological study of adolescents. *Journal of the American Academy of Child and Adolescent Psychiatry, 44,* 121–129.

Dabbs, J. M. & Morris, R. (1990). Testosterone, social class, and antisocial behavior in a sample of 4,462 men. *Psychological Science, 1,* 209–211.

Dadds, M. R. & Powell, M. B. (1992). The relationship of interparental conflict and global marital adjustment to aggression, anxiety, and immaturity in aggressive and nonclinic children. *Journal of Abnormal Child Psychology, 19,* 553–567.

Dadds, M. R., El Masry, Y., Wimalaweera, S. & Guastella, A. J. (2008). Reduced eye gaze explains 'fear blindness' in childhood psychopathic traits. *Journal of the American Academy of Child and Adolescent Psychiatry, 47,* 455–463.

Daleiden, E. L. & Vasey, M. W. (1997). An information-processing perspective on childhood anxiety. *Clinical Psychology Review, 4,* 407–429.

Daugherty, T. K. & Quay, H. C. (1991). Response perseveration and delayed responding in childhood behavior disorders. *Journal of Child Psychology and Psychiatry, 32,* 453–461.

Day, D. M., Bream, L. A. & Pal, A. (1992). Proactive and reactive aggression: An analysis of subtypes based on teacher perceptions. *Journal of Clinical Child Psychology, 21,* 210–217.

Deater-Deckard, K., Dodge, K. A., Bates, J. E. & Pettit, G. S. (1996). Physical discipline among African American and European American mothers: Links to children's externalizing behaviors. *Developmental Psychology, 32,* 1065–1072.

DeGarmo, D. S., Patterson, G. R. & Forgatch, M. S. (2004). How do outcomes in a specific parent training intervention maintain or wane over time? *Prevention Science, 5*, 73–89.

Delaney-Black, V., Covington, C., Templin, T. *et al.* (2000). Teacher-assessed behavior of children prenatally exposed to cocaine. *Pediatrics, 106*, 782–791.

Deluty, R. H. (1983). Children's evaluation of aggressive, assertive, and submissive responses. *Journal of Consulting and Clinical Psychology, 51*, 124–129.

Deming, A. M. & Lochman, J. E. (2009). The relation of locus of control, anger, and impulsivity to boys' aggressive behavior. *Behavioral Disorders* (in press).

Denham, S. A. (1998). *Emotional development in young children.* New York: Guilford Press.

Denham, S. A., Caverly, S., Schmidt, M. *et al.* (2002). Preschool understanding of emotions: Contributions to classroom anger and aggression. *Journal of Child Psychology and Psychiatry, 43*, 901–916.

De Wied, M., Goudena, P. P. & Matthys, W. (2005). Empathy in boys with disruptive behaviour disorders. *Journal of Child Psychology and Psychiatry, 46*, 867–880.

Dick, D. M., Li, T.-K., Edenberg, H. J. *et al.* (2004). A genome-wide screed for genes influencing conduct disorder. *Molecular Genetics, 9*, 81–86.

Diener, M. B. & Milich, R. (1997). Effects of positive feedback on the social interaction of boys with attention deficit hyperactivity disorder: A test of the self-protective hypothesis. *Journal of Clinical Child Psychology, 26*, 256–265.

Dishion, T. J. & Andrews, D. W. (1995). Preventing escalation in problem behaviors with high-risk young adolescents: Immediate and 1-year outcomes. *Journal of Consulting and Clinical Psychology, 63*, 538–548.

Dishion, T. J. & Dodge, K. A. (2006). Deviant peer contagion in interventions and programs: An ecological framework for understanding influence mechanisms. In K. A. Dodge, T. J. Dishion & J. E. Lansford (Eds.), *Deviant peer influences in programs for youth* (pp. 14–43). New York: Guilford Press.

Dishion, T. J. & McMahon, R. J. (1998). Parental monitoring and the prevention of child and adolescent problem behavior: A conceptual and empirical formulation. *Clinical Child and Family Psychology Review, 1*, 61–75.

Dishion, T. J., Reid, J. B. & Patterson, G. R. (1988). Empirical guidelines for a family intervention for adolescent drug use. *Journal of Chemical Dependency Treatment, 1*, 189–224.

Dishion, T. J., Patterson, G. R. & Griesler, P. C. (1994). Peer adaptations in the development of antisocial behavior: A confluence model. In L. R. Huesmann (Ed.), *Aggressive behavior: Current perspectives* (pp. 61–95). New York: Plenum Press.

Dishion, T. J., Andrews, D. W. & Crosby, L. (1995). Antisocial boys and their friends in early adolescence: Relationship characteristics, quality, and interactional process. *Child Development, 66*, 139–151.

Dishion, T. J., McCord, J. & Poulin, F. (1999). When interventions harm: Peer groups and problem behavior. *American Psychologist, 54*, 755–764.

Dishion, T. J., Poulin, F. & Burraston, B. (2001). Peer group dynamics associated with iatrogenic effects in group interventions with high-risk young adolescents. In D. W. Nangle & C. A. Erdley (Eds.), *The role of friendship in psychological adjustment* (pp. 79–92). San Francisco: Jossey-Bass.

Dishion, T. J., Dodge, K. A. & Lansford, J. E. (2006). Findings and recommendations: A blueprint to minimize deviant peer influence in youth interventions and programs. In K. A. Dodge, T. J. Dishion & J. E. Lansford (Eds.), *Deviant peer influences in programs for youth: Problems and solutions* (pp. 366–394). New York: Guilford Press.

Ditto, B. (1993). Familial influenced on heart rate, blood pressure, and self-reported responses to stress: Results from 100 twin pairs. *Psychophysiology, 30*, 635–645.

Dmitrieva, T. N., Oades, R. D., Hauffa, B. P. & Eggers, C. (2001). Dehydro-epiandrosterone sulphate and cortocotropin levels are high in young male patients with conduct disorder: Comparisons for growth factors, thyroid and gonadal hormones. *Neuropsychobiology, 43,* 134–140.

Dodge, K. A. (1986). A social information processing model of social competence in children. In M. Perlmutter (Ed.), *The Minnesota symposium on child psychology* (Vol. 18, pp. 77–125). Hillsdale, NJ: Lawrence Erlbaum.

Dodge, K. A. (1991). The structure and function of reactive and proactive aggression. In D. J. Pepler & K. H. Rubin (Eds), *Development and treatment of childhood aggression* (pp. 201–218). Hillsdale, NJ: Lawrence Erlbaum.

Dodge, K. A. (1993). Social cognitive mechanisms in the development of conduct disorder and depression. *Annual Review of Psychology, 44,* 558–584.

Dodge, K. A. & Coie, J. D. (1987). Social-information-processing factors in reactive and proactive aggression in children's peer groups. *Journal of Personality and Social Psychology, 53,* 1146–1158.

Dodge, K. A. & Newman, J. P. (1981). Biased decision making processes in aggressive boys. *Journal of Abnormal Psychology, 90,* 375–390.

Dodge, K. A. & Somberg, D. R. (1987). Hostile attributional biases among aggressive boys are exacerbated under conditions of threats to the self. *Child Development, 58,* 213–224.

Dodge, K. A., McClasky, C. L. & Feldman, E. (1985). Situational approach to the assessment of social competence in children. *Journal of Consulting and Clinical Psychology, 53,* 344–353.

Dodge, K. A., Petit, G. S., McClaskey, C. L. & Brown, M. M. (1986). Social competence in children. *Monographs of the Society for Research in Child Development, 51*(2).

Dodge, K. A., Pettit, G. S. & Bates J. E. (1994). Socialization mediators of the relation between socioeconomic status and child conduct problems. *Child Development, 65,* 649–665.

Dodge, K. A., Lochman, J. E., Harnish, J. D., Bates, J. E. & Pettit, G. S. (1997). Reactive and proactive aggression in school children and psychiatrically impaired chronically assaultive youth. *Journal of Abnormal Psychology, 106,* 37–51.

Dodge, K. A., Laird, R., Lochman, J. E., Zelli, A. & the Conduct Problems Prevention Research Group (2002). Multi-dimensional latent construct analysis of children's social information processing patterns: Correlations with aggressive behavior problems. *Psychological Assessment, 14,* 60–73.

Donovan, S. J., Stewart, J. W., Nunes, E. V. *et al.* (2000). Divalproex treatment for youth with explosive temper and mood lability: A double-blind, placebo-controlled crossover design. *American Journal of Psychiatry, 157,* 818–820.

Dornbusch, S. M., Glasgow, K. L. & Lin, I-C. (1996). The social structure of schooling. *Annual Review of Psychology, 47,* 401–429.

Dumas, J. E. & Albin, J. B. (1986). Parent training outcome: Does active parental involvement matter? *Behaviour Research and Therapy, 24,* 227–230.

Dumas, J. E. & Wahler, R. G. (1983). Predictors of treatment outcome in parent training: Mother insularity and socioeconomic disadvantage. *Behavioral Assessment, 5,* 301–313.

Dunn, J. F. (1988). Sibling influences on childhood development. *Journal of Child Psychology and Psychiatry, 29,* 119–127.

Dunn, S. E., Lochman, J. E. & Colder, C. R. (1997). Social problem-solving skills in boys with conduct and oppositional defiant disorders. *Aggressive Behavior, 23,* 457–469.

Durston, S. (2003). A review of the biological bases of ADHD: What have we learned from imaging studies? *Mental Retardation and Developmental Disabilities Research Reviews, 9,* 184–195.

D'Zurilla, T. J. & Goldfried, M. R. (1971). Problem solving and behavior modification. *Journal of Abnormal Psychology*, *78*, 107–126.

D'Zurilla, T. J. & Nezu, A. M. (1980). A study of the generation of alternative process in social problem solving. *Cognitive Therapy and Research*, *4*, 67–72.

Eddy, J. M. & Chamberlain, P. (2000). Family management and deviant peer association as mediators of the impact of treatment condition on youth antisocial behavior. *Journal of Consulting and Clinical Psychology*, *68*, 857–863.

Eddy, J. M., Reid, J. R., Stoolmiller, M. & Fetrow, R. A. (2003). Outcomes during middle school for an elementary school-based preventive intervention for conduct problems: Follow-up results from a standardized trial. *Behavior Therapy*, *34*, 535–552.

Eddy, J. M., Whaley, R. B. & Chamberlain, P. (2004). the prevention of violent behavior by chronic and serious male juvenile offenders: A 2-year follow-up of a randomized clinical trial. *Journal of Emotional and Behavioral Disorders*, *12*, 2–8.

Edelbrock, C. (1984). Developmental considerations. In T. Ollendick & M. Hersen (Eds.), *Child behavioral assessment: Principles and procedures* (pp. 20–37). Elmsford, NY: Pergamon Press.

Edens, J. F., Cavell, T. A. & Hughes, J. N. (1999). The self-systems of aggressive children: A cluster-analytic investigation. *Journal of Child Psychology and Psychiatry and Allied Disciplines*, *40*, 441–453.

Egger, H. L., Erkanli, A., Keeler, G., Potts, E., Walter, B. K. & Angold, A. (2006). Test–retest reliability of the Preschool Age Psychiatric Assessment (PAPA). *Journal of the American Academy of Child and Adolescent Psychiatry*, *45*, 538–549.

Eisenberg, N. & Fabes, R. A. (1998). Prosocial development. In W. Damon & N. Eisenberg (Eds.), *Handbook of child psychology*, Vol 3, *Social, emotional, and personality development* (pp. 701–778). New York: Wiley.

Eisenberg, N. & Miller, P. A. (1987). The relation of empathy to prosocial and related behaviors. *Psychological Bulletin*, *101*, 91–119.

Eisenberg, N., Sadovsky, A., Spinrad, T. L. *et al.* (2005). The relations of problem behavior status to children's negative emotionality, effortful control, and impulsivity: Concurrent relations and prediction of change. *Developmental Psychology*, *41*, 193–211.

Ellis, M. L., Weiss, B. & Lochman, J. E. (2009). Executive functions in children: Associations with aggressive behavior and social appraisal processing. *Journal of Abnormal Child Psychology* (in press).

Embry, D. D. (2002). The Good Behavior Game: A best practice candidate as a universal behavioral vaccine. *Clinical Child and Family Psychology Review*, *5*, 273–297.

Embry, D. D. & Straatemeier, G. (2001). *The PAX Acts Game Manual: How to apply the Good Behavior Game*. Tuscson, AZ: PAXIS Institute.

Erath, S. A., Bierman, K. L. & the Conduct Problems Prevention Research Group (2006). Aggressive marital conflict, maternal harsh punishment, and child aggressive-disruptive behavior: Evidence for direct and indirect relations. *Journal of Family Psychology*, *20*, 217–226.

Erel, O. & Burman, B. (1995). Interrelatedness of marital relations and parent–child relations: A meta-analytic review. *Psychological Bulletin*, *118*, 108–132.

Ernst, M., Bolla, K., Mouratidis, M. *et al.* (2002). Decision-making in a risk-taking task: A PET study. *Neuropsychopharmacology*, *26*, 682–691.

Ernst, M., Grant, S. J., London, E. D., Contoreggi, C. S., Kimes, A. S. & Spurgeon, L. (2003). Decision making in adolescents with behaviour disorders and adults with substance abuse. *American Journal of Psychiatry*, *160*, 33–40.

Essau, C. A. & Petermann, F. (1997). *Developmental psychopathology: Epidemiology, diagnostics, and treatment*. Amsterdam: Harwood Academic Publishers.

Etkin, A. E., Pittenger, C., Polan, H. J. & Kandel, E. R. (2005). Toward a neurobiology of psychotherapy: Basic science and clinical applications. *Journal of Neuropsychiatry and Clinical Neurosciences, 17*, 145–158.

Eveland, W. P., Seo, M. & Marton, K. (2002). Learning from the news in campaign 2002: An experimental comparison of TV news, newspapers, and online news. *Media Psychology, 4*, 355–380.

Eyberg, S. M., Nelson, M. M. & Boggs, S. R. (2008). Evidence-based psychosocial treatment for children and adolescents with disruptive behavior. *Journal of Clinical Child and Adolescent Psychology, 37*, 215–237.

Fairchild, G., Van Goozen, S. H., Stollery, S. J. & Goodyer, I. (2008). Fear conditioning and affective modulation of the startle reflex in male adolescents with early-onset or adolescence onset conduct disorder and healthy control subjects. *Biological Psychiatry, 63*, 279–285.

Faraone, S. V., Biederman, J., Jetton, J. G. & Tsuang, M. T. (1997). Attention deficit disorder and conduct disorder: Longitudinal evidence for a familial subtype. *Psychological Medicine, 27*, 291–300.

Farrell, A. D., Meyer, A. L. & White, K. S. (2001). Evaluation of Responding in Peaceful and Positive Ways (RIPP): A school-based prevention program for reducing violence among urban adolescents. *Journal of Clinical Child Psychology, 30*, 451–463.

Farrell, A. D., Meyer, A. L., Sullivan, T. N. & Kung, E. M. (2003). Evaluation of the responding in peaceful and positive ways (RIPP) seventh grade violence prevention curriculum. *Journal of Child and Family Studies, 12*, 101–120.

Farrington, D. P. (1993). Motivation for conduct disorder and delinquency. *Development and Psychopathology, 5*, 225–241.

Farrington, D. P. (2005). The importance of child and adolescent psychopathy. *Journal of Abnormal Child Psychology, 33*, 489–497.

Farrington, D. P., Jolliffe, D., Loeber, R., Stouthamer-Loeber, M. & Kalb, L. M. (2001). The concentration of offenders in families, and family criminality in the prediction of boys' delinquency. *Journal of Adolescence, 24*, 579–596.

Feindler, E. L. & Ecton, R. B. (1986). *Adolescent anger control: Cognitive-behavior techniques.* New York: Pergamon Books.

Felner, R. D., Brand, S., Adan, A. M. et al. (1993). Restructuring the ecology of the school as an approach to prevention during school transitions: Longitudinal follow-ups and extensions of the School Transitional Environment Project (STEP). *Prevention in Human Services, 10*, 103–136.

Felner, R. D., Favazza, A., Shim, M., Brand, S., Gu, K. & Noonan, N. (2001). Whole school improvement and restructuring as prevention and promotion: Lessons from STEP and the Project on High Performance Learning Communities. *Journal of School Psychology, 39*, 177–202.

Fergusson, D. M. (1999). Prenatal smoking and antisocial behaviors: Commentary. *Archives of General Psychiatry, 56*, 223–224.

Findling, R. L., McNamara, N. K., Branicky, L. A., Schluchter, M. D., Lemon, E. & Blumer, J. (2000). A double-blind pilot study of risperidone in the treatment of conduct disorder. *Journal of the American Academy of Child and Adolescent Psychiatry, 39*, 509–516.

Findling, R. L., Aman, M. G., Eerdekens, M., Derivan, A., Lyons, B. & the Risperidone Disruptive Behavior Study Group (2004). Long-term, open-label study of risperidone in children with severe disruptive behaviors and below-average IQ. *American Journal of Psychiatry, 161*, 677–684.

Findling, R. L., Reed, M. D., O'Riordan, M. A. et al. (2006). Effectiveness, safety, and pharmacokinetics of quetiapine in aggressive children with conduct disorder. *Journal of the American Academy of Child and Adolescent Psychiatry, 45*, 792–800.

Findling, R. L., Newcorn, J. H., Malone, R. P., Waheed, A., Prince, J. B. & Kratochvil, C. J. (2007). Pharmacotherapy of aggression in a 9-year old with ADHD. *Journal of the American Academy of Child and Adolescent Psychiatry, 46,* 653–658.

Fishbein, E. (2000). Neuropsychology function, drug use, and violence: A conceptual framework. *Criminal Justice and Behavior, 27,* 39–159.

Fisher, P. A. & Chamberlain, P. (2000). Mulltidimensional treatment foster care: A program for intensive parenting, family support, and skill building. *Journal of Emotional and Behavioral Disorders, 8,* 155–164.

Fiske, S. T. & Taylor, S. E. (1991). *Social cognition* (2nd ed.). New York: McGraw-Hill.

Fite, P. J., Colder, C. R., Lochman, J. E. & Wells, K. C. (2006). The mutual influence of parenting and boys' externalizing behavior problems. *Journal of Applied Developmental Psychology, 27,* 151–164.

Fite, P. J., Colder, C. R., Lochman, J. E. & Wells, K.C. (2007). Pathways from proactive and reactive aggression to substance use. *Psychology of Addictive Behaviors, 21,* 355–364.

Fite, P. J., Colder, C. R., Lochman, J. E. & Wells, K. C. (2008). The relation between childhood proactive and reactive aggression and substance use initiation. *Journal of Abnormal Child Psychology, 36,* 261–271.

Fite, P. J., Winn, P., Lochman, J. E. & Wells, K. C. (2009). The effect of neighborhood disadvantage on proactive and reactive aggression. *Journal of Community Psychology, 37,* 542–546.

Fletcher, A. C., Darling, N. & Steinberg, L. (1995). Parental monitoring and peer influences on adolescent substance use. In J. McCord (Ed.), *Coercion and punishment in long-term perspectives.* (pp. 259–271). New York: Cambridge University Press.

Flory, J. D., Newcorn, J. H., Miller, C., Harty, S. & Halperin, J. (2007). Serotonergic function in children with attention-deficit hyperactivity disorder. *British Journal of Psychiatry, 190,* 410–414.

Foley, D. L., Eaves, L. J., Wormley, B. *et al.* (2004). Childhood adversity, monoamine oxidase A genotype, and risk for conduct disorder. *Archives of General Psychiatry, 61,* 738–744.

Fontaine, R. G., Burks, V. S. & Dodge, K. A. (2002). Response decision processes and externalizing behavior problems in adolescents. *Development and Psychopathology, 14,* 107–122.

Forman, S. G. (1995). Organizational factors and consultation outcome. *Educational and Psychological Consultation, 6,* 191–195.

Foster, E. M., Jones, D. & the Conduct Problems Prevention Research Group (2006). Can a costly intervention be cost-effective? An analysis of violence prevention. *Archives of General Psychiatry, 63,* 1284–1291.

Fowles, D. C. (1980). The three arousal model: Implications of Gray's two-factor learning theory for heart rate, electrodermal activity, and psychopathy. *Psychophysiology, 17,* 87–104.

Fowles, D. C. (2000). Electrodermal hyporeactivity and antisocial behavior: Does anxiety mediate the relationship? *Journal of Affective Disorders, 61,* 177–189.

Frick, P. J. (1991). *The Alabama Parenting Questionnaire.* University of Alabama, Author.

Frick, P. J. & Hare, R. D. (2001). *The Antisocial Process Screening Device.* Toronto: Multi-Health Systems.

Frick, P. J. & White, S. F. (2008). Research review: The importance of callous-unemotional traits for developmental models of aggressive and antisocial behavior. *Journal of Child Psychology and Psychiatry, 49,* 359–375.

Frick, P. J., Kamphaus, R. W., Lahey, B. B. *et al.* (1991). Academic underachievement and the disruptive behavior disorders. *Journal of Consulting and Clinical Psychology, 59,* 289–294.

Frick, P. J., Kimonis, E. R., Dandreaux, D. M. & Farell, J. M. (2003). The 4 year stability of psychopathic traits in non-referred youth. *Behavioral Sciences and the Law, 21,* 713–736.

Fukui, H., Murai, T., Fukuyama, H., Hayashi, T. & Hanakawa, T. (2005). Functional activity related to risk anticipation during performance of the Iowa gambling task. *NeuroImage, 24,* 253–259.

Fung, M. T., Raine, A., Loeber, R. *et al.* (2005). Reduced electrodermal activity in psychopathy-prone adolescents. *Journal of Abnormal Psychology, 114,* 187–196.

Gabel, S., Stadler, J., Bjorn, J., Shindledecker, R. & Bowden, C. L. (1993). Dopamine-beta-hydroxylase in behaviorally disturbed youth. *Biological Psychiatry, 34,* 434–442.

Galvin, M., Shekar, A., Simon, J. *et al.* (1991). Low dopamine-beta-hydroxilase: A biological sequela of abuse and neglect? *Psychiatry Research, 39,* 1–11.

Gardner, F., Burton, J. & Klines, I. (2006). Randomized controlled trial of a parenting intervention in the voluntary sector for reducing child conduct problems: outcomes and mechanisms of change. *Journal of Child Psychology and Psychiatry, 47,* 1123–1132.

Garon, N., Bryson, S. E. & Smith, I. M. (2008). Executive function in preschoolers: A review using an integrative framework. *Psychological Bulletin, 134,* 31–60.

Garrison, S. R. & Stolberg, A. L. (1983). Modification of anger in children by affective imagery training. *Journal of Abnormal Child Psychology, 11,* 115–129.

Ge, X., Conger, R. D., Cadoret, R. J. *et al.* (1996). The developmental interface between nature and nurture: A mutual influence model of child antisocial behavior and parent behaviors. *Developmental Psychology, 32,* 574–589.

Ghuman, J. K., Riddle, M. A., Vitiello, B. *et al.* (2007). Comorbidity moderates response to methylphenidate in the Preschoolers Attention-Deficit/Hyperactivity Disorder Treatment Study (PATS). *Journal of Child and Adolescent Psychopharmacology, 17,* 563–579.

Glisson, C. & Schoenwald, S. K. (2005). The ARC organizational and community intervention strategy for implementing evidence-based children's mental health treatments. *Mental Health Services Research, 7,* 243–259.

Goldberg, S., Grusec, J. E. & Jenkins, J. M. (1999). Confidence in protection: Arguments for a narrow definition of attachment. *Journal of Family Psychology, 13,* 475–483.

Goldstein, A. P. & Glick, B. (1994). Aggression replacement training: Curriculum and evaluation. *Simulation and Gaming, 25,* 9–26.

Goodman, R. (1997). The Strengths and Difficulties Questionnaire: A research note. *Journal of Child Psychology and Psychiatry, 38,* 581–586.

Goodman, R. & Scott, S. (2005). *Child psychiatry.* Oxford: Blackwell.

Gorman-Smith, D. & Tolan, P. (1998). The role of exposure to community violence and developmental problems among inner-city youth. *Development and Psychopathology, 10,* 101–116.

Gotham, H. J. (2006). Advancing the implementation of evidence-based practices into clinical practice: How do we get there from here? *Professional Psychology: Research and Practice, 37,* 606–613.

Gouze, K. R. (1987). Attention and social problem solving as correlates of aggression in preschool males. *Journal of Abnormal Child Psychology, 15,* 181–197.

Graham, S., Bellmore, A. D. & Mize, J. (2006). Peer victimization, aggression, and their co-occurrence in middle school: Pathways to adjustment problems. *Journal of Abnormal Child Psychology, 34,* 363–378.

Grant, K., Poindexter, L., Davis, T., Cho, M., McCormick, A. & Smith, K. (2000). Economic stress and psychological distress among urban African American adolescents: the mediating role of parents. *Journal of Prevention and Intervention in the Community, 20*, 25–36.

Gray, J. A. (1982). *The neuropsychology of anxiety: An inquiry into the function of the septohippocampal system*. New York: Oxford University Press.

Gray, J. A. (1994). Framework for a taxonomy of psychiatric disorder. In S. H. M. van Goozen, N. E. van de Poll & J. E. Sergeant (Eds.), *Emotions: Essays on emotion theory* (pp. 29–59). Hillsdale, NJ: Lawrence Erlbaum.

Green, J. (2006). Annotation: The therapeutic alliance – a significant but neglected variable in child mental health treatment studies. *Journal of Child Psychology and Psychiatry, 47*, 425–435.

Greenberg, M. T. & Kusché, C. A. (2006). Building social and emotional competence: The PATHS curriculum. In S. R. Jimerson & M. Furlong (Eds.), *Handbook of school violence and school safety: From research to practice* (pp. 395–412). Mahwah, NJ: Lawrence Erlbaum.

Greenberg, M. T., Lengua, L. J., Coie, J. D., Pinderhughes, E. E. & the Conduct Problems Prevention Research Group (1999). Predicting developmental outcomes at school entry using a multiple-risk model: Four American communities. *Developmental Psychology, 35*, 403–417.

Greenberg, M. T., Domitrovich, C. & Bumbarger, B. (2001). The prevention of mental disorders in school-aged children: Current state of the field. *Prevention and Treatment, 4*. Available at: http://journals.apa.org/prevention/volume4/pre0040001c.html

Greenberg, M. T., Weissberg, R. P., O'Brien, M. U. *et al.* (2003). Enhancing school-based prevention and youth development through coordinated social, emotional, and academic learning. *American Psychologist, 58*, 466–474.

Greenhill, L., Kollins, S., Abikoff, H. *et al.* (2006). Efficacy and safety of immediate-release methylphenidate treatment for preschoolers with ADHD. *Journal of the American Academy of Child and Adolescent Psychiatry, 45*, 1284–1293.

Greenhill, L. L., Posner, K., Vaughan, B. S. & Kratochvil, C. J. (2008). Attention deficit hyperactivity disorder in preschool children. *Child and Adolescent Psychiatric Clinics of North America, 17*, 347–366.

Gresham, F. M. & Elliott, S. N. (1990). *The Social Skills Rating System*. Circle Pines, MN: American Guidance Service.

Gresham, F. M. & Lochman, J. E. (2008). Methodological issues in research using cognitive-behavioral interventions. In M. J. Mayer, R. Van Acker, J. E. Lochman & F. M. Gresham (Eds.), *Cognitive behavioral interventions for emotional and behavioral disorders: School-based practice* (pp. 58–81). New York: Guilford Press.

Gresham, F. M., MacMillan, D. L., Bocian, K. M., Ward, S. W. & Forness, S. R. (1998). Comorbidity of hyperactivity-impulsivity-inattention and conduct problems: Risk factors in social, affective, and academic domains. *Journal of Abnormal Child Psychology, 26*, 393–406.

Grossman, D. C., Neckerman, H. J., Koepsell, T. D. *et al.* (1997). Effectiveness of a violence prevention curriculum among children in elementary school. *Journal of the American Medical Association, 277*, 1605–1611.

Grych, J. H., Jouriles, E. N., Swank, P. R., McDonald, R. & Norwood, W. D. (2000). Patterns of adjustment among children of battered women. *Journal of Clinical and Consulting Psychology, 68*, 84–94.

Guerra, N. G. & Slaby, R. G. (1989). Evaluative factors in social problem solving by aggressive boys. *Journal of Abnormal Child Psychology, 17*, 277–289.

Guerra, N. G., Huesmann, L. R. & Spindler, A. (2003). Community violence exposure, social cognition, and aggression among urban elementary school children. *Child Development, 74*, 1561–1576.

Gutman, L. M., McLoyd, V. C. & Tokoyawa, T. (2005). Financial strain, neighborhood stress, parenting behaviors and adolescent adjustment in urban African-American families. *Journal of Research on Adolescence, 15*, 425–449.

Haapasalo, J. & Tremblay, R. (1994). Physically aggressive boys from ages 6 to 12: Family background, parenting behavior, and prediction of delinquency. *Journal of Consulting and Clinical Psychology, 62*, 1044–1052.

Haas, M., Karcher, K. & Pandina, G. J. (2008). Treating disruptive behaviour disorders with risperidone: A 1-year, open-label safety study in children and adolescents. *Journal of Child and Adolescent Psychopharmacology, 18*, 337–346.

Haberstick, B. C., Smolen, A. & Hewitt, J. K. (2006). Family-based association test of the 5HTTLPR and aggressive behavior in a general population sample of children. *Biological Psychiatry, 59*, 836–843.

Haenlin, M. & Caul, W. F. (1987). Attention deficit disorder with hyperactivity: A specific hypothesis to reward disfunction. *Journal of the American Academy of Child and Adolescent Psychiatry, 26*, 356–362.

Halperin, J. M., Sharma, V., Siever, L. J. et al. (1994). Serotonergic function in aggressive and nonaggressive boys with attention deficit hyperactivity disorder. *American Journal of Psychiatry, 151*, 243–248.

Halperin, J. M., Newcorn, J. H., Schwartz, S. T. et al. (1997). Age-related changes in the association between serotonergic function and aggression in boys with ADHD. *Biological Psychiatry, 41*, 682–689.

Hanish, L. D., Eisenberg, N., Fabes, R. A., Spinrad, T. L., Ryan, P. & Schmidt, S. (2004). The expression and regulation of negative emotions: Risk factors for young children's peer victimization. *Development and Psychopathology, 16*, 335–353.

Hare, R. D. (1993). *Without a conscience: The disturbing world of the psychopath among us.* New York: Pocket.

Harnett, P. H. & Dadds, M. R. (2004). Training school personnel to implement a universal school-based prevention of depression program under real-world conditions, *Journal of School Psychology, 42*, 343–357.

Hartman, C. A., Hox, J., Mellenbergh, G. J. et al. (2001). DSM-IV internal construct validity: When a taxonomy meets data. *Journal of Child Psychology and Psychiatry, 42*, 817–836.

Hawkins, J. D., Catalano, R. F. & Miller, J. Y. (1992). Risk and protective factors for alcohol and other drug problems in adolescence and early adulthood: Implications for substance abuse prevention. *Psychological Bulletin, 112*, 64–105.

Hawkins, J. D., Catalano, R. F., Kosterman, R., Abbott, R. D. & Hill, K. G. (1999). Preventing adolescent health-risk behaviors by strengthening protection during childhood. *Archives of Pediatrics and Adolescent Medicine, 153*, 226–234.

Hawley, K. M. & Weisz, J. R. (2002). Increasing the relevance of evidence-based treatment review to practitioners and consumers. *Clinical Psychology: Science and Practice, 9*, 225–230.

Hazell, P. L . & Stuart, J. F. (2003). A randomised controlled trial of clonidine added to psychostimulant medication for hyperactive and aggressive children. *Journal of the American Academy of Child and Adolescent Psychiatry, 42*, 886–894.

Hazell, P., Zhang, S., Wola czyk, T. et al. (2006) Comorbid oppositional defiant disorder and the risk of relapse during 9 months of atomoxetine treatment for attention-deficit/hyperactivity disorder. *European Child and Adolescent Psychiatry, 15*, 105–110.

Henderson, J. L., MacKay, S. & Peterson-Badali, M. (2006). Closing the research-practice gap: Factors affecting adoption and implementation of a children's mental health program. *Journal of Clinical Child and Adolescent Psychology, 35*, 2–12.

Henggeler, S. W. & Lee, T. (2003). Multisystemic treatment of serious clinical problems. In A. E. Kazdin & J. R. Weisz (Eds.), *Evidence-based psychotherapies for children and adolescents* (pp. 301–322). New York: Guilford Press.

Henggeler, S. W., Melton, G. B. & Smith, L. A. (1992). Family preservation using multisystemic therapy: An effective alternative to incarcerating serious juvenile offenders. *Journal of Consulting and Clinical Psychology, 60*, 953–961.

Henggeler, S. W., Melton, G. B., Brondino, M. J., Scherer, D. G. & Hanley, J. H. (1997). Multisystemic therapy with violent and chronic juvenile offenders and their families: The role of treatment fidelity in successful dissemination. *Journal of Consulting and Clinical Psychology, 65*, 821–833.

Henggeler, S. W., Schoenwald, S. K., Borduin, C. M., Rowland, M. D. & Cunningham, P. B. (1998). *Multisystemic treatment of antisocial behavior in children and adolescents.* New York: Guilford Press.

Henggeler, S. W., Lee, T. & Burns, J. A. (2002). What happens after the innovation is identified? *Clinical Psychology: Science and Practice, 9*, 191–194.

Henry, W. P. (1998). Science, politics, and the politics of science: The use and misuse of empirically validated treatment research. *Psychotherapy Research, 8*, 126–140.

Hernandez, L. M. & Blazer, D. G. (Eds.) (2006). *Genes, behavior, and the social environment: Moving beyond the nature–nurture debate.* Washington, DC: National Academies Press.

Herschell, A. D., McNeil, C. B. & McNeil, D. W. (2004). Clinical child psychology's progress in disseminating empirically supported treatments. *Clinical Psychology: Science and Practice, 11*, 267–288.

Hicks, B. M., Krueger, R. F., Iacono, W. G., McGue, M. & Patrick, C. J. (2004). Family transmission and heritability of externalizing disorders: A twin-family study. *Archives of General Psychiatry, 61*, 922–928.

Higley, J. D., Thompson, W. W., Champoux, M. *et al.* (1993). Paternal and maternal genetic and environmental contributions to cerebrospinal fluid monoamine metabolites in rhesus monkeys (*Macaca mulatta*). *Archives of General Psychiatry, 50*, 615–623.

Hill, J. (2002). Biological, psychological and social processes in the conduct disorders. *Journal of Child Psychology and Psychiatry, 43*, 133–164.

Hill, L. G., Lochman, J. E., Coie, J. D., Greenberg, M. T. & the Conduct Problems Prevention Research Group (2004). Effectiveness of early screening for externalizing problems: Issues of screening accuracy and utility. *Journal of Consulting and Clinical Psychology, 72*, 809–820.

Hilton, J. M. & Desrochers, S. (2000). The influence of economic strain, coping with roles, and parental control on the parenting of custodial single mothers and custodial single fathers. *Journal of Divorce and Remarriage, 33*, 55–76.

Hinshaw, S. P. (1992). Externalizing behavior problems and academic underachievement in children and adolescents: Causal relationships and underlying mechanisms. *Psychological Bulletin, 111*, 127–155.

Hinshaw, S. P. & Melnick, S. M. (1995). Peer relationships in children with attention-deficit hyperactivity disorder with and without comorbid aggression. *Development and Psychopathology, 7*, 627–647.

Hinshaw, S. P., Lahey, B. B. & Hart, E. L. (1993). Issues of taxonomy and comorbidity in the development of conduct disorder. *Development and Psychopathology, 5*, 31–49.

Hoffman, M. L. (2000). *Empathy and moral development.* Cambridge: Cambridge University Press.

Hogan, A. E. (1999). Cognitive functioning in children with oppositional defiant disorder. In H. C. Quay & A. E. Hogan (Eds.), *Handbook of disruptive behavior disorders* (pp. 317–335). New York: Kluwer Academic/Plenum Publishers.

Holden, G. W., Lavigne, V. V. & Cameron, A. M. (1990). Probing the continuum of effectiveness of parent training: Characteristics of parents and preschoolers. *Journal of Clinical Child Psychology, 19,* 2–8.

Holmbeck, G. (1997). Toward terminological, conceptual, and statistical clarity in the study of mediators and moderators: Examples from the child-clinical and pediatric psychology literatures. *Journal of Consulting and Clinical Psychology, 65,* 599–610.

Holmes, J., Payton, A., Barrett, J. et al. (2002) Association of DRD4 in children with ADHD and comorbid conduct problems. *American Journal of Medical Genetics, 114,* 150–153.

Holmes, K. J. & Lochman, J. E. (2009). Ethnic identity in African American and European American preadolescents: Relation to self-worth, social goals, and aggression. *Journal of Early Adolescence* (in press).

Hubbard, J. A., Smithmyer, C. M., Ramsdens, S. R. et al. (2002). Observational, physiological, and self-report measures of children's anger: Relations to reactive and proactive aggression. *Child Development, 73,* 1101–1118.

Huebner, R. R. & Izard, C. E. (1988). Mothers' responses to infants' facial expressions of sadness, anger, and physical distress. *Motivation and Emotion, 12,* 185–196.

Huebner, T., Vloet, T. D., Marx, I., et al. (2008). Morphometric brain abnormalities in boy with conduct disorder. *Journal of the American Academy of Child and Adolescent Psychiatry, 47,* 540–547.

Huesmann, L., Moise-Titus, J., Podolski, C.L. & Eron, L. (2003). Longitudinal relations between children's exposure to TV violence and their aggression and violent behavior in young adulthood: 1977–1992. *Developmental Psychology, 39,* 201–221.

Huey, S. J., Jr, Henggeler, S.W., Rowland, M.D., Halliday-Boykins, C.A., Cunningham, P. B. & Pickrel, S. G. (2005). Predictors of treatment response for suicidal youth referred for emergency psychiatric hospitalization. *Journal of Clinical Child and Adolescent Psychology, 34,* 582–589.

Hughes, C., Dunn, J. & White, A. (1998). Trick or treat?: Uneven understanding of mind and emotion and executive dysfunction in 'hard-to-manage' preschoolers. *Journal of Child Psychology and Psychiatry, 39,* 981–994.

Hughes, C., White, A., Sharpen, J. & Dunn, J. (2000). Antisocial, angry and unsympathetic: 'Hard-to-manage' preschoolers' peer problems and possible cognitive influences. *Journal of Child Psychology and Psychiatry, 41,* 169–179.

Hughes, J. H. (1988). *cognitive behavior therapy with children in schools.* New York: Pergamon.

Hughes, J. N, Cavell, T. A. & Grossman, P. B. (1997). A positive view of self: Risk or protection for aggressive children? *Development and Psychopathology, 9,* 75–94.

Hughes, J. N., Cavell, T. A. & Prasad-Gaur, A. (2001). A positive view of peer acceptance in aggressive youth risk for future peer acceptance. *Journal of School Psychology, 39,* 239–252.

Hutchings, J., Bywater, T., Daley, D. et al. (2007). Parenting intervention in Sure Start services for children at risk of developing conduct disorder: Pragmatic randomised trial. *British Medical Journal, 334,* 678–685.

Iaboni, F., Douglas, V. I. & Ditto, B. (1997). Psychophysiological response of AD/HD to reward and extinction. *Psychophysiology, 34,* 116–123.

Ialongo, N. S., Werthamer, L., Kellam, S. G., Brown, C. H., Wang, S. & Lin, Y. (1999). Proximal impact of two first-grade preventive interventions on the early risk behaviors for later substance abuse, depression, and antisocial behavior. *American Journal of Community Psychology, 27,* 599–641.

Ingoldsby, E. M. & Shaw, D. S. (2002). Neighborhood contextual factors and early-starting antisocial pathways. *Clinical Child and Family Psychology Review, 5,* 21–55.

Ireland, J. L. & Archer, J. (2004). Association between measures of aggression and bullying among juvenile and young offenders. *Aggressive Behavior, 30*, 29–42.

Jackson, M. F., Barth, J. M., Powell. N. & Lochman, J. E. (2006). Classroom contextual effects of race on children's peer nominations. *Child Development, 77*, 1325–1337.

Jacobs, L. & Joseph, S. (1997). Cognitive Triad Inventory and its association with symptoms of depression and anxiety in adolescents. *Personality and Individual Differences, 22*, 769–770.

Jaffee, S. R., Caspi, A., Moffitt, T. E. & Taylor, A. (2004a). Physical maltreatment victim to antisocial child: Evidence of an environmentally mediated process. *Journal of Abnormal Psychology, 113*, 44–55.

Jaffee, S. R., Caspi, A., Moffitt, T. E., Polo-Tomas, M., Price, T. & Taylor, A. (2004b). The limits of child effects: Evidence for genetically mediated child effects on corporal punishment, but not on maltreatment. *Developmental Psychology, 40*, 1047–1058.

Jenkins, J. (2008). Psychosocial adversity and resilience. In M. Rutter, D. V. M. Bishop, D. S. Pine *et al.* (Eds.), *Rutter's Child and adolescent psychiatry* (5th ed., pp. 377–391). Oxford: Blackwell.

Jensen, P., Roper, M., Fisher, P. *et al.* (1995). Test–retest reliability of the Diagnostic Interview Schedule for Children (DISC 2.1). *Archives of General Psychiatry, 52*, 61–71.

Jensen, P. S. (1999). Links among theory, research and practice: Cornerstones of clinical scientific progress. *Journal of Clinical Child Psychology, 28*, 553–557.

Jensen, P. S., Hinshaw, S. P., Kraemer, H. C. *et al.* (2001a). ADHD comorbidity findings from the MTA study: Comparing comorbid subgroups. *Journal of the American Academy of Child and Adolescent Psychiatry, 40*, 147–158.

Jensen, P. S., Hinshaw, S. P., Swanson, J. M. *et al.* (2001b). Findings from the NIMH Multimodal Treatment Study of ADHD (MTA): Implications and applications for primary care providers. *Journal of Developmental and Behavioral Pediatrics, 22*, 60–73.

Johnson, C. A., Pentz, M. A., Weber, M.D. *et al.* (1990). Relative effectiveness of comprehensive community programs for drug abuse prevention with high risk and low-risk adolescents. *Journal of Consulting and Clinical Psychology, 58*, 447–456.

Jones, A. P., Laurens, K. R., Herba, C. J. & Viding, E. (2009). Amygdala hypoactivity to fearful faces in boys with conduct problems and callous-unemotional traits. *American Journal of Psychiatry, 166*, 95–102.

Jones, D. P. H. (2008). Child maltreatment. In M. Rutter, D. V. M. Bishop, D. S. Pine, S. Scott, J. Stevenson, E. Taylor & A. Thapar (Eds.), *Rutter's child and adolescent psychiatry* (5th ed, pp. 421–439). Oxford: Blackwell.

Kandel, D. B. & Wu, P. (1995). Disentangling mother–child effects in the development of antisocial behavior. In J. McCord (Ed.), *Coercion and punishment in long-term perspectives* (pp. 106–123). New York: Cambridge University Press.

Kandel, E. R. (1998). A new intellectual framework for psychiatry. *American Journal of Psychiatry, 155*, 457–469.

Kandel, E., Brennan, P. A., Mednick, S. A. & Michelson, N. M. (1989). Minor physical anomalies and recidivistic adult violent criminal behavior. *Acta Psychiatrica Scandinavica, 79*, 103–107.

Kaplan, J. S. (1995). *Beyond behavior modification.* Austin, TX: Pro-Ed.

Kaplan, S., Heiligenstein, J., West, S. *et al.* (2004). Efficacy and safety of atomoxetine in childhood attention-deficit/hyperactivity disorder with comorbid oppositional defiant disorder. *Journal of Attention Disorders, 8*, 45–52.

Kazdin, A. (1992). *Research design in clinical psychology* (2nd ed.). New York: Macmillan.

Kazdin, A. E. (1995). Child, parent and family dysfunction as predictors of outcome in cognitive-behavioral treatment of antisocial children. *Behaviour Research and Therapy, 33,* 271–281.

Kazdin, A. E. (2000). Developing a research agenda for child and adolescent psycho-therapy. *Archives of General Psychiatry, 57,* 829–835.

Kazdin, A. E. (2003). Clinical significance: Measuring whether interventions make a difference. In A. Kazdin & J. Weisz (Eds.), *Methodological issues and strategies in clinical research* (3rd ed., pp. 691–710). Washington, DC: American Psychological Association.

Kazdin, A. E. (2005). *Parent management training. Treatment for oppositional, aggressive, and antisocial behaviour in children and adolescents.* New York: Oxford University Press.

Kazdin, A. E. & Nock, M. K. (2003). Delineating mechanisms of change in child and adolescent therapy: Methodological issues and research recommendations. *Journal of Child Psychology and Psychiatry, 44,* 1116–1129.

Kazdin, A. E. & Weisz, J. R. (2003). *Evidence-Based psychotherapies for children and adolescents.* New York: Guilford Press.

Kazdin, A. E. & Whitley, M. K. (2006). Pretreatment social relations, therapeutic alliance, and improvements in parenting practices in parent management training. *Journal of Consulting and Clinical Psychology, 74,* 346–355.

Kazdin, A. E., Esveldt-Dawson, K., French, N. H. & Unis, A. S. (1987). Problem-solving skills training and relationship therapy in the treatment of antisocial child behavior. *Journal of Consulting and Clinical Psychology, 55,* 76–85.

Kazdin, A. E., Bass, D., Siegel, T. & Thomas, C. (1989). Cognitive-behavioral therapy and relationship therapy in the treatment of children referred for antisocial behavior. *Journal of Consulting and Clinical Psychology, 57,* 522–535.

Kazdin, A. E., Bass, D. Ayres, W. & Rodgers, A. (1990). Empirical and clinical focus of child and adolescent psychotherapy research. *Journal of Consulting and Clinical Psychology, 58,* 729–740.

Kazdin, A. E., Siegel, T. C. & Bass, D. (1992). Cognitive problem-solving skills training and parent management training in the treatment of antisocial behavior in children. *Journal of Consulting and Clinical Psychology, 60,* 733–747.

Kazdin, A. E., Whitley, M. & Marciano, P. L. (2006). Child–therapist and parent–therapist alliance and therapeutic change in the treatment of children referred for oppositional, aggressive, and antisocial behavior. *Journal of Child Psychology and Psychiatry, 47,* 436–445.

Keenan, K., Wakschlag, L. S., Danis, B. *et al.* (2007). Further evidence of the reliability and validity of DSM-IV ODD and CD in preschool children. *Journal of the American Academy of Child and Adolescent Psychiatry, 46,* 457–468.

Keiley, M. K., Bates, J. E., Dodge, K. A. & Pettit, G. S. (2000). A cross-domain growth analysis: Externalizing and internalizing behaviors during 8 years of childhood. *Journal of Abnormal Child Psychology, 28,* 161–179.

Kellam, S. G. & Rebok, G. W. (1992). Building developmental and etiological theory through epidemiologically based preventive intervention trials. In J. McCord & R. Ernest (Eds.), *Preventing antisocial behavior: Interventions from birth through adolescence.* (pp. 162–195). New York: Guilford Press.

Kellam, S. G., Ensimger, M. E. & Simon, M. B. (1980). Mental health in first grade and teenage drug, alcohol, and cigarette use. *Drug and Alcohol Dependence, 5,* 273–304.

Kellam, S. G., Ling, X., Mersica, R., Brown, C. H. & Ialongo, N. (1998). The effect of the level of aggression in the first grade classroom on the course of malleability of aggressive behavior into middle school. *Development and Psychopathology, 10,* 165–185.

Kelly, J. G. (1971). The quest for valid preventive interventions. In G. Rosenblum (Ed.), *Issues in community psychology and preventive mental health* (pp. 109–125). New York: Behavioral Publications.

Kelly, J. J., Davis, P. O. & Henschke, P. N. (2000). The drug epidemic: Effects on newborn infants and health resource consumption at a tertiary perinatal centre. *Pediatric Child Health, 36,* 262–264.

Kempes, M., Matthys, W., de Vries, H. & van Engeland, H. (2005). Reactive and proactive aggression in children: A review of theory, findings and the relevance for child and adolescent physiatry. *European Child and Adolescent Psychiatry, 14,* 11–19.

Kempes, M., Matthys, W., Maassen, G., van Goozen, S.H.M. & van Engeland, H. (2006). A parent questionnaire for distinguishing between reactive and proactive aggression in children. *European Child and Adolescent Psychiatry, 13,* 38–45.

Kempes, M., Matthys, W., De Vries, H. & Van Engeland, H. (2009). Children's aggressive responses to their peer's neutral behavior: A form of unprovoked reactive aggression. *Psychiatry Research* (in press).

Kendall, P. C. (1993). Cognitive-behavioral therapies with youth: Guiding theory, current status, and emerging developments. *Journal of Consulting and Clinical Psychology, 61,* 235–247.

Kendall, P. C. (Ed.) (2000). *Child and adolescent therapy* (2nd ed.). New York: Guilford Press.

Kendall, P. (2002). Toward a research–practice–community partnership: Goin' fishing and showing slides. *Clinical Psychology: Science and Practice, 9,* 214–216.

Kendall, P. C. & Beidas, R. S. (2007). Smoothing the trail for dissemination of evidence-based practices for youth: Flexibility within fidelity. *Professional Psychology: Research and Practice, 38,* 13–20.

Kendall, P. C. & Braswell, L. (1982). Cognitive-behavioral self-control therapy for children: A components analysis. *Journal of Consulting and Clinical Psychology, 5,* 672–689.

Kendall, P. C. & Chu, B. C. (2000). Retrospective self-reports of therapist flexibility in a manual-based treatment for youths with anxiety disorders. *Journal of Clinical Child Psychology, 29,* 209–220.

Kendall, P. C., Chu, B., Gifford, A., Hayes, C. & Nauta, M. (1998). Breathing life into a manual: Flexibility and creativity with manual-based treatments. *Cognitive and Behavioral Practice, 5,* 177–198.

Kendler, K. S. (2005). Toward a philosophical structure for psychiatry. *American Journal of Psychiatry, 162,* 433–440.

Kendler, K. S., Kuo, P., Webb, B. T. *et al.* (2006). A joint genomewide linkage analysis of symptoms of alcohol dependence and conduct disorder. *Alcoholism: Clinical and Experimental Research, 30,* 1972–1977.

Kennedy, G. E. (2004). Promoting cognition in multimedia interactivity research. *Journal of Interactive Learning Research, 15,* 43–61.

Kim-Cohen, J., Caspi, A., Moffitt, T. E., Harrington, H., Milne, B. J. & Poulton, R. (2003). Prior juvenile diagnoses in adults with mental disorder: Developmental follow-back of a prospective-longitudinal cohort. *Archives of General Psychiatry, 60,* 709–717.

Kistner, J., Metzler, A., Gatlin, D. & Risi, S. (1993). Classroom racial proportions and children's peer relations: Race and gender effects. *Journal of Educational Psychology, 85,* 446–452.

Kitzmann, K. M., Gaylord, N. K., Holt, A. R. & Kenny, E. D. (2003). Child witnesses to domestic violence: A meta-analytic review. *Journal of Consulting and Clinical Psychology, 71,* 339–352.

Klein, K., Forehand, R., Armistead, L. & Long, P. (1997a), Delinquency during the transition to early childhood: Family and parenting predictors from early adolescence. *Adolescence, 32,* 61–80.

Klein, R. G., Abikoff, H., Klass, E., Ganales, D., Seese, L. M. & Pollack, S. (1997b). Clinical efficacy of methylphenidate in conduct disorder with and without attention deficit hyperactivity disorder. *Archives of General Psychiatry, 54,* 1073–1080.

Knutson, B., Adams, C. M., Fong, G. W. & Hommer, D. (2001a). Anticipation of increasing monetary reward selectively recruits nucleus accumbens. *Journal of Neuroscience, 21,* RC 159.

Knutson, B., Fong, G. W., Adams, C. M., Varner, J. L. & Hommer, D. (2001b). Dissociation of reward anticipation and outcome with event-related fMRI. *NeuroReport, 12,* 3683–3687.

Kochanska, G. & Aksan, N. (1995). Mother–child mutually positive affect, the quality of child compliance to requests and prohibitions, and maternal control as correlates of early internalization. *Child Development, 66,* 236–254.

Kochanska, G., Coy, K. C. & Murray, K. T. (2001). The development of self-regulation in the first four years of life. *Child Development, 72,* 1091–1111.

Koenen, K. C., Caspi, A., Moffitt, T. E., Rijsdijk, F. & Taylor, A. (2006). Genetic influences on the overlap between low IQ and antisocial behavior in young children. *Journal of Abnormal Psychology, 115,* 787–797.

Koretz, D. S. (1991). Prevention-centered science in mental health. *American Journal of Community Psychology, 19,* 453–458.

Kraemer, H. C., Kazdin, A. E., Offord, D. R., Kessler, R. C., Jensen, P. S. & Kupfer, D. J. (1997). Coming to terms with the terms of risk. *Archives of General Psychiatry, 54,* 337–343.

Kratochvil, C. J., Vaughan, B. S., Mayfield-Jorgenen, M. L. *et al.* (2007). A pilot study of atomoxetine in young children with attention-deficit/hyperactivity disorder. *Journal of Child and Adolescent Psychopharmacology, 17,* 175–185.

Krueger, R. F., Moffitt, T. E., Caspi, A., Bleske, A. & Silva, P. A. (1998). Assortative mating for antisocial behaviour: Developmental and methodological implications. *Behaviour Genetics, 28,* 173–186.

Kruesi, M. J., Rapaport, J. L., Hamburger, S. *et al.* (1990). Cerebrospinal fluid monoamine metabolites, aggression, and impulsivity in disruptive behavior disorders of children and adolescents. *Archives of General Psychiatry, 47,* 419–426.

Kruesi, M. J. P., Casanova, M. F., Mannheim, G. & Johnson-Bilder, A. (2004). Reduced temporal lobe volume in early onset conduct disorder. *Psychiatry Research: Neuroimaging, 132,* 1–11.

Kuczynski, L. (2003). *Handbook of dynamics in parent–child relations.* Thousand Oaks, CA: Sage.

Kuczynski, L. & Kochanska, G. (1990). Development of children's noncompliance strategies from toddlerhood to age 5. *Developmental Psychology, 26,* 398–408.

Kupersmidt, J. B., Griesler, P. C., DeRosier, M. E., Patterson, C. J. & Davis, P. W. (1995). Childhood aggression and peer relations in the context of family and neighborhood factors. *Child Development, 66,* 360–375.

Kusché, C. & Greenberg, M. (1994). *The PATHS curriculum: Promoting Alternative Thinking Strategies.* Seattle: Developmental Research and Programs.

Kutash, K., Duchnowski, A. J. & Lynn, N. (2006). School-based mental health: An empirical guide for decision makers. Tampa: University of Florida, Louis de la Parte Florida Mental Health Institute, Department of Child and Family Studies, Research and Training Center for Children's Mental Health.

Kutcher, S., Aman, M., Brooks, S. *et al.* (2004). International Consensus statement on attention-deficit/hyperactivity disorder (ADHD) and disruptive behavior disorders (DBDs): Clinical implications and treatment practice suggestions. *European Neuropsychopharmacology, 14*, 11–28.

Lacourse, E., Nagin, D., Tremblay, R. E., Vitaro, F., Vitaro, F. & Claes, M. (2003). Developmental trajectories of boys' delinquent group membership and facilitation of violent behaviors during adolescence. *Development and Psychopathology, 15*, 183–197.

Lahey, B. B. & Waldman, I., D. (2003). A developmental propensity model of the origins of conduct problems during childhood and adolescence. In B. B. Lahey, T. E. Moffitt & A. Caspi (Eds.), *Causes of conduct disorder and juvenile delinquency* (pp. 76–117). New York: Guilford Press..

Lahey, B. B., Loeber, R., Quay, H. C., Frick, P. J. & Grimm, J. (1992). Oppositional defiant and conduct disorders: Issues to be resolved for DSM-IV. *Journal of the American Academy of Child and Adolescent Psychiatry, 31*, 539–546.

Lahey, B. B., Loeber, R., Quay, H. C., *et al.* (1998). Validity of DSM-IV subtypes of conduct disorder based on age of onset. *Journal of the American Academy of Child and Adolescent Psychiatry, 37*, 435–442.

Lahey, B. B., Miller, T. L., Gordon, R. A. & Riley, A. W. (1999). Developmental epidemiology of the disruptive behavior disorders. In H. C. Quay & A. E. Hogan (Eds.), *Handbook of disruptive behavior disorders* (pp. 23–48). New York: Kluwer Academic/Plenum Press.

Lahey, B. B., Schwab-Stone, M., Goodman, S. H. *et al.* (2000). Age and gender differences in oppositional behavior and conduct problems: A cross-sectional household study of middle childhood and adolescence. *Journal of Abnormal Psychology, 10*, 488–503.

Lahey, B. B., Rathouz, P. J., Van Hulle, C. *et al.* (2008a). Testing structural models of DSM-IV symptoms of common forms of child and adolescent psychopathology. *Journal of Abnormal Child Psychology, 36*, 187–206.

Lahey, B. B., Van Hulle, C. A., Keenan, K. *et al.* (2008b). Temperament and parenting during the first year of life predict future child conduct problems. *Journal of Abnormal Child Psychology, 36*, 1139–1158.

LaHoste, G. J., Swanson, J. M., Wigal, S. B. *et al.* (1996). Dopamine D4 receptor gene polymorphism is associated with attention deficit hyperactivity disorder. *Molecular Psychiatry, 1*, 121–124.

Larson, J. & Lochman, J. E. (2002). *Helping school children cope with anger: a cognitive-behavioral intervention.* New York: Guilford Press.

Larsson, B., Fossum, S., Clifford, G., Drugli, M. B., Handegård, B. H. & Mørch, W.-T. (2009). Treatment of oppositional defiant and conduct problems in young Norwegian children: Results of a randomized controlled trial. *European Child and Adolescent Psychiatry, 18*, 45–52.

Laucht, M., Skowronek, M. H., Becker, K. *et al.* (2007). Interacting effects of the dopamine transporter gene and psychosocial adversity on attention-deficit/hyperactivity disorder symptoms among 15-year-olds from a high-risk community sample. *Archives of General Psychiatry, 64*, 585–590.

Laursen, B., Coy, K. C. & Collins, W. A. (1998). Reconsidering changes in parent–child conflict across adolescence: A meta-analysis. *Child Development, 69*, 817–832.

Lazarus, R. (1991). Cognition and motivation in emotion. *American Psychologist, 46*, 352–367.

Letendre, J. & Davis, K. (2004). What really happens in violence prevention groups? A content analysis of leader behaviors and child responses in a school-based violence prevention project. *Small Group Research, 35*, 367–387.

Leve, L. D. & Chamberlain, P. (2004). Female juvenile offenders: Defining an early-onset pathway for delinquency. *Journal of Child and Family Studies, 13*, 439–452.

Lewis, C., Watson, M. & Schaps, E. (2003). Building community in school: The Child Development Project. In M. J. Elias & H. Arnold (Eds.), *EQ + IQ = best leadership practices for caring and successful schools* (pp. 100–108). Thousand Oaks, CA: Corwin Press.

Lieberman, D. A. (2001). Using interactive media in communication campaigns for children and adolescents. In R. E. Rice & C. K. Atkin (Eds.), *Public communication campaigns* (3rd ed, pp. 373–388). Thousand Oaks, CA: Sage.

Linnoila, M., Virkkunen, M., Scheinen, M., Nuutila, A., Rimon, R. & Goodwin, F. K. (1983). Low cerebrospinal fluid 5-hydroxyindoleacetic acid concentration differentiates impulsive from nonimpulsive violent behaviour. *Life Sciences, 33*, 2609–2614.

Little, T. D., Jones, S. M., Henrich, C. C. & Hawley, P. H. (2003). Disentangling the 'whys' from the 'whats' of aggressive behaviour. *International Journal of Behavioural Development, 27*, 122–133.

Liu, J., Raine, A., Venables, P. H., Mednick, S. A. (2004). Malnutrition at age 3 years and externalizing behavior problems at ages 8, 11, and 17 years. *American Journal of Psychiatry, 161*, 2005–2013.

Livert, D. & Hughes, D. L. (2002). The ecological paradigm: Persons in settings. In T. A. Revenson & A. R. D'Augelli (Eds.), *A quarter century of community psychology: readings from the American Journal of Community Psychology*. New York: Kluwer Academic/Plenum Press.

Lochman, J. E. (1992). Cognitive-behavioral intervention with aggressive boys: Three year follow-up and preventive effects. *Journal of Consulting and Clinical Psychology, 60*, 426–432.

Lochman, J. E. (2001). Issues in prevention with school-aged children: Ongoing intervention refinement, developmental theory, prediction and moderation, and implementation and dissemination. *Prevention and Treatment, 4*, Article 4. Available at: http://journals.apa.org/prevention/volume4/pre0040004c.html

Lochman, J. E. (2003). Preventive intervention targeting precursors. In W. J. Bukoski & Z. Sloboda (Eds.), *Handbook of drug abuse prevention: Theory, science, and practice* (pp. 307–326). New York: Plenum Press.

Lochman, J. E. (2004). Contextual factors in risk and prevention research. *Merrill-Palmer Quarterly, 50*, 311–325.

Lochman, J. E. (2006). Translation of research into interventions. *International Journal of Behavioral Development, 31*, 31–38.

Lochman, J. E. (2007). Contextual factors in risk and prevention research. In G. W. Ladd (Ed.), *Appraising the human developmental sciences: Essays in honor of Merrill-Palmer Quarterly* (pp. 351–365). Detroit: Wayne State University Press.

Lochman, J. E. & Conduct Problems Prevention Research Group (1995). Screening of child behavior problems for prevention programs at school entry. *Journal of Consulting and Clinical Psychology, 63*, 549–559.

Lochman, J. E. & Curry, J. F. (1986). Effects of social problem-solving training and self-instruction training with aggressive boys. *Journal of Clinical Child Psychology, 15*, 159–164.

Lochman, J. E. & Dodge, K. A. (1994). Social-cognitive processes of severely violent, moderately aggressive and nonaggressive boys. *Journal of Consulting and Clinical Psychology, 62*, 366–374.

Lochman, J. E. & Dodge, K. A. (1998). Distorted perceptions in dyadic interactions of aggressive and nonaggressive boys: Effects of prior expectations, context, and boys' age. *Development Psychopathology, 30*, 495–512.

Lochman, J. E. & Gresham, F. M. (2008). Intervention development, assessment, planning and adaptation: Importance of developmental models. In M. J. Mayer, R. Van Acker, J. E. Lochman & F. M. Gresham (Eds.), *Cognitive behavioral inter-*

ventions for emotional and behavioral disorders: School-based practice (pp. 29–57). New York: Guilford Press.

Lochman, J. E. & Lampron, L. B. (1986). Situational social problem solving skills and self-esteem of aggressive and non-aggressive boys. *Journal of Abnormal Child Psychology, 14,* 605–617.

Lochman, J. E., & Lenhart, L. A. (1993). Anger coping intervention for aggressive children: Conceptual models and outcome effects. *Clinical Psychology Review, 13,* 785–805.

Lochman, J. E. & Pardini, D. A. (2008). Cognitive behavioral therapies. In M. Rutter, D. Bishop, D. Pine, S. Scott, J. Stevenson, E. Taylor & A. Thapar (Eds.), *Rutter's Child and Adolescent Psychiatry* (5th ed., pp. 1026–1045). London: Blackwell.

Lochman, J. E. & Wayland, K. K. (1994). Aggression, social acceptance and race as predictors of negative adolescent outcomes. *Journal of the American Academy of Child and Adolescent Psychiatry, 33,* 1026–1035.

Lochman, J. E. & Wells, K. C. (1996). A social-cognitive intervention with aggressive children: Prevention effects and contextual implementation issues. In R. De V. Peters & R. J. McMahon (Eds.) (pp. 111–143). *Prevention of childhood disorders, substance abuse and delinquency.* Thousand Oaks, CA: Sage.

Lochman, J. E. & Wells, K. C. (2002a). Contextual social-cognitive mediators and child outcome: A test of the theoretical model in the Coping Power Program. *Development an Psychopathology, 14,* 971–993.

Lochman, J. E. & Wells, K. C. (2002b). The Coping Power Program at the middle school transition: Universal and indicated prevention effects. *Psychology of Addictive Behaviors, 16,* S40–S54.

Lochman, J. E. & Wells, K. C. (2003). Effectiveness study of Coping Power and class-room intervention with aggressive children: Outcomes at a one-year follow-up. *Behavior Therapy, 34,* 493–515.

Lochman, J. E. & Wells, K. C. (2004). The Coping Power program for preadolescent aggressive boys and their parents: Outcome effects at the one-year follow-up. *Journal of Consulting and Clinical Psychology, 72,* 571–578.

Lochman, J. E., Nelson, W. M. III & Sims, J. P. (1981). A cognitive behavioral program for use with aggressive children. *Journal of Clinical Child Psychology, 10,* 146–148.

Lochman, J. E., Burch, P. R., Curry, J. F. & Lampron, L. B. (1984). Treatment and generalization effects of cognitive behavioral and goal setting interventions with aggressive boys. *Journal of Consulting and Clinical Psychology, 52,* 915–916.

Lochman, J. E., Lampron, L. B., Gemmer, T. C., Harris, R. & Wyckoff, G. M. (1989). Teacher consultation and cognitive-behavioral interventions with aggressive boys. *Psychology in the Schools, 26,* 179–188.

Lochman, J. E., White, K. J., Curry, J. F. & Rumer, R. (1992). Antisocial behavior. In V. B. van Hasselt & D. J. Kolko (Eds.), *Inpatient behavior therapy for children and adolescents,* New York: Plenum Press.

Lochman, J. E., Wayland, K. K. & White, K. J. (1993a). Social goals: Relationship to adolescent adjustment and to social problem solving. *Journal of Abnormal Child Psychology, 21,* 135–151.

Lochman, J. E., Coie, J. D., Underwood, M. & Terry, R. (1993b). Effectiveness of a social relations intervention program for aggressive and nonaggressive rejected children. *Journal of Consulting and Clinical Psychology, 61,* 1053–1058.

Lochman, J. E., FitzGerald, D. & Whidby, J. (1999). *Anger management with aggressive children.* In C. Schaefer (Ed.), *Short-term psychotherapy groups for children* (pp. 301–349). Northvale, NJ: Jason Aronson.

Lochman, J. E., Whidby, J. M. & FitzGerald, D. P. (2000). Cognitive-behavioral assessment and treatment with aggressive children. In P. C. Kendall (Ed.), *Child and*

Adolescent Therapy: Cognitive-Behavioral Procedures (2nd ed., pp. 31–87). New York: Guilford Press.

Lochman, J. E., Curry, J. F., Dane, H. & Ellis, M. (2001a). The Anger Coping Program: An empirically-supported treatment for aggressive children. *Residential Treatment for Children and Youth, 18,* 63–73.

Lochman, J. E., FitzGerald, D. P., Gage, S. M. *et al.* (2001b). Effects of social-cognitive intervention for aggressive deaf children: The Coping Power Program. *Journal of the American Deafness and Rehabilitation Association, 35,* 39–61.

Lochman, J. E., Magee, T. N. & Pardini, D. (2003). Cognitive behavioral interventions for children with conduct problems. In M. Reinecke & D. Clark (Eds.), *Cognitive therapy over the lifespan: Theory, research and practice* (pp. 441–476). Cambridge: Cambridge University Press.

Lochman, J. E., Barry, T. D. & Salekin, K. (2005a). Aggressive/oppositional behaviors (oppositional defiant and conduct disorders). In L. Osborn, T. DeWitt & L. R. First (Eds.), *Pediatrics* (pp. 1577–1585). Philadelphia: Elsevier.

Lochman, J. E., Barth, J. M. & Czopp, W. (2005b). Effects of therapeutic alliance in preventive intervention with aggressive children. Paper presented in a symposium (I. Granic, Chair) at the Twelfth Scientific Meeting of the International Society for Research in Child and Adolescent Psychopathology, New York, June.

Lochman, J. E., Powell, N. R., Whidby, J. M. & FitzGerald, D. P. (2006a). Cognitive-behavioral assessment and treatment with aggressive children. In P. C. Kendall (Ed.), *Child and adolescent therapy: Cognitive-behavioral procedures* (3rd ed., pp. 33–81). New York: Guilford Press.

Lochman, J. E., Powell, N., Clanton, N. & McElroy, H. (2006b). Anger and aggression. In G. Bear & K. Minke (Eds.), *Children's Needs III: Development, prevention, and intervention* (pp. 115–133). Washington, DC: National Association of School Psychologists.

Lochman, J. E., Boxmeyer, C., Powell, N., Roth, D. L. & Windle, M. (2006c). Masked intervention effects: Analytic methods addressing low doseage of intervention. *New Directions for Evaluation, 110,* 19–32.

Lochman, J. E., Powell, N. R., Jackson, M. F. & Czopp, W. (2006d). Cognitive-behavioral psychotherapy for Conduct Disorder: The Coping Power program. In W. M. Nelson III, A. J. Finch & K. J. Hart (Eds.), *Comparative treatment of conduct disorder* (pp. 177–215). New York: Springer.

Lochman, J. E., Boxmeyer, C. & Powell, N. (2008a). Contributions of developmental psychopathology. In C. R. Reynolds & T. B. Gutkin (Eds.), *Handbook of school psychology* (4th ed., pp. 173–190). New York: Wiley.

Lochman, J. E., Barry, T. D., Powell, N., Boxmeyer, C. & Holmes, K. (2008b). Externalizing conditions. In M. L. Wolraich, D. D., Drotar, P. H. Dworkin & E. C. Perrin (Eds.), *Developmental and behavioral pediatrics* (pp.603–626). Philadelphia: Elsevier.

Lochman, J. E., Wells, K. C. & Lenhart, L. A. (2008c). *Coping Power child group program: Facilitator guide.* New York: Oxford.

Lochman, J. E., Wells, K. C. & Lenhart, L. A. (2008d). *Coping Power child group program: Workbook.* New York: Oxford.

Lochman, J. E., Holmes, K. & Wojnaroski, M. (2008e). Children and cognition: Development of social schema. In J. K. Asamen, M. L. Ellis & G. L. Berry (Eds.), *Handbook of child development, multiculturalism, and media* (pp. 33–46). Thousand Oaks, CA: Sage.

Lochman, J. E., Powell, N. R., Boxmeyer, C., Young, L. & Baden, R. (2009a). Historical conceptions of risk subtyping among children and adolescents. In D. Lynam & R. Salekin (Eds.), *Handbook of child and adolescent psychopathy.* New York: Guilford Press (in press).

Lochman, J. E., Powell, N. R., Boxmeyer, C. L. & Baden, R. (2009b). Dissemination of evidence-based programs in the schools: The Coping Power program. In B. Doll, W. Pfohl & J. Yoon (Eds.), *Handbook of youth prevention science*. New York: Routledge (in press).

Lochman, J. E., Powell, N., Boxmeyer, C., Qu, L., Wells, K. & Windle, M. (2009c). Implementation of a school-based prevention program: Effects of counselor and school characteristics. *Professional Psychology: Research and Practice* (in press).

Lochman, J. E., Boxmeyer, C., Powell, N., Qu, L., Wells, K. & Windle, M. (2009d). Dissemination of the Coping Power program: Importance of intensity of counselor training. *Journal of Consulting and Clinical Psychology, 77*, 397–409.

Loeber, R. (1990). Development and risk factors of juvenile antisocial behavior and delinquency. *Clinical Psychology Review, 10*, 1–42.

Loeber, R. & Farrington, D. P. (2000). Young children who commit crime: Epidemiology, developmental origins, risk factors, early interventions, and policy implications. *Development and Psychopathology, 12*, 737–762.

Loeber, R. & Farrington, D. P. (2001). The significance of child delinquency. In R. Loeber & D. P. Farrington (Eds.), *Child delinquents: Development, intervention, and service needs* (pp. 1–22). Thousand Oaks, CA: Sage.

Loeber, R. & Hay, D. (1997). Key issues in the development of aggression and violence from early childhood to early adulthood. *Annual Review of Psychology, 48*, 371–410.

Loeber, R. & Stouthamer-Loeber, M. (1998). Development of juvenile aggression and violence: Some common misconceptions and controversies. *American Psychologist, 53*, 242–259.

Loeber, R., Burke, J. D., Lahey, B. B., Winters, A. & Zera, M. (2000). Oppositional defiant and conduct disorder: A review of the past 10 years. I. *Journal of the American Academy of Child and Adolescent Psychiatry, 39*, 1468–1484.

Lonczak, H. S., Huang, B., Catalano, R. F. *et al.* (2001). The social predictors of adolescent alcohol misuse: A test of the Social Development Model. *Journal of Studies on Alcohol, 62*, 179–189.

Lonigan, J., Elbert, J. & Johnson, S. (1998). Empirically supported psychosocial interventions for children: An overview. *Journal of Clinical Child Psychology, 27*, 138–145.

Lopez-Duran, N. L., Olson, S. L., Hajal, N. J., Felt, B. T. & Vazques, D. M. (2009). Hypothalamic pituitary adrenal axis functioning in reactive and proactive aggressive children. *Journal of Abnormal Child Psychology* (in press).

Lorber, M. F. (2004). Psychophysiology of aggression, psychopathy and conduct problems: A meta-analysis. *Psychological Bulletin, 130*, 531–552.

Lord, C., Rutter, M. & LeCouteur, A. (1994). Autism Diagnostic Interview-Revised: A revised version of a diagnostic interview for caregivers of individuals with possible pervasive developmental disorders. *Journal of Autism and Developmental Disorders, 24*, 659–685.

Lord, C., Risi, S., Lambrecht, L. *et al.* (2000). The Autism Diagnostic Observation Schedule-Generic: A standard measure of social and communication deficits associated with the spectrum of autism. *Journal of Autism and Developmental Disorders, 30*, 205–223.

Luman, M., Oosterlaan, J. & Sergeant, J. A. (2005). The impact of reinforcement contingencies on AD/HD: A review and theoretical appraisal. *Clinical Psychology Review, 25*, 183–213.

Luria, A. R. (1961). *The role of speech in the regulation of normal and abnormal behavior*. Oxford: Liveright.

Luthar, S. S. (1999). *Children in poverty: Risk and protective factors in adjustment.* Thousand Oaks, CA: Sage.

Luthar, S. S., Burack, J. A., Cicchetti, D. & Weisz, J. R. (1997). *Developmental psychopathology: Perspectives on adjustment, risk, and disorder.* Cambridge: Cambridge University Press.

Lynam, D. R. (1997). Pursuing the psychopath: Capturing the fledging psychopath in a nomological net. *Journal of Abnormal Psychology, 116,* 155–165.

Macmillan, R., McMorris, B. J. & Kruttschnitt, C. (2004). Linked lives: Stability and change in maternal circumstances and trajectories of antisocial behavior in children. *Child Development, 75,* 205–220.

Mahoney, M. J. (1974). *Cognition and behavior modification.* Oxford: Ballinger.

Malatesta, C. Z., Grigoryev, P., Lamb, C., Albin, M. & Culver, C. (1986). Emotion socialization and expressive development in preterm and full-term infants. *Child Development, 57,* 316–330.

Malone, R. P., Delaney, M. A., Luebbert, J. F., Cater, J. & Campbell, M. (2000). A double-blind placebo-controlled study of lithium in hospitalized aggressive children and adolescents with conduct disorder. *Archives of General Psychiatry, 57,* 649–654.

Manuck, S. B., Bleil, M. E., Petersen, K. L. *et al.* (2005). The socio-economic status of communities predicts variation in brain serotonergic responsivity. *Psychological Medicine, 35,* 519–528.

Markowitz, F. (2003). Socioeconomic disadvantage and violence: recent research on culture and neighborhood control as explanatory mechanisms. *Aggression and Violent Behavior, 8,* 145–154.

Marsh, A. A., Finger, E. C., Mitchell, D. G. V. *et al.* (2008). Reduced amygdala response to fearful expressions in children and adolescents with callous-unemotional traits and disruptive behaviour disorders. *American Journal of Psychiatry, 165,* 712–720.

Masten, A. S. (2006). Developmental psychopathology: Pathways to the future. *International Journal of Behavioral Development, 30,* 47–54.

Masten, A. S., Best, K. M. & Garmezy, N. (1990). Resilience and development: Contributions from the study of children who overcome adversity. *Development and Psychopathology, 2,* 425–444.

Matthys, W. (1997). Residential behavior therapy for children with conduct disorders. *Behavior Modification, 21,* 512–532.

Matthys, W., Walterbos, W., Van Engeland, H. & Koops, W. (1995a). Conduct disordered boys' perceptions of their liked peers. *Cognitive Therapy and Research, 19,* 357–372.

Matthys, W., De Vries, H., Hectors, H. *et al.* (1995b). Differences between conduct disordered and normal control children in their tendencies to escalate or neutralize conflicts when interacting with normal peers. *Child Psychiatry and Human Development, 26,* 29–41.

Matthys, W., van Loo, P., Pachen, P., de Vries, H., van Hooff, J. A. R. A. M. & van Engeland, H. (1995c). Behavior of conduct disordered children in interaction with each other and their normal peers. *Child Psychiatry and Human Development, 25,* 183–195.

Matthys, W., van Goozen, S., de Vries, H., Cohen-Kettenis, P. and van Engeland, H. (1998). The dominance of behavioural activation over behavioural inhibition in conduct disordered boys with and without attention deficit hyperactivity disorder. *Journal of Child Psychology and Psychiatry, 39,* 643–651.

Matthys, W., Cuperus, J. & Van Engeland, H. (1999). Deficient social problem-solving in boys with ODD/CD, with ADHD, and with both disorders. *Journal of the American Academy of Child and Adolescent Psychiatry, 38,* 311–321.

Matthys, W., Maassen, G. H., Cuperus, J. M. & van Engeland, H. (2001). The assessment of the situational specificity of children's problem behaviour in peer–peer context. *Journal of Child Psychology and Psychiatry, 42*, 413–420.

Matthys, W., van Goozen S. H. M., Snoek, H. & van Engeland, H. (2004). Response perseveration and sensitivity to reward and punishment in boys with oppositional defiant disorder. *European Child and Adolescent Psychiatry, 13*, 362–364.

Maughan, B. (2001). Conduct disorder in context. In J. Hill & B. Maughan (Eds.), *Conduct disorders in childhood and adolescence* (pp. 169–201). Cambridge: Cambridge University Press.

Maughan, B., Pickles, A. & Quinton, D. (1995). Parental hostility, childhood behavior, and adult social functioning. In J. McCord (Ed.), *Coercion and punishment in long-term perspectives* (pp. 34–58). New York: Cambridge University Press.

Maughan, B., Taylor, A., Caspi, A. & Moffitt, T. E. (2004). Pernatal smoking and early childhood conduct problems: Testing genetic and environmental explanations of the association. *Archives of General Psychiatry, 61*, 836–843.

Maxwell, S. E. (2004). The persistence of underpowered studies in psychological research: causes, consequences, and remedies. *Psychological Methods, 9*, 147–163.

Mayer, R. E. (2003). The promise of multimedia learning: Using the same instructional design across different media. *Learning and Instruction, 13*, 125–139.

Mazas, C. A., Finn, P. R. & Steinmetz, J. E. (2000). Decision-making biases, antisocial personality, and early-onset alcoholism. *Alcoholism: Clinical and Experimental Research, 24*, 1036–1040.

McBurnett, K., Lahey, B. B., Rathouz, P. J. & Loeber, R. (2000). Low salivary cortisol and persistent aggression in boys referred for disruptive behavior. *Archives of General Psychiatry, 64*, 38–43.

McCart, M. R., Priester, P. E., Davies, W. H. & Azen, R. (2006). Differential effectiveness of behavioral parent-training and cognitive-behavioral therapy for antisocial youth: A meta-analysis. *Journal of Abnormal Child Psychology, 34*, 527–543.

McCarty, C. A., McMahon, R. J. & the Conduct Problems Prevention Research Group (2003). Mediators of the relation between maternal depressive symptoms and child internalizing and disruptive behavior disorders. *Journal of Family Psychology, 17*, 545–556.

McClure, L. (1980). Community psychology concepts and research base: Promise and product. *American Psychologist, 35*, 1000–1011.

McClure, L. F., Chinsky, J. M. & Larcen, S. W. (1978). Enhancing social problem-solving performance in an elementary school setting. *Journal of Educational Psychology, 70*, 504–513.

McCord, J., Tremblay, R. E., Vitaro, F. & Desmarais-Gervais, L. (1994). Boys' disruptive behaviour, school adjustment, and delinquency: The Montreal prevention experiment. *International Journal of Behavioral Development, 17*, 739–752.

McGrath, E. P. & Repetti, R. L. (2002). A longitudinal study of children's depressive symptoms, self-perceptions, and cognitive distortions about the self. *Journal of Abnormal Psychology, 111*, 77–87.

McMahon, R. J. & Forehand, R. L. (2003). *Helping the noncompliant child: Family-based treatment for oppositional behavior* (2nd ed). New York: Guilford Press.

McMahon, R. J. & Frick, P. J (2005). Evidence-based assessment of conduct problems in children and adolescents. *Journal of Clinical Child and Adolescent Psychology, 34*, 477–505.

McMahon, R. J. & Wells, K. C. (1998). Conduct problems. In E. J. Mash (Ed.), *Treatment of childhood disorders* (2nd ed., pp. 111–207). New York: Guilford Press.

McMahon, R. J., Forehand, R., Griest, D. L. & Wells, K. C. (1981). Who drops out of therapy during parent training? *Behavior Counseling Quarterly, 1*, 79–85.

McMahon, R. J., Wells, K. C. & Kotler, J. S. (2006). Conduct problems. In E. J. Mash & R. A. Barkley (Eds.), *Treatment of childhood disorders* (pp. 137–268). New York: Guilford Press.

McMahon, S. D., Grant, K. E., Compas, B. E., Thurm, A. E. & Ey, S. (2003). Stress and psychopathology in children and adolescents: Is there evidence of specificity? *Journal of Child Psychology and Psychiatry, 44*, 107–133.

Meichenbaum, D. (1977). *Cognitive-behavioral modification: An integrated approach.* New York: Guilford Press.

Meichenbaum, D. H. & Goodman, J. (1971). Training impulsive children to talk to themselves: A means for developing self-control. *Journal of Abnormal Psychology, 7*, 553–565.

Mezzacappa, E., Tremblay, R. E., Kindlon, D. *et al.* (1997). Anxiety, antisocial behavior, and heart rate regulation in adolescent males. *Journal of Child Psychology and Psychiatry, 38*, 457–469.

Michelson, D., Allen, A. J., Busner, J. *et al.* (2002). Once-daily atomoxetine treatment for children and adolescents with attention deficit hyperactivity disorder: A randomized, placebo-controlled study. *American Journal of Psychiatry, 159*, 1896–1901.

Michelson, D., Buitelaar, J. K., Danckaerts, M. *et al.* (2004). Relapse prevention in pediatric patients with ADHD treated with atomoxetine: A randomized, double-blind, placebo-controlled study. *Journal of the American Academy of Child and Adolescent Psychiatry, 43*, 896–904.

Milich, R. & Dodge, K. A. (1984). Social information processing in child psychiatric populations. *Journal of Abnormal Child Psychology, 12*, 471–490.

Milich, R. & Landau, S. (1988). The role of social status variables in differentiating subgroups of hyperactive children. In L. M. Bloomingdale & J. M. Swanson (Eds.), *Attention deficit disorder* (Vol. 4, pp. 1–16). Oxford: Pergamon Press.

Miller-Johnson, S., Coie, J. D., Maumary-Gremaud, A., Lochman, J. & Terry, R. (1999a). Relationship between childhood peer rejection and aggression and adolescent delinquency severity and type among African American youth. *Journal of Emotional and Behavioral Disorders, 7*, 137–146.

Miller-Johnson, S., Winn, D. M., Coie, J. D. *et al.* (1999b). Motherhood during the teen years: A developmental perspective on risk factors for childbearing. *Development and Psychopathology, 11*, 85–100.

Miller-Johnson, S., Coie, J. D., Maumary-Gremaud, A., Bierman, K. & the Conduct Problems Prevention Research Group (2002). Peer rejection and aggression and early starter models of conduct disorder. *Journal of Abnormal Child Psychology, 30*, 217–230.

Mischel, W. (1973). Toward a cognitive social learning conceptualization of personality. *Psychological Review, 80*, 252–283.

Mischel, W. (1990). Personality disposition revisited and revised: A view after three decades. In L. Pervin (Ed.), *Handbook of personality: Theory and research* (pp. 111–134). New York: Guilford Press.

Moffitt, T. E. (1990). Juvenile delinquency and attention deficit disorder: Boys' developmental trajectories from age 3 to age 14. *Child Development, 61*, 893–910.

Moffitt, T. E. (1993). Adolescence-limited and life course persistent antisocial behavior: A developmental typology. *Psychological Review, 100*, 674–701.

Moffitt, T. E. (2003). Life-course-persistent and adolescence-limited antisocial behaviour: A 10-year research review and a research agenda. In B. J. Lahey, T. E. Moffitt & A. Caspi (Eds.), *Causes of conduct disorder and juvenile delinquency* (pp. 49–75). New York: Guilford Press.

Moffitt, T. E. (2005a). The new look of behavioral genetics in developmental psychopathology: Gene–environment interplay in antisocial behaviors. *Psychological Bulletin, 131*, 533–554.

Moffitt, T. E. (2005b). Genetic and environmental influences on antisocial behavior: Evidence from behavioral–genetic research. *Advances in Genetics, 55*, 41–104.

Moffitt, T. E. (2006). Life-course-persistent versus adolescence-limited antisocial behavior. In D. Cicchetti & D. Cohen (Eds), *Developmental psychopathology*. Vol. 3: *Risk, disorder, and adaptation* (2nd ed., pp. 570–598). Hoboken, NJ: Wiley.

Moffitt, T. E. & Caspi, A. (2001). Childhood predictors differentiate life-course persistent and adolescence-limited antisocial pathways among males and females. *Development and Psychopathology, 13*, 355–375.

Moffitt, T. E. & Scott, S. (2008). Conduct disorders in childhood and adolescence. In M. Rutter, D. V. M. Bishop, D. S. Pine *et al.* (Eds.), *Rutter's child and adolescent psychiatry* (5th ed., pp. 543–564). Oxford: Blackwell.

Moffitt, T. E., Caspi, A., Harrington, H. & Milne, B. J. (2002). Males on the life-course-persistent and adolescence-limited antisocial pathways: Follow-up at age 26 years. *Development and Psychopathology, 14*, 179–207.

Moffitt, T. E., Arsenault, L., Jaffee, S. R. *et al.* (2008). Research review: DSM-V conduct disorder: research needs for an evidence base. *Journal of Child Psychology and Psychiatry, 49*, 3–33.

Moore, T. M., Scarpa, A. & Raine, A. (2002). A meta-analysis of serotonin metabolite 5-HIAA and antisocial behavior. *Aggressive Behavior, 28*, 299–316.

Moos, R. H. (1974). *The social climate scales: An overview*. Palo Alto, CA: Consulting Psychologists Press.

Moos, R. H. (2002). The mystery of human context and coping: An unraveling of clues. *American Journal of Community Psychology, 30*, 67–88.

Morgan, A. B. & Lilienfeld, S. O. (2000). A meta-analytic review of the relation between antisocial behavior and neuropsychological measures of executive function. *Clinical Psychology Review, 20*, 113–136.

Moss, E., Smolla, N., Cyr, C., Dubois-Comtois, K., Mazzarello, T. & Berthiaume, C. (2006). Attachment and behavior problems in middle childhood as reported by adult and child informants. *Development and Psychopathology, 18*, 425–444.

Mowday, R. T. & Sutton, R. I. (1993). Organizational behavior: Linking individuals and groups to organizational contexts. In L. W. Porter & M. R. Rosenzweig, (Eds.), *Annual review of psychology* (Vol. 44, pp. 195–229). Palo Alto, CA: Annual Reviews.

Mrazek, P. J. & Haggerty, R. J. (1994). *Reducing risks for mental disorders: Frontiers for preventive intervention research*. Washington, DC: National Academy Press.

Murray, J., Janson, C.-G. & Farrington, D. P. (2007). Crime in adult offspring of prisoners: A cross-national comparison of two longitudinal samples. *Criminal Justice and Behavior, 34*, 133–149.

Murray, L., Stanley, C., Hooper, R., King, F. & Fiori-Cowley, A. (1996). The role of infant factors in postnatal depression and mother–infant interactions. *Developmental Medicine and Child Neurology, 38*, 109–119.

Nabuzoka, D. & Smith, P. K. (1993). Sociometric status and social behavior of children with and without learning difficulties. *Journal of Child Psychology and Psychiatry, 34*, 1435–1448.

Nadder, T. S., Rutter, M., Silberg, J. L., Maes, H. H. & Eaves, L. J. (2002). Genetic effects on the variation and covariation of attention deficit-hyperactivity disorder (ADAH) and oppositional defiant disorder/conduct disorder (ODD/CD) symptomatologies across informant and occasion of measurement. *Psychological Medicine, 32*, 39–53.

Nagin, D. & Tremblay, R. E. (1999). Trajectories of boys' physical aggression, opposition, and hyperactivity on the path to physically violent and nonviolent juvenile delinquency. *Child Development, 70*, 1181–1196.

Nagin, D., Pogarsky, G. & Farrington, D. (1997). Adolescent mothers and the criminal behavior of their children. *Law and Society, 31*, 137–162.

Najstrom, M. & Jansson, B. (2006). Unconscious responses to threatening pictures: Interactive effect of trait anxiety and social desirability on skin conductance responses. *Cognitive Behavior Therapy, 35,* 11–18.

Narayan, V. M., Narr, K. L., Kumari, V. *et al.* (2007). Regional cortical thinning in subjects with violent antisocial personality disorder or schizophrenia. *American Journal of Psychiatry, 164,* 1418–1427.

Nathan, P., Stuart, S. & Dolan, S. (2000). Research on psychotherapy efficacy and effectiveness: Between Scylla and Charybdis? *Psychological Bulletin, 126,* 964–981.

Neale, J. (1966). Egocentrism in institutionalized and non-institutionalized children. *Child Development, 37,* 97–101.

Neisser, U. (1967). *Cognitive psychology.* New York: Wiley.

Neugebauer, R., Hoek, H. W. & Susser, E. (1999). Prenatal exposure to wartime famine and development of antisocial personality disorder on early adulthood. *Journal of the American Medical Association, 282,* 455–462.

Newcorn J. H., Spencer T. J., Biederman J., Milton D. R. &Michelson, D. (2005). Atomoxetine treatment in children and adolescents with attention deficit/hyperactivity disorder and comorbid oppositional defiant disorder. *Journal of the American Academy of Child and Adolescent Psychiatry, 44,* 240–248.

Nigg, J. T. (2006a). Temperament and developmental psychopathology. *Journal of Child Psychology and Psychiatry, 47,* 395–422.

Nigg, J. T. (2006b). *What causes ADHD? Understanding what goes wrong and why.* New York: Guilford Press.

Nigg, J. T. & Casey, B. J. (2005). An integrative theory of attention-deficit/hyperactivity disorder based on the cognitive and affective neurosciences. *Development and Psychopathology, 17,* 785–806.

Nock, M. K. & Kazdin, A. E. (2005). Randomized controlled trial of a brief intervention for increasing participation in parent management training. *Journal of Consulting and Clinical Psychology, 73,* 872–879.

Nock, M. & Kurtz, S. M. S. (2005). Direct observation in school settings: Bringing science to practice. *Cognitive and Behavioral Practice, 12,* 359–370.

Nowak, C. & Heinrichs, N. (2008). A comprehensive meta-analysis of Triple P-Positive Parenting Program using hierarchical linear modeling: Effectiveness and moderating variables. *Clinical Child and Family Psychology Review, 11,* 114–144.

O'Brien, B. S. & Frick, P. J. (1996). Reward dominance: Associations with anxiety, conduct problems, and psychopathy in children. *Journal of Abnormal Child Psychology, 24,* 223–240.

O'Connor, T. G., Deater-Deckard, K., Fulker, D., Rutter, M. & Plomin, R. (1998). Genotype-environment correlations in late childhood and early adolescence: Antisocial behavioral problems and coercive parenting. *Developmental Psychopathology, 34,* 970–981.

Odgers, C. L., Milne, B. J., Caspi, A., Crump, R., Poulton, R. & Moffitt, T. E. (2007a). Predicting prognosis for the conduct-problem boy: Can family history help? *Journal of the American Academy of Child and Adolescent Psychiatry, 46,* 1240–1249.

Odgers, C. L., Caspi, A., Broadbent, J. *et al.* (2007b). Prediction of differential adult health burden by conduct problem subtypes in males. *Archives of General Psychiatry, 64,* 476–484.

Odgers, C. L., Moffitt, T. E., Broadbent, J. M. *et al.* (2008). Female and male antisocial trajectories: From childhood origins to adult outcomes. *Development and Psychopathology, 20,* 673–716.

Offord, D. R. (1996). The state of prevention of early intervention. In R. D. Peters & R. J. McMahon (Eds.), *Preventing childhood disorders, substance abuse, and delinquency.* (pp. 329–344). Thousand Oaks, CA: Sage.

Olweus, D. (1991). Bully/victims problems among schoolchildren: Basic facts and effects of a school based intervention program. In D. J. Pepler & K. H. Rubin (Eds), *Development and treatment of childhood aggression* (pp. 411–448). Hillsdale, NJ: Lawrence Erlbaum.

Olweus, D. (1992). Bullying among schoolchildren: Intervention and prevention. In R. D. Peters, R. J. McMahon & V. L. Quinsley (Eds.), *Aggression and violence throughout the life span* (pp. 100–125). Thousand Oaks, CA: Sage.

Olweus, D. (1993) Bully/victim problems among schoolchildren: Long-term consequences and an effective intervention program. In S. Hodgins (Ed.), *Mental disorder and crime* (pp. 317–349). Thousand Oaks, CA: Sage.

Oosterlaan, J., Logan, G. D. & Sergeant, J. A. (1998). Response inhibition in AD/HD, CD, comorbid AD/HD+CD, anxious and normal children: A meta-analysis of studies with the stop task. *Journal of Child Psychology and Psychiatry, 39,* 411–426.

Oosterlaan, J., Scheres, A. & Sergeant, J. A. (2005). Which executive function deficits are associated with AD/HD, ODD/CD and comorbid AD/HD+ODD/CD? *Journal of Abnormal Child Psychology, 31,* 69–85.

O'Reilly, C. A. (1991). Organizational behavior: Where we've been, where we're going. In M. R. Rozenzweig & L. W. Porter (Eds.), *Annual review of psychology* (Vol. 42, pp. 427–458). Palo Alto, CA: Annual Reviews.

Orobio de Castro, B., Veerman, J. W., Koops, W., Bosch, J. D. & Monshouwer, H. J. (2002). Hostile attribution of intent and aggressive behavior: a meta-analysis. *Child Development, 73,* 916–934.

Orobio de Castro, B., Bosch, J. D, Veerman, J. W. & Koops, W. (2003). The effects of emotion regulation, attribution, and delay prompts on aggressive boys' social problem solving. *Cognitive Therapy and Research, 27,* 153–166.

Ortiz J. & Raine A. (2004). Heart rate level and antisocial behavior in children and adolescents: A meta analysis. *Journal of the American Academy of Child and Adolescent Psychiatry, 43,* 154–162.

Ottenbacher, K. J. & Cooper, H. M. (1983). Drug treatment of hyperactivity in children. *Developmental Medicine and Child Neurology, 25,* 358–366.

Panak, W. F. & Garber, J. (1992). Role of aggression, rejection, and attributions in the prediction of depression in children. *Developmental Psychology, 4,* 145–165.

Pardini, D., Lochman, J. & Wells, K. (2004). Negative emotions and alcohol use initiation in high-risk boys: The moderating effect of good inhibitory control. *Journal of Abnormal Child Psychology, 32,* 505–518.

Pardini, D. A., Barry, T. D., Barth, J. M., Lochman, J. E. & Wells, K. C. (2006). Self-perceived social acceptance and peer social standing in children with aggressive-disruptive behaviors. *Social Development, 15,* 46–64.

Pardini, D. A., Lochman, J. E. & Powell, N. (2007). Shared or unique developmental pathways to callous-unemotional traits and antisocial behavior in children? *Journal of Clinical Child and Adolescent Psychology, 36,* 319–333.

Parke, R. D. & Slaby, R. G. (1983). The development of aggression. In P. H. Mussen (Ed.), *Handbook of child psychology: Socialization, personality and social development* (Vol. 4, pp. 547–641). New York: Wiley.

Parker, J. G. & Asher, S. R. (1987). Peer relations and later personal adjustment: Are low-accepted children at risk? *Psychological Bulletin, 102,* 357–389.

Patel, V. & Goodman, A. (2007). Researching protective and promotive factors in mental health. *International Journal of Epidemiology, 36,* 703–707.

Patterson, G. R. (1976). *Living with children: New methods for parents and teachers.* Champaign, IL: Research Press.

Patterson, G. R. (1982). *Coercive family process.* Eugene, OR: Castalia.

Patterson, G. R. (1993). Orderly change in a stable world: The antisocial trait as a chimera. *Journal of Consulting and Clinical Psychology, 61,* 911–919.

Patterson, G. R. (2002). The early development of coercive family process. In J. B. Reid, G. R. Patterson & J. Snyder (Eds.), *Antisocial behavior in children and adolescents: a developmental analysis and model of intervention.* (pp. 25–64). Washington: American Psychological Association.

Patterson, G. R. & Forgatch, M. (1987). *Parents and adolescents: Living together.* Eugene, OR: Castalia.

Patterson, G. R., Reid, J. B., Jones, R. R. & Conger, R. E. (1975). *A social learning approach to family intervention: Families with aggressive children.* Vol 1. Eugene, OR: Castalia.

Patterson, G. R., Chamberlain, P. & Reid, J. B. (1982). A comparative evaluation of a parent-training program. *Behavior Therapy, 13,* 638–650.

Patterson, G. R., DeBaryshe, B. D. & Ramsey, E. (1989). A developmental perspective on antisocial behavior. *American Psychologist, 44,* 329–335.

Patterson, G. R., Reid, J. B. & Dishion, T. J. (1992). *Antisocial boys.* Eugene, OR: Castalia.

Patterson, G. R., Forgatch, M. S., Yoerger, K. L. & Stoolmiller, M. (1998). Variables that initiate and maintain an early-onset trajectory for juvenile offending. *Development and Psychopathology, 10,* 531–547.

Pattij, T. & Vanderschuren, L. J. M. J. (2008). The neuropharmacology of impulsive behavior. *Trends in Pharmacological Sciences, 29,* 192–199.

Pearson, J. L., Ialongo, N. S., Hunter, A. G. & Kellam, S. G. (1994). Family structure and aggressive behavior in a population of urban elementary school children. *Journal of the American Academy of Child and Adolescent Psychiatry, 33,* 540–548.

Pelham, W., Wheeler, T. & Chronis, A. (1998). Empirically supported psychosocial treatments for attention deficit hyperactivity disorder. *Journal of Clinical Child Psychology, 27,* 190–205.

Pennington, B. F. (2002). *The development of psychopathology: Nature and nurture.* New York: Guilford Press.

Pennington, B. F. & Ozonoff, S. (1996). Executive functions and developmental psychopathology. *Journal of Child Psychology and Psychiatry, 37,* 51–87.

Pentz, M. A., Dwyer, J. H., MacKinnon, D. P. *et al.* (1989). A multicommunity trial for primary prevention of adolescent drug abuse: Effects on drug use prevalence. *Journal of the American Medical Association, 262,* 3259–3266.

Perry, D. G., Perry, L. C. & Rasmussen, P. (1986). Cognitive social learning mediators of aggression. *Child Development, 57,* 700–711.

Peterson, A. M. (1997). Aspects of school climate: A review of the literature. *ERS Spectrum, 15,* 36–42.

Petry, N. M., Bickel, W. K. & Arnett, M. (1998). Shortened time horizons and insensitivity to future consequences in heroin addicts. *Addiction, 93,* 729–738.

Pettit, G. S., Bates, J. E. & Dodge, K. E. (1997). Supportive parenting, ecological context, and children's adjustment: A seven year longitudinal study. *Child Development, 68,* 908–923.

Pfeffer, J. (1983). Organizational demography. *Research on Organizational Behavior, 5,* 299–357.

Phillips, N. C. & Lochman, J. E. (2003). Experimentally-manipulated traits change in children's proactive and reactive aggressive behavior. *Aggressive Behavior, 29,* 215–227.

Pinderhughes, E. E., Nix, R., Foster, E. M., Jones, D. & the Conduct Problems Prevention Research Group (2001). Parenting in context: Impact of neighborhood poverty, residential stability, public services, social networks and danger on parental behaviors. *Journal of Marriage and Family, 63,* 941–953.

Pliszka, S. R., Rogeness, G. A., Renner, P., Sherman, J. & Broussard, T. (1988). Plasma neurochemistry in juvenile offenders. *Journal of the American Academy of Child and Adolescent Psychiatry*, 27, 588–594.

Plomin, R. & Rutter, M. (1998). Child development, molecular genetics, and what to do with genes once they are found. *Child Development*, 69, 1223–1242.

Polman, H., Orobio de Castro, B., Koops, W., Van Boxtel, H. W. & Merk, W. W. (2007). A meta-analysis of the distinction between reactive and proactive aggression in children and adolescents. *Journal of Abnormal Child Psychology*, 35, 522–535.

Polman, H., Orobio de Castro, B., Thomaes, S. E. & Van Aken, M. A. G. (2009). New directions in measuring reactive and proactive aggression: Validation of a teacher questionnaire. *Journal of Abnormal Child Psychology*, 37, 183–193.

Popma, A., Vermeiren, R., Geluk, C. A. *et al.* (2007). Cortisol moderates the relationship between testosterone and aggression in delinquent males. *Biological Psychiatry*, 61, 405–411.

Porras, J. I. & Robertson, P. J. (1992). Organizational development: Theory, practice, and research. In M. D. Dunnette & L. M. Hough (Eds.), *Handbook of organizational psychology* (2nd ed., pp. 719–822). Palo Alto, CA: Consulting Psychology Press.

Posthumus, J. A., Böcker, K. B. E., Raaijmakers, M. A. J., Van Engeland, H. & Matthys, W. (2009). Heart rate and skin conductance in 4-year old children with aggressive behavior. *Biological Psychology* (in press).

Poulin, F. & Boivin, M. (1999). Proactive and reactive aggression and boys' friendship quality in mainstream classrooms. *Journal of Emotional and Behavioral Disorders* 7, 168–177.

Poulin, F. & Boivin, M. (2000a). Reactive and proactive aggression: Evidence of a two-factor model. *Psychological Assessment*, 12, 115–122.

Poulin, F. & Boivin, M. (2000b). The role of proactive and reactive aggression in the formation and development of boys' friendships. *Developmental Psychology*, 36, 233–240.

Poulin, F., Dishion, T. J. & Burraston, B. (2001). 3-year iatrogenic effects associated with aggregating high-risk adolescents in cognitive-behavioral interventions. *Applied Developmental Science*, 5, 214–224.

Price, J. (2005). Free will versus survival: Brain systems that underlie intrinsic constraints on behaviour. *Journal of Comparative Neurology*, 493, 132–139.

Price, J. M. & Dodge, K. A. (1989). Reactive and proactive aggression in childhood: relations to peer status and social context dimensions. *Journal of Abnormal Child Psychology*, 17, 455–471.

Price, J. M., Chamberlain, P., Landsverk, J., Reid, J. B., Leve, L. D. & Laurent, H. (2008). Effects of a foster parent training intervention on placement changes of children in foster care. *Child Maltreatment*, 13, 64–75.

Prinstein, M. J. & Cillessen, A. H. N. (2003). Forms and functions of adolescent peer aggression associated with high levels of peer status. *Merrill-Palmer Quarterly*, 49, 310–342.

Quay, H. C. (1988). The behavioral reward and inhibition system in childhood behavior disorder. In L. M. Bloomingdale (Ed.), *Attention deficit disorder* (Vol. 2, pp. 177–186). Elmsford, NY: Pergamon Press.

Quiggle, N. L., Garber, J., Panak, W. & Dodge, K. A. (1992). Social information-processing in aggressive and depressed children. *Child Development*, 63, 1305–1320.

Raaijmakers, M. A. J., Smidts, D. P., Sergeant, J. A. *et al.* (2008). Executive functions in preschool children with aggressive behavior: Impairments in inhibitory control. *Journal of Abnormal Child Psychology*, 36, 1097–1107.

Raine A. (1993). *The psychopathology of crime: Criminal behavior as a clinical disorder.* San Diego: Academic Press.

Raine, A., Venables, P. & Mednick, S. (1997a). Low resting heart rate at age 3 years predisposes to aggression at age 11 years: Evidence from the Mauritius Child Health Project. *Journal of the American Academy of Child and Adolescent Psychiatry, 36,* 1457–1464.

Raine, A., Brennan, P. & Mednick, S. A.(1997b). Interactions between birth complications and early maternal rejection in predisposing individuals to adult violence: Specificity to serious, early onset violence. *American Journal of Psychiatry, 154,* 1265–1271.

Raine, A., Lencz, T., Bihrle, S., LaCasse, L. & Colletti, P. (2000). Reduced prefrontal gray matter volume and reduced autonomic activity in antisocial personality disorder. *Archives of General Psychiatry, 57,* 119–127.

Raine, A., Moffitt, T. E., Caspi, A., Loeber, R., Stouthamer-Loeber, M. & Lynam, D. (2005). Neurocognitive impairments in boys on the life-course persistent antisocial path. *Journal of Abnormal Psychology, 114,* 38–49.

Rasanen, P., Hakko, H., Isobarmi, M., Hodgins, S., Jarvelin, M. R. & Tiihonen, J. (1999). Maternal smoking during pregnancy and risk of criminal behavior among male offspring in the northern Finland 1996 birth cohort. *American Journal of Psychiatry, 156,* 857–862.

Raudenbush, S. W. & Willms, J. D. (1991). The organization of schooling and its methodological implications. In S. W. Raudenbush & J. D. Willms (Eds.), *Schools, classrooms, and pupils: International studies of schooling from a multilevel perspective* (pp. 1–12). San Diego: Academic Press.

Reeves, J. C., Werry, J. S., Elkind, G. S. & Zametkin, A. (1987). Attention deficit, conduct oppositional, and anxiety disorders in children. II. Clinical characteristics. *Journal of the American Academy of Child and Adolescent Psychiatry, 26,* 144–155.

Reich, W. (2000). Diagnostic Interview for Children and Adolescents (DICA). *Journal of the American Academy of Child and Adolescent Psychiatry, 39,* 59–66.

Reid, J. B. & Eddy, J. M. (2002). Preventive efforts during the elementary school years: The Linking the Interests of Families and Teachers Project. In J. B. Reid & G. R. Patterson (Eds.), *Antisocial behavior in children and adolescents: A developmental analysis and model for intervention* (pp. 219–233). Washington, DC: American Psychological Association.

Reid, J. B., Eddy, J. M., Fetrow, R. A. & Stoolmiller, M. (1999). Description and immediate impacts of a preventive intervention for conduct problems. *American Journal of Community Psychology, 27,* 483–517.

Reid, J. B., Patterson, G. R. & Snyder, J. (2002). *Antisocial behavior in children and adolescents. A developmental analysis and model of intervention.* Washington, DC: American Psychological Association.

Reid, M. J., Webster-Stratton, C. & Hammond, M.. (2007). Enhancing a classroom social competence and problem-solving curriculum by offering parent training to families of moderate- to high-risk elementary school children. *Journal of Clinical Child and Adolescent Psychology, 36,* 605–620.

Reyes, M., Buitelaar, J., Toren, P., Augustyns, I. & Eerdekens, M. (2006). A randomized, double-blind, placebo-controlled study of risperidone maintenance treatment in children and adolescents with disruptive behaviour disorders. *American Journal of Psychiatry, 163,* 402–410.

Reynolds, C. R. & Kamphaus, R. W. (2004). *Behavior Assessment System for Children-2.* Bloomington, MN: Pearson Assessments.

Rhee, S. H. & Waldman, I. D. (2002). Genetic and environmental influences on antisocial behavior: A meta-analysis of twin and adoption studies. *Psychological Bulletin, 128,* 490–529.

Rhee, S. H., Willcutt, E. G., Hartman, C. A., Pennington, B. F. & DeFries, J. C. (2008). Test of alternative hypotheses explaining the comorbidity between attention-deficit/hyperactivity disorder and conduct disorder. *Journal of Abnormal Child Psychology*, *36*, 29–40.

Rhodes, J., Roffman, J., Reddy, R. & Fredriksen, K. (2004). Changes in self-esteem during the middle school years: A latent growth curve study of individual and contextual influences. *Journal of School Psychology*, *42*, 243–261.

Ridgeway, D., Waters, E. & Kuczaj, S. A. (1985). Acquisition of emotion-descriptive language: Receptive and productive vocabulary norms for ages 18 months to 6 years. *Developmental Psychology*, *21*, 901–908.

Rifkin, A., Karajgi, B., Dicker, R. *et al.* (1997). Lithium treatment of conduct disorders in adolescents. *American Journal of Psychiatry*, *154*, 554–555.

Rigby, K. & Cox, I. (1996). The contribution of bullying at school and low self-esteem to acts of delinquency among Australian teenagers. *Personality and Individual Differences*, *21*, 609–612.

Riggins-Caspers, K. M., Cadoret, R. J., Knutson, J. F. & Langbehn, D. (2003). Biology–environment interaction and evocative biology–environment correlation: Contributions of harsh discipline and parental psychopathology to problem adolescent behaviors. *Behavior Genetics*, *33*, 205–220.

Roberts, M. C., Lazicki-Puddy, T. A., Puddy, R. W. & Johnson, R. J. (2003). The outcomes of psychotherapy with adolescents: a practitioner-friendly research review. *Journal of Clinical Psychology*, *59*, 1177–1191.

Robins, L. N. (1966). *Deviant children grown up: A sociological and psychiatric study of sociopathic personality*. Oxford: Williams & Wilkins.

Rogeness, G. A., Hernandez, J. M., Macedo, C. A. & Mitchell, E. L. (1982). Biochemical differences in children with conduct disorder socialized and undersocialized. *American Journal of Psychiatry*, *139*, 307–311.

Rogeness, G. A., Javors, M. A., Maas, J. W., Macedo, C. A. & Fischer, C. (1987). Plasma dopamine-β-hydroxylase, HVA, MHPG, and conduct disorder in emotionally disturbed boys. *Biological Psychiatry*, *22*, 1158–1162.

Rogeness, G., A., Javors, M. A., Maas, J. W. & Macedo, C. A. (1990). Catecholamines and diagnoses in children. *Journal of the American Academy of Child and Adolescent Psychiatry*, *29*, 234–241.

Rogers, E. (1995). *Diffusion of innovations* (4th ed.). New York: Free Press.

Rogers, R. D., Everitt, B. J., Baldacchino, A. *et al.* (1999). Dissociable deficits in the decision-making cognition of chronic amphetamine abusers, opiate abusers, patients with focal damage to prefrontal cortex, and tryptophan-depleted normal volunteers: Evidence for monoaminergic mechanisms. *Neuropsychopharmacology*, *20*, 322–339.

Roisman, G. I., Aguilar, B. & Egeland, B. (2004). Antisocial behavior in the transition to adulthood: The independent and interactive roles of developmental history and emerging developmental tasks. *Development and Psychopathology*, *16*, 857–871.

Rolls, E. T. (2004). The functions of the orbitofrontal cortex. *Brain and Cognition*, *55*, 11–29.

Rotter, J. B., Chance, J. E. & Phares, E. J. (1972). *Applications of a social learning theory of personality*. New York: Holt, Rinehart & Winston.

Rowe, R., Maughan, B., Worthman, C. M., Costello, E. J. & Angold, A. (2004). Testosterone, antisocial behavior, and social dominance in boys: Pubertal development and biosocial interaction. *Biological Psychiatry*, *55*, 546–552.

Rowe, R., Maughan, B., Costello, E. J. & Angold, A. (2005). Defining oppositional defiant disorder. *Journal of Child Psychology and Psychiatry*, *46*, 1309–1316.

Rubenstein, A. K. (2003). Adolescent psychotherapy: An introduction. *Journal of Clinical Psychology*, *59*, 1169–1175.

Rubia, K., Halari, R., Smith, A. *et al.* (2008). Dissociated functional brain abnormalities of inhibition in boys with pure conduct disorder and in boys with pure attention deficit hyperactivity disorder. *American Journal of Psychiatry, 165,* 889–897.

Rubia, K., Smith, A. B., Halari, R. *et al.* (2009). Disorder-specific dissociation of orbitifrontal dysfunction in boys with pure conduct disorder during reward and ventrolateral prefrontal dysfunction in boys with pure ADHD during sustained attention. *American Journal of Psychiatry, 166,* 83–94.

Rudolph, K. D. & Clark, A. G. (2001). Conceptions of relationships in children with depressive and aggressive symptoms: social-cognitive distortion or reality? *Journal of Abnormal Child Psychology, 29,* 41–56.

Rutter, M. (1997). Nature–nurture integration. The example of antisocial behavior. *American Psychologist, 52,* 390–398.

Rutter, M. (2003). Crucial paths from risk indicators to causal mechanisms. In B. B. Lahey, T. E. Moffitt & A. Caspi (Eds.), *Causes of conduct disorder and juvenile delinquency* (pp. 3–24). New York: Guilford Press.

Rutter, M. (2006). *Genes and behavior: Nature–nurture interplay explained.* Oxford: Blackwell.

Rutter, M. (2008). Biological implications of gene–environment interaction. *Journal of Abnormal Child Psychology, 36,* 969–975.

Rutter, M. & Sroufe, L. A. (2000). Developmental psychopathology: Concepts and challenges. *Development and Psychopathology, 12,* 265–296.

Rutter, M. & Taylor, E. (2008). Clinical assessment and diagnostic formulation. In M. Rutter & E. Taylor (Eds.) *Rutter's Child and adolescent psychiatry* (5th ed., pp. 42–57). Malden, MA: Blackwell.

Rutter, M., Giller, H. & Hagell, A. (1998). *Antisocial behavior by young people.* New York: Cambridge University Press.

Rutter, M., Kim-Cohen, J. & Maughan, B. (2006a). Continuities and discontinuities in psychopathology between childhood and adult life. *Journal of Child Psychology and Psychiatry, 47,* 276–295.

Rutter, M., Moffitt, T. E. & Caspi, A. (2006b). Gene–environmental interplay and psychopathology: multiple varieties but real effects. *Journal of Child Psychology and Psychiatry, 47,* 226–261.

Rydell, A., Berlin, L. & Bohlin, G. (2003). Emotionality, emotion regulation, and adaptation among 5- to 8-year-old children. *Emotion, 3,* 30–47.

Sakai, J. T., Young, S. E., Stallings, M. C. *et al.* (2006). Case-control and within-family tests for an association between conduct disorder and 5HTTLPR. *American Journal of Medical Genetics Part B, 141B,* 825–832.

Salmivalli, C., Kaukianinen, A., Kaistaniemi, L. & Lagerspetz, K. M. J. (1999). Self-evaluated self-esteem, peer-evaluated self-esteem, and defensive egotism as predictors of adolescents' participation in bullying situations. *Personality and Social Psychology Bulletin, 25,* 1268–1278.

Sampson, J. H. & Laub, R. J. (1993). *Crime in the making: Pathways and turning points through life.* Cambridge, MA: Harvard University Press.

Sanbonmatsu, D. M. & Fazio, R. H. (1990). The role of attitudes in memory-based decision making. *Journal of Personality and Social Psychology, 59,* 614–622.

Sanders, M. R., Markie-Dadds, C. & Turner, K. M. T. (2003). Theoretical, scientific and clinical foundations of the Triple P-Positive Parenting Program: A population approach to the promotion of parenting competence. *Parenting Research and Practice Monograph, 1,* 1–21.

Sanson, A. Smart, D., Prior, M. & Oberklaid, F. (1993). Precursors of hyperactivity and aggression. *Journal of the American Academy of Child and Adolescent Psychiatry, 32,* 1207–1216.

Scaramella, L. V. & Conger, R. D. (2003). Intergenerational continuity of hostile parenting and its consequences: The moderating influence of children's negative emotional reactivity. *Social Development, 12,* 420–439.

Scarpa, A. & Raine, A. (2000). Violence associated with anger and impulsivity. In J. C. Borod (Ed.), *The neuropsychology of emotion* (pp. 320–339). London: Oxford University Press.

Scarpa, A., Bowser, F. M., Fikretoglu, D., Romero, N. & Wilson, J. W. (1999). Effects of community violence. II. Interactions with psychophysiologic functioning. *Psychophysiology, 36* (Supplement), 102.

Scarr, S. (1991). The construction of the family reality. *Behavioral and Brain Sciences, 14,* 403–404.

Schmidt, F. & Taylor, T. K. (2002). Putting empirically supported treatments into practice: Lessons learned in a children's mental health center. *Professional Psychology: Research and Practice, 33,* 483–489.

Schmidt, L. A., Fox, N. A., Rubin, K. H., Hu, S. & Hamer, D. H. (2002). Molecular genetics of shyness and aggression in preschoolers. *Personality and Individual Differences, 33,* 227–238.

Schoen, S.F. (1983). The status of compliance technology: Implications for programming. *Journal of Special Education, 17,* 483–496.

Schoenwald, S. K. & Hoagwood, K. (2001). Effectiveness, transportability, and dissemination of interventions: What matters when? *Psychiatric Services, 52,* 1190–1196.

Schultz, K. P., Newcorn, J. H., McKay, K. E. *et al.* (2001). Relationship between serotonergic function and aggression in prepubertal boys: Effect of age and attention-deficit/hyperactivity disorder. *Psychiatry Research, 101,* 1–10.

Schultz, W., Dayan, P. & Montague, P. R. (1997). A neural substrate of prediction and reward. *Science, 275,* 1593–1599.

Schutter, D. J. L. G., van Bokhoven, I., Vanderschuren, L. J. M. J., Lochman, J. E. & Matthys, W. (2009). Interrelations between impaired decision making in disruptive behaviour disorders and substance dependence (submitted).

Schwab-Stone, M. E., Ayers, T. S., Kasprow, W. *et al.* (1995). No safe haven: A study of violence exposure in an urban community. *Journal of the American Academy of Child and Adolescent Psychiatry, 34,* 1343–1352.

Schwartz, D., Dodge, K. A., Pettit, G. S., Bates, J. E. & the Conduct Problems Prevention Research Group (2000). Friendship as a moderating factor in the pathway between early harsh home environment and later victimization in the peer group. *Developmental Psychology, 36,* 646–662.

Schwartz, J. M., Stoessel, P. W., Baxter. L. R., Martin, K. M. & Phelps, M. E. (1996). Systematic changes in cerebral glucose metabolic rate after successful behavior modification treatment of obsessive-compulsive disorders. *Archives of General Psychiatry, 53,* 109–113.

Scott, S., Spender, Q., Doolan, M., Jacobs, B. & Aspland, H. (2001). Multicentre controlled trial of parenting groups for childhood antisocial behaviour in clinical practice. *British Journal of Medicine, 323,* 1–7.

Séguin, J. R. & Zelazo, P. D. (2005). Executive function in early physical aggression. In Tremblay, R. E., Hartup, W. W. & Archer, J. (Eds.), *Developmental origins of aggression* (pp. 307–329). New York: Guilford Press.

Senn, T. E., Espy, K. A. & Kaufmann, P. M. (2004). Using path analysis to understand executive function organization in preschool children. *Developmental Neuropsychology, 26,* 445–464.

Serketich, W. J. & Dumas, J. E. (1996). The effectiveness of behavioral parent training to modify antisocial behavior in children: A meta-analysis. *Behavior Therapy, 27,* 171–186.

Shadish, W., Cook, T. & Campbell, D. (2002). *Experimental and quasi-experimental designs for generalized causal inference*. New York: Houghton Mifflin.

Shaffer, D., Gould, M. S., Brasic, J. *et al.* (1983). A Children's Global Assessment Scale (CGAS). *Archives of General Psychiatry*, 40, 1228–1231.

Shaffer, D., Fisher, P., Lucas, C. P., Dulcan, M. K. & Schwab-Stone, M. E. (2000). NIMH diagnostic interview schedule for children version IV (NIMH DISC-IV): description, differences from previous versions and reliability of some common diagnoses. *Journal of the American Academy of Child and Adolescent Psychiatry*, 39, 28–38.

Shannon, C., Schwandt, M. L., Champoux, M. *et al.* (2005). Maternal absence and stability of individual differences in CSF 5-HIAA concentrations in rhesus monkey infants. *American Journal of Psychiatry*, 162, 1658–1664.

Shapiro, S. K., Quay, H. C., Hogan, A. E. & Schwartz, K. P. (1988). Response perse-veration and delayed responding in undersocialized aggressive conduct disorder. *Journal of Abnormal Psychology*, 97, 371–373.

Shaw, D. S. & Vondra, J. I. (1995). Infant attachment security and maternal predictors of early behavior problems: A longitudinal study of low-income families. *Journal of Abnormal Child Psychology*, 26, 407–414.

Shaw, D. S., Keenan, K. & Vondra, J. I. (1994). The developmental precursors of antisocial behavior: Ages 1–3. *Developmental Psychology*, 30, 355–364.

Shaw, D. S., Gilliom, M., Ingoldsby, E. M. & Nagin, D.S. (2003). Trajectories leading to school-aged conduct problems. *Developmental Psychology*, 39, 189–200.

Shaw, D. S., Lacourse, E. & Nagin, D. S. (2005). Developmental trajectories of conduct problems and hyperactivity from ages 2 to 10. *Journal of Child Psychology and Psychiatry*, 46, 931–942.

Shaw, D. S., Dishion, T. J., Supplee, L., Gardner, F. & Arnds, K. (2006). Randomized trial of a family-centered approach to the prevention of early conduct problems: 2-year effects of the Family Check-Up in early childhood. *Journal of Consulting and Clinical Psychology*, 74, 1–9.

Sheeber, L. & Johnson, J. (1992). Applicability of the impact on family scale for assess-ing families with behaviourally difficult children. *Psychological Reports*, 71, 155–159.

Sherman, L. W. (2007). The power few: Experimental criminology and the reduction of harm: The 2006 Joan McCord Prize Lecture. *Journal of Experimental Criminology*, 3, 299–321.

Shipman, K. L., Zeman, J., Nesin, A. E. & Fitzgerald, M. (2003). Children's strategies for displaying anger and sadness: What works with whom? *Merrill-Palmer Quarterly*, 49, 100–122.

Shirk, S. R. & Karver, M. (2003). Prediction of treatment outcome from relationship variables in child and adolescent therapy: A meta-analytic review. *Journal of Consulting and Clinical Psychology*, 71, 452–464.

Shoal, G. D., Giancola, P. R. & Kirillova, G. P. (2003). Salivary cortisol, personality, and aggressive behaviour in adolescent boys: A 5-year longitudinal study. *Journal of the American Academy of Child and Adolescent Psychiatry*, 42, 1101–1107.

Sholomskas, D. E., Syracuse-Siewert, G. & Rounsaville, B. J. (2005). We don't train in vain: A dissemination trial of three strategies of training clinicians in cognitive-behavioral therapy. *Journal of Consulting and Clinical Psychology*, 73, 106–115.

Sinzig, J., Döpfner, M., Lehmkuhl, G. and the German Methylphenidate Study Group (2007). Long-acting methylphenidate has an effect on aggressive behaviour in children with attention-deficit/hyperactivity disorder. *Journal of Child and Adolescent Psychopharmacology*, 17, 421–432.

Slep, A. M. S. & O'Leary, S. G. (2005). Parent and partner violence in families with young children: Rates, patterns, and connections. *Journal of Consulting and Clinical Psychology*, 73, 435–444.

Smith, C. L., Calkins, S .D., Keane, S. P., Anastopoulos, A. D. & Shelton, T. L. (2004). Predicting stability and change in toddler behavior problems: Contributions of maternal behavior and child gender. *Developmental Psychology, 40*, 29–42.

Smith, D. J. & Ecob, R. (2007). An investigation into causal links between victimization and offending in adolescents. *British Journal of Sociology, 58*, 633–659.

Smith, K., Landry, S. & Swank, P. (2000). The influence of early patterns of positive parenting on children's preschool outcomes. *Early Education and Development, 11*, 147–169.

Smith, S. W., Lochman, J. E. & Daunic, A. P. (2005). Managing aggression using cognitive-behavioral interventions: State of the practice and future directions. *Behavior Disorders, 30*, 227–240.

Snoek, H., Van Goozen, H. M., Matthys, W. *et al.* (2002). Serotonergic functioning in children with oppositional defiant disorder: A sumatriptan challenge study. *Biological Psychiatry, 51*, 319–325.

Snoek, H., Van Goozen, S. H. M., Matthys, W., Buitelaar J. K. & Van Engeland, H. (2004). Stress responsivity in children with externalising behavior disorders. *Development and Psychopathology, 16*, 389–406.

Snyder, J., Dishion, T. J. & Patterson, G. R. (1986). Determinants and consequences of associating with deviant peers during preadolescence and adolescence. *Journal of Early Adolescence, 6*, 29–43.

Snyder, R., Turgay, A., Aman, M., Binder, C., Fisman, S., Caroll, A. & the Risperidone Conduct Study Group (2002). Effects of risperidone on conduct disorder and disruptive behaviour disorders in children with subaverage IQs. *Journal of the American Academy of Child and Adolescent Psychiatry, 41*, 1026–1036.

Solomon, D., Battistich, V., Watson, M., Schaps, E. & Lewis, C. (2000). A six-district study of educational change: Direct and mediated effects of the child development project. *Social Psychology of Education, 4*, 3–51.

Sonuga-Barke, E. J. S. (2003). The dual pathway model of AD/HD: an elaboration of neuro-developmental characteristics. *Neuroscience and Biobehavioral Reviews, 27*, 593–604.

Sonuga-Barke, E. J. S. , Sergeant, J. A., Nigg, J. & Willcutt, E. (2008). Executive dysfunction and delay aversion in attention deficit hyperactivity disorder: Nosologic and diagnostic implications. *Child and Adolescent Psychiatric Clinics of North America, 17*, 367–384.

Soubrie, P. (1986). Serotonergic nerves and behaviour. *Journal of Pharmacology, 17*, 107–112.

Speltz, M. L., DeKlyen, M. & Greenberg, M. T. (1999). Attachment in boys with early onset conduct problems. *Development and Psychopathology, 11*, 269–285.

Spieker, S. J., Larson, N. C., Lewis, S. M., Keller, T. E. & Gilchrist, L. (1999). Developmental trajectories of disruptive behavior problems in preschool children of adolescent mothers. *Child Development, 70*, 443–458.

Spivack, G. & Shure, M. B. (1974). *Social adjustment of young children: A cognitive approach to solving real-life problems.* San Francisco: Jossey-Bass.

Spivack, G., Platt, J. & Shure, M. B. (1976). *The problem-solving approach to adjustment.* San Francisco: Jossey-Bass.

Sroufe, L. A. & Rutter, M. (1984). The domain of developmental psychopathology. *Child Development, 55*, 17–29.

Stadler, C., Sterzer, P., Schmeck, K., Krebs, A., Kleinschmidt, A. & Poustka, F. (2007). Reduced anterior cingulate activation in aggressive children and adolescents during affective stimulation: association with temperament traits. *Journal of Psychiatric Research, 44*, 410–417.

Stallings, M. C., Corley, R. P., Dennehey, B. *et al.* (2005). A genome-wide search for quantitative trait loci that influence antisocial drug dependence in adolescence. *Archives of General Psychiatry, 62*, 1042–1051.

Stanger, C., Achenbach, T. M. & Verhulst, F. C. (1997). Accelerated longitudinal comparisons of aggressive versus delinquent syndromes. *Development and Psychopathology, 9,* 43–58.

Stattin, H. & Klackenberg-Larsson, I. (1993). Early language and intelligence development and their relationship to future criminal behavior. *Journal of Abnormal Psychology, 102,* 369–378.

Stearns, E., Dodge, K. A., Nicholson, M. & the Conduct Problems Prevention Research Group (2008). Peer contextual influences on the growth of authority acceptance problems in early elementary school. *Merrill-Palmer Quarterly, 54,* 208–231.

Stein, A., Ramchandani, P. & Murray, L. (2008). Impact of parental psychiatric disorder and physical illness. In M. Rutter, D. V. M. Bishop, D. S. Pine S. *et al.* (Eds.), *Rutter's child and adolescent psychiatry* (5th ed., pp. 407–420). Oxford: Blackwell.

Steinberg, L. (1987). Familial factors in delinquency: A developmental perspective. *Journal of Adolescent Research, 2,* 255–268.

Steiner, H. & Dunne J.E. (1997). Summary of the practice parameters for the assessment and treatment of children and adolescents with conduct disorder. *Journal of the American Academy of Child and Adolescent Psychiatry, 36,* 1482–1485.

Stenberg, C. R., Campos, J. J. & Emde, R. N. (1983). The facial expression of anger in seven-month-old infants. *Child Development, 54,* 178–184.

Sterzer, P., Stadler, C., Krebs, A., Kleinschmidt, A. & Poustka, F. (2005). Abnormal neural responses to emotional stimuli in adolescents with conduct disorder. *Biological Psychiatry, 57,* 7–15.

Sterzer, P., Stadler, C., Poustka, F. & Kleinschmidt, A. (2007). A structural neural deficit in adolescents with conduct disorder and its association with lack of empathy. *Neuroimage, 37,* 335–342.

Stirman, S. W., Crits-Christoph, P. & DeRubeis, R. J. (2004). Achieving successful dissemination of empirically supported psychotherapies: A synthesis of dissemination theory. *Clinical Psychology: Science and Practice, 11,* 343–359.

Stoff, D. M., Ieni, J., Friedman, E., Bridger, W. H., Pollock, L. & Vitiello, B. (1991). Platelet ³H-imipramine binding, serotonin reuptake, and plasma alpha 1 acid glycoprotein in disruptive behaviour disorders. *Biological Psychiatry, 29,* 494–498.

Stoff, D. M., Pasatiempo, A. P., Yeung, J., Cooper, T. B., Bridger, W. H. & Rabinovich, H. (1992). Neuroendocrine responses to challenge with *dl*-fenfluramine and aggression in disruptive behavior disorders of children and adolescents. *Psychiatry Research, 43,* 263–276.

Stoiber, K. & Kratochwill, T. R. (2000). Empirically supported interventions and school psychology: Rationale and methodological issues. Part I. *School Psychology Quarterly, 15,* 75–105.

Stormshak, E. A., Bierman, K. L., Bruschi, C., Dodge, K.A., Coie, J. D. & the Conduct Problems Prevention Research Group (1999). The relation between behavior problems and peer preference in different classroom contexts. *Child Development, 70,* 169–182.

Stormshak, E. A., Bierman, K. L., McMahon, R. J., Lengua, L. J. & the Conduct Problems Prevention Research Group (2000). Parenting practices and child disruptive behavior problems in early elementary school. *Journal of Clinical Child Psychology, 29,* 17–29.

Sturge-Apple, M. L., Davies, P. T. & Cummings, E. M. (2006). Impact of hostility and withdrawal in inter-parental conflict on parental emotional unavailability and children's adjustment difficulties. *Child Development, 77,* 1623–1641.

Sugai, G. & Horner, R. H. (2002). Introduction to the special series on positive behavior support in schools. *Journal of Emotional and Behavioral Disorders, 10,* 130–135.

Sullivan, T. N., Farrell, A. D. & Kliewer, W. (2006). Peer victimization in early adolescence: Association between physical and relational victimization and drug use, aggression, and delinquent behaviors among urban middle school students. *Development and Psychopathology, 18*, 119–137.

Sutherland, E. (1939). *Principles of criminology.* Philadelphia: Lippincott.

Swanson, J. M. (1995). *SNAP-IV Scale.* Irvine, UC: Child Development Center.

Swanson, J. M., Sunohara, G. A., Kenedy, J. L. *et al.* (1998). Association of the dopamine receptor D4 (DRD4) gene with the refined phenotype of attention deficit hyperactivity disorder (ADHD): a family-based approach. *Molecular Biology, 3*, 38–41.

Swanson, J. M., Kinsbourne, M., Nigg, J. *et al.* (2007). Etiological subtypes of attention-deficit/hyperactivity disorder: Brain imaging, molecular genetic and environmental factors and the dopamine hypothesis. *Neuropsychology Review, 17*, 39–59.

Taub, J. (2001). Evaluation of the Second Step Violence Prevention Program at a rural elementary school. *School Psychology Review, 31*, 186–200.

Taylor, E., Schachar, R., Thorley, G., Wieselberg, H. M., Everitt, B. & Rutter, M. (1987). Which boys respond to stimulant medication? A controlled trial of methylphenidate in boys with disruptive behaviour. *Psychological Medicine, 17*, 121–143.

Taylor, T. K., Schmidt, F., Pepler, D. & Hodgins, C. (1998). A comparison of eclectic treatment with Webster-Stratton's Parents and Children Series in a children's mental health center: A randomized trial. *Behavior Therapy, 29*, 221–240.

Thapar, A., O'Donovan, M. C. & Owen, M. (2005). The genetics of attention deficit hyperactivity disorder. *Human Molecular Genetics, 14* (Spec. No. 2), R 275–R 282.

Thomas, A., Chess, S. & Birch, H. G. (1968). *Temperament and behavior disorders in children.* New York: New York University Press.

Thomas, D. E., Bierman, K. L. & the Conduct Problems Prevention Research Group (2006). The impact of classroom aggression on the development of aggressive behavior problems in children. *Development and Psychopathology, 18*, 471–487.

Thomas, D. E., Bierman, K. L., Thompson, C., Powers, C. J. & the Conduct Problems Prevention Research Group (2009). Double jeopardy: Child and school characteristics that predict aggressive-disruptive behavior in the first grade. *School Psychology Review, 37*, 516–532.

Thomas, R. M. (1996). *Comparing theories of child development* (4th ed.) Pacific Grove, CA: Brooks/Coles.

Thomas, R. & Zimmer-Gembeck, M. J. (2007). Behavioral outcomes of Parent–Child Interaction Therapy and Triple P- Positive Parenting Program: A review and meta-analysis. *Journal of Abnormal Child Psychology, 35*, 475–495.

Thorell, L. B. & Wåhlstedt, C. (2006) Executive functioning deficits in relation to symptoms of ADHD and/or ODD in preschool children. *Infant and Child Development, 15*, 503–518.

Thornberry, T. P. & Krohn, M. D. (1997). Peers, drug use, and delinquency. In D. M. Stoff, J. Breiling & J. D. Maser (Eds.), *Handbook of antisocial behavior* (pp. 218–233). New York: Wiley.

Todd, A. W., Horner, R. H., Anderson, K. & Spriggs, M. (2002). Teaching recess: Low-cost efforts producing effective results. *Journal of Positive Behavior Interventions, 4*, 46–52.

Tremblay, R. E., Vitaro, F., Bertrand, L., LeBlanc, M. *et al.* (1992). Parent and child training to prevent early onset of delinquency: The Montreal longitudinal-experimental study. In J. McCord & R. E. Tremblay (Eds.), *Preventing antisocial behavior: Interventions from birth through adolescence* (pp. 117–138). New York: Guilford Press.

Tremblay, R. E., Kurtz, L., Masse, L. C., Vitaro, F. & Pihl, R. O. (1995). A bimodal preventive intervention for disruptive kindergarten boys: Its impact through mid-adolescence. *Journal of Consulting and Clinical Psychology*, 63, 560–568.

Tremblay, R. E., Masse, L. C., Pagani, L. & Vitaro, F. (1996). From childhood physical aggression to adolescent maladjustment: The Montreal prevention experiment. In R. D. Peters & R. J. McMahon (Eds.), *Preventing childhood disorders, substance abuse, and delinquency* (pp. 268–298). Thousand Oaks, CA: Sage Publications.

Trickett, E. J. & Moos, R. H. (1973). Assessment of the psychosocial environment of the high school classroom. *Journal of Educational Psychology*, 65, 93–102.

Turkheimer, E. & Waldron, M. (2000). Nonshared environment: A theoretical, methodological, and quantitative review. *Psychological Bulletin*, 126, 78–108.

Turner, K. M. T. & Sanders, M. R. (2006). Dissemination of evidence-based parenting and family support strategies: Learning from the Triple P-Positive Parenting Program system approach. *Aggression and Violent Behavior*, 11, 176–193.

Turnipseed, D. (1994). The relationship between the social environment of organizations and the climate for innovation and creativity. *Journal of Applied Social Psychology*, 24, 782–800.

Underwood, M., Coie, J. & Herbsman, C.R. (1992). Display rules for anger and aggression in school-aged children. *Child Development*, 63, 366–380.

Unis, A. S., Cook, E. H., Vincent, J. G. *et al.* (1997). Platelet serotonin measures in adolescents with conduct disorder. *Biological Psychiatry*, 42, 553–559.

Vaden-Kiernan, N., Ialongo, N., Pearson, J. & Kellam, S. (1995). Household family structure and children's aggressive behavior: A longitudinal study of urban elementary school children. *Journal of Abnormal Child Psychology*, 23, 553–568.

Van Bokhoven, I., Matthys, W., van Goozen, S. H. M. & van Engeland, H. (2005). Prediction of adolescent outcome in children with disruptive behaviour disorders: A study of neurobiological, psychological and family factors. *European Child and Adolescent Psychiatry*, 14, 153–163.

Van den Oord, E. J. C. G., Verhulst, F. C. & Boomsma, D. I. (1996). A genetic study of maternal and paternal ratings of problem behaviors in 3-year-old twins. *Journal of Abnormal Psychology*, 105, 349–357.

Van de Wiel, N. M. H., Matthys, W., Cohen-Kettenis, P. & van Engeland, H. (2003). Application of the Utrecht Coping Power program and care as usual to children with disruptive behavior disorders in outpatient clinics: A comparative study of cost and course of treatment. *Behavior Therapy*, 34, 421–436.

Van de Wiel, N. M. H., Matthys, W., Cohen-Kettenis, P. T., Maassen, G. H., Lochman, J. E. & van Engeland, H. (2007). The effectiveness of an experimental treatment when compared with care as usual depends on the type of care as usual. *Behavior Modification*, 31, 298–312.

Van Goozen, S. H. M. & Fairchild, G. (2008). How can the study of biological processes help design new interventions for children with severe antisocial behaviour? *Development and Psychopathology*, 20, 941–973.

Van Goozen, S. H. M., Matthys, W., Cohen-Kettenis, P. T., Thijsen, J. H. H. & Van Engeland, H. (1998). Adrenal androgens and aggression in conduct disorder prepubertal boys. *Biological Psychiatry*, 43, 156–158.

Van Goozen, S., Matthys, W., Cohen-Kettenis, P., Westenberg, H. & van Engeland, H. (1999). Plasma monoamine metabolites and aggression: two studies of normal and oppositional defiant disorder children. *European Neuropsychopharmacology*, 9, 141–147.

Van Goozen, S. H. M., Matthys, W., Cohen-Kettenis, P.T., Buitelaar, J. K. & van Engeland, H. (2000a). Hypothylamic-pituitary-adrenal axis and autonomic nervous system activity in disruptive children and matched controls. *Journal of the American Academy of Child and Adolescent Psychiatry*, 39, 1438–1445.

Van Goozen, S., van den Ban, E., Matthys, W., Cohen-Kettenis, P. T., Thijssen, J. & van Engeland, H. (2000b). Increased adrenal androgen functioning in children with oppositional defiant disorder: A comparison with psychiatric and normal controls. *Journal of the American Academy of Child and Adolescent Psychiatry, 39*, 1446–1451.

Van Goozen, S. H. M., Snoek, H., Matthys, W., Van Rossum, I. & van Engeland, H. (2004a). Evidence of fearlessness in behaviourally disordered children: a study on startle reflex modulation. *Journal of Child Psychology and Psychiatry, 45*, 884–892.

Van Goozen, S. H. M., Cohen-Kettenis, P. T., Snoek, H., Matthys, W., Swaab-Barneveld, H. & Van Engeland, H. (2004b). Executive functioning in children: a comparison of hospitalized ODD and ODD/ADHD children and normal controls. *Journal of Child Psychology and Psychiatry, 45*, 284–292.

Van Goozen, S. H. M., Fairchild, G., Snoek, H. & Harold, G. T. (2007). The evidence of a neurobiological model of childhood antisocial behavior. *Psychological Bulletin, 133*, 149–182.

Van Honk, J., Hermans, E. J., Putman, P., Montagne, B. & Schutter, D. J. L. G. (2002). Defective somatic markers in sub-clinical psychopathy. *NeuroReport, 13*, 1025–1027.

Van Hulle, C. A., Corley, R., Zahn-Waxler, C., Kagan, J. & Hewitt, J. K. (2000). Early childhood heart rate does not predict externalizing behavior problems at age 7 years. *Journal of the American Academy of Child and Adolescent Psychiatry, 39*, 1238–1244.

Van IJzendoorn, M. H., Schuengel, C. & Bakermans-Kranenburg, M. J. (1999). Disorganized attachment in early childhood: Metaanalysis of precursors, concomitants, sequelae. *Development and Psychopathology, 11*, 225–249.

Van Nieuwenhuijzen, M., Bijman, E. R., Lamberix, I. C. W. *et al.* (2005). Do children do what they say? Responses to hypothetical and real-life social problems in children with mild intellectual disabilities and behaviour problems. *Journal of Intellectual Disability Research, 49*, 419–433.

Vaughn, B. E., Kopp, C. B. & Krakow, J. B. (1984). The emergence and consolidation of self-control from eighteen to thirty months of age: Normative trends and individual differences. *Child Development, 55*, 990–1004.

Venables, P. (1989). The Emanuel Miller memorial lecture 1987: Childhood markers for adult disorders. *Journal of Child Psychology and Psychiatry, 30*, 347–364.

Verhulst, F. C. & Van der Ende, J. (2008). Using rating scales in a clinical context. In M. Rutter & E. Taylor (Eds.) *Rutter's Child and adolescent psychiatry* (5th ed., pp. 289–298). Malden, MA: Blackwell.

Viding, E., Blair, J. R., Moffitt, T. E. & Plomin, R. (2005). Psychopathic syndrome indexes strong genetic risk for antisocial behaviour in 7-year-olds. *Journal of Child Psychology and Psychiatry, 46*, 592–597.

Vitaro, F. & Tremblay, R. E. (1994). Impact of a prevention program on aggressive children's friendships and social adjustment. *Journal of Abnormal Child Psychology, 22*, 457–475.

Vitaro, F., Tremblay, R. E., Kerr, M., Pagani, L. & Bukowski, W. M. (1997). Disruptive friends' characteristics and delinquency in early adolescence: A test of two competing models of development. *Child Development, 68*, 676–689.

Vitaro, F., Brendgen, M., Pagani, L., Tremblay, R. E. & McDuff, P. (1999). Disruptive behavior, peer association, and conduct disorder: Testing the developmental links through early intervention. *Development and Psychopathology, 11*, 287–304.

Vitaro, F., Brendgen, M. & Barker, E. D. (2006). Subtypes of aggressive behaviors: A developmental perspective. *International Journal of Behavioral Development, 30*, 12–19.

Volkow, N. D. & Insel, T. R. (2003). What are the long-term effects of methylphenidate treatment? *Biological Psychiatry, 54*, 1307–1309.

Volkow, N. D., Wang, G. J., Fowler, J. S. *et al.* (1998). Dopamine transporter occupancies in the human brain induced by therapeutic doses of oral methylphenidate. *American Journal of Psychiatry, 155*, 1325–1331.

Volkow, N. D., Wang, G. J., Fowler, J. S. *et al.* (2002). Relationship between blockade of dopamine transporters by oral methyphenidate and the increases in extracellular dopamine: Therapeutic implications. *Synapse, 43*, 181–187.

Vondra, J. I., Shaw, D. S., Swearingen, L., Cohen, M. & Owens, E. B. (2001). Attachment stability and emotional and behavioral regulation from infancy to preschool age. *Development and Psychopathology, 13*, 13–33.

Vorderer, P. & Ritterfeld, U. (2003). Children's future programming and media use between entertainment and education. In E. L. Palmer & B. M. Young (Eds.), *Faces of televisual media: Teaching, violence, selling to children* (2nd ed., pp. 241–262). Mahwah, NJ: Lawrence Erlbaum.

Vuchinich, S., Bank, L. & Patterson, G. R. (1992), Parenting, peers, and the stability of antisocial behavior in preadolescent boys. *Developmental Psychology, 28*, 510–521.

Vygotsky, L. S. (1962). *Thought and language.* Oxford: Wiley.

Wagner, E. E. (1996). *Children's peer preferences: Effects of classroom racial composition.* Unpublished master's thesis, Duke University, Durham, North Carolina.

Wakschlag, L. S. & Danis, B. (2004). Assessment of disruptive behavior in young children: A clinical-developmental framework. In R. DelCarmen-Wiggins & A. Carter (Eds.), *Handbook of infant, toddler, and preschool mental health assessment* (pp. 421–440). Oxford: Oxford University Press.

Wakschlag, L. S., Pickett, K. E., Kasza, K. E. & Loeber, R. (2006a). Is prenatal smoking associated with a developmental pattern of conduct problems in young boys? *Journal of the American Academy of Child and Adolescent Psychiatry, 45*, 461–467.

Wakschlag, L. S., Pine, D. S., Pickett, K. E. & Carter, A. S. (2006b). Elucidating early mechanisms of developmental psychopathology: The case of prenatal smoking and disruptive behavior. *Child Development, 77*, 893–906.

Wakschlag, L. S., Briggs-Gowan, M. J., Carter, A. S. *et al.* (2007). A developmental framework for distinguishing disruptive behaviour from normative misbehaviour in preschool children. *Journal of Child Psychology and Psychiatry, 48*, 976–987.

Wakschlag, L. S., Hill, C., Carter, A. S. *et al.* (2008a). Observational assessment of preschool disruptive behaviour. I. Reliablility of the Disruptive Behavior Diagnostic Observation Schedule (DB-DOS). *Journal of the American Academy of Child and Adolescent Psychiatry, 47*, 622–631.

Wakschlag, L. S., Briggs-Gowan, M. J., Hill, C. *et al.* (2008b). Observational assessment of preschool disruptive behaviour. II. Validity of the Disruptive Behavior Diagnostic Schedule (DB-DOS). *Journal of the American Academy of Child and Adolescent Psychiatry, 47*, 632–641.

Waldman, I. D. (1996). Aggressive boys' hostile perceptual and response biases: The role of attention in impulsivity. *Child Development, 67*, 1015–1033.

Waldman, I. D. & Rhee, S. H. (2002). Behavioural and molecular genetic studies. In S. Sandberg (Ed.), *Hyperactivity and attention disorders of childhood* (2nd ed., pp. 290–335). Cambridge: Cambridge University Press.

Walker, H. M., Ramsay, E. & Gresham, F. M. (2004). *Antisocial behavior at school: Evidence-based practices* (2nd ed.). Belmont, CA: Wadsworth/Thomson Learning.

Wallis, D., Russell, H. F. & Muenke, M. (2008). Genetics of attention deficit/hyperactivity disorder. *Journal of Pediatric Psychology, 33*, 1085–1099.

Walma van der Molen, J. H. & van der Voort, T. H. A. (2000). Children's and adults' recall of television and print news in children's and adult news formats. *Communication Research, 27*, 132–160.

Wanous, J. P., Reichers, A. E. & Austin, J. T. (1994). Organizational cynicism: An initial study. *Academy of Management Best Papers Proceedings*, 269–273.

Warr, M. (2002) *Companions in crime: The social aspects of criminal conduct.* Cambridge: Cambridge University Press.

Webster-Stratton, C. (1984). Randomized trail of two parent-training programs for families with conduct-disordered children. *Journal of Consulting and Clinical Psychology, 52*, 666–678.

Webster-Stratton, C. (1985). Predictors of treatment outcome in parent training for conduct disordered children. *Behavior Therapy, 16*, 223–243.

Webster-Stratton, C. (1990). Enhancing the effectiveness of self-administered video-tape parent training for families with conduct-problem children. *Journal of Abnormal Child Psychology, 18*, 479–492.

Webster-Stratton, C. (1998). Preventing conduct problems in Head Start children: Strengthening parenting competencies. *Journal of Consulting and Clinical Psychology, 66*, 715–730.

Webster-Stratton, C. (2001). *The Incredible Years. Parents and Children Videotape Series: A parenting course (BASIC).* Seattle: Incredible Years.

Webster-Stratton, C. (2002). *The Incredible Years. Parents and Children Videotape Series: A parenting course (ADVANCE).* Seattle: Incredible Years.

Webster-Stratton, C. (2005a). *The Incredible Years. A parenting guide: A trouble-shooting guide for parents of children aged 2–8 years.* Seattle: Incredible Years.

Webster-Stratton, C. (2005b). The Incredible Years: A training series for the prevention and treatment of conduct problems in young children. In E. D. Hibbs & P. S. Jensen (Eds.), *Psychosocial treatments for child and adolescent disorders: Empirically based strategies for clinical practice* (2nd ed., pp. 507–555). Washington, DC: American Psychological Association.

Webster-Stratton, C. & Hammond, M. (1997). Treating children with early-onset conduct problems: A comparison of child and parent training interventions. *Journal of Consulting and Clinical Psychology, 65*, 93–109.

Webster-Stratton, C. & Lindsay, D. W. (1999). Social competence and conduct problems in young children: Issues in assessment. *Journal of Clinical Child Psychology, 28*, 25–43.

Webster-Stratton, C. & Reid, M. J. (2003). The Incredible Years. Parents, Teachers, and Children Training Series: A multifaceted treatment approach for young children with conduct problems. In A. E. Kazdin & J. R. Weisz (Eds.), *Evidence-based psychotherapies for children and adolescents* (pp. 224–240). New York: Guilford Press.

Webster-Stratton, C., Kolpacoff, M. & Hollinsworth, T. (1988). Self-administered videotape therapy for families with conduct problem children: Comparison with two-cost effective treatments and a control group. *Journal of Consulting and Clinical Psychology, 56*, 558–566.

Webster-Stratton, C., Reid, M. J. & Hammond, M. (2001). Preventing conduct problems, promoting social competence: A parent and teacher training partnership in Head Start. *Journal of Clinical Child Psychology, 30*, 283–302.

Webster-Stratton, C., Reid, M. J. & Hammond, M. (2004). Treating children with early-onset conduct problems: Intervention outcomes for parent, child, and teacher training. *Journal of Clinical Child and Adolescent Psychology, 33*, 105–124.

Weich, K. E. & Quinn, R. E. (1999). Organizational change and development. In J. T. Spence, J. M. Darley & D. J. Foss (Eds.), *Annual review of psychology* (Vol. 50, pp. 361–386). Palo Alto, CA: Annual Reviews.

Weiss, B., Dodge, K. A., Bates, J. E. & Petit, G. S. (1992). Some consequences of early harsh discipline: Child aggression and maladaptive social information processing style. *Child Development*, *63*, 1321–1335.

Weiss, B., Caron, A., Ball, S., Tapp, J., Johnson, M. & Weisz, J. R. (2005). Iatrogenic effects of group treatment for antisocial youths. *Journal of Consulting and Clinical Psychology*, *73*, 1036–1044.

Weissman, M. M., Leaf, P. J., Tischler, G. L. *et al.* (1988). Affective disorders in five United States communities. *Psychological Medicine*, *18*, 141–153.

Weisz, J. R., Donenberg, G. R., Han, S. S. & Kauneckis, D. (1995). Child and adolescent psychotherapy outcomes in experiments versus clinics: Why the disparity? *Journal of Abnormal Child Psychology*, *23*, 83–106.

Weisz, J. R., Sandler, In. N., Durlak, J. A. & Anton, B. S. (2005). Promoting and protecting youth mental health through evidence-based prevention and treatment. *American Psychologist*, *60*, 628–648.

Weisz, J. R., Jensen-Doss, A. & Hawley, K. M. (2006). Evidence-based youth psychotherapies versus usual clinical care: A meta-analysis of direct comparisons. *American Psychologist*, *61*, 671–689.

Wells, K.C., Chi, T., Hinshaw, S. P. *et al.* (2006). Treatment-related changes in objectively measured parenting behaviors in the multimodal treatment study of children with attention-deficit/hyperactivity disorder. *Journal of Consulting and Clinical Psychology*, *74*, 649–657.

Wells, K. C., Lochman, J. E. & Lenhart, L. A. (2008a). *Coping Power parent group program: Facilitator guide*. New York: Oxford.

Wells, K. C., Lochman, J. E. & Lenhart, L. A. (2008b). *Coping Power parent group program: Workbook*. New York: Oxford.

Widom, C. S. (1997). Child abuse, neglect, and witnessing violence. In D. M. Stoff (Ed.), *Handbook of antisocial behavior*. (pp. 159–170). Hoboken, NJ: Wiley.

Wigal, T., Greenhill, L., Chuang, S. *et al.* (2006). Safety and tolerability of methylphenidate in preschool children with ADHD. *Journal of the American Academy of Child and Adolescent Psychiatry*, *45*, 1294–1303.

Willcutt, E. G., Doyle, A. E., Nigg, J. T., Faraone, S. V. & Pennington, B. F. (2005). Validity of the executive function theory of attention-deficit/hyperactivity disorder: A meta-analytic review. *Biological Psychiatry*, *57*, 1336–1346.

Williams, S. C., Lochman, J. E., Phllips, N. C. & Barry, T. (2003). Aggressive and nonaggressive boys' physiological and cognitive processes in response to peer provocations. *Journal of Clinical Child and Adolescent Psychology*, *32*, 568–576.

Wills, T. A., McNamara, G., Vaccaro, D. & Hirkey, A. E. (1996). Escalated substance use: A longitudinal grouping analysis from early to middle adolescence. *Journal of Abnormal Child Psychology*, *105*, 166–180.

Wilpert, B. (1995). Organizational behavior. In J. T. Spence, J. M. Darley & D. J. Foss (Eds.), *Annual review of psychology* (Vol. 46, pp. 59–90). Palo Alto, CA: Annual Reviews.

Wolfe, D. A., Crooks, C. V., Lee, V., McIntyre-Smith, A. & Jaffe, P. G. (2003). The effects of children's exposure to domestic violence: A meta-analysis and critique. *Clinical Child and Family Psychology Review*, *6*, 171–187.

World Health Organization (1996). *Multiaxial classification of child and adolescent psychiatric disorders: The ICD-10 classification of mental and behavioural disorders in children and adolescents*. Cambridge: Cambridge University Press.

Wright, C. A., George, T. P., Burke, R., Gelfand, D. M. & Teti, D. M. (2000), Early maternal depression and children's adjustment to school. *Child Study Journal*, *30*, 153–168.

Wright, J. C., Giammarino, M. & Parad, H. W. (1986). Social status in small groups: Individual-group similarity and the social 'misfit.' *Journal of Personality and Social Psychology*, *50*, 523–536.

Youngblade, L. M., Theokas, C., Schulenberg, J., Curry, L., Huang, I.-C. & Novak, M. (2007). Risk and promotive factors in families, schools, and communities: A contextual model of positive youth development in adolescence. *Pediatrics, 119,* S47–S53.

Zelazo, P. D. & Muller, U. (2002). Executive function in typical and atypical development. In U. Goswami (Ed.), *Handbook of childhood cognitive development* (pp. 445–469). Oxford: Blackwell.

Zelli, A., Dodge, K. A., Lochman, J. E., Laird, R. D. & the Conduct Problems Prevention Research Group (1999). The distinction between beliefs legitimizing aggression and deviant processing of social cues: Testing measurement validity and the hypothesis that biased processing mediates the effects of beliefs on aggression. *Journal of Personality and Social Psychology, 77,* 150–166.

Zonnevylle-Bender, M. J. S., Matthys, W., van de Wiel, N. M.H. & Lochman, J. (2007). Preventive effects of treatment of DBD in middle childhood on substance use and delinquent behavior. *Journal of the American Academy of Child and Adolescent Psychiatry, 46,* 33–39.

Zuckerman, M. (1979). *Sensation seeking: Beyond the optimum level of arousal.* Hillsdale, NJ: Lawrence Erlbaum.

Index

Oppositional Defiant Disorder and Conduct Disorder in Childhood   By Walter Matthys and
John E. Lochman
© 2010 John Wiley & Sons, Ltd.